DISCARDED

LAWRENCE HENRY GIPSON

AUTHOR

JARED INGERSOLL: A STUDY OF AMERICAN LOYALISM IN RELATION TO BRITISH COLONIAL GOVERNMENT

STUDIES IN CONNECTICUT COLONIAL TAXATION

THE MORAVIAN INDIAN MISSION ON WHITE RIVER

LEWIS EVANS

THE COMING OF THE REVOLUTION, 1763–1775

THE BRITISH EMPIRE BEFORE THE AMERICAN REVOLUTION

VOLUME I. THE BRITISH ISLES AND THE AMERICAN COLONIES: GREAT BRITAIN AND IRELAND, 1748–1754

VOLUME II. THE BRITISH ISLES AND THE AMERICAN COLONIES: THE SOUTHERN PLANTATIONS, 1748–1754

VOLUME III. THE BRITISH ISLES AND THE AMERICAN COLONIES: THE NORTHERN PLANTATIONS, 1748–1754

VOLUME IV. ZONES OF INTERNATIONAL FRICTION: NORTH AMERICA, SOUTH OF THE GREAT LAKES REGION, 1748–1754

VOLUME V. ZONES OF INTERNATIONAL FRICTION: THE GREAT LAKES FRONTIER, CANADA, THE WEST INDIES, INDIA, 1748–1754

VOLUME VI. THE GREAT WAR FOR THE EMPIRE: THE YEARS OF DEFEAT, 1754–1757

VOLUME VII. THE GREAT WAR FOR THE EMPIRE: THE VICTORIOUS YEARS, 1758–1760

VOLUME VIII. THE GREAT WAR FOR THE EMPIRE: THE CULMINATION, 1760–1763

VOLUME IX. THE TRIUMPHANT EMPIRE: NEW RESPONSIBILITIES WITHIN THE ENLARGED EMPIRE, 1763–1766

Every considerable library on American and British history will require Mr. Gipson's volumes as an indispensable work of reference, and most readers will be so captivated by the lively reports of this intelligent and humane historical surveyor as to look forward with impatience to future volumes.

SAMUEL ELIOT MORISON

THE BRITISH EMPIRE
BEFORE THE AMERICAN REVOLUTION

VOLUME I

THE BRITISH ISLES AND THE AMERICAN COLONIES: GREAT BRITAIN AND IRELAND

1748–1754

THE BRITISH EMPIRE
BEFORE THE AMERICAN REVOLUTION
VOLUME I

THE BRITISH ISLES AND *THE AMERICAN COLONIES*

GREAT BRITAIN AND IRELAND
1748–1754

BY

LAWRENCE HENRY GIPSON

MCMLVIII
ALFRED A. KNOPF
NEW YORK

L. C. Catalog card number: 58–9670

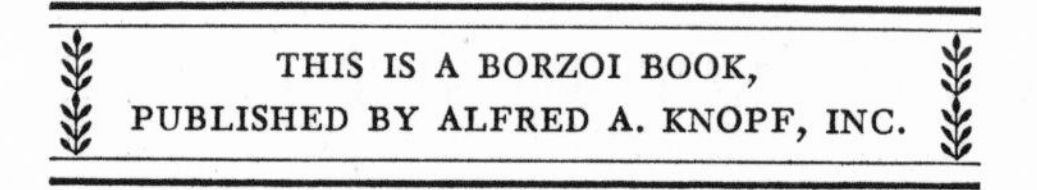

 Manufactured in the United States of America. Published simultaneously in Canada by McClelland & Stewart Ltd.

FIRST BORZOI EDITION

Originally published in 1936 by The Caxton Printers, Ltd., Caldwell, Idaho.

This edition completely revised, reset and printed from new plates.

IN MEMORY *of my Oxford tutor, the late* SIR OWEN MORGAN EDWARDS, *one time Fellow of Lincoln College, later Chief Inspector of Education for Wales, and always devoted friend of the Welsh people.*

Foreword

IN laying the plan for *The British Empire before the American Revolution,* which covers the years between the Peace of Aix-la-Chapelle in 1748 and the outbreak of the War for American Independence in 1775, it seemed best – in view of the comprehensive scope of the series – to divide it into "books," each with a distinct title, and further into volumes, each also carrying a separate title. Thus it is possible to present every book and volume as an entity. In this way each major theme achieves coherent treatment unencumbered by details not directly related to that theme, important as such details may be in another connection. The books are five in number:

THE BRITISH ISLES AND THE AMERICAN COLONIES

The first book, in three volumes, is concerned not only with the British Isles, but also with the older British colonies, including those planted on the islands of the North Atlantic and the Caribbean Sea. It seeks to make clear the nature of the civilization within these areas in the middle of the eighteenth century, with emphasis upon their political, economic, and social institutions.

Volume I carries the title *Great Britain and Ireland, 1748–1754,* and constitutes a broad survey of the centre of empire in an age of transition at mid-century, with chapters relating to England, Wales, Scotland, and Ireland. (The Channel Islands and the Isle of Man will be given consideration in a later volume.)

Volume II, *The Southern Plantations, 1748–1754,* deals with the southern North American British colonies and islands in the Atlantic where the plantation system prevailed, and with the tobacco and African slave trade and the struggle of the sugar colonies to retain their European markets in the face of the French competition, since slavery and the staple export products of slave labour were important elements the southern plantations had in common.

Volume III, *The Northern Plantations, 1748–1754,* is concerned with the older colonies in North America as far south as, but not including, Maryland. Chapters on Newfoundland with its fisheries and on the Hudson Bay region with its trade in fur are also included, as is one on the growing American iron industry, centred in Pennsylvania by 1750. The Province of Nova Scotia is reserved for treatment in a later volume as more pertinent to a subsequent theme.

Zones of International Friction

The second book embraces Volumes IV and V of the series. The theme is the rivalry between the British Empire and the French and Spanish Empires in the New World and in the Far East.

Volume IV, *North America, South of the Great Lakes Region, 1748–1754,* is concerned with Florida and the Mississippi Valley and Ohio Valley frontiers; it also embodies chapters on Spanish Florida and French Louisiana and the Illinois country.

Volume V, called *The Great Lakes Frontier, Canada, the West Indies, India, 1748–1754,* treats of French Canada, British Nova Scotia, the activities of the United East India Company in India, North American Indian relations, the Albany Congress of 1754, the problem of the so-called "Neutral" islands of the West Indies, and the efforts of an Anglo-French Commission to resolve conflicting New World territorial claims.

The Great War for the Empire

The third book is concerned with the world-wide struggle that arose out of Great Britain's efforts to protect the territorial claims of Virginia and Nova Scotia in face of what these colonies insisted were aggressive movements on the part of the French. It includes Volumes VI, VII, and VIII of the series.

Volume VI, *The Years of Defeat, 1754–1757,* covers the first four years of Anglo-French hostilities, with the French holding the upper hand at the end of 1757. While the main emphasis of the volume is on the war in North America, chapters on the exile of the Acadians, the reversal of the European system of alliances, and the conquest of British Minorca are included.

Volume VII, *The Victorious Years, 1758–1760,* follows the course of the war to the destruction of French power in the Ohio Valley and the conquest of Canada. Additional chapters are devoted to the statesmanship of William Pitt, the reversal of the system of European alliances, and the outbreak of the German Seven Years' War between Prussia, allied with Great Britain, and Austria, Russia, and Sweden, allied with France.

Volume VIII, *The Culmination, 1760–1763,* is primarily concerned with hostilities in Europe, in India, and in the West Indies, with chapters covering Spain's entrance into the Anglo-French war, the Peace of Paris of 1763, which terminated this war, and the Peace of Hubertusburg, which terminated the Seven Years' War.

The Triumphant Empire

The fourth book projected for the series will include Volumes IX, X, and XI. Covering the period 1763–1775, it will place emphasis on the problem of reconciling centralized political control within the eighteenth-century British Empire with the growing aspirations of the older colonies for freedom from interference in their internal affairs and for the recognition of the principle of government by consent. In developing this theme, various aspects of increasing colonial maturity and self-confidence will be stressed, as will also the failure of British statesmanship to find a way to surmount a major political and constitutional crisis that faced the government at the conclusion of the Great War for the Empire.

Volume IX, already published under the title *New Responsibilities within the Enlarged Empire, 1765–1766,* deals with problems presented by the immense increase in the territorial bounds of the Empire as a result of the peace treaty with France and Spain in 1763 and of the efforts to establish types of governments in harmony with British political principles within these acquisitions. It takes into account not only this imperial expansion in the New World, but also the growth of power of the United East India Company in the area of its operations.

Volume X will carry the title *Thunder Clouds in the West, 1763–1770.* It emphasizes the ominous nature of the crisis that developed within the old British Empire after the Peace of Paris of 1763, when the government of Great Britain sought in time of peace both a rigid enforcement of the navigation and trade acts and the securing of added revenue from the colonies by parliamentary statute to help support the heavy charges involved in providing adequate military protection for the new acquisitions in North America.

Volume XI, under the title *Britain Sails into the Storm, 1770–*

1775, will consider first the developments in those parts of the Empire which remained at peace with the mother country during these years, with special emphasis upon Ireland, India, and the West Indies. It will then concentrate upon the emergence after 1770 of an impasse in Anglo-American relations so serious in its constitutional and political implications as to lead to an appeal to arms.

Historiography and Bibliography, 1748–1775, and General Index

Volume XII will constitute the last book of the series and will be divided into three parts.

Part One, "Historiography," will seek to give some account of those writers who have made important contributions to the history of the British Empire covering the twenty-five years before the outbreak of the War for American Independence. Part Two, "Bibliography," will list under appropriate headings and subheadings the chief printed secondary and primary sources, and the important manuscript collections relating to this period. Part Three, "General Index," will embody in one unified index the indexes of the entire series.

Preface

SOME twenty-five years have elapsed since the first edition of this volume was written. During this time there has been great activity in eighteenth-century British studies, which has provided additional material and new points of view. I have sought to take these into account, as well as to correct the inevitable errors that crept into the earlier volume. Further, with a clearer realization now of how important it is to shed the fullest possible light on developments in the British Isles during the period under immediate consideration, I have introduced a chapter on the Principality of Wales and a summarizing chapter.

In addition, I have expanded greatly the footnotes, in the hope that these will more fully support particular observations and comments embodied in the text and will thus make this volume of greater use to students of the period and also to those general readers of history who may seek additional information on specific topics.

As was indicated in the first edition of this volume, the years from 1748 to 1754 – the period between the Treaty of Aix-la-Chapelle and the beginning of the Great War for the Empire, which lasted from 1754 to 1763 – is the last time in the history of the old British Empire when one can view it in a state of fair tranquillity and equilibrium. From the year 1754 to the year 1783 its condition was one of sustained crisis: there was, first of all, the great armed contest that the Empire waged with foreign powers; hardly had this ended triumphantly with the Peace of Paris of 1763 than there appeared a deep and dangerous cleavage within the Empire itself, which led in little over a decade to the outbreak of the War for American Independence. The purpose of the present volume and the two volumes that immediately follow it is to survey the Empire during this final period of tranquillity and equilibrium. This was the Empire, as will be noted, that Americans after 1763 and before 1775 lauded and looked back to with nostalgia, whether rightly or wrongly, and that foreigners envied. The present volume is limited to a consideration of certain aspects of civilization in the British Isles in the middle of the eighteenth century.

In the preparation of this volume I availed myself of the resources of the English Public Record Office; the British Museum; the Register Office of Scotland; the Public Record Office of Eire; the Public Record Office of Northern Ireland; the Merchant Ventures Hall and the Reference Library in Bristol; the Birmingham Reference Library; the Liverpool Reference Library; the National Library and University Library in Edinburgh; the University Library and Reference Library in Glasgow; the National Library and the Library of Trinity College in Dublin; and the Archives of Northern Ireland, the Linen Hall Library, and the Presbyterian Society Library at Belfast. I also drew upon the monumental collection of transcripts and photostats from British sources in the Library of Congress; the transcripts of the Board of Trade papers in the Historical Society of Pennsylvania; the collections of eighteenth-century books and pamphlets in the John Carter Brown Library at Brown University; the Wagner collection in the Sterling Library at Yale; and the equally important collection in the Widener Library at Harvard. It is also my good fortune to have at my constant disposal in the Library of Lehigh University a very fine collection of eighteenth-century material.

Before closing I must again acknowledge with deep appreciation grants that I received for the purpose of gathering materials for the original volume from the American Council of Learned Societies, the American Social Science Research Council, and the Lehigh University Institute of Research. A grant from the Rockefeller Foundation aided me in undertaking the present revision.

I must also express my gratitude to the administration of Lehigh University for its unwavering solicitude and generosity, which alone has made it possible to carry on the writing of this series; to my brother, James H. Gipson, president of the Caxton Printers, for publishing the original edition of this volume; to Jeannette Reed Gipson, my wife, for her aid at every stage of my labours; to Mrs. Jere Knight, my research assistant, for her work on the present volume; and to Alfred A. Knopf, for taking over the series after the appearance of the first three volumes, for continuing to issue the succeeding volumes in such an impressive format, and for authorizing the preparation of the present revision of Volume I.

Finally, a word of explanation may be in order. When Mr. Knopf became my publisher in 1939, he recommended that in subsequent volumes of the series, concerned as it is with the British Empire, I should follow English rather than American usage in spelling. This I did and the present volume therefore conforms to the style of Volumes IV to IX, as Volumes II and III will when reissued in revised editions.

L. H. G.

The Library,
Lehigh University,
Bethlehem, Pennsylvania,
July 17, 1957

Contents

CHAPTER I

WIDE SPREAD THE EMPIRE

CHAPTER II

THE HUB OF THE EMPIRE

Chapter III

SOCIAL AND ANTISOCIAL FORCES

CHAPTER IV

UNDER THE SHADOW OF THE PELHAMS

Chapter V

A GOVERNMENT OF LAWS

CHAPTER VI

THE MOUNTAINOUS PRINCIPALITY

Chapter VII

CALEDONIA GATHERS THE FRUITS OF THE UNION

CHAPTER VIII

NATIVE HIBERNIANS AND TRANSPLANTED BRITONS

Chapter IX

THE DEPENDENT KINGDOM

CHAPTER X

SUMMARIZATION

Maps

THE BRITISH EMPIRE
BEFORE THE AMERICAN REVOLUTION

VOLUME I

THE BRITISH ISLES AND THE AMERICAN COLONIES:
GREAT BRITAIN AND IRELAND
1748–1754

CHAPTER I

Wide Spread the Empire

BY THE MIDDLE of the eighteenth century the British Empire had spread from the British Isles into North America, Africa, and Asia; it also comprehended important islands of the Atlantic. The British flag was flying from outposts scattered from the Arctic to the equatorial belt, from the Great Lakes of North America to Borneo in the Far East. This Empire was peopled by nearly fifteen million white, bronze, black, and brown inhabitants whose status varied from group to group all the way from those having theoretical equality with the people of England to those possessing neither civic personality nor personal rights. Control of the lands embraced within it varied from mere economic penetration to theoretical proprietorship by the Crown with complete legal embodiment. Finally, the thirty-one governments subordinate to Great Britain ranged from the practically autonomous charter colonies with popular forms of government to the Crown possessions and the "factories" – as the foreign trading stations were called – of the United East India Company, which had none of these features.

The British Empire had come into existence as a result of overseas trade and colonization; also by wars of conquest and treaties of cession. There is, quite naturally, always much that is vague in the relations that exist between an expanding power, as was Great Britain at this period, and alien groups in the process of absorption. For example, while the people of the British West Indies had a sufficiently definite place within the Empire in 1750, the Iroquois Confederation, held to be a dependency of the Province of New York, had a most aggravatingly elusive relationship that demanded of the British the utmost tact in diplomacy. A child of political expediency of the home government and the economic impulses of individuals, the Empire necessarily presented a maze of legal inconsistencies. Indeed, strictly speaking in terms of constitutional law, there was no "British Empire," yet, in practice, the type of authority that Great Britain was extending over the lives and possessions of non-assimilable dependent peoples and its methods of economic exploitation of distant lands were distinctly imperialistic according to present-day conceptions. Even the writers of the eighteenth century employed the expression "empire" to describe those geographical and political limits within which the British government exercised some species of control.

In 1750 the Empire consisted of the following possessions and spheres of influence beyond the bounds of the British Isles: in North America, the territories claimed by the Hudson's Bay Company, Nova Scotia, New Hampshire, Massachusetts Bay with its dependency Maine, Rhode Island, Connecticut, New York, New Jersey, Pennsylvania, the Lower Counties on the Delaware, Maryland, Virginia, North Carolina, South Carolina, Georgia — all with boundaries to a certain degree indefinite and some of them with vast territorial claims to the hinterland which were absolutely irreconcilable with the counter-claims of the French and Spanish governments in North America; [1] in the North Atlantic, there were Newfoundland, the Bermuda Islands, the Bahamas, Jamaica, the Leeward Islands (St. Christopher, Antigua, Nevis, and Montserrat, with small adjacent islands), Barbados (the most easterly of all the islands of the Caribbean Sea), and claims to the Windward Islands (St. Lucia, Tobago, St. Vincent, and Dominica), as well as to the logwood region on the mainland along the Honduras Coast. On the continent of Europe there was but one possession, Gibraltar, an invaluable acquisition, and in the Mediterranean there was Minorca. Along the Gambia, the Gold Coast, the Wydah Coast, and the Bight of Benin the Royal African Company had established its posts under the British flag. Far in the South Atlantic and twelve hundred miles from the nearest point of Africa was the next British possession, St. Helena, over which Robert Jenkins, of "Jenkins's Ear" fame, had

[1] In the latter group were the claims of the Hudson's Bay Company, Nova Scotia, Massachusetts, Connecticut, New York, Pennsylvania, Virginia, North Carolina, South Carolina, and Georgia. A circular letter was sent in 1750 to the governors on the continent of North America, pointing out the necessity that the boundaries or limits of the British colonies be known. See P.R.O., C.O. 324:17, pp. 251–2.

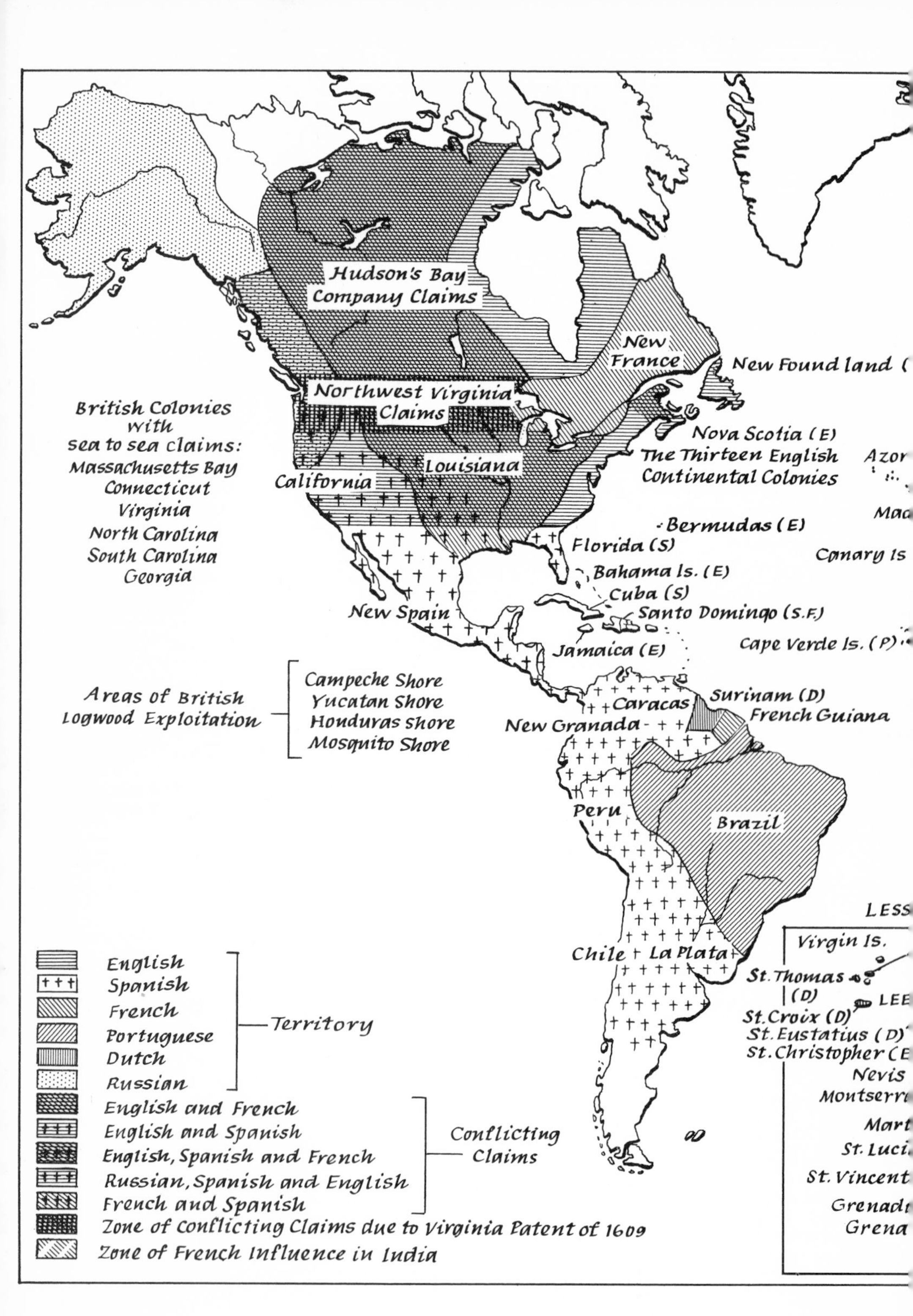

Hudson's Bay Company Claims
New France
New Found land
Northwest Virginia Claims
British Colonies with sea to sea claims:
Massachusetts Bay
Connecticut
Virginia
North Carolina
South Carolina
Georgia
Nova Scotia (E)
The Thirteen English Continental Colonies
Louisiana
California
Bermudas (E)
Florida (S)
Canary Is
Bahama Is. (E)
Cuba (S)
Santo Domingo (S.F.)
New Spain
Jamaica (E)
Cape Verde Is. (P)
Areas of British Logwood Exploitation
Campeche Shore
Yucatan Shore
Honduras Shore
Mosquito Shore
Caracas
Surinam (D)
French Guiana
New Granada
Peru
Brazil
Chile
La Plata
Virgin Is.
St. Thomas (D)
St. Croix (D)
St. Eustatius (D)
Nevis
English
Spanish
French
Portuguese
Dutch
Russian
Territory
English and French
English and Spanish
English, Spanish and French
Russian, Spanish and English
French and Spanish
Conflicting Claims
Zone of Conflicting Claims due to Virginia Patent of 1609
Zone of French Influence in India

The Britis

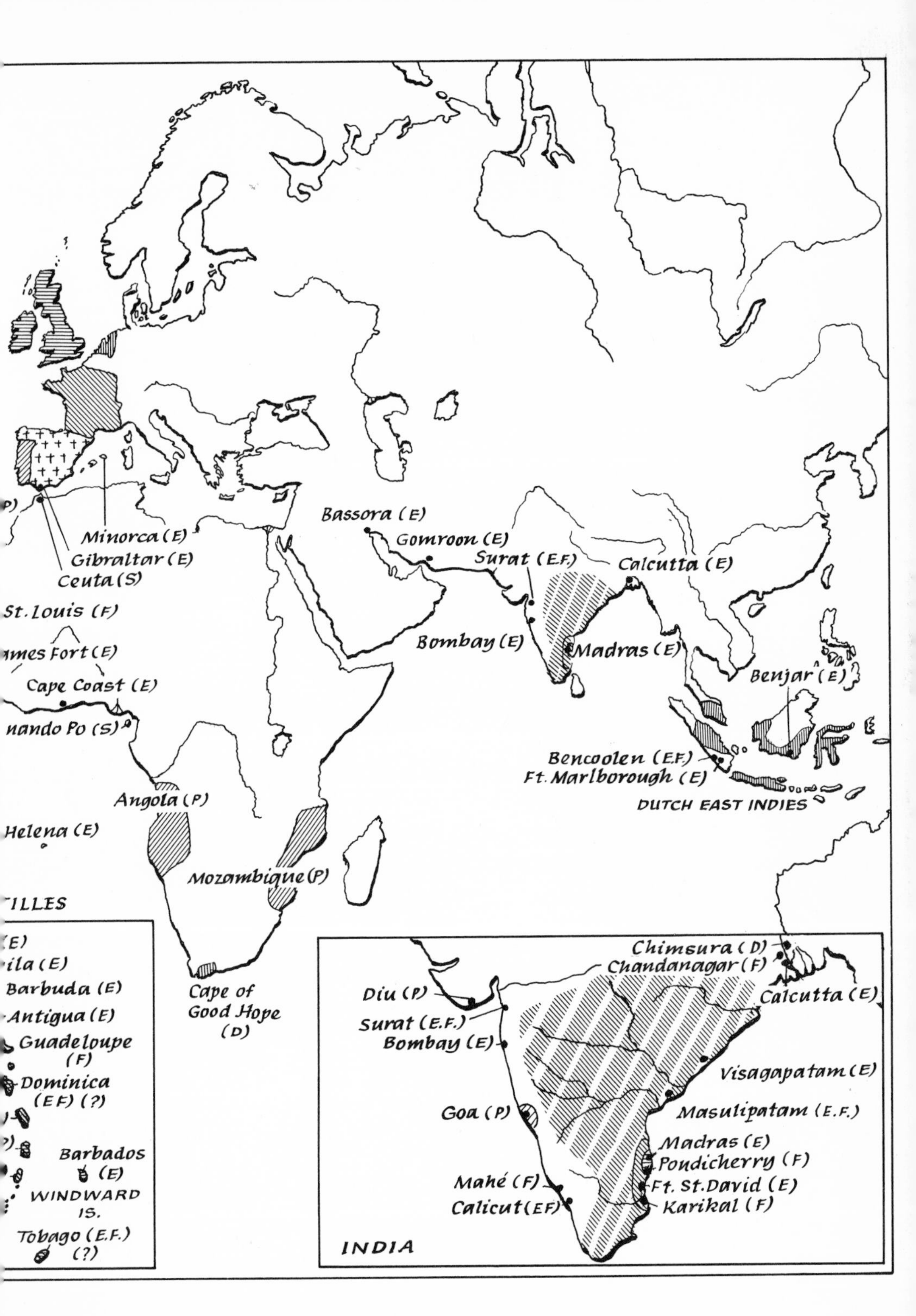

Minorca (E)
Gibraltar (E)
Ceuta (S)
St. Louis (F)
ames Fort (E)
Cape Coast (E)
nando Po (S)
Angola (P)
Helena (E)
Mozambique (P)
Cape of
Good Hope
(D)
Bassora (E)
Gomroon (E)
Surat (E.F.)
Calcutta (E)
Bombay (E)
Madras (E)
Benjar (E)
Bencoolen (E.F.)
Ft. Marlborough (E)
DUTCH EAST INDIES
ILLES
(E)
ila (E)
Barbuda (E)
Antigua (E)
Guadeloupe
(F)
Dominica
(E F) (?)
Barbados
(E)
WINDWARD
IS.
Tobago (E.F.)
(?)
Chimsura (D)
Chandanagar (F)
Calcutta (E)
Diu (P)
Surat (E.F.)
Bombay (E)
Visagapatam (E)
Masulipatam (E.F.)
Goa (P)
Madras (E)
Pondicherry (F)
Ft. St. David (E)
Mahé (F)
Calicut (EF)
Karikal (F)
INDIA

e in 1750.

ruled as governor in the early 1740's. During the period under consideration St. Helena belonged to the East India Company; the island was the last British land touched by ships bound eastward beyond the Cape from the mother country until their arrival at Bombay on the Arabian Sea in India, another "sovereignty" of the Company, which had come to England as a marriage gift from the King of Portugal in the day of Charles II. It was in 1750 perhaps the most valuable of the Company's posts, with its subordinate factories at such places as Calicut. Farther north, also along the Arabian Sea, there was the post at Surat in the Bay of Cambay, then also an important centre of British trade and influence, with subordinate factories scattered as far inland as Lahore; farther still to the north and west were the factories at Gomroon and at Balsora or Bassora, both on the Persian Gulf, the latter located at the confluence of the Tigris and Euphrates. In eastern India there was Fort St. George on the Coromandel Coast, which vied with Bombay in volume of business, with its adjoining black town of Madras and its dependent factories at Fort St. David, Masulapatam, and Vizagapatam; while northward along the Bay of Bengal in the kingdom of that name was the post of Fort William in Calcutta, also with its outlying factories. Farther east, on the island of Sumatra, were the posts of Bencoolen and Fort Marlborough, and finally, the factory at Benjar on the coast of the island of Borneo, the most eastward of the possessions of the East India Company, whose ships, however, regularly sailed beyond to China.[2]

In considering the government of the Empire, distinction must be made among company possessions, Crown possessions, and those politically organized with features identified with popular participation.

Little need be said at this point about the government of the possessions of the great companies — those in North America belonging to the Hudson's Bay Company, those in Africa belonging to the Royal African Company, and those in the Far East belonging to the United East India Company — except that in the ordinary processes of administering the Empire there was little disposition on the part

---

[2] In the year 1747 twenty European ships reached China: eight English, six Dutch, four Swedish, and two Danish; because of the war then in progress, France sent no ships there. See David Macpherson: *Annals of Commerce* (London, 1805), III, 259. For an account of the English forts, factories, and settlements in Asia in 1747 see Adam Anderson: *Origin of Commerce* (ed. William Coombe, Dublin, 1790), III, 532–4.

of the Crown to interfere with the companies in the exercise of their rights guaranteed by charter. In each instance there was something approaching a military cast in the management of the company's affairs; the officers in charge locally acted in a dual capacity as representatives of the companies in business matters and as local governors of territories or at least of factories, with limited powers in ordinary circumstances which, for example, required the sending of those accused of the more serious crimes back to England for trial. Government was rudimentary, and, as in the East India Company's possessions, complicated by many circumstances peculiar to the local situation. The control of Crown possessions, such as Minorca and Gibraltar, was purely military; in Newfoundland by 1750 there were the beginnings, but only the beginnings, of the establishment of a civil government with the chief authority in the hands of a naval commander; in Nova Scotia, authority was also concentrated in the hands of a governor and council, with the governor directly in command of a rather powerful garrison.

The possessions that were politically organized along lines based upon the principles of representative government were now twenty in number.[3] Of this group fourteen were so-called royal colonies, in the sense that they were supposed to be, legally at least, completely under the power of the Crown. Theoretically, the King might alter the form of government of any one of them, at any time that might seem best.[4] As a matter of fact, his Cabinet Council assumed the responsibility of selecting the governors, of outlining their powers as embodied in commissions issued under the Great Seal, of instructing them from time to time as to their course of action in particular situations, and of providing them with a council chosen chiefly from among the leading inhabitants of the particular province each was appointed to administer.

---

[3] The colonies with a representative form of government were New Hampshire, Massachusetts Bay, Rhode Island, Connecticut, New York, New Jersey, Pennsylvania, the Lower Counties on the Delaware, Maryland, Virginia, North Carolina, South Carolina, Georgia, the Bermudas, the Bahamas, Barbados, St. Christopher, Antigua, Nevis, and Montserrat.

[4] While theoretically this was true, in practice there were very grave obstacles to be confronted in making alterations in the government of these royal colonies. "Thus by the beginning of the eighteenth century all experiments with different varieties of government for the royal colonies in America came to an end, and a normal type of organization familiar to us as the 'old representative system,' became established" (C. M. Andrews: "The Government of the Empire, 1660–1763," *The Cambridge History of the British Empire* [ed. A. P. Newton, London, 1929], I, 409).

Under his commission the royal governor was, as a rule, commander-in-chief within his province; he was admiral of its harbours; he even might sit with his council acting as a court of final decision in judicial matters within the province; in legislation his council served as an upper chamber while he himself possessed an absolute veto on all bills issuing from the assembly, together with the authority to summon, adjourn,[5] prorogue, and dissolve that body. Acting in conjunction with his council, he disposed of vacant lands, negotiated with the Indians in North America for additional land cessions, made appointments to lesser posts that were not elective or the filling of which was not otherwise provided for by the Crown, and in other respects performed a multitude of functions. From time to time he reported on conditions within his province and asked for directions on vexed points or for specific authorization to act in cases where his commission or his instructions did not seem to cover contingencies. Or perhaps he acted and then reported to his superiors with the hope of approval. He was expected to be the eyes of the Crown as well as the strong arm for the enforcement of all those measures of the mother country affecting the people within his jurisdiction, in which he was assisted by all the other instrumentalities of the imperial authority that might be at hand.[6]

In addition to the royal colonies there were the three proprietary colonies of Pennsylvania, the Lower Counties on the Delaware, and Maryland. The first two — exclusive of the reserved rights that the Crown might still claim in the Lower Counties — were under the joint proprietorship of Thomas and Richard Penn; Maryland was under that of Charles, Lord Baltimore. Within the boundaries of these proprietaries the lands belonged to the proprietors, who had full rights to issue grants upon what terms they saw fit, which usually included levying annual quit-rents upon the grants. Further, with the approbation of the Crown, the proprietors selected governors and councillors and commissioned and instructed them, although the question of secret proprietorial instructions became a heated issue at this period both in the Pennsylvania and Maryland assemblies. In other respects the structure of these proprietorial governments corresponded closely to that of the royal colonies. In

[5] For the right of self-adjournment on the part of the provincial assemblies see L. W. Labaree: *Royal Government in America* (New Haven, 1930), pp. 207–11.

[6] For an illuminating discussion of the position of the royal governors see *ibid.*, pp. 92–134.

Pennsylvania, however, the legislature was really a unicameral body, and Maryland, alone of all the colonies, under her charter had been specifically exempt from taxation by the Crown and also claimed a freedom in lawmaking comparable only to that enjoyed by the colonies of purely corporate type.

Georgia, unique as a trusteeship, enjoyed its first legislative assembly in 1750. In fact, it was being prepared by its trustees to take its place among the royal colonies.

Finally, there were the corporate colonies – three in number: Massachusetts Bay, Rhode Island, and Connecticut, each possessed of a charter containing various privileges and exemptions with wide powers of self-government entrusted to the freemen under its provisions. In Rhode Island and Connecticut these powers extended to the making of laws without the necessity of submitting them to royal approval, and even to the selection of a governor, either by direct vote of the freemen, as in Connecticut, or through the action of the general court, popularly elected and co-operating with the freemen in a primary assembly, as in Rhode Island. In all three of these corporate colonies the governor's council or assistants were selected without reference to the mother country. However, the government of Massachusetts Bay was, under its charter of 1691, semiroyal in structure, providing among other things for the appointment of a royal governor and for the royal approval of all laws.

The colonial governors of the year 1750 were – taken as a group and without distinguishing the manner of their selection – men well fitted for their posts, the importance of which can scarcely be overemphasized at a period when grave issues were facing the plantations both on the continent of North America and in the West Indies.[7] It may, indeed, be questioned whether there existed in the world at that time a body of men assuming corresponding responsi-

[7] The following is a list of the governors of the British colonies in 1750: George Rodney, Newfoundland; Edward Cornwallis, Nova Scotia; Benning Wentworth, New Hampshire; William Shirley, Massachusetts Bay; William Greene, Rhode Island; Jonathan Law, Connecticut; George Clinton, New York; Jonathan Belcher, New Jersey; James Hamilton, Pennsylvania and the Lower Counties on the Delaware; James Ogle, Maryland; the Earl of Albemarle, Virginia, with Thomas Lee, President of the Council, acting for him within that province; Gabriel Johnston, North Carolina; James Glen, South Carolina; William Stephens, President of the colony under the Trustees, Georgia; William Popple, the Bermudas; John Tinker, the Bahamas; Edward Trelawny, Jamaica; William Mathew, the Leeward Islands; and Henry Grenville, Barbados and the Windward Islands.

bilities who brought to their work greater honesty and capacity, with zeal for decent government, than did these nineteen colonial governors. In the same breath one may say, however, that they were – with the exception of the governors of Connecticut and Rhode Island, who, selected annually, were not inclined to seek independent action and were weak in authority – likely to be in conflict with their assemblies, and this was as true in the royal colony of Jamaica as it was in the proprietary of Pennsylvania or in the corporate colony of Massachusetts Bay.[8]

This friction between the two branches of government representing opposing points of view, that of centralization of authority as against that of freedom of action in local issues, was recognized as unfortunate and undesirable. In 1748 it was reported from London that in the ensuing session of Parliament a very strict inquiry would be made into the conduct of governors of some of the colonies "in order to discover the true source of that spirit of dissatisfaction and distraction with which they have been disturbed of late years, to the no small detriment of the affairs of their mother country as well as their own."[9]

The governor, however, was but one of those links in the imperial administrative system which had come into existence by 1750 and which sought to bind the colonies to the mother country.[10] There was an expanded customs service that reached to all of the plantations, largely for the purpose of trade regulation, although in the case of Barbados and the Leeward Islands important revenues were secured through the collection of the four and one-half per cent export duty on all dead products.[11] The work of this service was supported by

---

[8] Agnes M. Whitson: *The Constitutional Development of Jamaica, 1660–1729* (Manchester, 1929), p. 158; see also J. F. Burns: *Controversies between Royal Governors and their Assemblies* (Boston, 1923), and especially L. W. Labaree: *Royal Government in America.*

[9] "London correspondence," September 8, 1748, *The Maryland Gazette* of January 11, 1749.

[10] For a useful study of the activities of the colonial governor in North America see E. B. Greene: *The Provincial Governor in the English Colonies in North America* (New York, 1898).

[11] In the course of the eighteenth century "a chain of officials came into being, located at forty-seven different ports and including nearly ninety surveyors, riding surveyors, comptrollers, collectors, searchers, preventive officers, land waiters and tide waiters" (C. M. Andrews: "Acts of Trade," *Cambridge History of the British Empire,* I, 292).

In 1750 Peter Randolph was acting as Surveyor General of the Southern Customs

courts of vice-admiralty, the judges of which were appointed by royal commission. In addition, there was the Surveyor General of the King's Woods in North America, with his subordinates; the receivers of the royal quit-rents; and a royal postal service, which in 1753 was placed under the joint supervision of Benjamin Franklin and William Hunter, acting as deputies for the Postmaster General. Finally, as an added means of articulating central and local authority, the colonies were expected to have their agents in London authorized to speak with a certain degree of authority for their principals, and, after some hesitation, this had been accepted as a desirable thing on the part of the colonial governments by the middle of the eighteenth century.

At this period the London agency plays so important a role in British colonial government that it would be well to summarize some of the many important aspects of its evolution as an institution.

The agent was the authorized representative in London of a colony,[12] or at least of some branch of a colonial government, and within certain limits, generally defined with care, he was competent to conclude matters in its name and in general served as a medium of constant communication between it and the home government. His sphere of activity, as a rule, was limited only by the character of his instructions,[13] which occasionally were expressly framed for the purpose of allowing him to refrain from giving an opinion regarding some delicate point involving colonial interests and to plead, instead, lack of authority.[14] While at times it was of incalculable ad-

---

District in America and the West Indies, which took in the West Indies and the continental possessions in North America from Georgia up to New York; the Northern District, which embraced the region north of the former, was under Thomas Lechmere. A list of customs officials in North America for the year 1749 is to be found in the Treasury Papers, Out-Letters, Customs, T. 11. 23, Public Record Office.

[12] For an illustration of the appointment of an agent and of a letter of agency see those accorded by Connecticut to Richard Partridge in 1750, *Wolcott Papers, 1750–1754* (Hartford, 1916), pp. 516–17.

[13] See instructions issued to Jared Ingersoll in 1758, *Conn. Col. Rec.*, XI, 127–8. For studies relating to the colonial agents see Ella Lonn: *Colonial Agents of the Southern Colonies* (Chapel Hill, 1945); J. J. Burns: *Colonial Agents of New England* (Washington, 1935); L. M. Penson: *Colonial Agents of the British West Indies* (London, 1924); M. P. Wolff: *Colonial Agency of Pennsylvania 1752–1757* (Philadelphia, 1933); M. Appleton: "Richard Partridge: Colonial Agent," *New Eng. Quart.*, V (1932); E. P. Tanner: "The Colonial Agent," *Political Science Quarterly* (1901), Vol. 14; B. W. Bond: "The Colonial Agent as a Popular Representative," *ibid.* (1920), Vol. 34.

[14] For example, two early colonial agents of Massachusetts Bay, William Stoughton and Peter Bulkely, in 1676 were furnished with two sets of instructions. One, signed by

vantage for a colony to be strongly represented in London,[15] yet, not infrequently, especially in the seventeenth century, those in authority in America were so disinclined to take any steps in this direction that the home government, after its repeated requests that this be done had been ignored, was led to complain vigorously.[16] For the process was a slow one that changed the London agency from an exceptional and not too welcome colonial mode of action into a confirmed and accepted institution.

It may be said that until the days of the English Revolution the London agencies almost without exception were in the nature of a special missions, although it is true that Virginia had made the agency a permanent feature by the latter part of the seventeenth century.[17] After the Revolution, however, none of the colonies appreciated more the importance of being well and continuously represented in Great Britain than did the corporate colonies Massachusetts Bay, Connecticut, and Rhode Island. They thereupon followed the example of Virginia and by the beginning of the new century had adopted the agency as perhaps the most important, effective, and regular means of maintaining contact with the various branches of the British government and of guarding both general and special colonial interests. The practice soon spread to other colonies and was especially encouraged by the Board of Trade,[18] which found its labours greatly facilitated, in preparing reports and

---

the Governor, commanded them to act only in matters that related to the claims of Gorges and Mason and to plead lack of instructions on all other points. When questioned on other matters they urged these restrictions, but were, in spite of this, forced to answer various questions and to receive orders which lay outside the range of the instructions. See R. H. Toppan and A. T. S. Goodrick: *Edward Randolph* (Prince Society Publications, Boston, 1898–1909), II, 275–86.

[15] The work of Rev. Increase Mather, Sir Henry Ashurst, Elisha Cooke, and Thomas Oakes, in the years 1689–90 undoubtedly preserved the corporate nature of the Massachusetts Bay government as embodied in the charter of 1691. See *A Brief Account concerning several of the Agents of New England, their negociation at the Court of England* (London, 1691), and *Andros Tracts*, II, 271–96.

[16] See C. M. Andrews: *Colonial Self-Government, 1652–1689* (New York, 1904), pp. 258–9.

[17] H. L. Osgood: *The American Colonies in the Seventeenth Century* (New York, 1904), I, 43.

[18] Board of Trade to Lord Bellomont, February 23, 1697/8, *Documents Relative to the Colonial History of the State of New York* (ed. E. B. O'Callaghan, 15 vols., Albany, N. Y., 1853–87), IV, 297–8; Board of Trade to Governor Hunter of New Jersey, April 23, 1713, *New Jersey Archives*, IV, 183; Board of Trade to Governor Hunter, July 23, 1718, *ibid.*, IV, 375.

representations to the Privy Council[19] and in corresponding with the colonial governors, by the presence of those in London who could give authoritative data on, and the point of view of, the colony or colonies under discussion. Indeed, so important in the eyes of the home government was this idea of having the agent in the fullest sense the responsible representative of the colony that it was finally laid down by the Crown in the 1760's that no agent should be received who was not appointed by concurrence of all branches of the colonial legislature.[20]

In characterizing the activities of the eighteenth-century London agents, it is necessary to bear in mind that no series of generalizations can be made that would cover accurately the work of each agency. For example, the agents of Connecticut, Rhode Island, and Maryland were not concerned with one of the most important responsibilities that confronted the others in connection with the review in England of colonial legislation.[21] When the other colonial governments, as required, had submitted their laws, their agents were thereupon expected to justify these in the eyes of the Attorney General, the Solicitor General, or the Board of Trade or its special legal adviser,[22] and to take every means to prevent disallowance and to secure confirmation.[23] The agents of the charter colonies, on the

[19] See C. M. Andrews: *List of Reports and Representations of the Plantation Councils, 1660–1674, The Lords of Trade, 1675–1696, and the Board of Trade in the Public* Record Office, Amer. Hist. Assoc. *Report* 1913.

[20] "It having been represented to his Majesty that the admission in the several public offices of Persons to act as Agents for the several Colonies and Islands in America under appointments from the lower Houses of Assembly only, without the Concurrence of the other Branches of Legislature, had been attended with great Prejudice and Inconvenience: It is His Majesty's Pleasure, that, for the future, no Person shall be received in any of the said public Offices in the Character of Agent for any Colony or Island, but such only as shall have been regularly appointed for that purpose by an Act or concurrent Vote of the whole Legislature of such Colony or Island" (P.R.O., C.O. 5:216, p. 67).

[21] These colonies were not required to submit their laws for confirmation, although this was done by Maryland during those years immediately succeeding the English Revolution when Baltimore was temporarily displaced. In 1734 and again in 1748 attempts were made by the Board of Trade to require this of them through an act of Parliament. See *Talcott Papers* (Conn. Hist. Soc. *Coll.*, IV, Hartford, 1892–96), Vol. I, 296–8; and G. S. Kimball: *Correspondence of the Governors of Rhode Island* (Boston and New York, 1903), I, 63, and the *Commons Journal*, XXV, 746.

[22] In 1718 the Board of Trade secured a special legal adviser. See C. M. Andrews: *Guide to the Materials of American History to 1783, in the Public Record Office of Great Britain* (Washington, 1912), I, 88–90; also, by the same scholar: *Connecticut and the British Government* (New Haven, 1933), p. 87 *et seq.*

[23] See C. M. Andrews: "The Royal Disallowance of Colonial Laws," Amer. Antiq.

other hand, had to be exceedingly active to thwart by hook or crook the plans that from time to time were formulated and urged by the Board of Trade for recalling the charters.[24] During the later French and Indian wars the securing of financial reimbursement for colonial military expenditures was also an exceptional and weighty task confronting all the agents. They were, moreover, expected at all times to defend the interests of the colonies they represented in judicial proceedings, and when necessary in this connection, to secure adequate legal assistance. Their activities were often exceedingly varied: they appeared before the Privy Council, secured audiences with whomsoever was acting head of the government, consulted with the Board of Trade, the Attorney General, the Lords of the Treasury, the Admiralty and other administrative branches of the government; they also were granted hearings before parliamentary committees, and when the occasion demanded, lobbied among the members of both houses. Indeed, it may be said that the influence of the agents was so great that no decision of importance affecting the colonies was ever arrived at without the most careful consideration of their informal testimony and arguments as well as their more formal memorials and petitions.

That this was an elaborate machinery of imperial control cannot be disputed. However, it should be emphasized that nowhere outside the old British Empire had there developed a system of government giving so much freedom of action and responsibility for self-government to the local units while so earnestly seeking to reconcile this latitude with the maintenance of an effective type of centralized supervision and direction.

The extension of the system of representative government to the various colonies as soon as conditions were favourable for its adoption in each case undoubtedly stands as a major contribution of England to the science and art of applied government. As we have noticed, most of the colonies were organized upon this basis. What-

---

Soc. Proc., XXIV, 342–63; E. B. Russell: *The Review of American Colonial Legislation by the King in Council* (New York, 1915); O. M. Dickerson: *American Colonial Government 1696–1765* (Cleveland, 1912), pp. 266–8. In the eyes of the Board of Trade the part played by the colonial agent was so important in this connection that in 1716 it refused to give its approval to the laws of New Jersey until the colony was represented in London by an agent. See *New York Col. Doc.*, V, 473.

[24] In 1701, 1706, and 1721 the Board of Trade made vigorous representations in favour of recalling the charters. See *North Car. Col. Rec.*, I, 535–7; 630–3, and *New York Col. Doc.*, V, 627–30.

ever may have been the attitude of those responsible for endowing them in the first instance with the powers of self-expression, it is certain that by the period under discussion the realization had come home to many if not most contemporaries that they differed, in some respects vitally, from the incorporated units of local government in England.[25]

Indeed, the development of so-called parliamentary privilege within the assemblies with the demand that the representatives of the people be endowed with powers and immunities similar to those enjoyed by members of the House of Commons is indicative of the nature of the evolution of British colonial government.[26] The political status of some of the colonies seemed to certain contemporaries little short of "independence." [27] Nevertheless, all the governments were based upon express or implied delegations of power. In other words, while it is true that they enjoyed an extraordinarily wide range of legislative competence and three of them [28] were highly privileged in that they were not obliged, as were the rest, to submit to the Crown the acts of their assemblies for acceptance or rejection, none enjoyed full autonomy. All important colonial legislation was subject under certain conditions to the processes of judicial appeal to the Privy Council functioning through its committee of the whole Council as the Lords of the Committee of Appeals.[29] No law passed in any of the plantations could stand in face of the refusal of the Council to uphold it.[30]

The colonies without exception had come into existence as the

---

25 See James Abercrombie's (Abercromby's) discussion of this in his "Examination," dated 1752 (Shelburne Papers, 47:1–25, Clements Library). For a contrasting opinion see Edward Channing: *History of the United States* (New York, 1925), II, 223, n. 2.

26 See Mary P. Clarke's *Parliamentary Privilege in the American Colonies* (New Haven, 1943), for elaboration of this point.

27 Abercrombie stresses the above view in his "Examination."

28 Connecticut, Rhode Island, and Maryland.

29 See J. H. Smith: *Appeals to the Privy Council from the American Plantations* (New York, 1950).

30 For a report of the Attorney and Solicitor General on the above question at this period, see C. O. 323:13, O, 117. For the most important work on colonial appeals see J. H. Smith: *op. cit.;* see also A. M. Schlesinger: "Colonial Appeals to the Privy Council," *Political Science Quarterly*, 1913, 279–97; H. D. Hazeltine: "Appeals from Colonial Courts to the King in Council," Amer. Hist. Assoc. *Report* for 1894, pp. 299–350; G. A. Washburne: *Imperial Control of the Administration of Justice in the American Colonies, 1684–1776* (New York, 1923), pp. 55–6; E. H. Turner: *The Privy Council of England in the Seventeenth and Eighteenth Centuries, 1603–1783* (Baltimore, 1928), II, 279–81, 287.

result of royal sanction expressed in the issuance of letters patent under the Great Seal. Legally, the King was still the source of authority in all matters having to do with the exercise of the powers embodied in those instruments that set forth the plan of government, whether in the form of the surviving charters or of a governor's commission and instructions. But by the middle of the eighteenth century, as the result of the shifting of the balance of power from the Crown to Parliament after the Revolution of 1689, and, also, due to the development of a powerful bureaucratic form of government, the King had come to play a minor part in the actual work of imperial administration, in view of the fact that his Privy Council was recognized to be that organ of government under Parliament entrusted with supreme supervisory powers. All matters of first importance automatically came before this body, and its decisions in the form of orders were considered definitive and binding by the royal officials.

There was, however, in the administration of the Empire a distribution of executive and administrative labours among the great officers of state. The Lords of the Treasury and the Exchequer were responsible for the collection and disbursement of the King's revenue; the Commissioners of the Customs, under the Treasury, and the Admiralty Board were concerned with the carrying out of the various regulations of Parliament regarding colonial trade; and the Bishop of London had oversight of matters pertaining to the Anglican Church wherever established within the colonies. These agencies were aided in some cases by lesser groups and subordinates to carry out the routine of administration.[31]

Beyond the range of activities just described lay those more definitely political in nature. In 1750 these were under the immediate oversight of the Secretary of State for the Southern Department. With him the governors corresponded and from him they received directions. He it was who recommended to the King in Council (that is, the Privy Council) the names of those, for example, to be appointed to the office of royal governor and who brought before that body issues of importance that had to do with political aspects of colonial affairs. Made up of great officers of state and busied with

[31] For a careful analysis of the imperial administration in the eighteenth century see C. M. Andrews: "The Government of the Empire, 1660–1763," *The Cambridge History of the British Empire*, I, Chapter XIV.

a multitude of problems, the Privy Council, after referring these matters thus brought before it to itself as a committee – known as the Lords of the Committee of Council for Plantation Affairs – in turn usually sought guidance from the Lords Commissioners for Trade and Plantations, popularly known as the Board of Trade.[32]

This Board, established in 1696 after the Crown had experimented with trade and plantations councils and a committee of the Privy Council duly commissioned under the Great Seal and known as the Lords of Trade, had been given a surprisingly wide range of interests as the objects of its attention. But it was created primarily to aid in the carrying out of the mercantilistic policies adopted by England, and, especially was designed to promote the trade of the Empire and the exploitation of its resources. During its first fifty years the Board had more than justified its existence, although in affirming this one must admit that it does not appear to have shown consistency either in activity or capacity.[33] Nevertheless, it was the only body permanently established and resident in England and carrying out prescribed functions which kept constantly in touch with colonial affairs, had a grasp on colonial problems, and could be depended upon, generally, to give enlightened advice in the solution of such problems.

The powers of the Board were carefully defined. It might investigate, hear complaints, and formulate representations to His Majesty as to lines of action to be adopted by his Council and especially as to laws proper to be passed in the assemblies; finally, it was expected to recommend suitable individuals for those offices in the plantations within the gift of the Crown. In practice, according to the Earl of Halifax, before 1750 the Board had not for many years made any representations or recommendations on its own initiative, having been given to understand that it should represent only such points as were referred to it by the Secretary of State for the Southern Department or by the King's Council. Therefore, it had automatically transmitted to the Secretary all correspondence received

---

[32] For the Board of Trade see O. M. Dickerson: *American Colonial Government, 1696–1765* (New York, 1912), and A. H. Basye: *The Lords Commissioners of Trade and Plantations . . .* (New Haven, 1926).

[33] For a discriminating statement by C. M. Andrews regarding the activities of the Board of Trade see *The American Historical Review*, XXXIV, 849–53; see also M. A. Thomson: *The Secretaries of State, 1681–1782* (London, 1932), pp. 47–50.

from America relating to Indian affairs, misconduct of officers, and all other matters that required the direction of the Privy Council.[34] But a situation had arisen within the government itself that now led to an expansion of the Board over colonial matters.

The Duke of Newcastle, who since 1724 had acted as Secretary of State for the Southern Department (with the exception of a few days in February, 1745/6), had been transferred early in 1748 by the chief minister, his brother Henry Pelham, to the Secretaryship of the Northern Department. In this post he took a leading part in the negotiations that ended in the Treaty of Aix-la-Chapelle. The Duke of Bedford succeeded Newcastle as Secretary for the Southern Department. Between the two Secretaries of State, no love was lost, and Newcastle sought means to weaken his rival. One of these was to strip his old office of much of its former importance by exalting the Board of Trade, which was under the presidency of his friend, the Earl of Halifax, acting as First Commissioner. During 1751 Newcastle was busy with the formulation of his plans, which comprehended the idea of allowing the Commissioners to act up to the letter of their commission "by presenting to the Council the names of proper people to be employed as Governors, Deputy Governors, Secretary, etc. and by taking cognizance of the government of the colonies." [35]

Halifax, who was heartily in sympathy with this proposal, sought, as an additional means of giving the Board prestige, an arrangement whereby it should be recognized that the First Commissioner would have frequent access to the King on all plantation matters. If this could not be arranged, Halifax signified that he was disposed to try to serve "with publick utility and satisfaction to himself" as the First Commissioner on this new footing suggested by Newcastle, provided that he had the honor of being appointed a Cabinet Councillor with added compensation and provided, also, that it would be fully understood by His Majesty's ministers that he should have the same weight in all plantation matters as if he were entitled by his post to have frequent access to His Majesty. These concessions were thereupon made. Bedford, doubtless well aware of the intentions of

---

[34] See George Montagu Dunk, Earl of Halifax, to the Duke of Newcastle, August 25, 1751, Newcastle Papers, B. M., Add. Mss. 32725, folio 91.

[35] L. H[alifax] to [the Duke of Newcastle] August 6, 1751, Newcastle Papers, B. M., Add. Mss. 32725, folio 17.

the brothers to reduce the importance of his office, had already resigned in disgust early in the summer of 1751.[36]

Under these circumstances the King's Cabinet Council determined to give new vitality to the Board of Trade, led by the aggressive, influential, and capable Halifax. Early in January of the following year, Lord Holderness, the new Secretary of State for the Southern Department, apparently much against his inclination,[37] addressed a letter to the President of the Board notifying him that in the future as vacancies arise in the plantations the Lords Commissioners should present to His Majesty in Council for approbation the names of persons deemed proper to be governors, deputy governors, councillors, and secretaries, as well as the names of inferior officers necessary for the administration of justice and the execution of government, excepting only those having to do with the customs and revenues or with the execution of powers relating to the jurisdiction of the Admiralty. Further, he declared that in the future the Board was also to prepare the commissions, warrants, and instructions for these appointees. Finally, he ordered that it should draft an additional instruction to the governors of all of the colonies signifying that in the future they were to transmit all accounts of their proceedings and matters relating to their governments to the Lords Commissioners *only,* except in such cases wherein they had previously received His Majesty's orders to the contrary "by one of his principal secretaries of state, or in such cases as might require His Majesty's more immediate direction by one of his principal secretaries of state." [38] By this means it was doubtless anticipated that the Board of Trade would be able to fulfill effectively its responsibilities of watching over the complicated processes involved in the proper articulation of the interests of a great Empire.

Under these arrangements the Board of Trade was undeniably now given a degree of importance in the eyes of colonial officials that could hardly have existed under the older system of administering the colonies, under which places in the overseas service had generally been filled without reference to the desires of the Lords

[36] M. S. Thomson: *The Secretaries of State, 1681–1782,* pp. 50–3.

[37] *Ibid.,* pp. 52 and 167–9.

[38] Lord Holderness to the Lord President, January 22, 1752, Newcastle Papers, B. M., Add. Mss. 33029, folios 88–9. For the order in council of March 11, 1752, see *Acts of the Privy Council, Col. Ser., 1745–1766,* pp. 154–6; for the order of May 16, 1761, revoking this authority, *ibid.,* p. 157. A. H. Basye's *The Lords Commissioners of Trade and Plantations* (New Haven, 1925) gives an excellent treatment of this aspect.

Commissioners. Appointment and, in consequence, tenure, depended now upon the pleasure of the Board, which was by no means illogical in the light of its specialized knowledge of colonial conditions.[39] This also gave to it a direct and inescapable responsibility in the administration of colonial affairs. How successful the Board would have been in meeting this responsibility at the beginning of the American crisis in the 1760's one cannot say, since in 1761 a shift took place by order in Council whereby it was deprived of the right to recommend appointments to office.[40]

Reference has been made to the authority of Parliament over the plantations. This came by a gradual extension of statutory regulation beginning with the acts relating especially to trade within the Empire [41] and finally including many matters quite outside of this field.[42] By 1750 Parliament had provided, among other plantation restrictions, that no place of trust in the law or in Treasury matters should be in the hands of other than natural born subjects in any of the colonies; [43] that lands should not be sold to aliens without the consent of the Crown; [44] that lands should be liable for the debts of the owners; [45] that debts owing in the plantations may be proved before a magistrate in England; [46] that unlawful stocks and business undertakings in the plantations should cease; [47] that foreigners who have resided seven years in the plantations and have taken the prescribed oaths should be deemed natural subjects; [48] that gover-

[39] For examples of appointments, on the basis of the Board's representations in 1754 and 1761, see *Acts of the Privy Council, Col. Ser.*, 1745–1766, pp. 257–8, 283–4.

[40] A. Berriedale Keith: *Constitutional History of the First British Empire* (Oxford, 1930), p. 275.

[41] The principal acts, not including the act of Oct. 19, 1651, regulating plantation trade are 12 Chas. II, c. 18; 13 and 14 Chas. II, c. 11; 15 Chas. II, c. 7; 25 Chas. II, c. 7; 7 and 8 Wm. III, c. 22; and 6 Geo. I, c. 21, Pars. 30–53. For a careful study covering parliamentary regulation of American colonial trade see L. A. Harper: *The English Navigation Laws . . .* (New York, 1939).

[42] For an interesting view that Parliament could not properly legislate for the colonies see C. H. McIlwain: *The American Revolution: a Constitutional Interpretation* (New York, 1923). For opposite views see E. S. Corwin's review of Professor McIlwain's book in the *American Historical Review*, XXIX, 775–8, and especially R. L. Schuyler's *Parliament and the British Empire: Some Constitutional Controversies Concerning Imperial Legislative Jurisdiction* (New York, 1929).

[43] 7 and 8 Wm. III, c. 22, Par. 12.

[44] 7 and 8 Wm. III, c. 22, Par. 16.

[45] 5 Geo. II, c. 7, Par. 4.

[46] 5 Geo. II, c. 7, Par. 2.

[47] 14 Geo. II, c. 37.

[48] 13 Geo. II, c. 7.

nors may be tried in England for offences charged against them; [49] that pine trees designated as serviceable to the Royal Navy should not be destroyed; [50] that the value of foreign coins in circulation in the colonies should be established; [51] that minors consenting thereto might be bound to service in the colonies; [52] that no wool, woollen yarn, or woollen manufactures should be exported from the plantations; [53] that beaver hats manufactured in any one plantation should not be sent to another; and that plantation hatters should have no more than two apprentices.[54]

During the period under consideration three other acts widened the scope of British statutory interference in colonial affairs: [55] the British act concerning the attestation of wills was extended to the plantations; [56] the New England colonies were placed under severe restraint in the issuing of bills of credit; [57] and a general prohibition was directed against the erection in any plantation of additional slitting mills or steel furnaces.[58]

It must not be understood that the passing of a statute meant its enforcement. This may be briefly illustrated with respect to the laws governing colonial commerce. So widespread was the violation of these acts that it seemed in the middle of the eighteenth century that the plantation trade was about to slip from the control of the mother country. In 1749 William Bollan, who had been acting as His Majesty's Advocate General in the Province of Massachusetts Bay, sent to the Board of Trade at its request his proposal for securing and regulating colonial commerce. He charged that great abuses were daily committed by ill-disposed persons who made a practice of importing into the colonies various commodities, the products of diverse countries, not shipped to Great Britain according to law, "to

---

[49] 11 and 12 Wm. III, c. 12.

[50] 3 and 4 Anne, c. 10, Par. 6; 9 Anne, c. 17; 8 Geo. I, c. 12, Par. 5; 2 Geo. II, c. 35.

[51] 6 Anne, c. 30.

[52] 4 Geo. I, c. 11, Par. 5.

[53] 10 and 11 Wm. III, c. 10, Par. 19.

[54] 5 Geo. II, c. 22.

[55] The voluntary adoption of English statute law by the colonial governments also represents an extension of this power, as in the act of the Assembly of Pennsylvania of 1718, "An Act for the Advancement of Justice and more certain Administration Thereof," which provided that those guilty of certain crimes should incur the same penalties, disabilities, and forfeitures incurred by persons convicted by the laws of Great Britain. See *Pennsylvania Statutes at Large*, III, 199.

[56] 25 Geo. II, c. 6, Par. 10.

[57] 24 Geo. II, c. 53.

[58] 23 Geo. II, c. 29.

the great Prejudice of the British Commerce and the utter loss to this Kingdom of a considerable Part of the Plantation Trade." To remedy this situation he proposed strengthening the authority of the vice-admiralty courts in the colonies and a modification of the plan whereby goods and ships of those guilty of evading the customs were forfeited.[59] In November of the following year, in answer to a letter from the Board of Trade requiring more definite information regarding complaints made of the illegal importation of foreign linens and silks into the Northern colonies, William Wood of the Customs Board wrote to Secretary John Pownall that this information had been communicated to the Customs Board from time to time by gentlemen who desired to conceal their names.[60] The vast contraband trade in foreign sugars and molasses carried on by the Northern colonies was taken into consideration by the House of Commons in March 1750 when it asked the Board of Trade for copies of the letters sent by the governments of Antigua and St. Christopher regarding this trade with the foreign sugar islands.[61]

These illustrations serve to indicate the nature of the problem of law enforcement that faced the government in its desire to extend parliamentary regulation to the colonies.

One explanation for this situation lies in the fact that colonials as a group were not favourably disposed toward a control which to them was not identified with the source of that authority, the royal prerogative. This had in the first instance given legal expression to the extension of British dominion into the New World and had in the main provided subsequent direction and guidance to imperial expansion. The growth of the colonies, in fact, during the period of a century and more, had the effect of gradually introducing new conceptions of the nature of the relations that existed between the mother country and her dependencies. To an ever increasing extent colonials had come to think of their own local governments not only as quite adequate to provide for their ordinary needs, but also as fully competent to do so while still theoretically accepting the supervisory authority of the Crown.[62]

---

59 "Proposals for securing and regulating the Plantation Trade by Mr. Bollan," Oct. 24, 1749, P.R.O., C.O. 323:12, O. 61.

60 See letter of November 22, 1750, P.R.O., C.O. 323:13, O. 79.

61 C.O. 323:13, O. 93. The struggle for the sugar markets will be more fully treated in Volume II of this series.

62 In the words of Governor Thomas Pownall, which can be considered almost as

Whereas the seventeenth century had witnessed the evolution of trade and plantation corporations and great proprietorial possessions into provinces, the first half of the eighteenth century saw these provinces changing into commonwealths and their legislative assemblies into parliaments. Implied in this was an inevitable challenge to all the conceptions of the older idea of delegated authority.

This change in attitude doubtless had its source in the growing sense of political maturity and self-sufficiency that reflected the extraordinary increase in population, growth in material resources, and social development of the colonies by 1750.

The old Empire had had as its basis the impulse of English people toward overseas colonization for religious purposes and for many other reasons, including the expansion of trade and industry. These English settlers were supplemented by large numbers of Ulster Scots, Germans, and other continentals, all influenced to migrate by a dual quest: for better standards of living and for a more favourable environment for individual self-expression. The Empire in 1750, it is important to keep in mind, was not so much the conscious achievement of far-seeing statesmanship as it was the unconscious creation of adventurous, hard-working, home-loving men and women of the middle and lower classes of society of the British Isles and Europe who were endowed with extraordinary initiative, tenacity of purpose, and resourcefulness in individually facing the problems of frontier life. As the wilderness gave place to permanent settlement so, too, the self-confidence of these pioneers grew in the midst of the slow moulding of a civilization distinctively their own. Their personal efforts almost from the beginning were supplemented by the institutions of white servitude and black slavery, the political as well as social and economic consequences of which were far-reaching. It is not without significance that the labour of over three hundred and eighty thousand Negroes, representing an invest-

---

applicable in 1750 as in 1765, "the people of the colonies say, that the inhabitants of the colonies are entitled to all the privileges of Englishmen; that they have a right to participate in the legislative power; and that no commands of the crown, by orders in council, instructions, or letters from Secretaries of State, are binding upon them, further than they please to acquiesce under such, and conform *their own actions* thereto; that they hold this right of legislation, not derived from the grace and will of the crown . . . that this right is inherent and essential to the community, as a community of Englishmen; and that therefore they must have all the rights, privileges, and full and free exercise of their own will and liberty in making laws . . . uncontrolled by any power of the crown. . . ." (Thomas Pownall: *Administration of the Colonies* [London, 1765], pp. 39–40).

ment, it would seem, of over £7,750,000 sterling,[63] was being exploited by these masterful British colonials. How far they were able, thus buttressed, to contribute to the material resources of the Empire may be gathered from computations made at this period which placed a valuation on their annual exports to the mother country of more than £5,000,000 sterling. Some three thousand ships were required for their trade, over one half of which were owned in the plantations.[64] Indeed, partly as the result of great activity in shipbuilding in the colonies and the favouring operation of the navigation and trade system, the British merchant marine enjoyed in 1750 an unquestioned supremacy over its rivals, which guaranteed the maintenance of communication between the various parts of the Empire and all those other advantages that accrue to any power in control of the seas.

---

63 For figures taken from Dinwiddie's report prepared in the early 1740's see James Abercrombie's "Examination," dated 1752, copies of which exist in both the Huntington and Clements libraries. Professor Andrews of Yale carefully collated the variations of these reports; this collation is deposited in the Yale University Library.

64 *Ibid.*

CHAPTER II

The Hub of the Empire

THE CENTRE of all imperial activity in the middle of the eighteenth century was England.

In population, the Kingdom, including Wales, contained some six and one half million persons.[1] Among these people great inequalities in wealth, education, and culture existed, and the scale of living varied from the luxurious and fastidious manner of life of the great landowning, fox-hunting aristocrats, merchant princes, and others – the Chestertons, Walpoles, Bedfords, and Beckworths – to the squalid dwellers of the unreclaimed fen country of Lincolnshire. It was an England of fairly sharply defined classes. The wealthy nobility at the top, then the landowning gentry, and following them, various groups, each more or less distinct from other groups, which by complex gradations of prestige constituted the so-called middle class. Beneath it was the lower order of people, also characterized by many social gradations, and made up of such groups as small shopkeepers, skilled artisans, and unskilled labourers, underneath which were the paupers and other unfortunates. Each class, except, of course, the very highest, seems to have sought to emulate the standard of living of the one immediately above it. Political, religious, educational, social, and economic leadership was provided in the middle of the century by the nobility, the landed gentry, the

---

[1] Sir John Chapham: *A Concise Economic History of Britain . . . to 1750* (Cambridge, 1949), p. 186; T. S. Ashton: *An Economic History of England. The Eighteenth Century* (London, 1955), p. 2; D. V. Glass: "The Population Controversy in the Eighteenth Century," *Population Studies* (July 1952); and E. C. K. Gonner: "The Population of England in the Eighteenth Century," *Journal of the Royal Statistical Society*, LXXVI, Part III, pp. 262–303.

"A New Map of England and Wales Divided into Counties. Drawn from the best Authorities."

(From D. Fenning and J. Collyer, *A New System of Geography*, 1765)

great merchants and financiers, and the professional groups, supplemented later in the century by promoters of the new enterprises created by the industrial revolution.

Compared with their European contemporaries, the English people were enjoying a rather comfortable and even in some respects rising, standard of living. Indeed, a Frenchman who prepared his observations of the Kingdom in 1742 asserted with surprise: "The whole people live in the greatest affluence. It is impossible to find in England a man in wooden shoes." [2] Another Frenchman, Plumard de Dangeul, declared, in comparing the agricultural population of France with that of England: "So far from being at their ease, the peasants in France have not even a necessary subsistence. They are a species of men, which begins to decline and wear out at the age of forty, for want of a reparation proportioned to its fatigues. Humanity is hurt by the comparison of them with other men, and above all with the English peasants." [3]

The English were, by all accounts, industrious, intelligent, resourceful, and practical-minded.[4] As a group they were moderately

[2] *"Observations sur le Royaume d'Angleterre, 1742,"* Loudoun Papers, Huntington Library, San Marino, California.

[3] See page 16 of Dangeul's *Remarks on the Advantages and Disadvantages of France and Great Britain,* published under the nom de plume Sir John Nickolls in 1754. Considering the advantages of the English over the French, he enumerated three he held to be of great importance: first, that France has forty more holidays than has England; as a consequence "the French workman must work one-ninth of time less than the English which must render his work a ninth dearer and his subsistence the harder in that class"; second, that whereas France keeps 400,000 men armed, Great Britain scarcely employes 100,000 by sea and land, "who are scarce missed out of the cultivation of the land, and the manufactures"; third, the commercial advantage that arises to England by reason of the fact that "no kind of land in it the most distant from the sea-coast is farther than seventy miles from it" (*ibid.*, pp. 20, 52, 53). The name of the author is given here as it appears in the Dictionary of *Anonymous and Pseudonymous English Literature* (Edinburgh and London, 1929); Dean Josiah Tucker, a contemporary, called him "the Marquis D'Angeul," though his work appeared in English, as indicated, under the borrowed name of Sir John Nickolls. See *Josiah Tucker. A Selection of his Economic and Political Writings* (ed. R. L. Schuyler, New York, 1931), p. 230. Tucker also pointed out that the Frenchman had drawn heavily upon his own (Tucker's) writings. William Mildmay, British Commissioner in Paris, writing on March 22, 1754, to his kinsman, the Earl of Fitzwalter, said that the French edition was having a great sale in Paris, and that it embodied "many Treatises written by different hands in English" (Mildmay Papers, Clements Library).

[4] Daniel Defoe in his detailed description of Great Britain which appeared in three volumes between 1724 and 1726 under the title *A Tour thro' the Whole Island of Great Britain . . .* and which went through nine editions in the eighteenth century (the last published in Dublin in 1779 with additions by Samuel Richardson and others to bring it up to date), stresses throughout these qualities of the English, whom he found busy im-

sober and law-abiding, yet favoured harsh laws against offenders — laws that were not considered to be inhuman according to the standards of that age. As a nation they were certainly opposed to treachery, but were frequently hard-handed and generally blunt. They were not so volatile as the French — who thought them stolid — were strongly conservative in instinct, and intensely proud of their freedom, which they tended to abuse by corrupt methods in political life, although in business relations they usually maintained high standards of probity.

In the middle of the eighteenth century England was filled with activity. Very naturally the centre of much of this was London, a great sprawling metropolis extending almost seven miles along the Thames, reaching far out beyond its narrow incorporation limits and in reality taking in not only the city of Westminster and borough of Southwark, but also many communities beyond the boundaries of either, with a total population probably of more than 600,000.[5] The city itself could boast of a great past, and its government still reflected the spirit of the days of the all-powerful guilds in the person of Sir Samuel Pennant, Knight, Alderman, and Ironmonger, who held the high office of Lord Mayor. Within the metropolitan confines were to be found all the fashionable vices and extravagances of a rather materialistic age; there were also deafening noises, dirt, pestilence, hunger, and crime.[6] The London prisons in 1750 were a

proving the face of the country. Another observer, the Portuguese merchant Gonzales, who travelled about England in 1730, afterwards declared: "The natives of England, taking them as they come out of the hand of Heaven, or as nature formed them, are brave, generous, sincere, modest, lovers of freedom, averse to tyranny, devout, benevolent, compassionate, open hearted, far from treachery or malice; their judgments are sound, and they bring arts and sciences to the greatest perfection" (John Pinkerton: *Voyages and Travels,* [17 vols., London, 1808–14], II, 143).

[5] See M. Dorothy George: *London Life in the Eighteenth Century* (London, 1925), p. 329; see also her chapter on London in *Johnson's England* (ed. A. S. Tuberville, Oxford, 1933), I.

[6] "A gentleman attended the Court of Aldermen on Tuesday last with a message from Lord Chief Justice Lee to acquaint them of the necessity of some new regulation concerning the gaol of Newgate or that it would be dangerous for persons to attend the business of the sessions at the Old Bailey. To the message was annexed a list of twenty persons that were at the last sessions who had since died, as it is thought from the noisome stench of the Prisoners" (London advices, May 24, *The Pennsylvania Journal,* August 16, 1750). See also William Maitland: *The History and Survey of London* (London, 1756), I, 709. It should be pointed out that in 1770 a new prison, commodious and sanitary, built of Portland stone and considered "a remarkable building," took the place of the old Newgate; it has since disappeared.

disgrace to civilization.[7] Those designed for debtors still swarmed with helpless prisoners despite the reforms carried out by Parliament in the early days of the reigning monarch, which had brought the release of some ten thousand of these unfortunates.[8]

London, however, was ranked among the most progressive of the larger cities of the world. Its principal streets were lighted at this time and partly paved with cobblestones. It also had a supply of water, recently introduced, which was considered quite excellent,[9] and a sewage disposal system that compared favourably with that of almost any large city, especially with Edinburgh and Madrid, where English travellers were amazed at the filth and stench of the streets.

Indeed, a Scottish writer of the period, after referring to London's healthful, unconfined situation, remarked: [10] "No less obvious are the neatness and accomodation of its private houses, the beauty and

---

[7] For a recent account of conditions in eighteenth-century English prisons see the chapter on "Poverty, Crime, and Philanthropy" by J. L. Hammond and Barbara Hammond in *Johnson's England.*

[8] 2 Geo. II, c. 22. For the release of debtors in 1729 see the *Diary of Percival,* Hist. Mss. Com., *16th Report* (London, 1920), I, 90.

[9] For a description of the water-works system of London in the eighteenth century see Defoe and Richardson's *Tour of Great Britain* (Dublin, 1779), II, 121–2; for a history of the London water supply by George Turnbull, see Sir Walter Besant: *London in the Nineteenth Century* (London, 1902) pp. 347–74.

[10] See 10 Geo. II, c. 22, passed in 1737, for statutory regulations regarding the above matters. It appears that the favourable conditions described in the text were largely confined to the city. Referring to Westminster, a writer in 1754 declared: "Let any man but reflect, what fatal Mischiefs have daily happened to men and Cattle in our Streets . . . by rough, unequal or broken Pavements; especially when these are so covered with Filth, as to make them scarcely visible to the most Cautious Passengers by Day, and much less so by night. . . . The wise Governors of that city London (amongst numberless other Advantages) reapt this Fruit of having their Streets equally and regularly light in Winter and Summer . . . that they are rarely infested with Robbers" (*A Proposal . . . for the better Paving, Lighting and Cleansing the Streets . . . of the City and Liberty of Westminster . . . by John Sanger,* [London, 1754]. It may be pointed out that Parliament beginning in 1757 passed a series of acts providing for the repair of the streets of Westminster (31 Geo. II, c. 17; 3 Geo. III, c. 23; 4 Geo. III, c. 39; 5 Geo. III, c. 50; and 6 Geo. III, c. 54). In 1759 an act was also passed for widening the streets of London (33 Geo. II, c. 30, explained and amended by 6. Geo. III, c. 27) whereby many new thoroughfares were opened and older passages widened. In fact, from the thirteenth year of the reign of Charles II down to 1775, eighty-five acts were passed by Parliament for the improvement of the streets, the lighting, and the sewage disposal of London, Westminster, and Southwark, and the liberties about them. See the Index to Eyre and Strahan's edition of the *Statutes at Large* (London, 1786).

conveniences of its numerous streets and open squares, of its buildings and bridges, its large parks and extensive walks." [11]

It is to the credit of London citizens that the shops were the most impressive in the world. Among the most magnificent buildings of the city were St. Bartholomew, the hospital for the sick and crippled, Bethlehem in Moorfields for the insane, the smallpox hospital, and St. Thomas's and Guy's for the sick and wounded, both of the latter splendid edifices located in Southwark. Within the walls of London were ninety-seven parish churches, and outside the walls, seventeen; Westminster had ten, and, including the so-called out-parishes in Middlesex and Surrey, the number totalled 146.

Of the wealth of the metropolis, it was asserted at this period that the County of Middlesex paid more taxes to the government than any other ten shires.[12] This is not surprising when one realizes that it was the heart of the financial, industrial, and commercial, as well as political, activities of the British Empire. Here were the Bank of England, the headquarters of the great trading companies, Blackwell Hall — the chief mart for woollen cloth in the world — and innumerable other important business establishments. Here, also, was the Thames, which at all times swarmed with ships and small craft of every type and description. In fact, two thirds of England's foreign commerce was concentrated at this point. Here, too, were St. James and other royal palaces, the Parliament buildings, Westminster Hall, where the great common-law courts and the High Court of Chancery sat, the Inns of Court, and the grim Tower. The metropolis had drawn to itself much of the talent and riches of the Kingdom and the Empire.

Next to London in commercial importance and wealth was Bristol with a spacious harbour on the Avon which at high tide allowed vessels under sail to move into the very heart of the city. It was estimated in 1725 that 2,000 ships were employed in trade by the mer-

---

[11] *Proposals for Carrying on Certain Public Works in the City of Edinburgh* (Edinburgh, 1752). Yet Paris was found to be greatly superior to London with respect to pavements and cleanliness by Dr. Douglas, who visited there in 1749. See C. Maxwell: *The English Traveller in France* (London, 1932), pp. 68–72.

[12] According to estimates of taxes paid in 1731, Middlesex paid more than the combined fourteen counties of Bedfordshire, Buckinghamshire, Cambridgeshire, Cheshire, Cornwall, Cumberland, Devonshire, Dorsetshire, Hampshire, Hertfordshire, Huntingdonshire, Rutlandshire, Westmoreland, and Shropshire. See "A Brief Account of the State of Each County in England, Anno. 1731," John Pinkerton: *Collection of Voyages and Travels*, II, 24–5.

cantile interests of the city, especially those concerned with the West Indian trade and African slaving.[13] In 1750 the population was about 75,000. Despite its vast importance for centuries as a centre for trade and industry, the city was considered by contemporaries unattractive with its many dark, narrow, dirty streets.[14] Of little less importance and more modern was Liverpool, which, with a population in 1750 of only 22,099, was characterized as "the most flourishing seaport (London excepted) in Great Britain." Its new merchants' exchange, it was asserted, in size and elegance was not to be paralleled in Europe.[15] This port was also deeply involved in the African trade and had surpassed Bristol in this field.[16]

Again, Manchester, a place without incorporate powers yet growing enormously and soon to enjoy a population of 50,000, boasted a vast production of fustians, cottons, tickings, and velvets. Indeed, all British cotton manufactures were significantly called by the keepers of shops "Manchester goods" irrespective of the particular place of their origin.[17] Other flourishing cloth-making centres, all of

---

[13] Alexander Pope, who visited Bristol in 1739, wrote that "in the middle of the street, as far as you can see, hundreds of ships, their masts as thick as they can be stand by one another, which is the oddest and most surprising thing imaginable. This street is fuller of them than the Thames from London Bridge to Deptford, and at certain times only, the water rises to carry them out; so that, at other times, a long street, full of ships in the middle, and houses on both sides, looks like a dream" (*Letters to Martha Blount*, pp. 326–7, quoted by C. M. MacInnes: "The Port of Bristol," *Essays in British and Irish History in Honour of James Eadie Todd* [London, 1949], p. 201).

[14] For Bristol see W. E. Minchinton: "Bristol — Metropolis of the West in the Eighteenth Century," Royal Hist. Soc. *Trans.*, 5th ser., IV, 69–79; see also S. Seyer: *Memoirs, . . . of Bristol* (Bristol, 1821–3).

[15] *Williamson's Liverpool Memorandum Book for the year* 1753; see also Wm. Indfield: *An Essay Toward the History of Liverpool drawn up from Papers Left by . . . George Perry . . .* 1774, p. 28. The rapid growth of Liverpool is indicated by the fact that not before the reign of William III was it even a distinct parish from that of Walton. A statute passed under George II (21 Geo. II, c. 24) not only provided additional facilities for attending Church of England services, but made "several regulations . . . for cleaning, paving and enlightening the streets" of the town. See A. Anderson: *Origin of Commerce* (ed. by Coombe, Dublin 1790) III, 540. In 1773 a survey of the population indicated the presence of 34,407 inhabitants. See Defoe and Richardson: *A Tour of Great Britain* (Dublin, 1779), IV, 265. Between 1685 and 1760 Liverpool had a tenfold increase in its population, Birmingham and Sheffield a sevenfold, and Manchester a fivefold. See H. de B. Gibbins: *Industrial History of England* (London, 1926), p. 152.

[16] One great advantage that Liverpool possessed over Bristol was that three of the great docks were enclosed by floodgates so that the ships in the harbour were not affected by the movement of the tides.

[17] Manchester established her reputation in the first instance in the making of "checks"; even so late as the year 1750, the wives of the most opulent traders would visit

which specialized in woollens, were Leeds, Norwich, Worcester, Taunton, Halifax ("the most populous parish in England"), and Warrington, where sailcloth was made for the Royal Navy — to name only a few communities justly renowned at this period for their spinning and weaving.[18]

Birmingham, like Manchester without incorporation and still governed by two constables and two bailiffs, was, with its environs, the most flourishing centre in England for all sorts of iron work and hardware; other centres were Wolverhampton, which produced implements of brass and iron and where the English locksmith trade was concentrated, and Sheffield, already famed for its cutlery, where in 1740 Benjamin Huntsman had introduced the manufacture of cast steel.[19] Nottingham, famed for its hosiery, together with Derby, Reading, and Abingdon, prospered also by the production of malt. The great malt vaults were hewn from the rock, and some are said to have been fifty feet beneath the surface of the ground.[20]

---

in check aprons. See Wallace: *A General and Descriptive History of the Ancient and Present State of Liverpool* (Liverpool, 1795), pp. 203–4.

"After the year 1750 the main burden of the Nation's wealth, as we know it today, has hung upon the single hinge of Lancashire: with its fate has been linked the commercial fate of Britain" (*The Victoria History of the County of Lancaster* [eds. W. Farrar and J. Brownbill, London, 1906], II, 30). For an extended description of Manchester at the end of the eighteenth century see John Aiken: *A Description of the Country from Thirty to Forty Miles round Manchester* (London, [1795]). For the production of cotton goods in England in the eighteenth century see A. P. Wadsworth and Julia de Lacy Mason: *The Cotton Trade and Industrial Lancashire, 1600–1780* (Manchester, 1931), and G. W. Daniels: *The Early English Cotton Industry* (London, 1920).

[18] For the woollen industry in the eighteenth century see Sir John Clapham: *A Concise Economic History of Britain . . . to 1750* (Cambridge, 1949), pp. 237–46; see also Herbert Heaton: *The Yorkshire Woollen and Worsted Industries from the Earliest Times to the Industrial Revolution* (Oxford, 1920), and E. Lipson: *History of the Woollen and Worsted Industries* (London, 1921). For Leeds in the eighteenth century see James Wardell: *The Municipal History of the Borough of Leeds* (London, 1846); for Norwich see *History and Antiquities of the County of Norfolk* (10 vols., Norwich, 1781); for Worcester see [T. R. Nash]: *Collections for the History . . . of Worcestershire* (2 vols., London, 1781–82); for Taunton see Joshua Toulmin: *History of Taunton* (ed. James Savage, London, 1836); and for Halifax see John Watson: *The History and Antiquities of the Parish of Halifax* (London, 1775).

[19] For Birmingham in the eighteenth century see Conrad Gill: *History of Birmingham* (London, 1952); for Wolverhampton see *The Victoria History of the County of Stafford* (London, 1908); for Sheffield see R. E. Leader: *Sheffield in the Eighteenth Century* (Sheffield, 1901).

[20] For Nottingham see J. D. Chambers: *Nottinghamshire in the Eighteenth Century . . .* (London, 1932), and a contemporary account by [George Charles]: *Nottinghamia Vetus et Nova; or, An Historical Account of the Ancient and Present State of the*

Other English towns were also of significant importance: Yarmouth in Norfolk was enriched by its red-herring fishery; Newcastle-upon-Tyne, Sunderland, Whitehaven, and Swansea, by collieries. (Newcastle shipped to London alone nearly 500,000 cauldrons of coal annually, and employed, according to an estimate in the early 1740's, at least 500 large vessels in which coal was carried to various ports of the Kingdom.) [21]

There were other busy and flourishing English ports in 1750. Woolwich, where British men-of-war were built; Portsmouth, in the spacious harbour of which the Royal Navy rested when not at sea; Weymouth, Dartmouth, and Lyme Regis, each with an important overseas trade, the two former with Spain, Portugal, and the American colonies, the latter especially with Holland, Norway, and the Baltic; and, finally, Hull, restricted in size by nature, but one of the busiest marts in England and having an immense trade with Hamburg.[22]

But some areas were hardly holding their own in the year 1750. The shifting of population and industry to regions more advantageously located for industrial development is indicated, among

---

Town of Nottingham (Nottingham, 1751); for Derby see W. Hutton: *History of Derby* (London, 1791), and R. Simpson: *History and Antiquities of Derby* (Derby, 1826); for Reading see C. Coates: *History of Reading* (Reading, 1806), for Abingdon see *The Victoria History of Berkshire* (London, 1906).

[21] England was the leading exporter of coal to Holland, France, Finland, Scandinavia, and Germany. In 1735 this export amounted to more than 100,000 cauldrons. New England in that year purchased more than 1,700 cauldrons and even Pennsylvania was importing a small amount. See the "Account of the Quantity of Coals exported for seven years," Custom House Report, May 6, 1737, P.R.O., Treas. 64. 273; see also "*Observations sur le Royaume d'Angleterre,*" 1742, Huntington Library, and especially Edward Hughes: *North Country Life in the Eighteenth Century. The North-East, 1700–1750* (Oxford, 1952), Chap. V, "The Coal Trade."

For the history of the English coal industry in the eighteenth century see T. S. Ashton and Joseph Sykes: *The Coal Industry of the Eighteenth Century* ([Manchester], 1929) and J. U. Nef: *The Rise of the British Coal Industry* (London, 1932); for Newcastle-upon-Tyne see John Brand: *The History and Antiquities of . . . Newcastle upon Tyne* (London, 1789); for Whitehaven see *Victoria History of the County of Cumberland* (London, 1905).

[22] For Woolwich see C. H. Grinling, T. A. Ingram, and B. C. Polkinghorne: *Survey and Record of Woolwich and West Kent* (London, 1909); for Portsmouth see *Victoria History of Hampshire* (London, 1908); for Weymouth see John Hutchins: *History and Antiquities of the County of Dorset* (London, 1908), which also deals with the history of Lyme Regis; for Hull see G. Hadley: *History of the Town and County of Kingston-upon-Hull* (Hull, 1788), and J. J. Sheaham: *General and Concise History of Kingston-upon-Hull* (London, 1864).

other ways, by the rapid growth of the population of some counties while in others it remained stationary or actually declined.[23]

In the middle of the eighteenth century, industry extended into the country districts. When they were not employed in the fields the farmers of Staffordshire and Warwickshire, for example, laboured at their own forges, fashioning with great perfection implements of iron, brass, and copper.[24] In Lancashire, Gloucestershire, Wiltshire, Somersetshire, Worcestershire, Shropshire, and Berkshire, especially, they were usually busily engaged with the loom in the home, at least during the winter months. Each locality, moreover, was likely to possess some specialty that had acquired a reputation. Somersetshire was famed for its fine cloth, Yorkshire for coarse weaves; long "ells" were produced at Exeter, a fine serge known as "says" was made at Sudbury, and Norwich led in crepes, Kendal in linseys, and Whitney in blankets. It was said of Worcester that the number of hands employed "in carding, spinning, and fulling, etc., is almost incredible"; the same could be said of the region in Lancashire near Manchester and of Norfolk in and about Norwich. In 1750, therefore, the independent domestic system of handicraft, although falling increasingly under the control of the entrepreneur, was still a major factor in the industrial life of England and was by no means limited to the counties enumerated above.[25] As Professor Ashton has pointed out, during the eighteenth century "English manufactures were offering increased opportunities to labour at rates of pay well

---

[23] In 1700 the nine most populous counties (outside of Middlesex) had the following order in density of population: Worcestershire, Somersetshire, Devonshire, Lancashire, Gloucestershire, Hertfordshire, Durham, Norfolk, and Bedfordshire. In 1750 the nine most densely populated counties were in the following order: Lancashire, Gloucestershire, Warwickshire, Somersetshire, Durham, Worcestershire, Hertfordshire, Staffordshire, and Berkshire. In 1801 the order was as follows: Lancashire, Warwickshire, West Riding of Yorkshire, Staffordshire, Gloucestershire, Worcestershire, Kent, Cheshire, and Somersetshire. The two counties with the least density throughout the century were Westmoreland and Cumberland. The maximum density of population (outside of London) in 1700 was up to 150 to the square mile; in 1750 Lancashire had a density of up to 200, and in 1801 this density increased to more than 250. See E. C. K. Gonner: "The Population of England in the Eighteenth Century," *op. cit.*, LXXVI, 287–8.

[24] For brass and copper manufacturing see H. Hamilton: *English Brass and Copper Industries to 1800* (London, 1926).

[25] Yorkshire was apparently the chief centre for the independent craftsmen among the weavers of wool. For an excellent description of conditions in the middle of the eighteenth century see the chapter on "Industry and Trade" by Herbert Heaton in *Johnson's England*, I, 225–60.

above those of most other countries," which had the effect of drawing workers from outside into the Kingdom.[26]

It must be remembered that in 1750 Richard Arkwright (1732–1792), one day to be knighted, was still a barber at Bolton,[27] James Hargreaves (d. 1778) was still a Blackburn carpenter, and James Watt (1736–1819), a delicate Scottish boy fourteen years of age, was still living at Greenock.[28] It would be three years until the birth of Samuel Crompton.[29] Nevertheless, heralds of the dawning industrial age of England already existed: Thomas Newcomen's "fire-engine," constructed in 1705, which displaced Thomas Savery's engine and was employed for mine pumping; the mechanical spinning inventions of Lewis Paul and John Wyatt[30] of 1738; and the famous Derby water-driven machine used extensively in Sardinia for the making of organzine, constructed about 1717 by Sir Thomas Comb. The spirit of invention animated many others. Well might Josiah Tucker affirm in 1758 that "Few Countries are equal, perhaps none excel the English in the Numbers and Contrivance of their Machines to Abridge Labour."[31]

Despite all such activity, England in 1750 was still predominantly agricultural and chiefly concerned in the raising of grain and livestock, although Kent was noted for its hops, the southwestern coun-

---

[26] T. S. Ashton: *op. cit.*, p. 11.

[27] For Arkwright see George Unwin, Arthur Hulme, and George Taylor: *Samuel Oldknow and the Arkwrights. The Industrial Revolution at Stockport and Marple* (Manchester, 1924).

[28] For Watt see H. W. Dickinson and Rhys Jenkin: *James Watt and the Steam Engine* (Oxford, 1927); see also H. W. Dickinson: *James Watt, Craftsman and Engineer* (Cambridge, 1936), and his *A Short History of the Steam Engine* (London, 1938), as well as *The Origin and Progress of the Mechanical Inventions of James Watt* (ed. J. P. Muirhead, London, 1854).

[29] For Crompton see G. W. Daniels: *The Early English Cotton Industry* (Manchester, 1920).

[30] For Wyatt see [Henry Pooley]: *John Wyatt, Master Carpenter and Inventor* (London, 1885).

[31] See Tucker's *Instructions for Travellers* (Dublin, 1758), reprinted in *Josiah Tucker, Selections from his Economic and Political Writings* (ed. R. L. Schuyler, New York, 1931), p. 240. In support of Tucker's assertions one need only turn to the large number of opinions of the Advocate, Attorney and Solicitor General on applications for patents under the Great Seal between the years 1760 and 1766 by those who had made improvements in the steam-engine, in the process of knitting by machines, in devices for unloading vessels by machines, as well as in other useful inventions too numerous to mention. These opinions are among the manuscripts in the Huntington Library, HM 220.

ties for their cider, and Hampshire for its honey and bacon. Somersetshire, Lincolnshire, Sussex, and Herefordshire were chiefly renowned for their beef cattle; Cheshire and Wiltshire for dairy farming. Leicestershire, Northamptonshire, and Suffolk bred the great draft and work horses; Durham, race horses and chargers. Shropshire, Dorsetshire, Gloucestershire, Leicestershire, and Yorkshire were perhaps the most important sheep-raising counties at this period, with the new Leicestershire breed of sheep to be developed by Bakewell soon to become especially famed.

Even in sheep-raising there was specialization in England by 1750. The most beautiful of the shorter wools came from the Cotswold Hills; the finest and nearest approaching those of Spain were secured in Herefordshire and Worcestershire; long wools for combing, favoured for their length as well as fineness, were produced in the counties of Warwickshire, Northamptonshire, Durham, and the Romney Marshes, and especially, in Lincolnshire and Leicestershire, where the pelts were valued not only for these qualities, but also for their softness and gloss.[32] It is estimated that seventeen million sheep were shorn in England in 1741, providing an exceedingly important domestic staple, valued at £3,000,000 – the larger sheep yielded from five to eight pounds of wool each year.[33] So great was the demand on the part of the spinners and weavers that even this large supply of wool was inadequate, especially in light of the fact that a considerable quantity of the total was exported to France. England therefore purchased this article from Ireland in quantity and also bought large amounts of merino wool from Spain.[34] In fact, in 1753 she gave additional facilities for the importation of Irish wool.[35]

Whereas the western and northern parts of England were chiefly devoted to grazing and stock-raising in 1750, the eastern, southern, and midland parts seem to have supplied the great surplus of corn.[36]

[32] Dangeul's *Remarks on the Advantages and Disadvantages of France and Great Britain*, p. 74.

[33] It was computed that in the salt marshes of Romney alone, which contained 45,000 acres, 130,000 sheep were grazing. See *ibid.*, p. 75–6, and also H. de B. Gibbins: *Industrial History of England*, p. 136.

[34] From 1729 to 1743 England secured from Spain a total of 65,905 bags. See London Custom House Report, 1744, P.R.O., Treas. 64. 273.

[35] For the debate upon the above issue see *Parliamentary History*, (Hansard), XIV, 1297–1317.

[36] According to a tabular account of the various counties of England drawn up in 1731 (giving the chief commodities ranked in order of importance) in the following list

In the middle of the century this crop was still grown under the old system of crop rotation and field rest. In 1754 it was said that a favourable year's harvest would supply five years of plenty to inhabitants of the island.[37]

Undoubtedly, what most stimulated grain-raising was the unique practice of providing a bounty on the export of corn when prices went below an established level,[38] which resulted in the exportation in 1750 of 1,651,417 quarters of wheat and the payment of bounties that totalled £325,405.[39] This bounty certainly acted as a check upon the conversion of arable lands into sheep walks and must have had a beneficial effect on the rural population. Nevertheless, Charles, Lord Townshend, (the son of the second Viscount Townshend, who was one of the most enlightened and active contributors to the agricultural revolution in England) published in 1752 his *National Thoughts* against the subsidy. In the same year, in a letter to the Rev. Josiah Tucker, he denounced it as "an absurd piece of extrava-

---

the raising of corn was placed first, with other commodities occupying a secondary position: Bedfordshire, Cambridgeshire, Cheshire, Devonshire, Dorsetshire, Essex, Gloucestershire, Hampshire, Herefordshire, Huntingdonshire, Norfolk, Nottinghamshire, and Oxfordshire. Those in which cattle ranked as the product of first importance were Lancashire, Lincolnshire, and Northamptonshire; those in which sheep occupied first place were Rutlandshire and Wiltshire; those in which wood-products ranked first were Buckinghamshire, Warwickshire, and Shropshire (fuel); those in which coal was of first importance were Derbyshire, Durham, and Staffordshire; those in which cloth ranked first were Berkshire (sailcloth), Westmorland, and Yorkshire. Fish stood first in Cornwall, copper in Cumberland, fuller's earth in Surrey, lead in Northumberland, cast-iron in Sussex, lapis caliminaris in Somersetshire, and cider in Worcestershire. See "A Brief Account of the State of Each County in England, Anno. 1731," John Pinkerton: Voyages *and Travels*, II, 24–5. For Professor Ashton's analyses of agricultural specialization see his *An Economic History of England: The Eighteenth Century*, pp. 30–2.

[37] Dangeul's *Remarks on the Advantages and Disadvantages of France and Great Britain*, p. 57.

[38] The bounty on corn when priced at £2.8 per quarter or four bushels, Winchester measure, was five shillings for this amount; rye, barley, and malt also enjoyed bounties, but of lesser amounts. See 1 Wm. and Mary, c. 12; 2 Geo. II, c. 18; see also Henry Saxby: *The British Customs* (London, 1750), p. 360. For an exhaustive account of the corn laws see D. G. Barnes: *History of the English Corn Laws from 1660–1846* (London, 1930).

[39] *Parliamentary History* (Hansard), XIV, 576; see also Dangeul's *Remarks on the Advantages and Disadvantages of France and Great Britain* (1754), p. 63. These figures are based upon "The State of the Exportation of Grain" laid before the House of Commons in 1751. According to this, in four years 5,289,847 quarters were exported. *Ibid.*

"They write from Cadiz that there were upwards of 150 English, 14 Dutch, 9 Danish and two Swedish ships in this Bay, all laden with corn; it was not doubted but they would all soon be discharged and their cargoes sold off" (London advices of July 26, 1750, *Pennsylvania Journal*, October 4, 1750).

gance" which allowed foreign countries to feed their "Manufacturers and Labourers of all kinds at a cheaper rate with our own produce than we can feed our own – thereby aiding the foreign competition with English-made goods." [40]

That these corn bounties were unpopular, moreover, with the non-agricultural population is indicated by the act of 1738 [41] which provided for the punishment of those who through violent means hindered the exportation of corn. Significantly, this law declared in the preamble that many "disorderly and evil-minded persons had of late committed great disorders whereby many of his Majesty's subjects had been deterred from purchasing corn." [42] It appears that the subsidy did not advance the price of English corn to the local consumer. At least it was calculated in 1751 by those who prepared a "state of the Exportation of Grain," which was laid before the House of Commons, that the average price for forty-three years preceding 1689 had been £2.10.8 per quarter of grain whereas the average price since 1689, a period of sixty-two years, had not been more than £2.2.6. Between 1746 and 1750 the average price before exportation was £1.8.[43]

Naturally, the agricultural interests – the great landowners and also the small farmers – favoured this subsidization of the export of

[40] "Townshend Papers," Hist. Mss. Com., *19th Report*, p. 372. However, a contrary view of the effect of the corn laws was expressed by a contemporary: "The effect of the bounty is not to lower the price of corn abroad in favour of foreign workers but . . . to enable us to carry ours to sale . . . on a par of price with that of Poland, Denmark, Hamburgh, Africa, Sicily and even with our own colonies who furnish Spain, Portugal and Ireland itself cheaper than we can. It gives our labour a bounty of £200,000 a year that England may gain £1,500,000" (Dangeul's *Remarks on the Advantages and Disadvantages of France and Great Britain* [1754], p. 64). Adam Smith in his *Wealth of Nations* (Vol. II, p. 8) indicated that the effect of these laws was to maintain the high price of corn; this is also the view of Professor Ashton (*op. cit.*, pp. 49–50). E. Lipson in his *The Economic History of England* (Vol. II, 457–8) took the position that the effect of the laws was to maintain the abundance of corn.

[41] 11 Geo. II, c. 22.

[42] Those twice convicted of the above offence were guilty of a felony. Injured parties were permitted to recover damages from the hundred where the violence occurred. See *ibid.* The importance of the price of corn in the national economy may be emphasized by pointing out that the average per capita consumption of wheat each year in England at this period was six bushels. See C. E. Russell: "Population and Wheat Production in the Eighteenth Century," *History Teachers' Miscellany*, VII, (New York, 1929), 65–8.

[43] Dangeul's *Remarks on the Advantages and Disadvantages of France and Great Britain*, pp. 58–9. See the table for the price of wheat from 1704 to 1800 in Ashton: *op. cit.*, p. 239, and particularly J. E. T. Roger: *A History of Agriculture and Prices* (Oxford, 1906), VIII, 2–229.

corn. In 1742 a foreign observer testified to the prosperous conditions in agriculture aided by this subvention. "The number of farmers who have £50, £100, and £200 in rent," he wrote, "is almost inconceivable; there are some in Kent who raise from their lands an income of £1,000." [44]

Yet, the movement of field crops to export markets was fraught with difficulties. In 1750 transportation was still very primitive in many parts of the Kingdom despite the building of numerous toll roads. Only near populous seaports such as London were roads kept in good condition; secondary roads might be almost impassable for periods at a time. Canals, such as the one promoted by the Duke of Bridgewater, were still to come.

In the middle of the eighteenth century rural England was in the midst of a great revolution under the stimulus of improved methods of agriculture sponsored by such men as Jethro Tull, a Berkshire gentleman who stressed the importance of crop cultivation and its concomitant drill-sowing and horse-hoeing,[45] and Charles, second Viscount Townshend, who introduced at Raynham a four-course system of crop rotation, known as the Norfolk system, which included the growing of turnips as a winter cattle food.[46]

But the agricultural revolution was only beginning. Experiments in stock-breeding had hardly begun and even the planting of clover and turnips was apparently localized. Progress depended on the freedom with which farmers could test new methods.

At the beginning of the eighteenth century one half of the arable land was still unenclosed. Improvement could hardly take place so

---

[44] "*Observations sur le Royaume d'Angleterre, 1742*," Loudoun Papers, Huntington Library.

[45] See Jethro Tull: *New Horse-hoeing Husbandry* (London, 1733); see also R. E. Prothero (Baron Ernle): *English Farming Past and Present* (London, 1912), p. 169; T. H. Marshall: "Jethro Tull and the New Husbandry," *Economic History Review*, II, (1929), 41–60; and E. R. Wicker: ". . . Jethro Tull: Innovator or Crank," *Agricultural History*, XXXI, 46–8. That many others were interested in improved methods of cultivation is indicated by the following news item: "This day an experiment was try'd with a new inverted plow, which is called a Dave's Mathematical or Universal plow, which plows three complete furrows at the same time, can sow, harrow or roll all as it goes on, which in about 5 minutes can be made to heel, weed, or level ground, all which, and several other things, can be made with it without any more horses than what is usual to a common plow. The encouragement the inventor has met with has engaged him to send models to every county in the Kingdom . . ." (London advices, Dec. 2, 1749, *Pennsylvania Gazette*, March 27, 1750).

[46] For the early but limited practice of growing turnips in England for stock feeding, see Sir John Clapham: *A Concise Economic History of Britain . . . to 1750*, p. 219.

long as the old open and common field system of landholding and land-utilization so characteristic of most of southern, midland, and eastern England prevailed.[47] Men of enterprise and capital with landed interests and progressive ideas were, in fact, becoming increasingly aware of the inadequacies of those traditional methods of exploiting the land, which had been evolved after the break-up of the mediæval manorial system. Self-interest therefore led them to work for large, individual estates, portions of which could be leased under advantageous terms for periods between seven and twenty-one years. This enclosure movement was, of course, not merely the product of eighteenth-century forces, for it had its beginning at least as early as the sixteenth century.[48] Nevertheless, it was not until the reign of George II that enclosure by means of private acts of Parliament came to possess great significance. This is clear from the fact that of the 110 enclosure acts passed from 1700 to 1750, 91 were enacted during the early years of that monarch's reign (1727–1760), which saw the passage of 240 of these acts as against a total of but 19 from 1700 to 1727 (that is, for the period of the eighteenth century preceding his coming to the throne). Further, it is of interest to note that during the first six years of his reign, 1727–1733, only 30 of these acts were passed, while during the last six years, 1755–1760, there were more than four times as many; indeed, but 4 enclosure acts were passed in the first year, while during the last year there were 35.[49] The year 1755, when England was facing a great war, marks the beginning of the period of acceleration of this movement, and an avalanche of enclosure legislation followed during the reign of George III after the passage of the very comprehensive general

[47] The open field system was unknown in Kent. In this connection see T. S. Ashton: op. cit., pp. 36–48; see also C. S. Orwin's chapter on "Agriculture and Rural Life" in *Johnson's England*, I, 261–99, and H. L. Gray: *English Field Systems* (Cambridge, Mass., 1915), pp. 404–9.

[48] Among important works relating to enclosures, see Gilbert Slater: *The English Peasantry and the Enclosure of Common Fields* (London, 1907); E. C. K. Gonner: *Common Land and Enclosure* (London, 1912); W. H. R. Curtler: *The Enclosure and Distribution of our Land* (Oxford, 1920); E. F. Gay: "Enclosures in England in the Sixteenth Century," *Quarterly Journal of Economics*, Vol. XVII; and A. H. Johnson: *The Disappearance of the Small Landowner* (Oxford, 1909). Dorothy Marshall in her *English People in the Eighteenth Century* (London, 1956, pp. 232–6), in summing up the results of research on the effects of parliamentary enclosures upon the small agriculturist, arrives at the conclusion that those which were adverse have been exaggerated.

[49] These private acts can be found among the titles of acts in the *Statutes at Large*, published by Charles Eyre and Andrew Strahan in 1786, which extends and revises Ruffhead's editions of 1762–1765 and of 1769.

enclosure act of 1773 in the thirteenth year of the reign of that monarch.[50]

The parliamentary enclosure acts differed in scope. Some ratified previous agreements for the enclosing of particular meadows or waste lands, such as the act reducing the "stint" of the horse and beast pastures and sheep commons within the manor of Castle Donnington in Leicestershire,[51] or the act of confirming certain articles of agreement between the lord of the manor of Hunmanby in Yorkshire and the vicar and freeholders.[52] Other acts provided for the dividing and allotting of all lands, including the open arable fields as well as the pastures and other common lands. That enclosing the lands of Sulgrave, Northamptonshire, the old home of the Washingtons, is quite typical of the latter group, for it brought about the dividing and enclosing of the open and common fields, the common meadows, the common pastures, the common grounds, and the commonable lands in general within the parish, township, and liberties of that place.[53]

The distribution of the lands affected by the enclosure acts is not difficult to ascertain. One fifth of the acts during the reign of George II concerned Yorkshire, with the counties of Warwickshire, Leicestershire, Northamptonshire, Lincolnshire, and Nottinghamshire following in order of the number of acts obtained. All told, twenty-eight of the forty counties were involved between the years 1727 and 1760, not including the County of the City of Coventry. The movement, however, was largely concerned with a group of northern and midland counties, some of them especially famed at this period for sheep and for their great production of wool, and would seem to point to the increase in many cases of the number of enclosed sheep walks.[54] At the same time, much hitherto uncultivated

[50] 13 Geo. III, c. 81, "An Act for the better Cultivation, Improvement, and Regulation, of the Common Arable Fields, Wastes, and Commons of Pasture, in this Kingdom."

[51] 11 Geo. II, c. 19, Private Acts, *Statutes at Large* (Eyre and Strahan), VI, "A Table of the Publick and Private Statutes, containing the Titles of the Acts from the Ninth Year of the Reign of George II. to the Twenty-sixth Year of the Reign of George II."

[52] 12 Geo. II, c. 10, Private Acts, *ibid.*, VI.

[53] 33 Geo. II, c. 5, Private Acts, *ibid.*, VII, "A Table of the Publick and Private Statutes, containing the Titles of the Acts from the Twenty-fifth Year of the Reign of George II. to the Seventh Year of the Reign of George III."

[54] From 1700 to 1741 there was, it has been estimated, an increase in the number of sheep from 12 millions to 17 millions. See H. de B. Gibbins: *Industrial History of England* (19th edn., London 1913), p. 36.

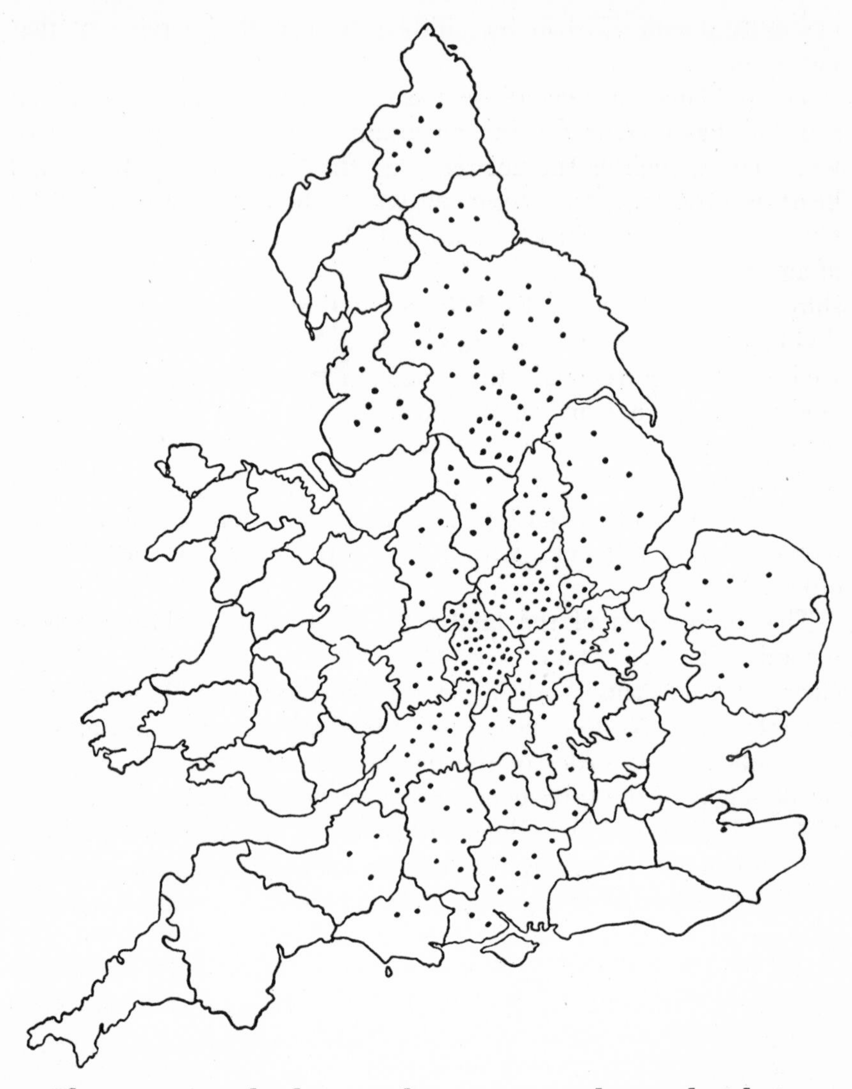

The areas involved in parliamentary enclosure legislation, 1699–1760.

land, it appears, also went into tillage. Nevertheless, tillage did not keep pace with public demand for cereal. With the steady increase in the industrial population, especially after the middle of the century, and perhaps also as the result of a change in dietary habits, it was necessary to import wheat from time to time.[55]

[55] T. S. Ashton: *op. cit.*, p. 50.

In dealing with the problems of food supplies there arises the difficult question of the standard of living of the labourers in the period under consideration. It appears that, on the basis of such studies as those by Miss Elizabeth Gilboy, real wages increased in the course of the eighteenth century in the area about London and in many of the other larger industrial centres, particularly in the northern part of England, whereas in the western part little change can be noted, at least for the better.[56]

One further aspect must be stressed in considering conditions in rural England in the middle of the century. This was the decline now noticeable in the yeoman class, "that middle mass of men higher than the peasant, and lower than the gentleman" who "hath subsisted independent; who, like an isthmus hath divided and withstood the fury of popular insurrections; and the arrogant encroachments of greatness; saving alike this *founded monarchy* from *confusion* and *tyranny*." [57] To "that good class of men," complained the same writer in 1749, "a race succeeds, of *puny, abject wretches*, tamed by *want* into *servitude*." According to him, an unbearable weight of taxation fell upon the yeomanry not only as small landowners, but as consumers of articles the price of which had been enhanced beyond their reach by the needs of the public treasury. He also saw, as the result of this public pressure, the disappearance very soon of the smaller gentry, and declared most pessimistically: "*An independent country gentleman* will then be just as much a phenomenon as an *independent farmer is now*." [58] Another contemporary made comparable assertions, which, he declared,

> "every man must know who has taken a ride in the country at Eighty or a Hundred miles distant from London . . . ; let him proceed from Village to Village through the Kingdom, and except some few

[56] Elizabeth Gilboy: *Wages in Eighteenth Century England* (Cambridge, Mass., 1934), especially pages 240–3; see also T. S. Ashton: *op. cit.*, pp. 219–26, who pays tribute not only to Miss Gilboy's work but to the observations of Adam Smith; P. J. Mantoux in his *The Industrial Revolution in the Eighteenth Century* (trans. M. Vernon, rev. edn., London, 1947, Chap. III of Part III) also throws light on the standard of living of the labouring class.

[57] R. Nugent: *Considerations upon a Reduction of the Land-Tax* (London, 1749), p. 22.

[58] *Ibid.*, p. 23. Sir Matthew Decker, in *An Essay on the Causes of the Decline of the Foreign Trade* (2nd edn. with additions, London, 1750, p. 3), refers to the great arrears of rent on the part of tenants all over England. For a brief discussion of the decay of the yeomanry see H. de B. Gibbins: *Industrial History of England*, pp. 115–16.

> places which have had the fortune to strike out some Manufacture, he will find numerous signs of decay at least if not of desolation. . . . The township were [where] I was born consists of Twenty houses; Eighteen of these about Fifty years ago were inhabited by Freeholders, from Sixty to Two Hundred Pounds a year, who all lived upon their own Estates; at present there is but One man in it who owns a bit of the land that he occupies. In the parish were [where] you now live, you observed, that there are Seventy odd Families, and that at the same distance of time, Forty of them were Freeholders, and Six of these worth above Two Hundred Pounds a year each. There is not a man in the parish now, except yourself and the Vicar, who is not a Tenant at will: And the Poor's Levy, which in 1708 was not Seven Pounds for that year is now above Fifty."[59]

The explanation of decline in the number of small freehold farmers and lesser gentry, according to Professor Habakkuk, was that their financial reserves were so small that with the heavy land tax they could not tide themselves over unfavourable seasons in face of the competition of the large wealthy landowners, who, in adding to their acreage, leased their lands in large units to efficient tenant-farmers.[60]

Although the agricultural revolution was in its earlier stages and the industrial revolution had not begun, England, despite the decline of the yeomanry, was nevertheless considered by contemporaries to be in 1750 the greatest wealth-producing country in the world.[61] The value of natural products and manufactures in 1749 was placed by one writer at £48,000,000. Under ordinary circumstances the country had a large exportable surplus that was estimated at one sixth of the total output from year to year. The prosperity of the people rested on England's ability to market this surplus abroad advan-

---

[59] *The Present Taxes Compared to the Payments made to the Publick within the Memory of Man, a Letter to a member of Parliament from a Country Farmer* (London, 1749), pp. 47–8.

[60] The above statement is based upon Professor H. J. Habakkuk's important article, "English Landownership, 1680–1740," *Economic History Review*, X, 2–17; see also Dorothy Marshall: *The English People in the Eighteenth Century*, pp. 42–3. For a recent scholarly study of the English land tax and its inequalities see W. R. Ward: *The English Land Tax in the Eighteenth Century* (Oxford, 1953), especially Chapters 6 and 7.

[61] "*J'accordera que le peuple anglais est plus riche que les autres peuples,*" wrote Rousseau in his "*Gouvernement de Pologne,*" *Political Writings of Rousseau* (ed. C. V. Vaughan, Cambridge, 1915), II, 480.

tageously, as well as on the export of the excess over local demands of certain of her great importations, especially those from her own colonies and possessions.[62]

It appears that at this time the value of British commodity exports in certain parts of the world was greater than the value of imports. This was manifestly true of the New England and Middle Atlantic colonies; it also seems to be true of Holland, Flanders, Portugal, Spain, and much of the Mediterranean region. On the other hand, Scandinavia, Russia, the East Indies, the West Indies, the Carolinas, Newfoundland, and Hudson Bay sent commodities the value of which was in excess of the imports received from Great Britain.[63] This does not, however, take into account certain invisible exports and imports. Most of the shipping employed in these activities was British – ships built in Great Britain and manned by British crews – which with the cargoes was also insured by the underwriters at Lloyd's Coffee House; foreign shipping was likewise insured on a large scale.[64]

That business was thriving in most branches is indicated by the vast growth of commercial centres and improvements undertaken within them and the construction of innumerable country-seats, many of them sumptuous. Moreover, the credit of the country was high and money relatively plentiful in the middle of the eighteenth

---

[62] *The Present Taxes Compared . . . to a Member of Parliament from a Country Farmer* (London, 1749), p. 15. "But the most important ingredient in English prosperity was to be found in her export of textiles. Of these, woollens still took the first place, even as late as 1785, when Macpherson estimates that some £16,000,000 worth were being exported every year" (Dorothy Marshall: *English People in the Eighteenth Century*, p. 5).

[63] Report on imports and exports, 1702–1750, B. M., Add. Mss. 29903. The difficulty of using with confidence such tables as those just cited is stressed by a contemporary, Malachy Postlethwait. In his *Universal Dictionary of Trade and Commerce. Translated from the French . . . of Monsieur Savary . . . with large Additions* (2nd edn., London, Vol. I, 184–9) in dealing with the difficult problem of the balance of trade he shows how unsatisfactory are the official tables of exports and imports. David Hume, in his *Political Discourses* (Edinburgh, 1752) in Essays V and VI also deals perceptively with the intricacies of balances of trade. In this connection the reader should consult Sir George Clark's *Guide to English Commercial Statistics, 1696–1782* (London, 1938), as well as W. Schlote's *British Overseas Trade from 1700 to 1930* (trans. from the German by W. O. Henderson and W. H. Chaloner, Oxford, 1952), pp. 15–26, and E. Lipson's *Economic History of England*, III, 62–116.

[64] For marine insurance in the mid-eighteenth century see Principal Lucy Sutherland's *A London Merchant, 1695–1774* (Oxford, 1933), pp. 42–80; see also Frederick Martin: *The History of Lloyd's and of Marine Insurance in Great Britain* (London, 1876).

century with the interest on the consolidated debt reduced from 4 per cent to 3 per cent in 1748.

Whereas, as a rule, there was little attempt during this period to check the natural movement of precious metals in the course of international and imperial trade, Spain and Portugal sought to prohibit the export of specie and bullion. This they found to be impossible in practice, despite occasional arbitrary measures.[65] For example, in 1752 the British Trading Committee of Lisbon was forced to appeal to the government in London for assistance because of hostile demonstrations of Portuguese officials against those who sought to transport out of that kingdom specie that had been accumulated in the course of trade. It was reported that on January 19 three officers of His Majesty's Ship *The Lime* were attacked by customs officers while on their way to the ship with a considerable amount of money, and that one of them was seized before the palace of the Portuguese King. The money, which was forcibly taken from them, belonged to one of the local British merchants, who was seeking to send it home. Further attempts were made to prevent other traders from doing the same. What alarmed the British merchants particularly was evidence that those in power at the Court were really determined to prevent the exportation of any specie out of the country; a judicial inquiry, they declared, was actually in agitation against a British merchant house that also in 1722 had suffered an unaccountable sequestration of its funds.[66] Faced by this attitude of the Portuguese government, the merchants also appealed to Commander George Brydges Rodney, who had just come into the port of Lisbon convoying the sack-ships from Newfoundland, to delay his departure until the crisis had passed. The local British consul, John Russell, had recently died, and

---

[65] "In Spain and Portugal, it is, by the law, death to ship off gold and silver; and yet we see this daily exported" (Malachy Postlethwait: *A Dissertation on . . . Trade and Commerce; Translated from the French of M. Savary with additions* ([London, 1749] p. 33); see also *Parliamentary History* (Hansard), XIV, 1313. It was, of course, unlawful to export from England the money of the realm. However, merchants were permitted to re-export the specie they received in the course of trade (27 Ed. I in *Statutum De falsa Moneta* in the Norman French of this period; 9 Ed. III, Stat. 2, c. 1; 17 Ed. IV, c. 1; 4 Henry IV, c. 16). They also melted the silver coin of the realm and thus exported it as bullion. See C. P. Nettels: *The Money Supply of the American Colonies before 1720* (Madison, Wis., 1934), p. 166.

[66] British Trading Committee of Lisbon to the Earl of Holderness, September 7, 1752, Rodney Papers, P.R.O., G.D. 20: 12; see also *Transactions of the Royal Historical Society* (fourth series), XVI, 230–2.

Rodney agreed to stay.[67] The crisis, indeed, was so grave that the Earl of Holderness wrote to Rodney that it seemed necessary to select some person of high rank and great reputation whose character was such as to impress the Portuguese ministers, in order to carry through negotiations in behalf of the British factory group at Lisbon. He finally sent Lord Tyrawly, who for a considerable time had been employed in that country and who understood the Portuguese people.[68]

A somewhat more detailed analysis of England's commercial relations with the outer world is important to an understanding of the economic situation at this period.

There is sharp diversity of opinion as to whether or not the commercial relations with her great rival, France, were beneficial, at least so far as Great Britain was concerned.[69] John Cary, a merchant who lived in the early eighteenth century and wrote on questions of trade, insisted that the French trade was a loss to England:

> "France being like a Tavern with whom we spend what we get by other nations; and 'tis strange we should be so bewitcht to that People, as to take off their growth, which consists chiefly of things for Luxury, and receive a value only for the esteem we put on them, whilst at the same time they prohibit our Manufactures in order to set up the like among themselves which we encourage by furnishing them with Wool." [70]

He asserted that the balance of trade with France, as well as with the East Indies, was always against Great Britain.[71] In 1749 this was also

---

67 The British Merchants to Commander Rodney, February 7, 1752, Rodney Papers, P.R.O., G.D. 20: 6. This was signed by ten merchants. The chairman of this committee was John Alten. Rodney, who later won great fame as an admiral in the Navy, was Governor of Newfoundland in 1752.

68 The Earl of Holderness to Commander Rodney, February 1752, *ibid.*, G. D. 20: 12.

69 See E. Lipson: *The Economic History of England* (London, 1931), III, 99–111, and Dorothy Marshall: *The English People in the Eighteenth Century*, Chapter I, "The Commercial Framework."

70 See John Cary: See *A Discourse on Trade* . . . (London, 1745), pp. 78–9.

71 *Ibid.*, pp. 80–1. It was also asserted by a writer of this period in the *Journal d'Economique* of Paris that after 1726, when the trade of the French East India Company began to counterbalance that of the English and Dutch, the course of exchange was always in favour of France. He presents a table of exchanges between Paris and the principal towns of Europe indicating the balance of trade (*Select Essays on Commerce, Agriculture, Mines, Fisheries* [London, 1754], pp. 501–7).

the contention of the Secretary of State for the Southern Department, the Duke of Bedford, in a discussion with M. Rouillé, the French minister in London, of the terms of the treaty of commerce concluded at Utrecht in 1713 between Great Britain and France.[72] Rouillé, on the other hand, insisted that the opposite was true.[73]

France, indeed, in 1750 supplied articles to her rival into which highly skilled and artistic labour had gone, such as laces, linens, cambrics, lawns, and other expensive fabrics, together with brandies, wines, dried fruits, and olive oil, while receiving from Great Britain tin and lead, great quantities of plantation tobacco, coal, meat, and butter, and, in years of scarcity, corn.[74]

According to the mercantilistic conceptions of international trade, a country to be highly favourably situated should import raw materials and export manufactured articles. To this extent France in her relations with England was more happily circumstanced than the reverse, a situation that led one writer, reflecting the popular English point of view, to state in 1765: "This trade is of very great disadvantage to England." [75] However that may be, France's dependence on English commodities was such that even in time of war she was compelled to buy through indirect means from her enemy.

One commodity that England could supply and France eagerly

---

[72] Duke of Bedford to the Duke of Albemarle, August 3, 1749, Newcastle Papers, B. M., Add. Mss. 32917.

[73] Bedford refers to "the extraordinary language held by Mr. Rouillé on this subject. . . . The chief tenor of this conversation and upon which he founded all his reasonings seemed to be that the advantage in trade between Great Britain and France was in favour of the former, and that at the time of the making of the treaty of 1713 they did not understand commerce as well as they do now, for which reasons he, Mr. Rouillé, asserts that they are not bound to comply with a Treaty which he himself cannot deny to be still existing. The two assertions, upon which he founds this reasoning, may, I think, be indisputably proved to be fallacious . . . that the Ballance of Trade is not in their Favour, and that they understand their commercial interest better now than they did when that treaty was made" (*ibid.*).

[74] For a detailed description of French commerce in the middle of the eighteenth century see the manuscript volume in the Library of Trinity College, Dublin, entitled, "*Commerce Général de la Nation Française Dans les Quatre Parties du Monde en l'Année Mil Sept Cinquante Deux*," Ms. 903, K. 2, 18.

[75] See D. Fenning and J. Collyer: *A New System of Geography* (London, 1765), II, 499. "Several duties upon the manufactures of France have lately been reduced, and great care has been taken to make the necessaries of life as cheap as possible to the manufacturers; by which means they hope to render their manufactures so cheap as to beat foreigners out of their markets" (London advices of November 5, 1749, *Pennsylvania Gazette*, June 30, 1749). The term "manufacturers" as used at this period refers to the workmen engaged in the labour of manufacturing articles.

sought was wool, the export of which, however, was forbidden on pain of transportation to the colonies by act of Parliament in the twelfth year of the reigning King (12 Geo. II, c. 21, Par. 26). Nevertheless, by all accounts of the period, great quantities were spirited into France by rings of wool smugglers who also carried abroad gold and silver. It was asserted in 1765 that the volume of wool smuggled was so great as to have led to the decline of cloth-making in Gloucestershire, where this industry "before our wool was smuggled to France has been known to return 500,000 pounds [sterling] per annum." [76]

Much the same type of exchange existed with Flanders as with France. With Scandinavia the balance of trade was unfavourable, as there was no large market for any of the English staples except coarse woolens and tobacco; thus the importation from this area of considerable quantities of timber, naval stores, copper, iron, skins, and other articles obliged the payment of ready money. But with Holland and Germany the trade was considered advantageous. Many kinds of woollen manufactures were sent to these countries together with other commodities, raw and finished, in return for such things as linens, thread, spices, dyeing-drugs, whale fins, and goat skins. Although Russia also took quantities of worsted stuffs, coarse cloth, tobacco, tin, lead, and other products, it made repayment by sending potash, hemp, flax, yarn, beeswax, hides, and sundry articles that in 1750 apparently greatly surpassed the value of British commodities sent.[77]

In southern Europe, Italy, Spain, and Portugal imported an immense volume of cod,[78] herring, and salmon, together with East India goods, broadcloth, and other English manufactures, including frequently large quantities of corn. These were exchanged for wine, oil, olives, silk, fruit, Spanish wool, indigo, and varied other commodities; in connection with this, both Spain and Portugal, as was suggested, were obliged to make annually large remittances in gold and silver to settle accounts.[79] The African trade of Bristol and Liverpool

---

[76] A *New System of Geography*, II, 533.

[77] B. M., Add. Mss. 29903.

[78] The cod was carried in the English sack ships directly from Newfoundland to Spain and Portugal.

[79] The above point with respect to Portugal is well illustrated in Lucy S. Sutherland's *A London Merchant, 1695–1774* (Oxford, 1933), pp. 33–40. Indeed, to combat this continuous draining of specie, Spain at this period was seeking to set up manufactures

was also highly lucrative, supplying slaves for the West Indies, gold-dust, ivory, and other valuable products. But to maintain trade with the East Indies it was necessary to send annually a considerable amount of silver for the finished and unfinished silk, calicoes, tea, and other commodities brought in by the East India Company, which was obliged by law to re-export all finished fabrics so as to prevent these from coming into competition with the products of British labour in the domestic market.

Trade to the New World was also of great importance to the English economy. The British West Indies and the North American plantations not only supplied raw materials for home industry but helped to absorb the surplus of British manufactures. The West India islands and the southern continental plantations especially were ideal colonies from the point of view of maintaining and furthering British enterprise. These absorbed all manner of clothing, house furnishings, and hardware from the mother country, and in return they produced things that would not compete in the markets with the results of English labour, such as sugar, tobacco, rice, indigo, molasses, deer skins, pitch, and tar. The Northern colonies also offered a great market for English manufactures, but they could furnish in return only ready-built ships, furs, and timber, together with logwood and other commodities secured in their Caribbean trade, which meant that as a rule they had balances to pay to the British in the form of bills of exchange.[80]

One should also bear in mind that the value of New World possessions to Great Britain, especially the Southern staple colonies, consisted not only in the supply of raw commodities secured from them and in the ready market that they offered for finished products, but their value also in supporting both the shipping of the mother country and the other agencies that profited by overseas trade, such as those that supplied insurance, sales on commission, and other such essential services, as the discounting of bills of exchange.[81]

---

that could supply her needs, especially for cloth, and would lessen her dependence on the outside world. She endeavoured to attract English artisans, and many hundreds from Lancashire and the surrounding regions, mostly Catholic in religion, it was reported, had been induced to settle there by 1750. See London advices of July 12, 1750, *Pennsylvania Journal*, September 20, 1750.

[80] For the trade of New England with the mother country in the early part of the eighteenth century see C. P. Nettels: "England's Trade with New England and New York, 1685–1720," Colonial Society of Massachusetts *Transactions*, February 1933.

[81] For a study of invisible items see C. P. Nettels: *The Money Supply of the American Colonies before 1720*, pp. 47–59.

How great a commercial asset the American colonies were to the mother country can be appreciated from the fact that during the period from 1739 to 1748, a period of almost continuous warfare when many of the lucrative markets were closed, it was calculated that England was able to sell to the overseas dependencies almost £7,500,000 worth of goods, including domestic manufactures and those commodities produced elsewhere, entered at an English port, and re-exported to the plantations by certificate.[82] Well might Horatio Walpole declare in 1754: "The American Colonies are great to this Country in general and indeed very justly, as being the principal sources of our balance in trade, and consequently of our riches and strength, by the Great Quantity of shipping employed, of manufactures vended and of the useful returns of their growth. . . ."[83] The West Indies possessions took a very large part of the exports to the American colonies. According to the figures cited above, Jamaica was by far the best customer, purchasing during this decade almost as much as Virginia and Maryland combined, more than New York and Pennsylvania combined, more than all New England, and more than the Carolinas and Georgia.[84]

That the mother country itself was producing those things that met the desires of the plantations is indicated by the fact that only about one fourth of the total exports to the latter were certificated goods; in Montserrat they were but one tenth of the total, in St. Christopher one seventh, in Antigua one sixth. In Bermuda, however, these constituted more than one half the total.[85] In 1750 the balance

---

[82] "An Account of Goods Exported from England . . ." Custom House, London, April 15, 1751, B. M., Add. Mss. 29903.

[83] H. Walpole to Duke of Newcastle, June 18, 1754, Newcastle Papers, B. M., Add. Mss. 32735, folios 485–9.

England's trade with the colonies, which amounted to about one tenth of the external trade during the first decade of the reign of Charles II, had by 1770 so increased that it equalled one third of this trade. See G. L. Beer: *Old Colonial Systems* (New York, 1912), I, 15; see also David Macpherson: *Annals of Commerce* (London, 1805), III, 508; and C. P. Nettels: *The Money Supply of the American Colonies before 1720*, pp. 45–6.

[84] The figures are as follows: goods sent to Jamaica between 1739 and 1748 were valued at £2,187,649.13.10; to Virginia and Maryland, £2,507,626.18.4; to New York and Pennsylvania, £1,916,023.15.5; to New England, £1,812,894.12.10; to Carolina, £1,245,091.16.1. See "An Account of Goods Exported from England," Custom House, London, April 15, 1751, B. M., Add. Mss. 29903.

[85] "Certificated" goods in the language of that period were goods brought to Great Britain from Europe and elsewhere for re-exportation to the plantations. The ship mas-

due the mother country from the plantations in North America amounted, according to the Custom House report under consideration, to the large sum of £592,769.8.6.

From 1721 England had been very consciously working to maintain a favourable balance of trade, and to promote that end most of the old duties on exports were swept away. This helped to realize one of the aims of those responsible for the maintenance of the navigation and trade system, of making the mother country the *entrepôt* for the commerce that her colonies had with the outside world. The system also aimed at the building up of the merchant marine and at securing from colonials – by duties on their imports from England – some contribution to the very great national charge of policing the seas for the protection of the commerce of the Empire.[86]

At that period the sugar, tobacco, ginger, cotton-wool, dyeing woods, molasses, furs, copper ore, rice, hemp, pitch, tar, turpentine, resin, masts, yards, and bowsprits procured in the English colonies were on the so-called "enumerated" list, with relaxations regarding rice and sugar.[87] Under the terms of the regulatory acts these commodities, unless otherwise provided for, could only be sent in the first instance to Great Britain or to one of the other English New World possessions. Further, all British plantation trade, including the coastal, was limited to ships flying the British colours, British or colonial owned and manned. This limitation also held for ships carrying British manufactures abroad. Finally European commodities for colonial consumption were expected, with some minor exceptions, to enter the colonies by way of British ports. Through these and other measures, based upon numerous statutes or royal decrees extending from the year 1081 and including some eighty acts of Par-

ter, before sailing from the mother country, was given a certificate to indicate that the goods were brought to America in accordance with the trade and navigation laws and had paid British custom duties.

[86] Professor Nettels makes clear that, during a period of but four years in the course of the War of the Spanish Succession, Great Britain expended £414,000 in defending the commerce and the coasts of the mainland colonies. See his "British Payments in the American Colonies, 1685–1715," *The English Historical Review*, April 1933, and also his *Money Supply of the American Colonies before 1720*, p. 195.

[87] An enumerated list first appeared in the Act of 1660 and was confirmed in the comprehensive Act of 1696, and enlarged in 1706 and still further in 1733. In 1764 the enumerated list was made to embrace not only the articles listed above but also whale fins, hides, iron, lumber, raw silk, and pearl ashes. For the acts of 1660, 1696, 1704 and 1733 see 12 Chas. II, c. 18, Par. 18; 7 and 8 Wm. III, c. 22; 3 and 4 Anne, c. 5, Par. 12; 6 Geo. II, c. 13.

liament from 1660 to 1751,[88] the Kingdom not only sought the prosperity of its people engaged in manufacturing,[89] trade, and shipping, but the means of guaranteeing the security and permanency of all the intimate and advantageous commercial relations established between itself and its plantations. This system that had been erected for monopolizing the resources of the Empire was characteristic of the spirit of the age and in keeping with the regulations of other maritime powers with overseas possessions. But could Britain continue to maintain it?

[88] For a "List of Acts of Parliament relating to Plantation Trade" see the Shelburne Papers, 49: 99–116, Clements Library.

[89] For the importance of the merchant class during the period under consideration see the article by W. E. Minchinton: "The Merchants in England in the Eighteenth Century, "The Entrepreneur. *Papers Presented at the Annual Conference of the Economic History Society at Cambridge, England, April 1957*, pp. 22–31.

CHAPTER III

Social and Antisocial Forces

England was an aristocracy in the eighteenth century. The royal court and the great landholding nobility set the standard of social aspiration, and, to a large extent, of conduct. To be of some account socially as well as politically one was expected to own a country estate, adorned with as fine a mansion and staffed with as complete a retinue of servants as one could possibly afford. No highly successful upper middle-class merchant was likely to forego such luxury in view of the fact that his family, if not he himself, would be aided thereby, especially by a fortunate marriage, to become one with the country gentry and possibly in time even to join the nobility. For it was the aristocracy that occupied almost all offices of great honour and profit within the gift of the King and also enjoyed great prestige in the local affairs of the shires. Its members automatically assumed leadership in most affairs of moment.

This English aristocracy had its gradations of eminence, with the royal family in the most privileged position, followed on the scale of precedence by non-royal dukes, marquesses, earls, viscounts, and barons, all of the peerage, beneath which were the gentry. There were also classes within each rank of the aristocracy; each individual was well aware of the one in which he belonged. Yet there was constant movement from one social group to another. As Edward Hughes pointed out in his recent *North Country Life in the Eighteenth Century* (Introduction, p. xviii), ". . . thanks to the profits to be made in coal-mining and satellite trades, the social process which transmuted yeomen into merchants and merchants into gentry was here greatly accelerated."

Whereas the countryside was the natural *milieu* of aristocratic activity – outside of that which took place in London during the sessions of Parliament – it was in the cities, towns, and villages that the middle classes played a dominant role. The liveried companies of London, for example, occupied a position of great social and political importance. Guildhall was and still is the centre of activity of the corporation of the city. In 1750 the Lord Mayor, Sir Samuel Pennant, Bachelor Knight, was, as was indicated in the preceding chapter, a member of the Guild of Ironmongers. His public position was an impressive one in the eyes of the common people; it was especially so when he appeared in his official capacity on state occasions. This high and honourable post as the chief representative of the capital city and metropolis of England placed him at the top of the middle classes, within which were many shadings of social distinction. To a lesser extent the same thing was true of those groups that had not attained middle-class standing. For the spirit of England in the middle of the eighteenth century was aristocratic from top to bottom.

At the top of the social ladder in 1750 was the King, George II. He could not, in some respects at least, be regarded as a model for his people. Yet he is by no means to be reckoned among England's bad monarchs.[1] Like most of the rulers on the Continent in that age, he made not the slightest pretence of conjugal fidelity. At the same time he never hesitated to insist that he was a very good husband. Whereas Lady Yarmouth had his love, he nevertheless held Queen Caroline in the highest respect, and it appears that he frequently submitted to her wise counsel in matters of statecraft.

The royal family was, unfortunately, not a particularly happy group. The King manifested an implacable hatred of his son and heir, Frederick, Prince of Wales, and, strangely enough, he was joined in this by the Queen and the Princesses, Emily and Caroline. The Prince returned this animosity with equal lack of restraint. The young man, the father of the future George III, was destined to die in 1751. He undoubtedly had very serious defects of character, although his virtues were lauded by the faction that surrounded him at Leicester House. Yet he appears to have been at heart a

[1] For George II see Reginald Lucas: *George II and his Ministers* (London, 1910), Lord Hervey: *Memoirs of the Reign of George II* (ed. R. Sedgewick, London, 1952), and Horace Walpole: *Memoirs of the Reign of George II* (ed. Lord Holland, London, 1847).

thorough-going Briton, unlike his father, who was always much more of a Hanoverian and never ceased to disparage, at least when he was in ill humour, all things English in favour of whatever existed in his native land. He blusteringly berated even his ministers as "puppies," "liars," and "idiots."

George II was, however, personally brave; at Dettingen he had led the allied troops in person. Further, in the maintenance of his court he was certainly not extravagant; in fact, he sought to check such a tendency in government and was even accused of great parsimony in personal expenditures. One would doubtless be justified therefore in saying that the nation, while not excessively fond of the reigning monarch, honoured him, and, as on the occasion of the crisis of 1746, gave abundant tokens of loyalty to him and his line.

The people of the second of the Hanoverian kings – from dukes to keel-men – cannot be thought of as particularly sober. The rich grew gouty with overindulgence in heavy wines; after the fox-hunt country gentlemen – with the parson sometimes thrown in to boot – still unhesitatingly drank one another under the table amidst scenes of great hilarity. All accounts testify to the injury to public morals and private industry resulting from the excessive consumption of domestically distilled Holland gin by the lower classes. The writer Smollett speaks of the gin shops as "hideous receptables of the most filthy vice, resounding with riot, execration and blasphemy." Josiah Tucker, in 1751, refers to the pernicious effects of ardent liquors as "raging, and in some respects even worse than pestilential Infection." Beyond the moral and spiritual losses involved he calculated that gin-drinking impoverished the nation by almost £4,000,000 after deducting the profits of the distilling business.[2] The Bristol Merchant Venturers, in fact, were so alarmed over the situation that in March of the preceding year they memorialized the House of Commons. "Your Petitioners," they declared, "cannot but reflect with the utmost concern on the excessive drinking of spirituous liquors by the frequent instances of sudden death of many of his Majesty's Subjects of both sexes. . . . For Drunkenness, the confessed leader of all other vices, was never so glaringly known in this Nation as at Present." [3] It appears that even the Masters of the Distillers Company of London and "a consider-

---

2 Josiah Tucker: *An Impartial Inquiry* (London, 1751), pp. 1–2, 24–6.

3 Merchants Hall, Bristol, Book of Charters, p. 320.

able body of the most respectable distillers of that city," felt impelled to wait upon the Commissioners of Excise to acquaint them that for a long time they had seen with the utmost concern the consequences arising from the bad manner of disposing of spirituous liquor. They pointed out that they had before now remonstrated against the growth of the present evil and observed that the primary, the real source of the evil was the vending of liquor in small quantities. Therefore they recommended that no spirituous liquor whatsoever be vended in less quantity than a pint and that this should not be drunk in the house of the vendor.[4]

Intimately associated with alcoholic excesses, as a rule, are many other agencies of social demoralization. Josiah Tucker estimated — perhaps with the reformer's pardonable tendency for exaggeration — that there were at least 10,000 loose women walking the streets of London. "In short, it has been often remarked," he declared in 1749, "that the greatest Rakes that all Europe can produce, when they arrive in England, and come to London, are quite shocked and scandalized at the unparalleled Lewdness and Debauchery reigning among us, so far beyond any thing they could have imagined."[5] Henry Fielding, referring to the common masquerades so popular at this period, affirmed that these were no other than occasions for "Drunkenness, Lewdness, and all kinds of Debauchery."[6] Eighteenth-century evangelicalism in Great Britain undoubtedly came as a revulsion against widespread human depravity.

Beyond gin-drinking the great national pastimes of the common

---

[4] For the effects of gin-drinking on the death rate and birth rate in London see M. Dorothy George: *London Life in the XVIIIth Century* (London, 1925), pp. 27, 28, 56, and 333. Thomas Alcock, in his *Observations on the Defects of the Poor Laws* (London, 1752), in listing the causes of poverty declared that dram drinking was perhaps worse in its effects upon the people than all the other concomitant causes combined (*ibid.*, p. 49). J. L. Hammond and Barbara Hammond deal illuminatingly with the efforts to check the excessive drinking of gin in their chapter on "Poverty, Crime and Philanthropy," in *Johnson's England* (ed. A. S. Tuberville, Oxford, 1933), I, especially pp. 312–4. Hogarth illustrates the prevailing evil of intemperance in series of engraved prints: "March to Finchley" (1750), and "Beer Street," "Gin Lane," and "The Four Stages of Cruelty" (1751).

[5] *A Brief Essay on the Advantages and Disadvantages which Respectively attend France and Great Britain* (London, 1749), p. 48; see also Mark Pattison: *Essays and Reviews*, (1860), p. 254, and G. V. Portus: *Caritas Anglicana* (London, [1912]), p. 29. Hogarth, in his "A Harlot's Progress" (1731–2), represented in six striking engravings, gives one a visual view of London's underworld.

[6] *An Enquiry into the Causes of the Late Increase of Robberies* (London, 1751), p. 19.

people at this period seem to have been such sports as cock-fighting, just as fox-hunting was the passion of the country gentry. As the cricket teams of English cities and counties now meet in championship contests, so then did the fighting cocks of various counties, and this was especially true in the Midlands. There was, for example, a tendency for the sporting groups of Worcestershire and Herefordshire to match their birds against those from Warwickshire and Staffordshire. On April 11, 1748, a great match of cocks occurred with 41 birds, at 10 guineas a battle and 200 for the main struggle.[7] Prize-fighting, without any of the present restraining regulations, was also a favourite amusement. In 1748 a boxing-match took place on the College Green in Bristol between a "short-sized" sailor and a soldier of the foot guards, "a lusty man"; despite his formidable appearance the soldier was beaten in so violent a manner by his sinewy antagonist that he was carried off the field almost dead, and the application of palm oil and spirits had to be made to keep him from expiring.[8] These sports were the occasion, moreover, for reckless gambling, which in all its forms was indeed another of the passions of the English. Thousands of people witnessed the winning of a wager laid in 1749 that a little girl eighteen months old could walk the length of the Mall in St. James's Park (which is half a mile long) in thirty minutes.[9] Ladies of quality kept roulette tables and profited thereby.[10] The most notorious gambling-house in England in the 1740's was probably Lord Mordington's at Covent Garden, although there was, it appears, a reaction against it by 1748. At least in October of that year a London correspondent of the *Maryland Gazette* wrote: "We hear that several of the principal inhabitants of Covent Garden and the places adjacent design to petition his Grace the Duke of Bedford in order to have the gaming-house . . . suppressed, it being attended with the worst consequences to the pub-

[7] Many news items in *Aris's Birmingham Gazette* refer to cock-fighting; these were gathered together by John A. Landford in his *A Century of Birmingham*, 1741–1841 (Birmingham, 1870); see also Sir Walter Gilbey: *Sport in Olden Time* (London, 1912).

[8] Bristol correspondence to the *Maryland Gazette*, March 8, 1749; see also for prize-fighting, H. O. Miles: *Pugilistica: Bring one hundred and forty-four Years of the History of British Boxing* (3 vols., London, [1880–]). For an admirable account of English sports in the eighteenth century see E. D. Cuming's chapter in *Johnson's England*, I, 362–84.

[9] London advices, *Maryland Gazette*, September 6, 1749.

[10] For gaming see John Ashton: *The History of Gambling in England* (London, 1898).

lic." [11] Lotteries also enjoyed almost a universal patronage. "The high prices you may have observed on lottery tickets during the course of the drawing," wrote Bishop Trevor in 1751, "will give you some Idea of the general spirit of Gaming arising from what Dr. Young calls the luxurious poverty of the Age." [12]

In addition to the social tendencies just described, many of the people, it must be confessed, displayed on occasion certain traits that were little short of barbarous. The conduct of the country people about Bideford in the winter of 1750, on the occasion of the wreck off that coast of a 400-ton French ship, *La Carpe,* loaded with timber, fish, and wine, was hardly above that of a group of North American Indians. Although this occurred in a time of peace, hardly had the survivors from this ship landed than more than 2,000 country people, it is estimated, boarded the ship, drank five hogsheads of wine, carried off 1,400 quintals of cod and the boxes and chests of the officers and crew, and in spite of everything the local customs officers could do to protect the property for its owners, set about breaking up the ship and carrying off the materials in their wagons. It is true that after some delay, warrants were issued for the apprehension of a great many of these looters.[13]

In other ways unsettled social conditions were manifested. The year 1749 saw great rioting. About Newcastle-upon-Tyne 6,000 keelmen refused to work and at one of their gatherings the Pretender was proclaimed.[14] In the western part of England, especially in Somersetshire and Gloucestershire, serious disturbances took place over the issue of the establishment of the system of turnpikes. The rioters, mostly miners and cottiers, blackened their faces and called themselves "Jack-a-Lints." Armed with rusty swords, pitchforks, axes, guns, pistols, and clubs, and made irresponsible through strong drink, they proceeded to destroy many of the toll-houses and gates and even the homes of people who had aroused their enmity. The civil authorities were helpless and it was necessary to call in a body

---

[11] London advices, *Maryland Gazette,* March 8, 1749.

[12] Bishop Trevor to Edward Weston, December 24, 1751, C. F. Weston Underwood Papers, Hist. Mss. Com., *10th Report,* p. 306; see also John Ashton: *A History of English Lotteries* (London, 1893).

[13] See *The Gentleman's Magazine,* February 1750. A letter from Lynn of February 3, 1750 adds the information: "They are the same fellows that plundered the money ship that came on shore there about 6 months ago" (*Pennsylvania Gazette,* May 3, 1750).

[14] London advices of May 5 to the *Pennsylvania Journal,* July 12, 1749.

of armed seamen and six troops of dragoon guards.[15] Ultimately, scores of them were tried at Bristol by special commission. Those guilty incurred the penalty of transportation for seven years with death for returning before the time allotted. To those responsible for the public welfare it seemed necessary to repress the savage tendencies of the people by means of exceedingly rigorous laws.[16]

The problem of law enforcement in England presented many difficulties. This was especially so with respect to the acts restricting and regulating trade. As has been pointed out in the preceding chapter, there was a prohibition against the exportation of wool to France upon pain of transportation, yet smuggling of wool appears to have been carried on upon a vast scale and for many years was a most lucrative business. Although the act was passed in 1738, it appears that the first execution for its violation occurred in 1748 when "at Maidstone assizes James Toty, an old smuggler, was capitally convicted on an indictment (being the first tried on the Statute) for carrying wool to France."[17] The following year at the Rochester assizes for the county of Kent there were 47 up for capital offences, 20 of whom were accused of wool smuggling. In these trials, one Butler, "a notorious smuggler," who for twenty years had been at the head of a gang, turned king's evidence, giving information not only regarding all the wool that had been exported to France, but the names of those individuals implicated in this traffic.[18] When not engaged in carrying wool abroad the smugglers were

---

[15] Excellent accounts of the disturbances are contained in communications from Bristol to the *Maryland Gazette,* December 20, 1749, and February 7, 1750.

[16] For the law covering the destruction of turnpikes see 1 Geo. II, stat. 2, c. 19, re-enacted by 5 Geo. II, c. 33; this was made perpetual by 27 Geo. II, c. 16. For rioting in eighteenth-century England see T. S. Ashton: *An Economic History of England: the Eighteenth Century* (London, 1955), pp. 226–8; see also T. S. Ashton and J. Sykes: *The Coal Industry of the Eighteenth Century* ([Manchester], 1929), Chap. VIII.

[17] London advices, the *Maryland Gazette,* October 25, 1748. Although the statement above is made that Toty was "capitally convicted," the law provided transportation for seven years and the death penalty only if the convicted man returned from America before the expiration of the period.

[18] London advices, *ibid.,* June 21, 1749. One writer of this period declared: "The English wools have yielded to the smuggler of them a profit of 50 per cent and yet do not exceed in price those of the wools in France of the same quality" (*Remarks on the Advantages and Disadvantages of France and of Great Britain* [London, 1754], p. 80); for wool smuggling see W. D. Cooper: *Smuggling in Sussex,* Sussex Archeological *Coll.,* Vol. X.

likely to be busy landing other dutiable articles in England.[19] For example, in February 1748 an armed band broke open a government warehouse at Pool and recovered 1,300 pounds of seized tea. One member of the band, alarmed at the arrest of a colleague, decided to save his neck by turning king's evidence and was proceeding to a justice of the peace with a local customs officer when the two fell into the grasp of the band and were killed – the smuggler only after his former associates had inflicted upon him the most unmentionable tortures. It was, in fact, estimated that at least 20,000 people were involved in the smuggling of tea.[20]

Enormous quantities of other dutiable goods, especially tobacco, brandy, arrack, and rum, were undoubtedly run, according to the Treasury records. The Isle of Man was a perfect haven for smugglers. They could flee there when in danger of arrest, and it was asserted in 1751 that through the use of this island as a smuggling base the King in the course of the past 16 years had been defrauded of more than £1,000,000 in duties on smuggled East India, West India, French, and Spanish goods.[21] The Sussex shore was also a maze of smuggling operations. Many were the ingenious devices employed for carrying commodities landed in this region into London for sale. One group of smugglers at Shoreham made use of a hearse and four horses to convey tea, gold and silver, French lace, and French cambrics.[22] So futile were the efforts of the local customs officials to control the situation that in 1753 it was proposed to employ dra-

[19] The method employed in dealing with smugglers is thus described by a contemporary: "After information given against any one on the Act of Smuggling or aiding and assisting in the landing and running of uncustomed Goods, his name is published in *The Gazette*, and a Proclamation directed to be published and fixed up in two market-towns near to the Place where the offence is charged to be committed requiring him to surrender himself in such a limited Time, within 40 days, to a justice of the peace or in Default thereof he becomes attainted and convicted of Felony" (*A Free Apology in Behalf of the Smugglers* [London, 1749], p. 13).

[20] Letter from Portsmouth, October 8, 1748, *Maryland Gazette*, February 15, 1749; see also the *Gentleman's Magazine*, January 1749, and especially *A Full and Genuine History of the Inhuman and Unparalleled Murders of Mr. William Galley and Mr. Daniel Chater by Fourteen Notorious Smugglers. By a Gentleman of Chichester* (London, 1752); see further E. Lipson: *The Economic History of England* (London, 1943), III, 144–5.

[21] Wm. Mercer to the Duke of Newcastle, August 29, 1751, Newcastle Papers, B. M., Add. Mss. 32725, folios 99–100. For an excellent brief survey of tobacco smuggling see Alfred Rive: "A Short History of Tobacco Smuggling," *Economic History*, January 1929, pp. 554–69.

[22] *Aris's Birmingham Gazette*, February 18, 1751.

goons to assist in the enforcement of both the customs and excise laws.[23] The following year they were required to assist the revenue officials in Scotland.[24]

However, the means of detection apparently had been sufficiently refined so that a goodly proportion of the offenders were certainly brought to justice. Between 1732 and 1750 more than a million and a quarter pounds of smuggled tobacco were seized in England alone, the confiscation of which was sued for in the Exchequer.[25]

One thing that doubtless added to the prevalence of smuggling was the disposition on the part of officials to "compound" with the convicted for a cash payment based on the provisions of a statute passed in 1736.[26] For example, in February 1749 William Harrison, master of the ship *Pennington* of Whitehaven, made a false report on the cargo, which on oath he stated was only deals and fir timber. He carried a quantity of wines, tea, and coffee valued at £48.8, which was seized; in addition to this loss he was allowed to compound for the trivial sum of £33.6.8.[27] In the course of the year 1751 twenty-six cases of smuggling were recorded in which the offenders were allowed to compound.[28] Old smugglers unable to compound also were from time to time released from jail. Thomas Cotton, who smuggled in goods valued at £5,025 and was imprisoned in Norwich jail in 1738, was released by order of the customs commissioners in 1749, as were other smugglers imprisoned in 1739 and 1740.[29]

All that has been said above – and even more that might be – hardly reflects credit on the social standards of England of the eighteenth century and may, in fact, be included under the common denominator of antisocial forces.

---

[23] "Proposals for quartering Dragoons," September 1, 1753, B. M., Add. Mss. 32733, folio 48.

[24] Secretary James Stewart to Col. Whitmore, September 7, 1754, Bland Letter Book, Nat. Lib., Edinburgh.

[25] During the above period 172,378 pounds of tobacco were seized at Bideford; 144,247, at Liverpool; 142,811, at Fowey in Cornwall; 139,334¾, in London; at Falmouth it was 88,748 pounds; at Whitehaven 77,600¼; at Plymouth 52,982½; at Bristol 50,642. See "An Account of the several quantitys of Tobacco seized and Prosecuted in the Exchequer from Christmas, 1732 to Christmas, 1750," B. M., Lansdowne Collection, No. 661, pp. 1–48.

[26] 9 Geo. II, c. 35.

[27] Customs, Treas. 11. 23, p. 534, P. R. O.

[28] *Ibid.*, Treas. 11. 20, *passim.*

[29] *Ibid.*, Treas. 11. 23, pp. 526–7.

There was, happily, a brighter side, one that seems to have escaped only too frequently the attention of many contemporary critics, who, living in London or in some other populous center, were probably depressed and made perhaps just a little feverish by glaring evidences of depravity and lawlessness – in contrast to the more normal behaviour of most people about them. Apparently they seldom ventured beyond the urban areas and therefore knew little of conditions prevailing elsewhere, especially in rural England where at this period the vast majority of the people were living rather isolated from centers of social infection. For it cannot be doubted that the heart of the nation was sound. Most of the millions who made up the population: merchants, shopkeepers, artisans, yeomen farmers, agricultural labourers, and others who by their energy, foresight, and ambition had made England the richest and in many respects the most progressive and enlightened of all the countries of the world, were without doubt people of solid qualities – honest, clearheaded, ingenious, and distinguished, certainly among most of their contemporaries living in the British Isles, for habits of cleanliness and industry.

The manner of life of the English people in 1750 varied from group to group. The greater nobility dwelt in spacious country mansions, the most impoverished groups in mere huts or in cellars. England was still largely rural and therefore most of its population was to be found living in the country. Without going into detail regarding the many rather striking differences in domestic architecture to be found in various parts of England, it may be said that the house of the average fairly prosperous farmer, which was normally built of stone and timber, seems to have included a kitchen, a parlor, a dairy, a pantry, and a closet on the ground floor, with some four bedrooms above; the labourer's family very commonly satisfied itself with a thatched-roof cottage perhaps of mud and stud, with a floor of earth, or at best with one built of timber or stone, containing two rooms on the ground floor and a bedroom or two above. Corresponding variations also existed among the inhabitants of the larger towns and cities, with shopkeepers and artisans frequently living above their shops.[30]

---

[30] Most of the works on English domestic architecture of the eighteenth century are concerned with the larger houses. However, see A. E. Richardson and A. D. Eberlein: *The Smaller English House of the Later Renaissance, 1660–1830* (London, 1933); S. C. Ramsey: *Small Houses of the Late Georgian Period, 1750–1820* (2 vols., London

In most portions of England, which means the villages, life still tended to be largely self-sufficing and therefore retained its characteristic isolation. Bishop Berkeley drew a charming picture of it in the middle of the century, the fidelity of which can hardly be questioned as characterizing English villagers as a group. It was customary, he declared in 1749, for the labourers, at least in northern England, thriftily to betake themselves, after the work in their fields was over, to one another's homes, where merrily and frugally they passed the long and dark winter evenings, with perhaps several families by the same light and open fire working up their wool, flax, and hemp, mutually cheering and provoking one another to labour. On summer evenings he found them sitting in front of their cottages also busily engaged and profiting thereby. Even in the field their steadiness of purpose was in evidence, for they could not be easily distracted from their industrious pursuits. He records that a friend of his on a journey from London to Bristol took particular note of the fact that whenever he stopped to ask directions these were given by workers without cessation of their labour or even so much as their lifting their eyes from the task in hand.[31]

Again, among the people of the cities and towns the middle classes, always reputed for their respectability, ordinarily found pleasure outside of gross dissipation. They resorted to church, to the theatre, the opera, the oratorio. In London they also, in family groups, visited Vauxhall Gardens or Ranelagh, great pleasure resorts, where they decently enough spent the evening refreshing themselves at supper while listening to the music of an orchestra.[32]

It is undoubtedly true that Englishmen, as was emphasized by contemporary writers, enjoyed a degree of personal freedom that only too frequently ended in licence and debauchery on the part of those weak both in character and in life-purposes; but this freedom,

---

1919–23); and N. Lloyd: *A History of English Houses from Primitive Times to the Victorian Period* (London, 1931). The agricultural population of southern England was apparently better housed than that of northern England. See G. E. Farrell and Constance Goodmay: "The Housing of the Rural Population in the Eighteenth Century," *Economic History*, II, 63–90.

[31] G. Berkeley: *A Word to the Wise* [first published in 1749 and reprinted in Dublin in 1752], in *A Miscellany, Containing several Tracts on various Subjects*, p. 78.

[32] Henry Fielding in his *An Enquiry into the Causes of the late Increase of Robberies* (page 15), published in 1751, refers to the passion for places of pleasure, which he declared were almost numberless in and near the metropolis. For a recent excellent account of the amusements of the London populace see M. Dorothy George's chapter on London in *Johnson's England*, I, especially pp. 177–93.

on the other hand, made for individual initiative and was largely responsible for the rather high standard of living enjoyed by the nation as compared with most of eighteenth-century Europe.[33] There seems to be little doubt that the greater part of the English people was living comfortably, if not at their ease, as a result of the intelligent direction of their efforts; and thousands of families of the middle class were enjoying many real luxuries.

Indeed, Thomas Alcock, writing in 1752, was very much alarmed with what to him were the extravagances of the masses. He not only found the custom of smoking and chewing tobacco very common among the poor, but also the new habit of doing away with the simple milk and broth in favour of tea, sugar, cream, bread, and butter "at an expense of near treble" that of the earlier type of breakfast. Further, he declared that in these "later Times" another species of expense had made its way among the poor who now demanded "Ribbons, Ruffles, Silks, and other slight foreign Things, that come dear, and do but little Service. Have not Extravagance in these Articles," he asked, "Contributed greatly to make Labour and Servants Wages run so high?"[34]

There was, in general, a marked contrast in basic necessities between the unskilled labourer of town and country who, depending upon the area in which he lived, often had to spend more than half his wages on food; the prosperous farmer who ate well of all that he grew, and the even more prosperous squire who was no absentee landlord but administered and enjoyed the fruits of his enclosures. Similarly, the wage-earner in town found the purchase of clothes a difficult matter and would rather lose his purse than his coat, whereas the country man's clothes were coarse homespun, but warm and adequate. By contrast, the gentry and nobility, returning from the Grand Tour of Europe, wore, at least on more formal occasions, silks, satins, and brocades of luxurious quality. The health of the country by 1750 reflected the diet of a nation still, by and large, agricultural. This, moreover, was not the century of the plagues.

[33] See Elizabeth W. Gebbon: "Wages in Eighteenth-Century England," *Journal of Economic and Business History*, II 603–29.

[34] Thomas Alsock: *Observations on the Defects of the Poor Laws* (London, 1752), pp. 45–8. For a study of domestic service in England see J. J. Hecht: *The Domestic Servant Class in Eighteenth Century England* (London, 1956). For the labouring class in general see Dorothy Marshall: *English People in the Eighteenth Century* (London, 1956), Chapter V, "The Labouring Poor"; for the eating habits of the English in the Hanoverian era see J. B. Botsford: *English Society in the Eighteenth Century* (New York, 1924), Chapter III, "The National Diet."

Dean Josiah Tucker assumed, in discussing the standard of living of this period, that a man with apparently the minimum income of thousands of people, that is, £250 a year, would have paintings and prints on the walls of his home, a service of chinaware, a sideboard of plate, a stock of port wine, rum, brandy, and spirits, with a man in livery to wait on table; that he would enjoy a wheeled chaise, riding horses, a pack of hounds, greyhounds, guns, and nets, and that his wife would possess necklaces, solitaires, rings, and earrings, all of value, and that both of them would have, for occasions, fabrics of gold and silver and silk stuffs.[35]

Among the less material aspects of English civilization, one is impressed by the fact that out of the religious impulses of the latter part of the seventeenth century an educational movement had developed which by 1750 was assuming national importance. This was the so-called system of charity schools fostered by the Society for the Promotion of Christian Knowledge.[36] It was stated in 1742 that over 1,746 schools were in existence in which more than 36,000 boys and girls within Great Britain and Ireland were receiving free maintenance and the foundations of an education while being prepared for various useful activities that would guarantee self-support. By 1764 the number had increased to 46,177 children cared for in 1,953 of these schools, according to one contemporary. Of this number

---

[35] *A Brief Essay on the Advantages and Disadvantages which Respectively attend France and Great Britain . . .* (London, 1749), pp. 71–2.

On the difficult problem of determining the income of various social and economic groups in England in the eighteenth century and also the size of each group, the writer Joseph Massie sought in 1760 to throw light. In a broadside, *A Computation of the Money . . . Raised on the People of Great Britain . . .* , he divides the people into some fifty groups at the top of which are ten families with an annual income or expense of £20,000 or over, and at the bottom of which (excluding common soldiers) were country labourers, who at five shillings a day were able to earn £12.5 annually. He estimated, for example, that there were over eighteen thousand families (not including those of officers in the Army and Navy) that made up the nobility and gentry and that enjoyed incomes of £200 or over. For a critique of his calculations see Peter Mathias, "The Social Structure in the Eighteenth Century: A Calculation by Joseph Massie," *Economic History Review*, 2nd ser., X, 30–45.

For a general picture of domestic life see Rosamond Bayne-Powell: *Housekeeping in the 18th Century* (London, 1956).

[36] See D. W. R. Bahlman: *The Moral Revolution of 1688* (New Haven, 1957), W. O. B. Allen and E. McClure: *Two Hundred Years: The History of the Society for Promoting Christian Knowledge, 1698–1895* (London, 1898), Mary G. Jones: *The Charity School Movement, a Study of Eighteenth Century Puritanism in Action* (Cambridge, 1938), and Betsy Rogers: *Cloak of Charity; Studies in Eighteenth Century Philanthropy* (London, 1949).

almost 153 schools were in and about London. Moreover, in the villages of England elementary education was provided, it would seem, quite generally by endowment and gifts and less frequently by means of parish rates.[37] "Even the people of the lowest rank can read and write," recorded with surprise a foreign observer of this period.[38]

Above this primary system of education, which was generally in the form of parsons' or dames' schools, there were the grammar and public schools, a good many of the latter old and aristocratic establishments.[39] There were also the academies for the education of dissenters, many of them excellent institutions of collegiate standing, and the two great English universities, Oxford and Cambridge, which at this period were notably quiescent, at least intellectually,[40] and the Inns of Court in London – Lincoln's Inn, Inner Temple, Middle Temple, and Gray's Inn – all splendid foundations with their

---

[37] In *A Tour of Great Britain*, by Daniel Defoe, revised by Samuel Richardson and others, and published in Dublin in 1779 in four volumes, repeated references are made, in describing the towns, to specific provision for the elementary education of children. See also J. W. Adamson: *A Short History of Education* (Cambridge, 1919), and particularly Jacques Pons: *L'éducation en Angleterre entre 1750 et 1800 . . .* (Paris, 1919).

[38] "*Observations sur le Royaume d'Angleterre*," 1742, Loudoun Papers, Huntington Library.

For the inadequacies of elementary education in the eighteenth century see M. Dorothy George: *London Life in the XVIIIth Century* (London, 1925), pp. 218–32; see also Rosamond Bayne-Powell: *The English Child in the Eighteenth Century* (New York, 1939), pp. 45–124. For the role of the coffee houses in spreading knowledge see Aytroun Ellis: *The Penny Universities. A History of Coffee Houses* (London, 1956).

[39] R. Ackermann and W. Combe: *The History of the Colleges of Winchester, Eton, and Westminster, with Charterhouse, the Schools of St. Paul's, Merchant Taylors', Harrow, and Rugby, and the free-school of Christ's Hospital* (London, 1816); see also Sir H. C. M. Lyte: *Eton* (London, 1911); W. H. D. Rouse: *Rugby* (London, 1898) H. C. Adams: *Winchester* (London, 1878); J. F. Williams: *Harrow* (London, 1901); G. S. Davies: *Charterhouse* (London, 1921); John Sargeaunt: *Westminster* (London, 1898); M. F. J. McDonnell: *St. Paul's* (London, 1909); E. H. Pearce: Christ's *Hospital* (London, 1901). There were many other schools with classical traditions of education such as that at Canterbury, at Bath, and at Otley.

[40] For the education of dissenters see Irene Parker: *Dissenting Academies in England* (Cambridge, 1914); for Oxford see Sir Charles E. Mallet: *A History of the University of Oxford* (London [1924–7], Vol. III); A. D. Godley: *Oxford in the Eighteenth Century* (London, 1908); and G. C. Broderick: *A History of the University of Oxford* (London, 1886); for *Cambridge in the Eighteenth Century* see D. A. Winstanley: *The University of Cambridge in the Eighteenth Century* (Cambridge, 1922), and also his *Unreformed Cambridge . . .* (Cambridge, 1935); another useful book is by Christopher Wordsworth: *Social Life at the English Universities in the Eighteenth Century* (Cambridge, 1874).

benchers, barristers, and students.[41] Oxford, however, was under attack as a centre of Jacobite disaffection,[42] whereas Cambridge, with strong Whig leanings and under the chancellorship of the Duke of Newcastle, was in general public favour and was busy with an elaborate building program.

Culturally, England in 1750 was under the spell of no great living personality, but was rather rehearsing the ideas expressed by men of letters and of science of the past, such men as the philosopher Locke, the scientists Harvey and Newton, and the poets and essayists Shakespeare, Swift, Dryden, Addison, and Pope — the latter almost a contemporary, surviving until 1744. Almost contemporary, too, was the saintly writer of hymns Isaac Watts, who died in 1748, but whose "When I Survey the Wondrous Cross," "Joy to the World, the Lord is Come," and "O God, our Help in Ages Past," are still among the favourite hymns of the English-speaking world.

Outstanding in the musical world of this period was George Frederick Handel, who deserted his post as *Kapellmeister* to the Elector of Hanover to become a naturalized Englishman in a musical age when Italian opera was the vogue in England. Handel competed successfully with the Italians in a series of Italian operas which captured the imagination of the British, but added little to his musical reputation or to his purse. Only when he turned to writing oratorios — a reflection of the growing preoccupation of the people of that time with religious music — did he reach his greatest success.

---

[41] For the Inns of Court see R. R. Pearce: *History of the Inns of Court* (London, 1848); see also W. P. Baildon: *The Records of the Society of Lincoln's Inn* (London, 1897–1902), R. J. Fletcher: *The Pension Book of Gray's Inn* (London, 1901–10), A. R. Ingpen: *Master Worsley's Book on the History and Constitution of the . . . Society of Middle Temple* (London, 1910), and R. A. Roberts: *A Calendar of the Inner Temple Records* (London, 1933–6). American students, numbering some 200 and mostly from the South, were enrolled before 1775 in one or another of the Inns of Court, with Middle Temple receiving the bulk of them. At this period they received at the Inns little formal legal education, but when at last qualified, by whatever means, were certified to act as barristers. See W. L. Sachse: *The Colonial American in Britain* (Madison, Wis., 1956), pp. 63–9.

[42] "Since the Defeat of the Rebels at Culloden, I myself spent some time at Oxford and had the Honour of the Friendship and Intimacy of a worthy Gentleman, the Head of a very considerable College. This Gentleman assur'd me, that its surprising to consider and reflect on the Disaffection and Disloyalty of that university" (*A Blow at the Root . . . a further Reformation . . . of our National Church, Universities and Schools* [1749], p. 58). See also *Oxford Honesty, or a Case of Conscience, Humbly Put to the Worshipful . . . The Vice-Chancellor, the Heads of Houses, the Fellows, etc. of the University of Oxford* (1749). These two are among the English tracts in the Widener Library, Harvard University.

With this development in his career also came some affluence, so that when the Foundling Hospital was opened in London on May 15, 1750, and the occasion was celebrated with a performance of his masterpiece *Messiah*, Handel presented an organ to the institution.

In the person of the Scot, David Hume, the age possessed an intellectual collossus. He had published his monumental *Treatise of Human Nature* in 1739 and at mid-century he was busy with his *Political Discourses*, which would appear in 1752 and which in turn made way for the ultrapartisan but financially rewarding *History of England*, an effort utterly unworthy of a man of incomparable talents in the field of philosophical abstraction.[43] The profound metaphysician George Berkeley, Bishop of Cloyne, author of the *Principles of Human Knowledge* and of the *Dialogues*, both of which appeared early in the century, was still living.[44] William Blackstone, a Fellow of All Souls at Oxford, was busy laying the foundations for his great *Commentaries on the Laws of England*, which, appearing in print between 1765 and 1769, was destined to exert a lasting influence on the law throughout the English-speaking world.[45]

In 1750 Thomas Gray sent to Horace Walpole his masterpiece, the famous "Elegy"; he had already written the beautiful "Ode on a Distant Prospect of Eton College" and the "Hymn to Adversity."[46] Samuel Richardson, more than three score years of age, was at this time at the height of his remarkable literary career; his moralizing *Pamela, or Virtue Rewarded*, published in 1740, was followed in 1747 by *Clarissa, or The History of a Young Lady*. His works had taken England by storm and nothing could check their popularity,

---

[43] For David Hume see his *A Treatise of Human Nature: being an Attempt to Introduce the Experimental Method of Reasoning into Moral Subjects* (London, 3 vols., 1739–40), *Political Discourses* (Edinburgh, 1752), and the *History of England* (London, 1754–61). His various writings edited by T. H. Green and T. H. Grose appeared in 4 volumes (1874–5); the best life of Hume is that by J. H. Burton (2 vols., Edinburgh, 1846).

[44] For Berkeley's writings see the edition of his works and life by A. C. Fraser in 4 volumes (Oxford, 1901); see also John Wild: *George Berkeley: A Study of his Life and Philosophy* (Cambridge, Mass., 1936). For English intellectual activity in the eighteenth century see Sir Leslie Stephen: *History of English Thought in the Eighteenth Century* (2 vols., London, 1876).

[45] There is, unfortunately, no standard life of Sir William Blackstone. The sketch in the *Dictionary of National Biography* is perhaps the most balanced.

[46] For Gray's poems see Leonard Whibley's revision of A. L. Poole's edition (London, 1937); for Gray's life see two works in French by Roger Martin: *Chronologie de la Vie et de l'Oeuvre de Thomas Gray* (London, 1931), and *Essai sur Thomas Gray* (London, 1934).

especially that of *Pamela.*[47] Henry Fielding the year before had given to the world his *Tom Jones; or the History of a Foundling,* the antithesis of Richardson's novels in its stark realism.[48] Tobias Smollett, a Scot, who with his plotless *Roderick Random* had placed his name as a novelist beside those of Richardson and Fielding, was now about to send to the press *The Adventures of Peregrine Pickle,* another novel filled with inimitable situations, rich humour, and savage thrusts, and in common with *Tom Jones,* decidedly coarse, judged by later standards.[49] Henry St. John, Viscount Bolingbroke, broken in health but still living had at last authorized the publication of his political essay *The Idea of a Patriot King,* which, appearing in 1749, was to exert, it has been thought, some influence on the mind of the future George III.[50] Among the greatest of contemporary writers was Samuel Johnson, busy with his *Dictionary of the English Language,* on which he had been engaged since 1747. In March 1750 he launched a semi-weekly, *The Rambler,* which continued to appear for two years and attained an importance not to be gauged by its limited circulation.[51]

Besides her men of literary attainments, England possessed in 1750 William Hogarth, who had established his fame as a painter

[47] The latest edition of Richardson's works was published in eighteen volumes in Oxford in 1930–1; for Richardson's life see Paul Dottin: *Samuel Richardson, 1689–1761, Imprimeur de Londres, Auteur de Pamela, Clarisse et Grandison* (Paris, 1931).

[48] For Fielding's writings see *The Works of Henry Fielding* (ed. Sir Leslie Stephen, 10 vols., London, 1882); for his life see Wilbur L. Cross: *The History of Henry Fielding* (3 vols., New Haven, 1918).

[49] The best collection of Smollett's work is *The Shakespeare Head* edition (11 vols., Oxford, 1925–6); for Smollett's life see L. M. Knapp: *Tobias Smollett: Doctor of Men and Manners* (Princeton, 1949). In spite of the coarseness of Fielding and Smollett, the literary taste of England seems to have been elevated by 1750; for example, the bawdy poetry so popular at the beginning of the century had disappeared. See R. O. Havens: "Changing Taste in the Eighteenth Century," The Modern Language Association *Publications,* XLIV, 501–36.

[50] The first authorized edition of Bolingbroke's *Letters on the Spirit of Patriotism: on the Idea of a Patriot King: and on the State of Parties, at the Accession of King George the first* appeared in London in 1749, as indicated above; an unauthorized edition was published some six years earlier; for Bolingbroke's life see W. S. Sichel: *Bolingbroke and his Times* (2 vols., London, 1901–2).

[51] Johnson's *Works* were edited by Sir John Hawkins in 11 volumes (London, 1787), supplemented by 3 volumes edited by J. Stockdale (London, 1787–8) and a final volume, edited by G. Gleig (London, 1789). For Johnson's *Dictionary of the English Language* see the edition published in 1773 in 2 volumes; for Johnson's life see J. W. Krutch: *Samuel Johnson* (New York, 1944), J. L. Clifford: *Young Sam Johnson* (New York, 1955), and, the greatest biography in the English language, by James Boswell, published in London in 1791.

and engraver of high rank. Although a master in colour on canvas, he is best remembered as a relentless satirist for his faithful portrayal of the more unseemly aspects of eighteenth-century England in three series of engravings, "The Harlot's Progress," "The Rake's Progress" and "Marriage à la Mode." [52] James Gibbs, the distinguished Scottish architect, was also active. He had but recently finished the building of that beautiful classical rotunda, the Radcliffe Library at Oxford, and was the creator of two of the finest of the London churches, St. Mary-le-Strand and St. Martins-in-the-Fields.[53] Moreover, there were Thomas Chippendale, one of the greatest designers of furniture,[54] and the sculptor Louis Roubiliac (Roubillac), an expatriated Frenchman, whose "Nightingale" monument in Westminster Abbey and whose "Shakespeare," executed by commission for Garrick and now in the British Museum, exhibit high qualities of technique.[55] Joshua Reynolds was but on the threshold of great achievement at this period, haunting the galleries of Italy.[56] Robert Adam, a Scot soon to win fame for his domestic architecture and home furnishings in co-operation with his brother James, was also in Italy at mid-century, studying classic remains.[57] George Romney [58]

---

[52] For Hogarth see W. *Hogarth: The Analysis of Beauty* (ed. J. Burke, Oxford, 1955), also H. A. Dobson: *William Hogarth,* with an introduction by Sir Walter Armstrong (London, 1902), and R. B. Becket: *Hogarth* (London, 1949).

[53] See James Gibb: *A Book of Architecture . . .* (London, 1739), and his *Bibliotheca Radcliviana, or, a Short Description of the Radcliffe Library at Oxford* (London, 1747). For English architecture in the eighteenth century see J. Summerson: *Architecture in Britain,* 1530–1830 (London, 1953), S. Sitwell: *British Architects and Craftsmen . . . 1600–1830* (London, 1945), and J. A. Gotch: *The English House from Charles I to George IV* (London, 1918).

[54] See Thomas Chippendale: *The Gentleman and Cabinet-Makers' Director, Being a Collection of . . . Designs of Household Furniture . . .* (London, 1754). His life, written by O. Brackett, appeared in London in 1924. For interior decoration of homes in the eighteenth century see F. Lenygon: *The Decoration and Furniture of English Mansions . . .* (London, 1909), and H. Cascinsky: *English Furniture in the Eighteenth Century* (3 vols., London, 1909–11).

[55] For Roubiliac (Roubillac) see K. A. Esdaile: *The Life and Works of Louis Françoise Roubiliac* (London, 1928).

[56] For Reynolds see Edmund Malone: *The Works of Sir Joshua Reynolds . . .* (5th edn., 3 vols., London, 1819); for his life see that by C. R. Leslie and T. Taylor (2 vols., London, 1865), and that by E. K. Waterhouse published in London in 1941.

[57] See Robert and James Adam: *Works in Architecture* (3 vols., London, 1778–1822); see also A. T. Bolton: *The Architecture of Robert and James Adam, 1758–1794* (2 vols., London, 1922).

[58] See T. H. Ward and W. Roberts: *Romney: A Biographical and Critical Essay with a Catalogue Raisonné of his Works* (London, 1904).

and Thomas Gainsborough [59] were still unknown painters; Goldsmith had just finished his studies at Dublin; [60] the future author of that masterpiece on the Roman Empire, Edward Gibbon, a delicate child of 13, was a student at Westminster School;[61] and the Scot, James Boswell, the future biographer of Johnson, was but ten years of age.[62] The period, as can be seen, was one of promise rather than one of the highest artistic achievement.

The middle of the eighteenth century was, however, notable for the dissemination of ideas. The Royal Society of London for Improving Natural Knowledge, to give its official name, had come into existence in the seventeenth century and was very active. It not only held regular meetings devoted largely to scientific subjects but by 1750 had published almost five hundred numbers of its *Philosophical Transactions* in forty-six volumes. In the field of *belles-lettres* men of fashion, such as Chesterfield [63] and Walpole,[64] were busy correspondents and helped to make it a golden age of letter-writing. Richardson even employed the epistle as the chief device in the construction of his novels.

The press was the leading agency for spreading information. From it poured forth books and innumerable pamphlets; it is estimated that in 1753 the aggregate number of copies of newspapers printed and sold annually in the Kingdom, by averaging the previous ten

---

[59] See W. T. Whitney: *Thomas Gainsborough* (London, 1915), and especially the biography by M. Woodall, which was published in 1949, also in London.

[60] See *The Works of Oliver Goldsmith* (ed. J. W. M. Gibbs, 5 vols., London, 1884–6), and the life of Goldsmith by A. Dobson: *The Citizen of the World* (2 vols., London, 1891).

[61] See John, Lord Sheffield: *Miscellaneous Works of Edward Gibbon, Esq., with Memoirs of his Life and Writings* (5 vols., London, 1814), and D. M. Low: *Edward Gibbon, 1736–1794* (London, 1937).

[62] Boswell, in addition to writing the incomparable life of Johnson, left a vast reservoir of writings in the form of journals and notes. See the *Private Papers of James Boswell* (ed. G. Scott and F. A. Pottle, 18 vols., London, 1928–34); the Yale edition in some forty or more volumes is also under way with the publication of three volumes that appeared between 1952 and 1956.

[63] See *The Letters of Philip Dormer Stanhope, 4th Earl of Chesterfield*, (ed. B. Dobree, 6 vols., London, 1932); see also W. H. Craig's *Life* (London, 1907) and S. Shellabarger: *Lord Chesterfield and His World* (Boston, 1951).

[64] See *The Letters of Horace Walpole, fourth Earl of Oxford . . .* (ed. Mrs. P. Toynbee, 19 vols., Oxford, 1903–25), and the even more elaborate *Yale Edition of Horace Walpole's Correspondence* (by various editors, 29 vols. up to date, New Haven, 1937–55); for Walpole's life see that by R. W. Ketton-Cremer (London, 1940) and also that by the French writer Paul Yvon: *La Vie d'un Dilettante: Horace Walpole* (Paris, 1924).

years, was no less than 7,411,751.[65] According to a report prepared in that year by the Stamp Office,[66] there were sixty London publishers of newspapers in arrears, among them, for example, one Thomas Paine (almost certainly not the revolutionist of later American fame), who owed stamp duties amounting to £87.18 for advertisements carried in his *Evening Post* and his *Universal Journal,* while James Standen owed as much as £201.2. Although this list was apparently limited to London, it includes 112 so-called newspapers published during this fiscal year by particular individuals for longer or shorter periods – an almost unbelievable number.[67]

The age of newspaper consolidations had not yet arrived, although it is true that certain publishers were adding to the number of their own publications by taking over those started by others. John Nicholson, for example, was responsible for the *Penny London Post, The British Spy, The London Evening Post, The Weekly Advertiser, Walker's Journal,* and the *London Morning Penny;* William Rayner *was credited with the St. James Weekly, The Packet, Rayner's Halfpenny Post, The Royal Oak Journal, The Morning Advertiser, The Universal Weekly Journal,* and *The London Tattler;* Thomas Warner attempted to intrigue the public with *The Daily Journal, The Post Boy, The Unusual Craftsman, The Craftsman Supplement, The Entertainer, The Shuffler,* and *The Renegade.*

Most of these publications given official but not the most complimentary recognition by the Stamp Office were undoubtedly ephemeral, and others passed from publisher to publisher. For example, the name *The Craftsman* was attached to six newspapers listed opposite the name of as many publishers; the *Penny Post* occurs four times. Nevertheless, in the list of 112 papers referred to above there were 79 without counting duplication of names, and the list, as has

---

[65] See Harold Herd: *The March of Journalism. The Story of the British Press from 1622 to the Present Day* (London, 1952), Chaps. IV and V, for the rise of the periodical and the development of the newspaper; see also the article "Newspapers" in *Encyclopedia Britannica,* 11th edition.

[66] "Sundry Publishers of Newspapers for Arrears of the Duties on Advertisements: An Account of the Duty on Several Kinds," General Account of Stamp Duties, 1752–1753, P.R.O., E. 351, 2930.

[67] For a balanced brief account of English newspapers in the eighteenth century see the chapter by D. Nichol Smith in *Johnson's England;* see also A. Andrews: *The History of British Journalism, from the Foundation of the Newspaper Press in England to . . . 1855* (2 vols., London, 1859), and H. R. F. Bourne: *English Newpapers; Chapters in the History of Journalism* (2 vols., London, 1887).

been stated, represents only those publications that had failed to pay the stamp duty on advertisements.

Whatever their defects — and these were many — the eighteenth-century newspapers voiced and moulded public opinion.[68] For "notwithstanding all . . . wise Regulations," declared a contemporary, William Smith, soon after arriving in America from Great Britain, " 'tis well known that Slavery would insensibly steal in upon us, were we not extremely watchful to prevent its Progress and were not the Press an easy and ready method of conveying the Alarum throughout the Nations." And he adds: ". . . we may understand what an inestimable Blessing Foreigners reckon the extreme Liberty we Britons enjoy, of speaking or writing what we please and of openly censuring every Measure entered into by the King or his Ministry [as] this Liberty is not indulg'd in by any other Government either Monarchical or Republican." [69]

The theatre was also an instrument for the shaping of public opinion as well as public taste, and both Covent Garden and Drury Lane were attracting the pleasure-seeker.[70] Drury Lane was managed by David Garrick, who was then at the height of his powers as England's greatest Shakespearean actor and who made the plays of Shakespeare prime favourites with the theatre-going public. During January 1750 *The Tempest* was offered four times, and performances were given also of *Hamlet, King Lear, Much Ado About Nothing,* and *Macbeth.*[71] However, *Edward the Black Prince,* by William Shirley, a play appealing to national sentiments, ran nine times — two of the performances were benefits for the author — at this theatre in 1750, in spite of the lack of a certain dramatic unity and

---

[68] W. T. Laprade: "The Power of the English Press in the Eighteenth Century," *South Atlantic Quarterly,* XXVII, 426–34.

[69] William Smith on "The Liberty of the Press," New York *Gazette,* July 28, 1752. Smith soon became Provost of the new College of Philadelphia. A copy of this essay is among the William Smith Papers, Brinton Collection, Hist. Soc. of Pennsylvania.

[70] See John Genest: *Some Account of the English Stage, from the Restoration in 1660 to 1830* (10 vols., Bath, 1832), published anonymously; see also Charles Dibdin: *A Complete History of the English Stage* (5 vols., London [1800]); H. S. Wyndham: *The Annals of Covent Garden Theatre from 1732 to 1897* (2 vols., London, 1906); and *Drury Lane Calendar, 1747–1776* (ed. D. W. Macmillan, Oxford, 1938).

[71] For Garrick see *The Dramatic Works of David Garrick . . . to which is Prefixed a Life of the Author* (3 vols., London, 1798); *The Private Correspondence of David Garrick* (ed. J. Boaden, 2 vols., London, 1831–2); P. Fitzgerald: *Life of David Garrick* (2 vols., London, 1899); and Margaret Barton: *Garrick* (New York, 1949).

coherence.[72] The giving of plays was under sharp restrictions. Those taking part in unauthorized performances were to be treated as vagabonds. To secure authorization it was necessary to send to the Chamberlain of the King's household a copy of the play fourteen days before the performance. A law of 1737 forbade, moreover, under penalty, players acting within five miles of either of the universities.[73]

However, with all these instrumentalities for enlightenment, it must be confessed that the public exhibited an extraordinary degree of credulity on occasions. In 1749 a performance was advertised at the New Theatre in the Haymarket at which the entertainer promised to play on a common cane the music of every instrument now in use, to allow people to come in disguise and to inform them who they were, to conjure up the dead relative of any person in the audience so that the latter could see and converse with the apparition, and finally, as the crowning act, to place a wine bottle of common size upon a table on the stage and in the sight of all to enter it and sing while within it, permitting the curious-minded to handle it and to prove that it did not exceed in size an ordinary tavern bottle. The announcement of the proposed performance created great excitement and on the night of the proposed entertainment the theatre was crowded with "prodigious numbers." Even dukes and duchesses vied for seats. At seven o'clock the theatre was lighted up, but the audience waited in vain for the appearance of the mighty man. The unsuspecting proprietor attempted to keep the audience in good humour, but cat-calls began and a riot soon developed. When the enraged audience at last realized it had been tricked, the younger men tore up the benches, broke to pieces the scenery, pulled down the boxes, and after dismantling the theatre carried its contents into the street for a great bonfire. " 'Tis thought the conjurer vanished away with the bank," wrote one commentator, leaving the deluded theatre-owner with nothing but a wrecked building. This writer went on to observe that not only the curious-minded were dis-

[72] *The Gentleman's Magazine*, 1750, p. 44. According to *The Companion to the Play-House*, published in 1764, the writer of the play *Edward the Black Prince* was not the distinguished Governor of Massachusetts Bay who was in England at the time, but a gentleman who for some years had been residing in Portugal and who had returned to England in 1749.

[73] For legislation restricting the giving of plays see 10 Geo. II, c. 19 and c. 28, and 17 Geo. II, c. 5, Par. 2.

appointed by the non-appearance of the conjurer inside of his wine bottle, but so also were the "many enemies to a late celebrated book concerning the ceasing of miracles." For these latter imagined, and rightly, "that his jumping into it would have been the most convincing proof possible that miracles are not yet ceased." [74]

Any people with the varied and world-wide contacts possessed by the English at this period, interested intensely as they were in the furtherance of certain large commercial ends and in the midst of building a far-flung empire, faced also as they were by great economic changes that struck at stratification of ideas and produced great dislocations in population, would hardly find time or inclination to be actively intolerant in the realm of the imponderables of theology and religious experience.[75] As a matter of fact, despite the prestige and privileges enjoyed by the Established Church, it was not exactly in a crusading mood in 1750. On the contrary, it was displaying a strong tendency toward latitudinarianism, which, incidentally, ultimately became a source of great vitality to it.[76] The Church, in fact, was perhaps feeling somewhat exhausted after its successful struggles in the early half of the century over the issue of Jacobitism, on the one hand, and deism, on the other.[77]

---

[74] *The London Magazine,* January 1749. It appears that this great hoax was actually perpetrated by John, second Duke of Montagu, not many months before his death. See the sketch of his life in the *Dictionary of National Biography*. The duke, it seems, left a reputation for his addiction to practical jokes, as well as for his philanthropy.

[75] A foreign observer makes this comment on religion in England in 1742: "Upon the whole among the great number of different religions properly speaking, there is no religion at all, especially among the great, and people of the lowest rank. Of which debauchery, corruption, perjury, and suicide so frequent in this Kingdom are melancholy proofs" ("*Observations sur le Royaume d'Angleterre,*" Loudoun Papers, Huntington Library).

[76] Leslie Stephen in his *English Thought in the Eighteenth Century* (London, 1881), I, 79, describes this as the golden period of English theology because of the alliance established by the latitudinarians between reason and Christian theology; see also C. J. Abbey and J. H. Overton: *The English Church in the Eighteenth Century* (London, 1878), I, 279, and Norman Sykes: *Edmund Gibson . . .* (Oxford, 1926), pp. 262–4.

[77] The Rev. Joseph Butler, in his *Analogy of Religion, Natural and Revealed, to the Constitution and Course of Nature,* (London, 1736), produced one of the most profound and original contributions to religious thought in the English language, which had the effect of placing deism on the defensive. For Butler see E. C. Mossner: *Bishop Butler and the Age of Reason: A Study in the History of Thought* (New York, 1936), and W. J. Norton: *Bishop Butler, Moralist and Divine* (New Brunswick, N. J., 1940). See also R. N. Stromberg: *Religious Liberalism in Eighteenth Century England* (Oxford, 1954), for a scholarly discussion of the controversy over deism and its aftermath.

Whereas numbers of the clergy were men of real piety and devoutness, others were given over to worldliness and at best were busy politicians seeking ecclesiastical promotion for themselves and friends. Commendams and pluralities still existed as an abuse and were eagerly sought, although many of the lesser clergy could easily be justified in these.[78] The Weston Papers, among others, throw a flood of light on conditions within the Church, especially the alliance between certain of the Whig politicians and leading clergymen. For example, a Dr. Newcomb who sought to secure the deanery of Peterborough in 1743, was informed by the Duke of Newcastle that he could not succeed to that post "without promising a firm attachment to Lord Fitzwilliam's Interest, wch the Dr. has accordingly promised" [79] Dr. John Thomas, successively Dean of Peterborough, Bishop of Lincoln, and Bishop of Salisbury, was called upon in the election at Huntington in 1747 to throw his influence at least quietly in support of the rather notorious "Lord Sandwich's Interest." [80]

The clergy were subject during this period to unusually bitter

---

[78] The following newspaper item is characteristic of the sort of thing going on in the church: "On Wednesday last, a Dispensation passed the Great Seal of England to enable the Rev. Edward Dicey to be a chaplain to the Right Hon. Earl of Sussex, to hold the Rectory of Walton in the county of Bucks and Diocese of Lincoln, with the Rectory of Mardwell, in the County of Northampton and Diocese of Peterborough, being presented thereto by the Hon. Lord Chancellor" (*Aris's Birmingham Gazette*, March 18, 1751). For an able defence of pluralities at this period see the Norman Syke's *Edmund Gibson*, pp. 223–31. This volume is also recommended for an excellent account of conditions within the Establishment during the first half of the eighteenth century. For a more exhaustive treatment of pluralities see C. J. Abbey and J. H. Overton's standard work, *The English Church in the Eighteenth Century* (2 vols., London, 1878).

[79] Dr. John Thomas to Edward Weston, June 26, 1743, C. F. Weston Underwood Papers, Hist. Mss. Com., *10th Report*, p. 278.

[80] Bishop Thomas to Edward Weston, January 1, 1747, *ibid.*, p. 296. "Sir, If the Bishop of Salisbury has mett with you he will have acquainted you that L^rd O—rd has agreed to Mr. Seech succeeding Dr. Bland, not doubting but that care will be taken to fill his fellowship with a Whig" (Horace Walpole to Edward Weston, November 30, 1743, *ibid.*, p. 279). While the bishops' bench was strongly Whig—thanks to the efforts of Bishop Edmund Gibson, whose influence over ecclesiastical promotions had been decisive for many years during Walpole's administration—nevertheless, his successor at Fulham, Thomas Sherlock, had been for many years the leader of the Tory clergy. The latter were strongly entrenched in the country districts. See Norman Sykes: *Edmund Gibson, Bishop of London, 1669–1748. A Study in Politics and Religion in the Eighteenth Century* (Oxford, 1926), and *The Works of Bishop Sherlock, with some Account of his Life* (ed. T. S. Hughes, 5 vols., London, 1830).

attacks by their enemies.[81] They did not so much influence the point of view of the government, it would appear, especially after the withdrawal of Bishop Gibson from political activity, as the government did that of the clergy, at least the higher clergy. Yet the government was opposed to persecution.

There was scarcely a community of any size that did not support one or more dissenting meeting houses, which were protected under the Toleration Act. In greater London these meeting houses numbered about 100; there were also Jewish synagogues, in spite of the existence of express laws against them,[82] as well as "several popish chapels for the use of foreign ambassadors." The number of nonconforming chapels is quite impressive in the light of the fact that not more than 111 churches of the Establishment were to be found within the same metropolitan area.[83]

Although many laws designed to enforce conformity remained on the statute books since their passage in the days of Elizabeth I and her successors to James II; although political disqualifications for religious nonconformity were still in force under the Test and Corporation Acts (despite the annual passage since 1727 of the Indemnity Act, which relieved the less sensitive dissenters of civil disabilities); [84] and although the universities were still monopolized by those of the Church of England persuasion, there was very little tendency to bother people because of their religious beliefs.[85] Of course, everyone – irrespective of his religious affiliation – was re-

---

[81] Mark Pattison: *Essays and Reviews*, p. 315, Norman Sykes: *op. cit.*, pp. 149–52, and Dorothy Marshall: *English People in the Eighteenth Century* (London, 1956), pp. 94–103.

[82] *Parliamentary History* (Hansard), XIV, 1382. In 1753 the Jewish naturalization bill was passed (26 Geo. II, c. 26), strongly supported by the bench of bishops in the upper house of Parliament (*ibid.*, XIV, 1365–1431). It was repealed the following year (27 Geo. II, c. 1), however, as a result of popular outcry.

[83] Sir Walter Besant: *London in the Eighteenth Century* (London, 1902), Appendix I.

[84] Only those professing the established religion or conforming to it could be magistrates of a city or borough or hold any office of honour or profit under the government. See *Parliamentary History* (Hansard), XIV, 1384.

[85] Occasionally, however, one comes across some such item in the press as the following: "We hear a bill will be brought into Parliament the next Session to lay a large Penalty on any person or persons who send their children to be educated in Seminaries abroad, whereby great Numbers of Persons are brought up" (London advices, Glasgow *Courant*, October 9, 1749). Bishop Gibson would have proceeded vigorously against various groups had he not lacked the support of the government. See his life by Dr. Sykes, already cited.

quired to make payment of tithes for the support of the Establishment.[86]

The Roman Catholics, it should be pointed out, were still legally excluded from public office, from positions in the army and navy, and from seats in Parliament; they could neither practice law nor medicine, nor could they become schoolmasters; further, they were incapable of inheriting land or purchasing it. They were forbidden to have arms, and on pain of fine were prohibited to send their children abroad for an education; moreover, their taxes were doubled and should a Protestant venture to tender one of them a sum beyond £5 for a horse in their possession, this must be surrendered; they were expected to register both their names and estates; their priests were still liable to the Elizabethan penalties for treason should they even appear in the Kingdom or should they try to convert Englishmen; and an act of William III still remained on the statute books providing life imprisonment for the exercise of their priestly office. Only in the chapels of the embassies in London could mass be openly celebrated, and Roman priests were forced to appear in public in the garb of laymen.[87]

Happily, there was little disposition during this period to enforce these statutes and thus to molest Catholics, who as a group were very quiescent and circumspect. Few of them even ventured openly to support the Young Pretender in 1746, in spite of the fact that there were many thousands of them in London.

On occasion, it is true, some old sixteenth- or seventeenth-century statute was dragged forth for temporary rehabilitation, as an inci-

---

[86] For the payment of tithes see 3 Wm. and Mary, c. 3, 7; 8 Wm. III, c. 6 and c. 34, Par. 4; and 1 Geo. I, c. 26. Par. 2. That there existed a good deal of opposition to the payment of tithes in the middle of the eighteenth century is indicated by the following excerpt from a letter: "I doubt we have a number of Incendiarys in this Town or Neighborhood: Monday last about one ye morning Richd Berkit's Tyth Barn at Hawton was set on fire, burnt to ye ground in two hours time, corn therein . . . if the Wind had been high the Church must inevitably have shared ye same fate" (Alex. Holden to ——, Newark, February 17, 1753, Newcastle Papers, B. M., Add. Mss. 32731, folio 197).

[87] Norman Sykes: *op. cit.*, pp. 292–5. The statutes that still bound Roman Catholics were, among others, the following: 23 Eliz. I, c. 1; 27 Eliz. I, c. 2; 25 Charles II, c. 2; 1 Wm. and Mary, c. 15; 7 and 8 Wm. III, c. 24; 11 and 12 Wm. III, c. 4; and 1 Geo. I, Stat. 2, c. 55. For accounts of the Roman Catholics in England see J. Gillow: *A Literary and Biographical History . . . of English Catholics, from the Breach with Rome, in 1534, to the Present Time* (5 vols., London, 1885–1902), and John Kirk: *Biographies of English Catholics in the Eighteenth Century* (ed. J. H. Pollen and Edwin Burton, London, 1909).

dent in the year 1748 will illustrate. It appears that two ladies had a house called the "Nunnery" near Micklegate Bar in York; they were indicted in September of that year for not attending church and in open court were fined, for the use of the poor, £4.7 each.[88] Yet, in 1754 a large gathering of Roman Catholics took place in this same city, "as they say to chuse a Receiver of their Taxes." Moreover, on the evening of one of their meetings the heads of two participants in the rebellion of 1746 were removed from the top of Micklegate, which gave great scandal to the more zealous subjects of His Majesty.[89]

Indeed, the religious situation in England was in most striking contrast to that in contemporary France, where the Huguenots, even in this age of the freethinker Voltaire, were faced by fierce persecution that led to the massacre of numbers of their pastors and caused panic-stricken congregations secretly to flee the country to escape the galleys.[90] South of France the Inquisition was still operating to stamp out freedom of belief.[91] "Many authors," wrote one at this period,

> "have exclaimed with great heat of the many sects in England; but let it be considered that civil and religious liberty are closely connected, and that it does not become any church who makes no pretentions to infallibility to set up that standard of persecution. May

[88] York advices to *The Maryland Gazette*, March 8, 1748.

[89] Rockingham to Newcastle, February 17, 1754, Newcastle Papers, B. M., Add. Mss. 32734, folios 146–7.

[90] On January 17, 1750, a royal ordinance was published at Versailles calling for the execution of the former edicts against the Protestants. Letters written by Huguenot ministers to their friends in England speak of attacks of armed dragoons on defenceless congregations, with the killing of many people, and of the consignment of others to the galleys, where they were chained to the oars. See *Sympathy with our Suffering Brethren — In Two Discourses: Occasioned by the Cruel Oppressions of the Protestants in France, and Enlarged with a recent and particular Account of the State of the Persecution in that Kingdom*, by Thomas Gibbons, (London, 1755); see also *The Annals of the Rise, Progress, and Persecutions, of the Reformed Churches of France*, by Isaac Tomes (London, 1753).

[91] "They write from Lisbon that the Design manifested by his Portuguese majesty to soften the rigorous Proceedings of the Inquisition occasioned a general joy in all ranks of People but especially among the trading Part of his subjects. . . . As yet the present King has done nothing more in this Matter than ordering provisionally, that no Person detained in the Prisons of the Inquisition shall be committed to the Flames, nor undergo any other corporal punishment, till the whole Proceedings on his Trial shall be examined in the King's Council and declared to be fair and Equitable. But they suppose that this is only the first Step to try the civil Magistrate's Strength against Ecclesiastical Tyranny" (*Aris's Birmingham Gazette*, February 18, 1751).

the minds of Britons ever be free and in affairs which relate solely to another life, may they be accountable to their conscience and their God!" [92]

Besides the Roman Catholics, the principal Christian groups outside the Establishment were the Congregationalists,[93] Presbyterians,[94] Unitarians,[95] Baptists,[96] Quakers,[97] and United Brethren or Moravians,[98] with a considerable number of French Protestants and Lutherans. It is estimated that there were ten thousand Jews in England.[99] To these groups must be added the Methodists, who, while asserting firm adherence to the Thirty-nine Articles and claiming at this period a place within the fold of the Established Church, were now gathered into their own societies.[100]

---

[92] D. Fenning and J. Collyer: *New System of Geography*, II, 497. "They [the English] know better than any other people upon earth how to value, at the same time, three great advantages — religion, commerce, and liberty," declared Montesquieu (*Spirit of the Laws*, Book XX, Sec. 7).

[93] For the Congregationalists see J. Waddington: *Congregational History, 1700–1800. In Relation to Contemporaneous Events* (London, 1876), and R. W. Dale: *History of English Congregationalism* (ed. A. W. W. Dale, London, 1907).

[94] For the Presbyterians see O. M. Griffiths: *Religion and Learning: A Study in English Presbyterian Thought from the Bartholomew Ejections (1662) to the Foundation of the Unitarian Movement* (Cambridge, 1935), and A. H. Drysdale: *History of the Presbyterians in England, their Rise, Decline, and Revival* (London, 1889).

[95] For the Unitarians see H. McLachlan: *The Unitarian Movement in the Religious Life of England* (London, 1934), and R. Wallace: *Antitrinitarian Biography . . . to which is Prefixed a History of Unitarianism in England* [to 1800] (3 vols., London, 1850). In this connection it should be noted that there was no distinct Unitarian church until after 1773.

[96] For the Baptists see W. T. Whitley: *A History of British Baptists* (London, 1932), and J. Ivimey: *A History of the English Baptists, Including a History of Baptism in England* (4 vols., London, 1811–30).

[97] For the Quakers see John Gough: *A History of the People called Quakers* (4 vols., Dublin, 1789–90), and Thomas Clarkson: *A Portraiture of Quakerism, as taken from a View of the Moral Education, Discipline, Peculiar Customs, Religious Principles, Political and Civil Economy, and Character of the Society of Friends* (3 vols., London, 1806).

[98] For the Moravians see *Memoirs of James Hutton: Comprising the Annals of his Life, and Connection with the United Brethren* (ed. D. Benham, London, 1856), and David Cranz: *The Ancient and Modern History of the Brethren* (trans. from the German by D. Cranz, London, 1780).

[99] For the Jewish people see M. Margoliouth: *The History of the Jews in Great Britain* (3 vols., London, 1851), and J. Picciotto: *Sketches of Anglo-Jewish History* (London, 1875).

[100] For the Methodists see G. Smith: *History of Wesleyan Methodism* (3 vols., London, 1857–61), A. Stevens: *The History of the Religious Movement of the Eighteenth Century, called Methodism* (3 vols., New York, 1858–61), and Umphrey Lee: *The Historical Backgrounds of Early Methodist Enthusiasm* (London, 1931).

By 1750 Methodism was exerting so powerful an influence in the British Isles and in America as to demand more than passing reference. For the movement started by John and Charles Wesley and George Whitefield some twenty years previous had attracted and held many supporters, although in the course of time the Wesleys and Whitefield had parted company because of theological differences.[101] Horace Walpole in 1749 complained to Sir Horace Mann that "this sect increases as fast as almost ever any religious nonsense did." The leaders at this period were at the height of their mental and physical powers. Whitefield, indeed, may be considered the greatest evangelist of his century. Some idea of his labours can be gained from a letter written on October 23, 1749, by a clergyman at Haworth in Yorkshire to a friend in London:

> "In these several weeks past Mr. Whitefield has been preaching in these Parts; in my Churchyard three times, as it was supposed, to 7000, and assisted me in administering the Lord's Supper to 1000; at Leeds, Newcastle, Halifax . . . and in several Places, particularly in Lancashire and Cheshire, at Raehdale, Rosedale, Bolton on the Moors, and Manchester, to several thousands. . . . He is now at Leeds again and I suppose you will shortly see him at London." [102]

In vain ministers of the Established Church of England and of Scotland attempted to exclude him from ministering to their flocks.[103]

The Methodist movement did not, of course, escape public attack. "*Amicus Veritatis*," writing in November 1749, warned the people against "this whimsical enthusiastical Society" that filled

---

[101] For John Wesley see *The Works of the Rev. John Wesley* (32 vols., Bristol, 1771–4), and J. H. Simon: *John Wesley and the Methodist Societies* (London, 1933), and *John Wesley, the Master Builder* (London, 1927) as well as other works by the same author relating to the life of Wesley. For Charles Wesley see *The Journal of the Rev. Charles Wesley . . .* (ed. T. Jackson, 2 vols., London, 1849) and T. Jackson: *Life of the Rev. Charles Wesley . . .* (2 vols., London, 1841). For Whitefield see *The Works of the Rev. George Whitefield . . .* (6 vols., London, 1771–2); Luke Tyerman: *The Life of . . . George Whitefield* (2 vols., London, 1876–7); J. P. Gladstone: *George Whitefield: Field Preacher* (London, 1900); and David Belden: *George Whitefield, the Awakener . . .* (Nashville, Tenn., 1930).

[102] Printed in the Bristol *Weekly Intelligencer*, November 11, 1749; see also the Glasgow *Courant*, November 6, 1749 for further comments on Whitefield's preaching.

[103] Among the Lang manuscripts at the University of Edinburgh is a copy of a resolution passed in one of the Scottish presbyteries November 1, 1748, and signed by nine ministers: "That it is the judgment of the Presby. that ministers Employing Mr. George Whitefield to preach in their pulpits is an Irregular Practice and y^r^fore Recommend to all ministers not to employ him in time coming."

"their Heads with imaginary nonsense." He asked in scorn if a wise, benevolent Deity indispensably required "their meeting at Midnight, at Five o'clock every Morning (even in the most rigorous inclement winter season), twice or thrice more in every day of the year." He also criticized "their childish Love Feasts upon Bread and Water – Dividing themselves into Classes or Tribes with divers other little whimsical Tricks and Rules, which none but a member can Enumerate." [104]

"A Friend to the Protestant Religion," writing in reply to these charges, summarized, as he saw it, the benefit that the Methodist movement had brought. Although denying that he himself was a Methodist, he stressed

> "the real Good produced from the Preachings of Messrs. W——tf—d and the W—y's, particularly among the Inhabitants of Kingswood (as well as many other Parts) where from a Native State of Ignorance, and Kind of Barbarism the People are become civilized and humane; brought into true Knowledge and Belief of the Principles of the Protestant Religion; – Order among themselves; – A due Respect to the Holy Profession of the Clergy; – Obedience to the Magistracy; and a proper Dread of the Laws. These good Effects have, at least, resulted from Methodism." [105]

The times were ripe for such a movement to spread.[106]

Hand in hand with religion goes the idea of solicitude for the welfare of the unfortunate. As will be seen in the chapter to follow, the English were strongly committed to the notion of strict if not harsh justice; they were, happily, equally committed to the notion that a duty rested on those who enjoyed a competence to share it with the needy. The poor rates in some of the parishes, for example, amounted in the middle of the century to as much as five and six shillings on the pound, particularly in Oxfordshire and in Essex; in some of the parishes of Cambridgeshire, it was asserted, these

[104] The Bristol *Weekly Intelligencer* for November 1, and 17, 1749. For the Bishop of London's attack upon the Methodists in 1739 see Norman Sykes: *Edmund Gibson*, pp. 307–8); for that by Joseph Trapp, also in that year, see his *The Nature, Folly, Sin and Danger of being Righteous Overmuch . . .* (London, 1739). In 1749 George Livingston also put out his anonymous *The Enthusiasm of Methodists and Papists Compared* (2nd edn., London, 1754).

[105] Bristol *Weekly Intelligencer*, November 25, 1749. See on the above point also W. J. Warner: *The Wesleyan Movement in the Industrial Revolution* (London, 1930), especially pp. 166–80, 207–48.

[106] See F. J. Klingberg: "The Evolution of the Humanitarian Spirit in the Eighteenth Century," *Penna. Mag. of Hist. and Biog.*, LXVI, 260.

were even higher.[107] One can indeed hardly doubt the assertion of Thomas Alcock, writing in 1752, that despite the defects of the poor laws there was abundant proof that the English were "a kind, a compassionate, a generous People." He called on men to "witness the many grand structures, and large endowments for Charity-Schools, for Hospitals, Infirmaries, etc. which have been erected and established only within a century past. Witness the handsome subscriptions and generous collections that even now are commonly made when the call is pressing, and the Object truly deserving." [108]

The provision for the unfortunate in London was so varied that those who made the 1754 revision of Stow's *Survey* proudly asserted that "there is almost in every parish a quantity of cloathes and coals for firing yearly bestowed and often times money too for their relief and subsistence so that by these charities . . . it is rarely or never heard of, that any die in this city, merely of famine or perish in the streets for want, as in many other countries they do." [109] A list of gifts and charities annually made by the twelve great liveried companies and incorporated in the *Survey* is almost wearisome in its extent. The guilds of lesser importance also had their benevolences. These benefits, moreover, were by no means limited to the families of members.[110]

Nor were there lacking those with a fervour to combat the tendencies toward dissolute living. The Society for the Reformation of Manners was established in 1690 by "many virtuous persons of the several Denominations of Protestants, readily agreed to give Hearts

---

107 Thomas Alcock: *Observations on the Defects of the Poor Laws* (London, 1752), p. 4.

108 *Ibid.*, p. 52.

109 John Strype: *A Survey of the Cities of London and Westminster . . . by John Stow . . . brought down . . . to the Present Time* (6th ed., London, 1754–5), II, 157.

110 A description has come down from this period of a curious procession of members of the Drapers' Guild in 1751. Leaving their Hall they paraded to St. Peter's Cornhill headed by the master, the wardens, and court of assistants, who were followed by a number of the Company's poor, each carrying a pair of shoes and stockings and a suit of clothes, the annual gift of the Company. See A. H. Johnson: *The History of the Worshipful Company of the Drapers of London* (Oxford, 1914–22), III, 399; see also P. H. Ditchfield: *The History of the City Companies of London and their Good Works* (London, 1904). For English philanthropy in the eighteenth century see B. K. Gray: *A History of English Philanthropy from the Dissolution of the Monasteries to the taking of the first Census* (London, 1905); W. S. Lewis and R. M. Williams: *Private Charity in England, 1747–1757* (New Haven, 1938); and E. Caulfield: *Infant Welfare Movement in the Eighteenth Century* (New York, 1931).

and Purses . . . to prevent the spreading of the Leprosy of Sin." During a period of 45 years before 1754 this society brought about the prosecution of more than 100,000 cases involving debauchery and profaneness in and about London.[111] The Society for the Promotion of Christian Knowledge, established in 1698, operated by the year 1750 in most parts of the Empire, "that so Piety and Knowledge and Devotion might be brought in among the Poor and Ignorant." In particular the members dedicated themselves to the setting up of schools for the education of poor children and in providing parochial libraries for communities in Great Britain and the plantations overseas; nor were their benefits limited to Englishmen or English speaking people. To rescue the Salzburg Protestants from persecution in 1732 they so strained their resources as to endanger their other charitable undertakings.[112] The Society for the Propagation of the Gospel in Foreign Parts, dating from 1701, the thirteenth year of the reign of King William, gave a further outlet to those who were animated with devout and kindly impulses. It was generously supplied with funds and was active in good works, especially in the British plantations.[113]

It is well to emphasize these facts somewhat in order to modify an impression that one gets in studying certain aspects of eighteenth-century English life that most people were cynical regarding their religious and moral obligations, heartless, and dissolute. Even the debtor prisons were not overlooked by the kind-hearted. The law passed the second year of the reign of George II (2 Geo. II, c. 22) resulted in the release of as many as ten thousand debtors, according to Viscount Percival.[114] Unhappy as the lot of these unfortunate peo-

---

111 See Stow's *Survey of London* (revision of 1754), II, 143. For an account of the Society for the Reformation of Manners and kindred societies see G. V. Portus: *Caritas Anglicana, or, An Historical Inquiry into those Religious and Philanthropical Societies that Flourished in England between 1678 and 1740* (London [1912]).

112 For a history of the above society see W. O. B. Allen and E. McClure: *Two Hundred Years: the History of the Society for Promoting Christian Knowledge, 1698–1898* (London, 1898); see also W. K. L. Clarke: *Eighteenth Century Piety* (London, 1944), which is also concerned with the activities of the S.P.C.K.

113 See C. F. Pascoe: *Two Hundred Years of the S.P.G.: An Historical Account of the Society for the Propagation of the Gospel in Foreign Parts, 1701–1900* (2 vols., London, 1901).

114 Percival's *Diary, Hist. Mss. Com. 16th Report* (London, 1920), I, 90. For an account of the condition of eighteenth-century debtors in English prisons see the chapter by J. L. Hammond and Barbara Hammond in *Johnson's England*, I, especially pp. 324–8; see also J. Ashton: *The Fleet: its River, Prison and Marriages* (London,

ple continued to be, it is recorded in the *Survey of London* that "many well-disposed citizens do frequently send the Prisoners Relief unknown who they be; and discharge poor Debtors . . . paying their Debts and several Ministers in London have considerable sums sent them by good Christians . . . where they shall see most need." [115] Moved with pity, wealthy people frequently came to the rescue of debtors. For Example, in 1749 the executors of a Mrs. Blondel, "late of Hemstead," pursuant to her will discharged 42 prisoners from White Chapel gaol; in that year another charitable lady discharged the debtors from Gatehouse and Bridwell; [116] and the Countess of Huntingdon – whom Horace Walpole called "the queen of the Methodists" – in co-operation with other ladies, released 27 prisoners at Newgate, Bristol.[117]

Many others in England were worthy of the eulogy pronounced in the *Gentleman's Magazine* at the death of Sir Walkin Wynne of Derbyshire, Bart., in 1749: "An Excellent pattern of generosity and hospitality, a steady senator, a firm patriot, a keen enemy to the corruption and venality of ye time. . . . His house was a daily relief to the poor – and none let to go away empty." [118] John, second Duke of Montagu, who also died in that year, was beloved by many as "the soul of all Benevolence, Husband to the Widow, Father to the Orphan, Sincere and Steady Friend of the Distressed." [119]

One final point should be stressed in this all too brief survey of social England in the middle of the eighteenth century. The nation was in the process of great transformations not only economically, but spiritually. Although people would run to see a man enter a tavern bottle, they were rapidly learning, and to their credit they had largely given up many of the credulous beliefs of the seventeenth century, as well as some of its fanaticism. Among other spiritual achievements they had in the main freed themselves from the age-

---

1888). For English prisons in the eighteenth century see J. Howard: *The State of the Prisons in England and Wales . . .* (Warrington, 1777), and W. Smith: *The State of the Gaols in London, Westminster and the Borough of Southwark* (London, 1776).

[115] Stow's *Survey of London* (revision of 1754), II, 160.

[116] London advices, *Maryland Gazette*, October 25, 1749.

[117] *Ibid.* It may be pointed out that R. N. Stromberg in his *Religious Liberalism in Eighteenth Century England*, a work already cited, emphasizes the fact (p. 150) that there was "no real humanitarian movement until the last quarter of the century" – granting the existence of benevolence and charity before that period.

[118] *Gentleman's Magazine*, 1749, p. 430.

[119] London advices to the *Maryland Gazette*, October 25, 1749.

old terror of the power of the black art: of witches and sorcerers.[120] While too many of them were still rather barbarous, many more brutalized by intemperance and distinctly antisocial in their attitudes, they nevertheless were being gradually moulded by new religious, educational, and economic forces into what was to become one of the most civilized, humane, socially-minded, and self-disciplined peoples that the world has yet seen.

One need not therefore be surprised, in view of the growing emphasis in England on the social responsibilities of the individual, that the colonial Benjamin Franklin, with his broad cultural interests, should have been so charmed with life in the mother country during the period of his first sojourn there in the late fifties and early sixties that he seriously contemplated settling in London for the remainder of his days.[121] Some foreigners were in like manner happily impressed with the civilization of the English. Henri Misson, a Frenchman who was acquainted with many of the nations of Europe and had resided in England for several years, declared in almost extravagant praise:

> "What brave men do I know in England! What moderation! What generosity! What uprightness of heart! What piety and charity! There are in England persons that may be truly called accomplished; men who are wisdom and goodness itself; if we may say so much of any thing besides God. Peace and prosperity be eternally to England!" [122]

Likewise, Jacques Henri Meister in his *Souvenirs de mes Voyages en Angleterre* (1795) wrote about the English:

> "These people are honourable, distinguished by sentiments of decorum, magnanimity and uprightness, by private attachments and universal benevolence, by affections of every gentle, constant and generous kind, which the heart is capable of feeling." [123]

---

[120] It is true, however, that even so highly an educated man as John Wesley seems to have retained a belief in witchcraft. At least in defence of the Scriptures he declared that "the giving up witchcraft is, in effect, giving up the Bible" (*Dictionary of National Biography*, quoting from the *Arminian Magazine*, 1782, p. 366).

[121] Thomas Bridges to Jared Ingersoll, Hedley, England, September 30, 1762, *Jared Ingersoll Papers*, 1758–1764 (New Haven, 1918), p. 278.

[122] John Pinkerton: *Voyages and Travels*, II, 143. H. Misson's *Memoirs and Observations in his Travels over England*, translated from the French by John Ozell, was published in London in 1719.

[123] See R. Bayne-Powell: *Travellers in Eighteenth-Century England* (London, 1951), p. 5.

But not all foreigners, it is needless to say, were so happily impressed. César de Saussure, who was in England between 1725 and 1729, complained in his *Lettres et Voyages*:

> "I do not think there is a people more prejudiced in its own favour than the British people and they allow this to appear in their talk and manners."

He also affirmed that when crowds gathered on state occasions, a foreigner ran "a great risk of being insulted by the vulgar populace which is the most cursed brood in existence." [124]

This then was the England that had attached to itself not only the rest of the British Isles, but also an overseas Empire that already was displaying enormous potentialities; an Empire, however, that could only be maintained in unity and loyalty through the display of great qualities of political leadership. What had the government of the country to offer in 1750?

[124] *Ibid.*, pp. 5 and 71.

CHAPTER IV

Under the Shadow of the Pelhams

IN THE MIDDLE of the eighteenth century England was governed by the Whigs, a distinct party which made its appearance as such in 1679 during the reign of Charles II and which stood for the supremacy of parliamentary authority in matters of state as against the claims of "the hereditary indefeasible rights" of the King, who was supported by the so-called Tories. Also involved in this struggle was the issue of toleration for those who dissented from the doctrines and forms of the established Anglican Church, with the Whigs supporting toleration and the Tories opposed to it. With the Revolution of 1688 and the repudiation thereby of the Catholic James II and the recognition of William and Mary by the nation at large, the Tories were compelled to shift their position on the fundamental matter of royal supremacy. Under Queen Anne, during the War of the Spanish Succession, they became the peace party against the Whigs, who demanded the continuation of the war to a satisfactory conclusion. With the death of Anne and the coming of the first of the Hanoverian line to the throne, largely through the instrumentality of a group of powerful Whig leaders, the Tory party disintegrated, leaving as supporters of its seventeenth-century principles a small residue of nonjuring clergy, high churchmen, and isolated individuals, mostly country gentlemen without personal political ambitions although they might sit in Parliament.

With the field of political manoeuvre left to themselves, the Whigs from the beginning of the reign of George I in 1714 tended to divide into rival groups generally headed by some powerful member of the nobility who was also a great landowner. Each group was intent on gaining control of the government, of legislative policy and also of the patronage that came with political power. This was the situation in 1750. With places too few for the many aspirants for office, those who were left out in the cold not unnaturally sought grounds for displacing those basking in the King's favour. They therefore constituted what may accurately be called His Majesty's loyal opposition – supporting as they did the principles of 1688 and the Hanoverian line of succession. This opposition rested, at least ostensibly, on the advocacy of different policies or on the assumption that an accepted policy could be more effectively directed by new leaders. In other words, within Parliament not all supported the King's ministers, but all were claimed to be loyal subjects of the King. This was not an unhealthy condition. It is axiomatic that no people will long enjoy good government if those responsible for the conduct of public affairs are not subject to open criticism and their misdeeds or supposed misdeeds given the full glare of publicity. As a result, the ministry, fully aware of the dangers lying in the pathway of those who acted with irresponsibility in public matters, moved with wary feet.

Given the Whig-dominated Parliament and ministry, what about the structure of the government of the country? One intelligent foreigner, the Portuguese merchant Don Manoel Gonzales, who travelled through England in the early 1730's and showed a keen interest in the institutions of the Kingdom, declared:

> "The policy or government of England is a limited monarchy, such as secures the people's liberty under the grandeur of a king; a monarchy without slavery; a great king, and yet a free people. It is an instrument of three strings, which, being well sorted, yields an admirable harmony, to the benefit and glory of the kingdom. A mixed government of monarchy in the king, aristocracy in the lords, and democracy in the commons. Here the king makes the figure of a great monarch, the lords keep up their state, and the commons their liberty." [1]

Another traveller, who visited England a decade later, a nameless Frenchman, found to his surprise that the King, although in the possession of three grand prerogatives and enjoying very extensive powers – through his right to convoke, adjourn, prorogue, and dissolve

---

[1] See John Pinkerton: *Collection of Voyages and Travels* (17 vols., London, 1808–14), II, 127.

Parliament, through his right of appointment to great posts and benefices in the Church and state, and through his power to make peace, pardon criminals, coin money, and confer titles of nobility — was nevertheless "subjected in all other Respects to the laws as much as the lowest subject." [2]

It would doubtless be exceedingly difficult to state in all respects the exact extent of the British Crown powers in the middle of the eighteenth century. The actual exercise of the more important of these rested in the Cabinet Council,[3] advised, and at times admonished and even opposed — though rarely — by the King, who in the last resort could take the responsibility of overruling that body in all executive measures, due to his ability to choose his own ministers.[4]

This Cabinet Council, which had come into existence in the course of the first half of the eighteenth century, had grown out of the all-embracing activities of the Privy Council, which it had gradually supplanted as the centre of administrative activity.[5] This took place despite the fact that it was not recognized in the constitution and consequently did not in the final analysis, possess legal authority. Whereas in the seventeenth century the Privy Council had assumed directly the great responsibilities of advising the King and formulating policies, these functions had now largely become the work of a small, extra-constitutional body made up of great officers of state. The Cabinet Council, it would seem, sought formal sanction of its measures but infrequently from the Privy Council, which still oper-

---

[2] "*Observations sur le Royaume d'Angleterre*," Loudoun Papers, Huntington Library. The King's person and the royal residence were, however, exempt from all ordinary processes.

[3] Lord Hervey declared to King George: "The titles of Government belong not to persons who exercise all the authority of it; your Majesty bears the name of King and wears the Crown, whilst all the authority of the one and the power of the other is exercised by another" (Reginald Lucas, *George II and His Ministers* [London, 1910], p. 11).

[4] See H. W. V. Temperley: "Inner and Outer Cabinet and Privy Council," *English Hist. Rev.*, XXVII, 683; E. R. Turner: *The Cabinet Council in England* (Baltimore, 1930–32, 2 vols.); Sir William R. Anson: *The Law and Custom of the Constitution*, Vol. II (4th edn., ed. A. B. Keith, London, 1935); and R. R. Sedgwick: "The Inner Cabinet Council from 1739 to 1741," *English Hist. Rev.*, XXXIV, 290–302. With respect to the ability of the King to choose his ministers freely see Sir Lewis Namier: *England in the Age of the American Revolution* (London, 1930), Chap. 1, Richard Pares: *King George III and the Politicians* (Oxford, 1953), Chap. 4, and Herbert Butterfield: *George III and the Historians* (London, 1957), pp. 40–50, *passim*.

[5] See E. T. Williams: "The Cabinet in the Eighteenth Century," *The Making of English History* (eds. R. L. Schuyler and H. Ausubel, New York, 1952, pp. 378–92) for an illuminating discussion of the above point.

ated effectively only when organized as a committee of the whole — and then only with respect to Irish and colonial affairs and questions of trade.[6] Even then the Privy Council was dominated, as a rule, by those who made up the Cabinet Council. So far had its earlier authority waned as an effective instrumentality of government. Under this system the King was allowed in practice the most ample opportunity of giving direction to the administration of affairs. The principle of full ministerial responsibility for all acts emanating from the Crown had been firmly established as a fundamental of the constitution only to the extent that measures arising from this source must bear the signature of at least one minister who would thereupon assume legal responsibility for them.[7]

Indeed, so great was the respect enjoyed by the King, whoever he might be, and so honoured was his high position within the state, that the exact limits of his influence on government would be impossible to circumscribe in a formal manner. It is certain that at this period, according to memoranda preserved in the Newcastle Papers, matters of importance rarely came before the Cabinet Council for decision before being submitted by the minister to the King.[8] George Augustus, the second of the Hanoverian line, was still much of a German princeling at heart and naturally still much of an Elector of the Holy Roman Empire in outlook.

Enjoying the royal confidence in 1750 was Henry Pelham, a quiet, compromising, peace-loving, industrious, unimaginative commoner who, firmly established as chief minister, was holding the offices of First Lord of the Treasury and Chancellor of the Exchequer.[9] In that year the other great offices of state were filled as follows: the Lord

---

[6] See E. R. Turner: *The Privy Council of England in the Seventeenth and Eighteenth Centuries* (2 vols., Baltimore, 1927–8), II, 415–32.

[7] Sir William Anson pointed out in his *The Law and Custom of the Constitution* (3rd edn., Vol. II, 100) that collective responsibility of the Cabinet Council did not exist during the period under consideration in this series.

[8] There were, of course, exceptions to the above. "My friend Holderness has wrote a very short but not improper letter of what passed at your meeting at the Lord Chancellor's, but he has referred to your letter, which I could not shew [the King] & therefore was obliged to suppress Lord Holdernesse's letter also," wrote Newcastle to his brother Henry Pelham on April 29, 1752, Newcastle Papers, B. M., Add. Mss. 32727, folio 27–9. See E. R. Turner and G. Megaro: "The King's Closet in the Eighteenth Century," *American Historical Review*, XLV, 761–76.

[9] For Pelham see William Coxe: *Memoirs of the Administration of the Right Honourable Henry Pelham* (2 vols., London, 1829); for the earlier political activities of the Pelham brothers between 1741 and 1747, see J. B. Owen: *The Rise of the Pelhams* (London, 1957).

President was Lionel Cranfield Sackville, Duke of Dorset, who somewhat earlier had been described as "the gayest man in Ireland" during his Lord-Lieutenancy; the Lord Privy Seal was John, Lord Gower, a mild Tory; Philip Yorke, Lord Hardwicke, an able jurist, occupied most acceptably the office of Lord High Chancellor; [10] the Duke of Newcastle, the brother of Henry Pelham, was the Secretary of State for the Northern Department; John, Duke of Bedford, was the Secretary of State for the Southern Department.[11] Bedford, a member of the great Russell family, was, however, growing weary of office under the existing conditions. Like Newcastle, his chief opponent in the Cabinet, he was a great landowner, but unlike him he was exceedingly arrogant and independent and was accused of being more addicted to the pursuit of pleasure than to the conscientious fulfillment of his duties – much to Pelham's dissatisfaction.

Among other great office-holders were John Montagu, Earl of Sandwich, a Bedford Whig, a man of some ability, but of evil reputation so far as his personal life was concerned, who served as First Lord of the Admiralty until his retirement the following year; [12] William Stanhope, Earl of Harrington, who had won some distinction as a diplomat and was acting as Lord Lieutenant of Ireland; and William Pitt, who was at this juncture Paymaster General of Forces.[13]

This was the so-called "Coalition" or "Broad-Bottom" ministry. In their deliberations Hardwicke was probably the most convincing, as his legal opinions carried great weight, although he enjoyed no influence with the King comparable to that of the Pelhams. In the

---

[10] For Hardwicke see P. C. Yorke: *The Life and Correspondence of Philip Yorke, Earl of Hardwicke, Lord High Chancellor of Great Britain* (3 vols., Cambridge, 1913).

[11] For Bedford see the *Correspondence of John, fourth Duke of Bedford . . .* (3 vols., London, 1842–6).

[12] For the private papers of Sandwich, covering a later period, see *The Private Papers of John, Earl of Sandwich, First Lord of the Admiralty, 1771–1782* (ed. G. R. Barnes and J. H. Owen, 4 vols., *Publications* of the Navy Record Society, London, 1932–8).

[13] Many of Pitt's letters covering the years 1741 to 1778 are printed in the *Correspondence of William Pitt, Earl of Chatham* (ed. W. S. Taylor and J. H. Pringle, 4 vols., London, 1838–40). For Pitt's life see Basil Williams: *The Life of William Pitt, Earl of Chatham* (2 vols., London, 1913); Albert von Ruville: *William Pitt, Earl of Chatham* (trans. H. J. Chaytor and M. Morison, 3 vols., London, 1907); J. C. Long: *Mr. Pitt and America's Birthright* (New York, 1940); and for Pitt's early years see Lord Roseberry: *Chatham: his Early Life and Connections* (London, 1922). Pitt's statesmanship is also acutely analyzed in a recent scholarly work by John Brooks: *The Chatham Administration, 1766–1768* (London, 1956); see also O. A. Sherrard: *Lord Chatham . . .* (London, 1952), and D. A. Winstanley: *Lord Chatham and the Whig Opposition* (Cambridge, 1912).

House of Commons, Pitt, Pelham, William Murray (the Solicitor General),[14] and Henry Fox spoke with authority for the ministry.[15] In the upper house there was Hardwicke; Newcastle was equally active there and enjoyed the reputation of an effective debater in spite of the somewhat muddled manner in which, according to Lord Hervey [16] and other contemporaries, he carried on the affairs of his office.

The ministry was, in truth, not a particularly harmonious group. Even the Pelhams were at odds. Thomas (Newcastle), who for more than twenty-seven years had acted as a Secretary of State, was reputed to be one of the wealthiest men in Great Britain and certainly was one of the most extensive landowners and a master at parliamentary management.[17] At times he tended to overshadow his younger brother, whom in the main he had supported since the latter took office in 1744 as head of the ministry. At the period under consideration their hostility was hardly veiled. "The cause of all this misunderstanding," wrote the Duke in 1751 to his private secretary, Andrew Stone, "I take shortly to be the uneasiness and dissatisfaction which my Brother had at the credit, the superior credit, which I was thought to have for some years with the King." [18] He then went on to explain the situation: "This credit he [Pelham] apprehended was obtained by the Foreign measures I was pursuing (though nobody ever doubted but they were thoroughly agreeable to my opinion) and by the great countenance and support of the Duke of Cumberland [19] and the Princess Amalie." [20]

Newcastle, however, had by 1750 lost the support of these two

[14] For Murray see John Holliday: *Life of William Murray, late Earl of Mansfield* (London, 1797), and John, Lord Campbell: *The Lives of the Chief Justices of England . . . till the Death of Lord Mansfield* (4 vols., London, 1874).

[15] For Fox see the Earl of Ilchester: *Henry Fox, first Lord Holland* (2 vols., London, 1920), and T. W. Riker: *Henry Fox, first Lord Holland: A Study of the Career of an Eighteenth Century Politician* (2 vols., Oxford, 1911).

[16] For Lord Hervey's picture of the times see his *Memoirs of the Reign of King George II* (ed. R. Sedgwick, London, 1952). Hervey's life is presented by A. C. Ewald in his *Studies Re-studied: Historical Sketches from Original Sources* (London, 1885).

[17] For Newcastle's early years see J. B. Owen, *op. cit.*, and S. H. Nulle: *Thomas Pelham-Holles Duke of Newcastle* (Philadelphia, 1931).

[18] Duke of Newcastle to Andrew Stone, December 26, 1751, Newcastle Papers, B. M., Add. Mss. 32725, folios 558–68.

[19] For Cumberland, son of George II, see A. N. C. MacLacklan: *William Augustus, Duke of Cumberland: Being a Sketch of his Military Life and Character* (London, 1876), and E. E. Charteris: *William Augustus, Duke of Cumberland, his early Life and Times, 1721–1748* (London, 1913).

[20] Princess Amalie, second daughter of George II.

members of the royal family, much to his anguish, especially when the Princess gave a series of parties to which all the members of his family but himself were invited. The injury was compounded by the presence of the Duke of Bedford "for carrying on the scheme and contributing to the pleasures and diversions of the young people." Both Cumberland and Amalie were now showering their favours on Brother Henry.[21] Thomas insisted that they had now entered a "cabal" to drive him from power, using his own great dissatisfaction with the conduct of the office of Secretary of State for the Southern Department by the Duke of Bedford, whom they were supporting, as a foil, as it were, against him.

Doubtless realizing the insecurity of his isolated position, Newcastle offered his brother a basis for compromise and complete reconciliation which gives one so much insight into the sources of political power at the time that it would be well to present it briefly. He stipulated, first of all, that the altercations that had occurred between them should never in the future be mentioned; that by mutual promises each should inform the other of everything that passed relative to public affairs and the administration of the government, and more particularly his respective situation "at Court with the King, the Duke of Cumberland, the Princess Amalie, Lady Yarmouth [22] and Mr. Fox"; that all employments either in the Church, the administration, or the House of Commons should be discussed between them before any person should be proposed to the King; that all public measures, either parliamentary or foreign, should be agreed upon between them; that in all conversations with the King it should be assumed that His Majesty had been pleased to confide equally in them both, and particularly that Pelham should take every occasion to show both the King and Lady Yarmouth that any coolness toward his brother would weaken the administration; and, finally, "that the Foreign system for the preservation of the peace, which has been followed since the conclusion of the war should be continued and supported." [23] These terms were accepted by Henry.

[21] Newcastle, acting at this period as Secretary of State for the Northern Department, had been especially responsible for the Peace of Aix-la-Chapelle and in connection with the negotiations preliminary to it sharp differences had arisen between him and the Earl of Sandwich, First Lord of Admiralty, who was ultimately supported vigorously by Cumberland.

[22] Amalie Sophie Marianne Wallmoden, the Countess of Yarmouth, was the mistress of George II.

[23] See Newcastle to Stone, December 26, 1751, *loc. cit.*

The power exercised by the Pelhams within Parliament itself may be judged by the fact that in 1746 the King attempted to displace them by giving his confidence to William Pulteney, Lord Bath, who after a three-day struggle to establish a ministry was compelled to recommend their recall to His Majesty.[24] The explanation for this great influence will become clearer in the course of this chapter; but it may be said here that, over and beyond their personal control of votes of Parliament, the policies of the brothers were not unenlightened. Upon the conclusion of the War of the Austrian Succession, Henry turned to a program of sharp retrenchment to lighten the public burdens; the annual charge on the national debt alone amounted in 1748 to £3,000,000. The personnel of the navy was thereupon reduced from 50,000 to 10,000 and that of the army from 40,000 to 19,000. Further, Pelham scored a real triumph when he succeeded in refunding on a 3 per cent basis the public debt, which had been paying 4 per cent.

The problem of filling offices, especially important offices, is a major responsibility in every form of government. It is also an important source of political influence. No individuals since the days of Walpole grasped at that instrumentality of authority more fully than did the Pelhams, even to bending the King to their will. An incident that occurred in 1752 illustrates not only the hostility sometimes shown by the King to their recommendations, but also his reluctance to break with them, especially now that they had composed their differences and were presenting a solid front to all rivals. George II had gone to Hanover accompanied by Newcastle; the latter, writing to his brother after an encounter over appointments, declared:

> "I had yesterday a very strong battle for Lord Breadalbane,[25] but it ended as I wished, though with hearing many disagreeable things of

---

[24] "The King could no longer run counter to them [the Pelhams] nor look for advice elsewhere than to his official counsellors" (I. S. Leadam: *The Political History of England, 1702–1760*, [London, 1909], p. 411). Pulteney wrote a number of pamphlets on political matters, among others *An Enquiry into the Conduct of our Domestic Affairs* . . . (London, 1734) and *A Letter . . . to two Great Men* (London, 1759), which was an attack on Pitt and Newcastle. For a careful treatment of the above episode see J. B. Owen: *op. cit.*, pp. 292–7.

[25] Reference above is made to John Campbell, third Earl of Breadalbane (1696–1782), who was a student at Christ Church, Oxford, served as ambassador to Russia and also in the Admiralty and in 1746 became Master of the Royal Jewels office. In January 1752 he succeeded to the title and was later chosen a representative peer for Scotland in the House of Lords.

myself & my friends, that we always recommended our own Creatures, that H. M. thought Lord B. a Jacobite but that he was my Lord Chancellors relation; that we never considered whether a man was a Jacobite or not if he was our Creature & many things to ye same purport." [26]

To Andrew Stone, Newcastle went into more particulars, emphasizing the hostility of the King to the recognition given to relatives of the Lord High Chancellor, Lord Hardwicke. The King had complained that all of Hardwicke's family had been heaped with favours, "his eldest son, a Teller of the Exchequer, another son, a boy, a plenip^{y} in Holland, another all the things in the Law, which meant the Clerk of the Crown, etc." [27]

It is evident that the King viewed with intense disfavour the processes by which the Pelhams were continually adding to their strength.[28] The Breadalbane case involved their securing His Majesty's approbation that this lord should succeed the ailing Earl of Dunmore as one of the sixteen peers of Scotland, the selection of whom was virtually in the hands of the government.[29] To Newcastle

---

[26] Duke of Newcastle to Henry Pelham, May 10, 1752, Newcastle Papers, B. M., Add. Mss. 32727, folios 27–9.

[27] Duke of Newcastle to Andrew Stone, May 2/13, 1752, *ibid.*, 32727, folios 63–5. Hardwicke had five sons, all of whom were talented. Philip Yorke, the eldest, who succeeded his father to the title, was chief author of the so-called *Athenian Letters* . . . (4 vols., London, 1741); he was styled Viscount Royston and represented Cambridge in the House of Commons. Charles Yorke, the second son, also a member of the House of Commons, enjoyed in 1752 the sinecure place of Joint-Clerk of the Crown in Chancery; in 1756 he became Solicitor General, and in 1770 succeeded Lord Camden as Lord High Chancellor, but died under tragic circumstances before actually serving in this capacity. Joseph Yorke, the third son, after serving in the army with credit, entered upon a diplomatic career and in 1752 was British minister at the Hague and in 1761 ambassador at the same court. The fourth son, John, also became Clerk of the Crown in Chancery. The fifth son, James, took orders and later became Bishop of Ely.

[28] The intensely personal quality of the loyalty expected by the Pelhams of the recipients of ministerial favour is indicated by the application that young Charles Townshend made to Newcastle in the year 1754, after the death of Henry Pelham had necessitated changes. "I beg leave to declare, your Grace," he wrote after calling in vain at Newcastle's door, "that if you should think it for your service to put me into an office of consequence and rank, you will always find me a diligent officer & a grateful man, attached & most strictly attached to your Grace personally & to Your honour and interest only" (Charles Townshend to the Duke of Newcastle, [March 11, 1754], B. M., Add. Mss. 32734, folios 216). For the career of Charles Townshend see P. H. Fitzgerald: *Charles Townshend, Wit and Statesman* (London, 1866).

[29] Lord Hardwicke to the Duke of Newcastle, May 5, 1752, B. M., Add. Mss. 32727, folios 81–3. William Murray, the third Earl of Dunmore, passed away in 1756.

the King's behaviour toward such a man as Hardwicke was almost incomprehensible. "It is amazing," he wrote, "that any body should endeavour to set the King against so good, so great & so valuable a man." [30]

The reconciliation of the brothers synchronized with the withdrawal from the Cabinet in 1751 of the Duke of Bedford and the Earl of Sandwich in favour of Robert D'Arcy, Earl of Holderness, who took over as Secretary of State for the Southern Department, and George, Lord Anson, who became First Lord of the Admiralty. Although Bedford and his supporters did not sit idle but proceeded to launch against the ministry a paper called *The Protector*,[31] there was unusual harmony within the government circle [32] until 1754. In the spring of that year came confusion caused by the death of Henry Pelham.

But no one could challenge the Newcastle ascendancy. He agreed to carry on the government and chose for himself the office of First Lord of the Treasury, one of the two his brother had enjoyed, giving the other, the Chancellorship of the Exchequer, to the Hon. Henry Bilson Legge; he also transferred the Earl of Holderness from the Secretaryship of State for the Southern Department to that of the Northern Department, which he himself had just vacated, and apparently acting in harmony with the King's wishes, offered the former, a most coveted post, to Henry Fox, Secretary at War. It appears that Fox had been living in expectation of that honour and for years had been a powerful factor with which the Pelhams had had to reckon.[33]

In the temporary bewilderment following his brother's death Newcastle had promised to Fox "the management of . . . affairs in the

---

[30] Duke of Newcastle to Andrew Stone, May 2/13, 1752, *ibid.*, 32727, folios 63–5.

[31] R. Blacow to the Duke of Newcastle, May 13, 1753, *ibid.*, 32731, folios 533–4; Pelham to Newcastle, July 17, 1753, *ibid.*, 32732, folios 295–300.

[32] Newcastle, writing to Pitt from Hanover, September 29, 1752, regarding the delicate negotiations in which he was engaged at this juncture with reference to the settlement of the imperial succession, declared: "I flatter myself that you will be glad to hear that I have sent constant accounts to my Brother of every step which I have taken, and that I can say I have his thorough approbation in the most kind and affectionate manner possible. This is the greatest comfort and the greatest encouragement to me, and I am sure will be extremely agreeable to one who wishes us both so well as you do" (*ibid.*, 32729, folios 386–7).

[33] For an excellent treatment of the politics of this period see T. W. Riker: *Henry Fox; First Lord Holland* (Oxford, 1911), I, especially Chapter 3.

H. of Commons. This," declared Fox in a letter to Newcastle, "was the whole tenor of your Grace's messages by Lord Hartington." [34] The Duke, however, at last made it clear to both Fox and Hartington that the office would carry with it no more control over the secret service funds used in securing the continued control of the Commons by the ministry than was enjoyed by Holderness when he held that position. There was no rival and there was to be no rival in Newcastle's control of government. Fox felt that he had reason to believe that the King desired it otherwise – doubtless with the idea of being able then to pit him against the Duke as for years he had done with Henry Pelham. He was undoubtedly correct about George II's desire to make a show of independence against his minister.

Therefore, when the offer of the Secretaryship of State, under the above limiting conditions, was made, Fox wisely declined to give up the very lucrative post he then enjoyed for one that would allow little play for his peculiar talents. Nevertheless, he could not, in refusing, forbear to make clear to Newcastle that this was because he himself was "unable therefore to answer, what I dare say is His Majesty's expectation (tho' your Grace has frankly declar'd it not to be yours). . . ." [35] All of which is sufficient to make clear the extent to which Newcastle had made the government temporarily his own.

No sooner had Fox written his refusal than he repented of it and made an "aggravated representation" to the King of the part played by the chief minister in defeating him in his anticipations; but he found little sympathy in that quarter, since the King was decidedly displeased with his behaviour at this juncture and therefore had come to favour another for the post in question.[36] The offer of this post to Sir Thomas Robinson did not fail to raise resentment among others in addition to Fox and his followers. Robinson had been the chief negotiator of the Treaty of Aix-la-Chapelle – although Newcastle had received the credit for this treaty – and had also represented the government at Vienna. He was a man excellently versed in the complexities of international diplomacy and was intimately

---

[34] William Cavendish (1720–1764), Marquis of Hartington and later fourth Duke of Devonshire.

[35] Henry Fox to the Duke of Newcastle, March 14, 1754, B. M., Add. Mss. 32734, folios 243–4.

[36] Lord Hardwicke to the Duke of Newcastle, March 19, 1754, *ibid.*, 32734, folios 281–2.

attached to Newcastle. Yet he was without influence in the House of Commons and was lacking in qualities of leadership.

To the aspiring Pitt it was almost an insupportable mortification to see even the nominal leadership of the House of Commons, which went with the Secretaryship, in the hands of one so inexperienced in parliamentary affairs as Robinson, while he, a veteran, was ignored.[37] "I shou'd have felt myself far less personally humiliated had Mr. Fox been placed by the King's favour, at the Head of the House of Commons than I am at present," he wrote with undisguised chagrin. He confessed that the appointment of Fox would have wounded him, but solely, he declared, because of his attachment to the chief minister and the Lord Chancellor, who might be adversely affected by it.[38] Newcastle could not only console him by pointing out the King's unwillingness to consider him for such a post, confessing his inability under the present situation to bring His Majesty into a favourable attitude toward a proposal of this nature,[39] while making clear that he was able to advance the interest of the Great Commoner's friends, Legge, George Littelton, and George Grenville.

In the exercise of these great powers of appointment the Pelhams, it should in justice be stated, sought undoubtedly for capable men, but also for men who would not challenge their authority. In the main they were successful in filling effectively the various posts within their gift. Newcastle, in fact, prided himself on the quality of his appointments, asserting "that my point is always to serve honest deserving men." [40] Opening his mind to Horatio Walpole on the colonial situation in 1754, he declared: "I wish I knew who were the two best men in all England for New York and Jamaica and I would

[37] With reference to the appointment of Robinson, Newcastle wrote to Pitt, April 2, 1754: "Those who are honoured with your friendship thought that the most favourable measure that could be obtained; an honourable and able man, extremely well qualified in every respect for the execution of that office, sincerely attached to our system, and who without departing from that rank & figure which belonged to his office, had not those Parliamentary talents which could give jealousy, or in that light set him above the rest of the King's servants there" (Duke of Newcastle to William Pitt, April 2, 1754, *ibid.*, 32735, folios 8-12).

[38] William Pitt to the Duke of Newcastle, April 4, 1754, *ibid.*, 32735, folios 26–9.

[39] Newcastle in attempting to soften the blow to Pitt wrote in the letter just referred to: "and since, from circumstances (which you know I have long lamented) it was impossible to put one into that office, who had all the necessary qualifications, both within & out of the House, nothing surely could show so great a desire to soften or alleviate that misfortune as the giving in to the nomination of Sir Thomas Robinson, under the description above mentioned" (*ibid.*, 32735, folios 8–12).

[40] Duke of Newcastle to Andrew Stone, May 2/13 1752, *ibid.*, 32727, folios 63–5.

recommend them immediately against all competitors; for we will have the best men we can find." [41] The fact that the Pelhams had had the unswerving support of William Pitt, Hardwicke, Legge, William Murray, and Sir Dudley Ryder,[42] certainly the most capable men in public life at this period, is to their credit, even accepting the fact that these men all enjoyed public office and favour at their hands; it is also to the credit of Newcastle that he leaned especially upon Hardwicke and Murray for advice, as his correspondence indicates.

We turn now to the composition and activities of Parliament in the middle of the eighteenth century. There were about 200 peers, but seldom did more than 160 of them sit in the House of Lords; the remainder were disqualified as Catholics or as minors. According to an enumeration made in the early 1740's, there were in attendance at the House 3 dukes,[43] 2 marquesses, 85 earls, 15 viscounts, 66 barons, 2 archbishops, and 24 bishops, together with the 16 elected peers from Scotland.[44] In reality, only a handful of peers met frequently to conduct business; only on great occasions or when an issue was pressing was the House filled.

The real influence of the House of Lords on government at this period, however, must not be underrated.[45] Indeed, many of the peers performed a variety of public services, or at least secured the emoluments, financial or otherwise, of a series of posts. John, second Duke of Montagu, enjoyed the following offices and honours in the 1740's, the last decade of his life: he was Marquis of Monthermer, one of the lords of His Majesty's most honourable Privy Council, Master General of Ordinance, Master of the Great Wardrobe, Colonel of the Second Regiment of Dragoonguards (the Queen's Regiment), a

---

[41] Duke of Newcastle to Horatio Walpole, May 14, 1754, *ibid.*, 32735, folios 268–72.

[42] Sir Dudley Ryder in 1733 became Solicitor General and in 1737 Attorney General; he was knighted in 1740 and in 1754 became Chief Justice of the Court of King's Bench and two years later became Baron Ryder of Harrowby, but died before the ceremony of kissing the King's hands took place.

[43] However, A. S. Tuberville, in his *House of Lords in the Eighteenth Century* (Oxford, 1927, p. 256), makes clear that in the Broad-Bottom Ministry eight dukes were given places.

[44] In 1765 there were 202 peers on the Roll of Peers. See L. G. Pine: *The Story of the Peerage* (London, 1956), Appendix IV. For Scottish peers, see *ibid.*, Appendix V.

[45] "The Commons might do most of the talking — they were welcome — but the Peers managed the country" (A. S. Tuberville: *The House of Lords in the Eighteenth Century*, p. 256).

General of horse, one of the knights of the most noble Order of the Garter, Grand Master of the Order of Bath, Lord Lieutenant and *custos rotulorum* of Northamptonshire and Warwickshire, Master of Geddington chase, and Warden of the west bailiwick of Rockingham forest.[46] Nothing perhaps is more strikingly characteristic of this period than the offices showered upon those who were already politically powerful and independently wealthy. Doubtless one of the things that somewhat reconciled the public to this situation was the possibility of a commoner who had achieved eminence and rendered important service to the nation being awarded with a peerage and many other honours.[47]

The House of Commons was composed of 558 members, 45 of whom were Scotsmen. The membership was divided between county members and those from boroughs, cities, universities, and the Cinque Ports.[48] The emphasis on landholding is shown by the requirement, frequently evaded however, that county members possess £600 sterling yearly in land rent and the others £300. Excluding Wales, the 40 counties each sent two knights,[49] and the 25 cities two citizens, with the exceptions that London sent four and that Ely was unrepresented; there were 167 boroughs entitled to two burgesses each and 5 to one each. The two universities were entitled to two each; the Cinque Ports and their dependent ports sent sixteen.

In order to vote in a county election, it was only necessary to possess within the shire a freehold of the yearly value of forty shillings.[50] The qualifications for the borough franchise varied from borough to borough. In some it was the payment of rates, in others the posses-

---

[46] London advices, *Maryland Gazette*, October 25, 1749. Montagu's country place, "Boughton" in Northamptonshire, was built, although on a more modest scale, on the pattern of Versailles.

[47] One of the most striking differences between the constitution of Great Britain and the constitutions of the states of continental Europe was the comparative ease with which a commoner could move into the rank of the nobility. It is well to bear in mind that all men in Great Britain were commoners irrespective of birth unless they succeeded to a title of nobility by the fact of birth itself.

[48] See Sir Lewis B. Namier: *Structure of Politics at the Accession of George III* (2nd edn., London, 1957); see also Edward and Annie G. Porritt: *The Unreformed House of Commons* (2 vols., Cambridge, 1909).

[49] Under the terms of the Act of Union of England and Wales of 1536, supplemented by that of 1542, each of the twelve Welsh shires was accorded one member in the House of Commons.

[50] For the liberal interpretation of the qualification for voting see the Porritts: *op. cit.*, I, 82.

sion of a freehold, in others the ownership of a hearth, in still others membership in a guild or in the borough council.[51]

In some cases the number of electors was respectably large, as was true of the city of Westminster, where at the polls in 1749 there were 9,465 votes cast,[52] and of Nottingham, where during the same period there were something over 1,200 voters.[53] In other instances, however, once flourishing towns with borough privileges had almost or quite disappeared because of shifts in population. As a result, the right of nominating their representatives had become, as it were, the possession of some great landowner who frequently sat in the upper house of Parliament.

In the case of a borough such as Mitchell in Cornwall, there was much complication. The place was "a manor and borough by prescription," of which John, fourth Baron Arundell of Wardour was high lord and Hugh Boscawen, Viscount Falmouth, George, Earl of Edgcumbe, Sir Richard Vyvyan, Thomas Scawen, and Captain Charles Courtenay of Tremere, were mesne lords, who alternately acted as port reeve of the manor, making returns for the members of Parliament chosen by forty-two of the tenants paying scot and lot,

---

[51] The following classes of boroughs are to be distinguished: Scot and lot boroughs; inhabitant householder and potwalloper boroughs; burgage boroughs; freeman boroughs; and corporation boroughs. See *ibid.*, I, 4–5.

That even at this period and in spite of the Last Determinations Act of 1729 (2 Geo. II. c. 24) the qualifications for the parliamentary franchise in many of the boroughs were not beyond dispute is indicated by the fact that at Worcester it was finally resolved in 1748 that the right of election was "in the citizens not receiving alms, and admitted to their freedom by birth or servitude, or by redemption, in order to trade within the city" (*Parliamentary History* [Hansard], XIV, 82). A serious dispute also arose in connection with the Westminster election of the following year. The supporters of Sir George Vandeput insisted that the right to return members was in the inhabitants, the householders within the city and liberty paying scot and lot, and the occupiers of chambers in the several inns of chancery within the same. The supporters of Granville Gower, Viscount Trentham, on the other hand, insisted that it was limited to the householders. The high bailiff, called upon to make a decision, after two days of deliberation and perhaps hesitation declared: "That the right of election for the city and liberty of Westminster is in the inhabitants, householders . . . paying or being liable to pay scot and lot; and in the occupiers in the several inns of chancery and in the inhabitants, householders of Whitehall, Scotland Yard, the Mews, and Stable-yard, St. James (not being the King's menial servants) and those belonging to the chest" (*Gentleman's Magazine*, 1750, p. 41); see also *The London Magazine*, 1751, p. 291.

[52] *Bristol Weekly Intelligencer*, December 9, 1749.

[53] "A certification of the Canvass of the Town of Nottingham," Newcastle Papers, B. M., Add. Mss. 32733, folio 150. Sir Lewis Namier, in his *Structure of Politics at the Accession of George III* (pp. 74–81), makes clear that only 112 out of 405 borough representatives were returned by electorates of five hundred or more.

that is, rates to the Church and to the poor. Seventeen of these "belonged" to Sir Richard, nine to Lord Arundell and seven to other mesne lords. In the election of 1747 it was harmoniously arranged — since all the mesne lords were supporting the ministry — that Scawen and Courtenay should name the member; subsequently these part-owners began a struggle among themselves that was aired in Westminster Hall.[54]

Such boroughs as Chippenham, Malmesbury, Old Sarum, and Wootton Bassett were regularly on the market and in the election of 1747 were picked up by Frederick, Prince of Wales, then engaged in building up an opposition party.[55] Many other boroughs were virtually in the giving of the ministry, such as Hastings, Harwich, Queenborough, Rye, Sandwich, and Winchelsea. Newcastle's personal control of patronage extended into three shires. Among these rotten boroughs, the Cinque Ports and their dependencies in the late 1740's provided for Pitt; John Cleveland, joint secretary to the Admiralty; Andrew Stone, Newcastle's private secretary; young James Pelham; Lord George Sackville, son of the Duke of Dorset; and for other pillars of the administration.

In both county and borough elections, voters frequently, if not generally, expected to be rewarded in some fashion or other for their votes.[56] This was true in spite of laws against the use of bribery at parliamentary elections[57] and the provisions of the law regulating

[54] Edward Boscawen to the Duke of Newcastle, March 22, 1754, Newcastle Papers, B. M., Add. Mss. 32734, folios 303–4. In the election of 1760 Admiral Boscawen had taken the place of his brother, Lord Falmouth, as one of the mesne lords. This is indicated in the "State of Cornish Burroughs from Lord Edgcumbe; received June . . . 1760." See Sir Lewis Namier: *The Structure of Politics at the Accession of George III* (2nd edn., London, 1957), p. 304.

[55] *Parliamentary History* (Hansard), XIV, 81–2.

[56] It may be noted that in the year 1771, 57 members of the so-called Christian Society of New Shoreham in Sussex, who had organized themselves for the express purpose of selling seats in Parliament, were disfranchised by name by act of Parliament. See II Geo. III, c. 55. There were therefore limits beyond which voters could not go in seeking rewards.

[57] For the laws against the use of bribery see 2 Geo. II, c. 24; 9 Geo. II, c. 38; and for the act of 1740 directed against fraudulent means of acquiring the franchise see 13 Geo. II, c. 20. The elector's oath in 1750, provided for by 2 Geo. II, c. 24, was, "I, A.B. do swear (or being one of the People called Quakers, I, A.B. do solemnly affirm) I have not received or had by my self, or any Person whatsoever in Trust for me, or for my Use and Benefit, directly or indirectly any Sum or Sums of Money, Office, Place or Employment, Gift or Reward, or any Promise or Security for any Money, Office, Employment or Gift, in order to give my Vote at this Election and that I have not been before polled at this Election."

county elections passed in 1745, which provided for the erection of election booths at the expense of the candidates, the appointment by the sheriff of clerks of election, and the preparation and use of electoral lists of the towns, villages, and parishes.[58]

The least that voters might anticipate was abundant food and drink. At Lewes in Sussex in 1754 dinners at the two taverns, refreshments at the eight public houses, and breakfast at the coffee house came to some £350 despite the lack of competition for the candidates of the government.[59] Thomas Vernon and Robert Tracy, standing for Worcester, estimated that they would be obliged to spend at least £1,200 between them to secure from London two hundred voters entitled to the franchise in the former place. In addition, Tracy calculated the total expense of retaining his seat at £3,000.[60] He besought the government for assistance. Worcester, in fact, was considered an expensive seat to hold for the government. Pelham had apprehended it would require from £4,000 to £5,000, and although he advanced some money, "seemed desirous to break off all engagements . . . if he had known how to extricate himself." [61]

To keep Robert Bristow in his seat for New Shoreham in Sussex, Pelham had agreed to pay all election costs beyond £1,000. To procure for Mr. Amyand a seat for Barnstaple and for Mr. Alderman Porter one for Evesham, he was obliged to make pledges to defray all expenses exceeding £1,500 in each case. He supported Sir Wil-

[58] See 18 Geo. II, c. 18. The Porritts in their *The Unreformed House of Commons* give a wealth of detail regarding the above point; see also Sir Lewis Namier: *Structure of Politics at the Accession of George III*.

[59] John Greening to the Duke of Newcastle, April 15, 1754, Newcastle Papers, B. M., Add. Mss. 32735, folio 94. For the election of 1747 see J. B. Owen: *op. cit.*, pp. 314–17; see also S. H. Nulle: *Thomas Pelham-Holles, Duke of Newcastle*, for Newcastle's relations with the Sussex boroughs in the early part of the eighteenth century.

For the purpose of purifying elections, Josiah Tucker took the position that the qualification for voting in the county elections should be changed from a 40 shillings freehold to a £20 freehold and for borough franchise the tradesman should have £200 "stock in trade." This would make the franchise comparable to what it was when Parliament laid down the qualifications in the reign of Henry VI (8 Henry VI, c. 7). See his *A Brief Essay on the Advantages and Disadvantages which respectively attend France and Great Britain with regard to Trade* (London, 1750), pp. 50–3.

[60] Robert Tracy to the Duke of Newcastle, December 11, 1753, Newcastle Papers, B. M., Add. Mss. 32735, folio 421. Henry Fox is said to have spent £4,000 to retain his seat for Windsor in 1757. See the Provost of Eton to Edward Weston, July 9, 1757, C. F. Weston Underwood Papers, Hist. Mss. Com., *10th Report*, pp. 313–14.

[61] "In Mr. West's letter of March 13, 1754," Newcastle Papers, B. M., Add. Mss. 32734, folio 239.

liam Yonge at Honiton in Devonshire with "a certain sum," and the campaign of Sir John Strange, Master of the Rolls, for the retention of his seat at Totnes, also in Devonshire, was understood to be entirely at the expense of the government. In the same election secret service money also went to aid its candidates at Reading, Gloucester, Wallingford, and Old Sarum.[62]

Nor did the Pelhams limit themselves to mere financial assistance to get their followers into office. A rather notorious case of direct interference occurred in the election for Seaford in Sussex, one of the boroughs of the Cinque Ports, in the year 1747. Pitt stood for reelection in this borough together with another supporter of the administration, William Hay; their opponents were Charles Sackville, commonly called Lord Middlesex, and William Hall Gage, both put forward by the Prince of Wales. The two last-named candidates, in a petition to the House of Commons after the poll, desired to have the election of Pitt and Hay invalidated, They claimed that "a noble peer of this realm," who was also a minister, entertained at his house most of the voters of the town, and on that occasion solicited each individually for his vote, "by means whereof several persons, who had promised to vote and would have voted for the petitioners, were prevailed upon by the said noble peer." This in itself, they urged, was a high infringement of the liberties and privileges of the Commons. Moreover, on the day of the election, in order to awe and influence the voters in favour of the sitting members, this peer and minister came into the court accompanied by other peers of the realm, and taking seats near the returning officer, they continued there until the poll was closed, even in the face of protests on the part of one of the petitioners that such conduct was an obstruction of freedom of election and in violation of repeated resolutions of the House of Commons.[63]

When the petition came before the Commons on November 20, it was treated by Pitt as beneath his consideration and turned into a mere jest. But Thomas Potter, son of the Archbishop of Canterbury, spoke strongly favouring it, and according to the account of the debate that has come down to us, declared:

---

[62] See Namier, *Structure of Politics*, pp. 196–9. For the disbursements actually made from the secret service money in 1754 see *ibid.*, pp. 199–205.

[63] At the end of the voting Pitt and Hay each received 23 votes and Middlesex and Gage 19 each. See J. B. Owen: *op. cit.*, p. 315, n.

"To my very great amazement I see this question treated with the greatest contempt and ridicule, by an hon. gentleman whose weight may, perhaps, persuade a majority to be of his opinion. . . . I believe history is not able to produce an instance equal to the present, of a wise and great statesman taking upon himself the honourable employment of being an agent to a borough. . . . In what other light, Sir, can it appear to us than as the last and utmost effort of one who was determined, at any rate, to procure a majority in this House, of persons attached to himself, his own creatures, the tools of his power; I wish to God, Sir, nothing may happen to-day, to give the people room to suspect that he has been too successful."

Nevertheless, when the question was put, the petition was rejected by a vote of 247 to 96.[64]

The practice by great personages of controlling weak boroughs and influencing county elections had virtually put the power of the state into the hands of an oligarchy. That this was possible was due, among other things, to the grossly unequal distribution of representation in the House of Commons. For example, by controlling the elections in only two counties, that is, in Cornwall, which returned 44 members, and in Wiltshire, which returned 34, it was possible to count on a group in the House equal to the entire representation from Middlesex, Northumberland, Nottinghamshire, Cambridgeshire, Cumberland, Hertfordshire, Warwickshire, Bedfordshire, Cheshire, Derbyshire, Durham, Huntingtonshire, Leicestershire, Westmorland, and Rutlandshire, given in order of their respective total representation.[65] The combined population of these two counties, calculated in 1731 at about 160,000, had a voting strength, on another basis of calculation, equal to that of eleven other counties containing a total estimated population of about 1,869,000 at that period. Further, by controlling the representation from but nine counties, that is, from Cornwall, Wiltshire, Yorkshire, Devonshire, Hampshire, Dorsetshire, Sussex, Somersetshire, and Suffolk, it was

---

[64] For an account of the disputed Seaford election see *Parliamentary History* (Hansard), XIV, 101–8. It may be noted, as Sir Lewis Namier points out (*The Structure of Politics at the Accession of George III*, p. 157), that Pitt while in the House of Commons was provided with a seat between the years 1735 and 1756 by three rotten boroughs in turn: Old Sarum, Seaford, and Aldborough; and from 1756–1766, the date of his elevation to the House of Lords, he was returned to the House by the 32 members of the Bath Corporation.

[65] *Parliamentary History*, XIV, 67–84.

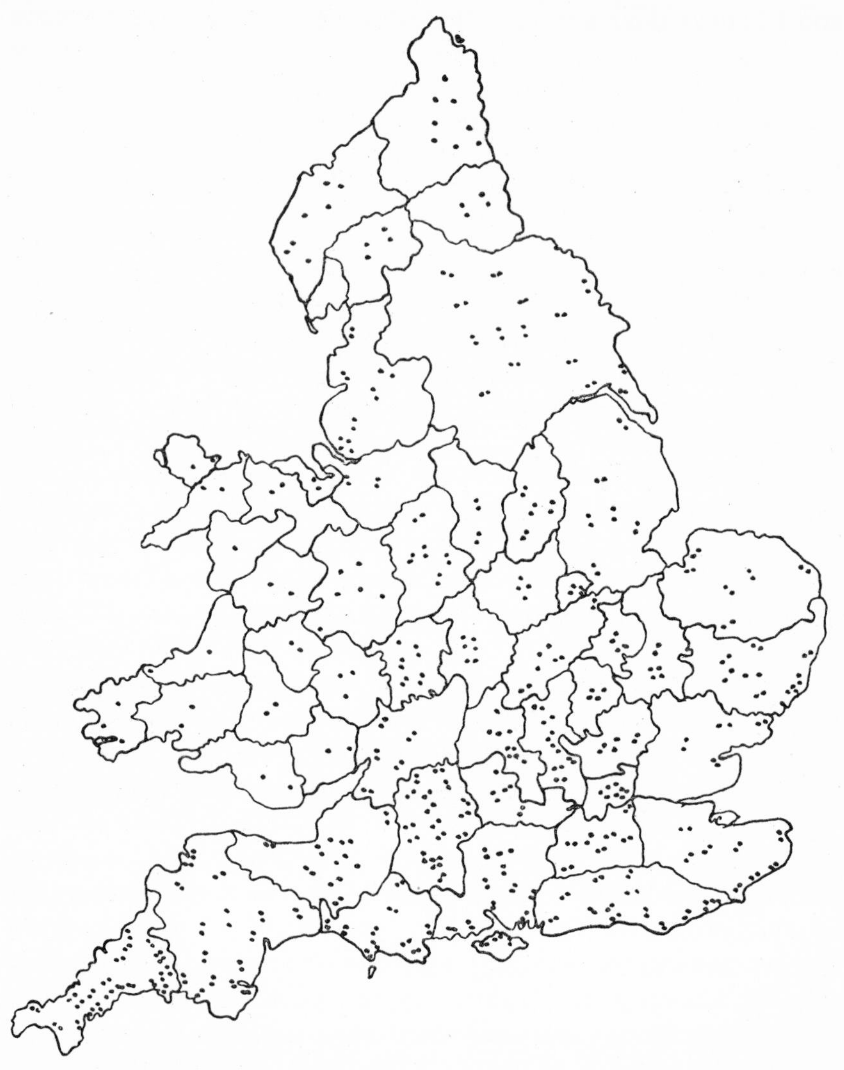

Distribution of representation in the House of Commons in the middle of the eighteenth century.

possible to command a clear majority of the votes in the House of Commons.[66]

In the light of this ministerial interference, it is not at all surprising that after the elections of 1754 Newcastle was able to write to Horatio Walpole: "The Parliament is good beyond my expectations,

---

[66] John Pinkerton: *Voyages and Travels*, II, 24–5.

and I believe there are more Whigs in it & generally well disposed Whigs, than in any Parliament since the Revolution. . . . For many places (as Bristol, Canterbury, etc.) we have chose Whigs where there did not appear to have been any hopes of doing it. The great point will be to keep our Friends together, and that they should do right when they are chose; for from the enemy we have nothing to fear."[67] In fact, reporting to the King, Newcastle stated that the majority was 213 – four more than in the last Parliament.[68]

The election of 1754 represented the height of the Newcastle political "system." It was the triumph of an oligarchy which saw that the government was conducted along the lines of its own interests and conceptions of statecraft, with places and pensions going to those who in the eyes of the leaders were complaisant and could advance some claim to these favours. In 1739, under Walpole, of 169 peers some 110 held places in his gift to the amount of £209,400; in the House of Commons, of 558 members, 224 enjoyed among them £212,956 in places. Under the Pelhams in the year 1750, at least 167 members of the House of Commons had positions of profit.[69]

It should, of course, be pointed out that those who gave their services in Parliament were not paid, and therefore many of the members undoubtedly felt that they were legitimately entitled to some salaried post at the gift of the Crown; not every man of ability in public life enjoyed wealth. Pitt, for example, never a financier, was Paymaster General of Forces.

While the practice of the Pelhams of providing places for influential supporters brought with it a variety of evils, it was perhaps not so reprehensible as might be hastily concluded. Even under Walpole the average income from places held by commoners was less than £1,000. Moreover, the evidence is not lacking that under the Pelhams efforts were made to punish those guilty of misconduct in office. Just as the gift of places, as has been previously made clear,

[67] Letter of May 14, 1754, B. M., Add. Mss. 32735, folios 268–72. It will be noted that Newcastle was inclined to limit the term "Whig" in 1754 to those well-disposed to the ministry. This is of course inaccurate. K. G. Feiling (*The Second Tory Party, 1714–1832*, London, 1938, p. 55) estimated that in 1751 "the fragment called Tories" had hardly more than sixty votes in Parliament, although in the 1747 election "they held a majority of the English shires, where representation was most real." As for the election of 1754, he writes (*ibid.*, p. 60): "If we look for the Tories, Hardwicke reckoned 124 'country gentlemen' in a total Opposition of 152."

[68] B. M., Add. Mss. 32735, folio 298.

[69] See the List of the House of Commons with employments in *Parliamentary History* (Hansard), XIV, 61–87.

was the source of great power and subject to abuse in the hands of the minister, just so was the possession of the secret service money. As Henry Pelham wrote somewhat cynically to Lord Harrington in November 1749 regarding the latter's administration of Ireland: "The condition that your publick revenue is in, must be a great consolation to you, as I, by experience know, that when you have that weapon to fight with advantageously, other squibs vanish in air." [70]

But it must not be supposed that this system could be maintained without exposing its supporters to attack. *The Remembrancer* of June 27, 1749, bitingly declared, referring to the Broad-Bottom ministry:

> "The C[abine]t is now in the custody of a *coalition* of *apostate patriots,* and hackney'd m[inister]s; that has all of W[alpole] but his abilities; and *patriots* that have *out jobbed* every *job* that they formerly made it their pride and glory to oppose; so that more is to be apprehended from *such a coalition* than even *such a sole* m[inister] as W[alpole]; for it is obvious to every man's understanding, that he who had no rival in his way, had nobody to outbid and consequently could be under no necessity to flee [flay] the subject he professed only to shear. But when two factions are forced to purchase the ground they stand on, and find *All* too narrow for the subsistence of their greedy followers, it is but natural for them to make their court at each others' expense, or rather the nation's." [71]

That some of these attacks were resented by the government is clear. The lashings of the Duke of Bedford's *Protector* forced from the mild Pelham a protest in a letter to his brother. "The infamous personal abuse upon me," he declared, "for serving under all administrations, I really despise. I am sure I never did, or ever will, serve under His Grace of Bedford's administration. But the paper is

---

[70] The C. F. Weston Underwood Papers, Hist. Mss. Com., *10th Report,* p. 304. For a correction of many misconceptions regarding the use of secret service funds by the Pelhams see Sir Lewis Namier: *The Structure of Politics at the Accession of George III,* Chap. 4 and the Appendix entitled "The Secret Service Accounts of the Duke of Newcastle."

[71] Doubtless many Englishmen felt as did a Mr. Newell, a member of the corporation of Harwich, who met with other members of the corporation on the occasion of the King's birthday to drink his health. When the Duke of Newcastle's health was going round it stopped at Newell, who damned the Pelhams, declaring they were all rogues "for that Mr. Pelham rob'd us of our liberties, and the Duke was worse than him . . ." (G. Davis to the Duke of Newcastle, Nov. 15, 1750, Newcastle Papers, B. M., Add. Mss. 32735, folios 316–17).

serious Jacobitism, a comparison in favour of the Tory ministry in Queen Anne's time against the Whig ministers at all times." [72]

Given this system of packing the Parliament and of filling the great offices of state, given this vast power lodged in the hands of the Pelhams — somewhat restricted, it is true, by the King — how was it employed? In what fashion was so great a national responsibility assumed? What were the fruits of the system?

In order to answer these questions one must understand what were the objectives of the state in that age. Upon what basis could a government be called good or bad in the middle of the eighteenth century? For surely the criteria for justifying or condemning the conduct of the affairs of state could not in all respects be the same in 1750 as it is today. According to the pamphleteers of that period, the administration of the Pelhams was an iniquitous mixture of corruption and ineptitude; while their creatures fed at the public expense, great national interests were neglected; the people groaned under taxes for the payment of which there was little or no return except in the reflected splendour of those who were guilty of this exploitation.

There is a very natural tendency for the present-day student to sympathize with the point of view just expressed and to echo it. The unfair accumulation of honours and lucrative posts and pensions in the hands of influential politicians, while men of equal capacity were ignored; the neglect of vast fields of social activity — such as all governments today undertake — with social amelioration as the objective; the most unblushing employment of public moneys for the maintenance of a group in power, which, were this to happen today, would bring down upon those guilty not only the severest public censure, but penalties for the commission of high crimes and misdemeanours — all this can justly be urged against the government of England under the Pelhams.

Nevertheless, the people of Great Britain best acquainted with the conduct of its government would not have exchanged it for any one of the governments of the Continent. If Henry Pelham was "the minister for the King in the House of Commons," he was equally "the

---

[72] For the above letter, dated July 17, 1753, see *ibid.*, 32732, folios 295–300. Pelham went on to say: "How this will serve the views of the Duke of Bedford and his great Friends, I don't see. I am sorry, however, that they have got this pen, for we shall be thus entertained every week. I intend to take an opportunity of talking to the King upon it."

minister for the House of Commons in the [royal] closet." [73] Further, under this government there was an equality among men in the presence of the laws that were made by Parliament, as will be emphasized in the chapter that follows – granted that the laws were made to serve the ends of particular interest. There was no exemption of the higher classes, as in France, from the carrying of the public burdens. In fact, the rich and powerful who controlled Parliament paid with the poor and weak and, it was asserted, in such a manner as to give them actually a higher rate. "In Your Grandfather's Time," wrote a correspondent to his friend in 1750, "the annual Income of the Estate you now have, produced in Cash to him £870, after all Deductions for Taxes and Duties; but you now pay out of the same Estate by the vast Increase of Taxes and Duties at least £450 a year: So that one half of the Income of your Estate is gone from you, and you also pay £90 per annum for interest of the £2,000 due on the Mortgage." [74] Here, in fact, lies one of the secrets of the continued popularity among the masses of Englishmen of this government by aristocracy: the willingness of the latter to bear at all times a substantial share of the nation's taxes. In other words, the men who voted for the levying of taxes played their part in the payment of them, which made them, as a rule, rather cautious and opposed to waste.

Further, in studying the operation of the Parliamentary system in the middle of the eighteenth century, one notes with interest the declarations of a writer of this period who challenged "the most malicious mal-content, during all the time in which the Clamours against Corruption have run so very high . . . to produce one single instance of any Law, which hath struck at the Root of our Constitution, which hath attempted to undermine our Liberties." [75] Perhaps Rousseau was not far wrong in his assertion that, in spite of the continued complaints of Englishmen, and one might add, most justifiable complaints, their government was the best in Europe.[76]

The government of Great Britain stood, first of all, for the maintenance of great traditions and precedents. With Chief Justice For-

[73] J. B. Owen: *op. cit.*, p. 319.

[74] *A letter from a Gentleman in Town to his Friend in the Country Recommending the Necessity of Frugality* (London, 1750), p. 6.

[75] *An Historical Essay upon the Balance of Civil Power in England* (London, 1748), Preface, xiii.

[76] *The Political Writings of Rousseau* (Vaughan), I, 328.

tescue (1394?–1476?) it could still affirm, in a world of despotisms in 1750, that *Angliae jura in omni cause Libertati dant Favorem,* that is, the laws of England do in all cases favour liberty. This government was still the child of the Revolution of 1689, the Bill of Rights, and the Act of Settlement; it acknowledged loyalty to the parliamentary principles of Whiggism, and was therefore opposed to the return of the Stuarts and the conceptions of the state for which they stood; it was also opposed to a revival of the political authority of Roman Catholicism and sought its real mandate from the Parliament and not from the King. "As our government was so happily settled at the Revolution I have endeavoured in every step of my life according to the principals [principles] of the said Revolution more and more to strengthen the Protestant succession in His Majesty's illustrious Family, his heirs and successors for ever, as the only means to make the nation peaceable, prosperous, and happy," declared Henry Pelham in addressing the people of Lewes the year before his death.[77]

In the minds of most Englishmen, the Pelhams were among those few of the elder statesmen who had never once faltered in their devotion to the Revolutionary settlement and the Hanoverian succession; in season and out, their loyalty was unquestioned and this was the source of immense influence. They further possessed a quality of loyalty to associates, a quality of dependability that gave them the friendship of some of the ablest and best men in political life of their age. Their frankness was disarming, the worst acts they committed were done, as it were, in the open, known to all men of understanding, blazoned from the housetops – and they went their way unashamed.

The explanation for this attitude lies in the fact that the Pelhams had grasped the national temper of the day. They well understood the existence of a general feeling, aroused by the renewed activities of the Stuarts to regain the throne in the 1740's that the spirit of faction was the thing most to be feared; that only by that process, only by the splitting up of the Whigs, could there ever be a return of Jacobitism to England, as the spirit of faction alone had led to its restoration in the previous century. Harmony must be maintained by quieting, by whatever means, those who had the power to dis-

---

[77] The speech of Pelham of August 29, 1753, is among the Newcastle Papers, B. M., Add. Mss. 32732, folios 570–1.

turb the tranquillity, and the Pelhams knew that most Englishmen would be complacent as to those means, even in the face of charges of corruption. The Pelhams, moreover, were the champions of the agricultural and trading interests of the nation and these were dominant during the period under examination. Henry Pelham was speaking to these interests throughout the Kingdom when, in the address referred to above, he declared:

> "As Trade and particularly the corn trade is the chief concern of the County of Sussex, it shall be my constant care to encourage and support the same, for by encouraging our farmers in their agriculture and extending our Commerce abroad we have no reason to fear of not being what we ever have been, a rich and powerful people."

Lastly, it was well known that in their private lives the Pelhams enjoyed a reputation for unimpeachable integrity. "Providing honestly for my wife and children is all I have thought of, personal advantages to myself, you must see, I have never proposed," wrote Pelham to his brother in 1752.[78] He then added: "I have always looked to your misfortunes as my own."

Newcastle had been, it should be pointed out, so absorbed in the task of maintaining the spirit of harmony among the Whigs and loyalty to the administration, that he had become oblivious of his own personal affairs. By 1752 he found himself confronted by a huge debt, with his lesser creditors beginning to murmur.[79] Beautiful "Claremont" was mortgaged, and so were other properties. He owed the Earl of Lincoln great sums, the Earl of Bradford £30,000, his friend Andrew Stone and others £20,000 and a Mr. Horne £15,000. Early in the following year, in 1753, he suffered the intense humiliation of having a writ issued against his personal effects. Among people of fashion the gossip ran that his chariot was seized and that he had been seen going to court in a chair. "In the City the execution was said to be by Kent, the Fishmonger; in other places . . . by Graham, the Apothecary." [80]

But the writ was the work of the Duke's enemies. In this crisis of his affairs he turned to his friend William Murray, the future Lord

---

[78] Date of November 9, 1752, *ibid.*, 32730, folios 226–9.

[79] See S. H. Nulle: *Thomas Pelham-Holles Duke of Newcastle* (pp. 83–4), for a brief account of Newcastle's earlier financial embarrassments.

[80] "Mr. Murray's Paper," January 16, 1753, Newcastle Papers, B. M., Add. Mss. 32731, folios 39–44.

Mansfield, for a plan whereby he might be saved from disgrace and utter ruin. Murray's scheme called for the payment of £5,000 a year out of a total income of £11,000 from his office and his various properties. It is to Newcastle's credit that he took this avenue of honour for relieving the situation rather than questionable means that might have suggested themselves to one in his high political station.[81] The principal creditors accepted a reduction of the interest and many of the debts were consolidated. Pelham, commenting on this crisis in the affairs of the Duke, wrote in a truly brotherly vein: "The next thing is your continuing in business with honour, for without that, I shall never desire you to do so." [82] The latter, it appears, fully lived up to those expectations and at the end of his political career went out of office, it is asserted, some £300,000 poorer than when he had entered. Although he was the means of procuring pensions for many importunate, as well as unfortunate people, he never would bring himself to accept one, in spite of the fact that he was offered the opportunity more than once to do so.[83]

The estimation in which Newcastle was held at this period is indicated by his elevation to the high office of Chancellor of Cambridge University, which, however titular it may have been in the case of some of those who have enjoyed this honour, was something far more than this during his incumbency. He felt in 1753 that both his word and honour were concerned to promote the subscription for completing the buildings. "There is," he declared, "no trouble that I will spare for that purpose," and he desired from the buttery books of the several colleges the names of peers, bishops, peers' sons, and other persons of distinction who had attended the university. He also interested himself in the selection of a vice chancellor who should be active and capable, and directed the architect Wright to prepare "a complete design for building a wing to answer the Senate House in front and [extending] to the Regent Walk, and also

---

[81] The Duke of Newcastle to the Duchess, May 27, 1753, *ibid.*, 32731, folios 490–1.

[82] Pelham to Newcastle, November 9, 1752, *ibid.*, 32730, folios 226–9.

[83] See James Earl Waldegrave: *Memoirs from 1754–58* (London, 1821), pp. 12–14; Sir Lewis Namier: *The Structure of Politics at the Accession of George III*, Chap. 8; A. S. Tuberville: *The House of Lords in the Eighteenth Century*, pp. 261–3. For other favourable estimates of Newcastle see the writers mentioned by S. H. Nulle: *Thomas Pelham-Holles Duke of Newcastle*, p. 170, n. For an unfavourable view of Newcastle see Sir Lewis Namier: *England in the Age of the American Revolution* (London, 1930), pp. 77–8.

of a new front to the Library and schools, to front the Regent Walk, with arcades to Caius College and King's College to join the schools with the other buildings." [84] At all times an indefatigable worker, he sought to preserve and foster in many ways those things that, from his perhaps narrow point of view, were fundamental factors in the maintenance of the civilization of which he was a part.

Here, it would seem, is the secret to the power of the Pelhams, who gave the people enjoying civic responsibility and influence in public life the sort of government they favoured – one standing for the objectives that met their approval. Moreover, under this system of government the nation, far from going to ruin, was able to realize certain great material objectives and to become by 1750 the richest in the world, the most powerful on the sea, and the most successful as a colonizer and empire-builder.

Reprehensible as were many of the features of the old Cabinet Council form of government – features that would only pass away with the growth of a finer sense of political morality, especially after 1783 with the appearance of the later cabinet system in which the ministers were fully responsible to the House of Commons and exhibited elements of solidarity under the acknowledged leadership of the Prime Minister – one should, nevertheless, point out that much of the technique of government worked out by the old Whigs still survives. This is true not only in the constitutional practice that accords to the ministry in all parliamentary matters an acknowledged leadership and in all matters of public finance decisive control, but also in the now fully acknowledged principle, which even Newcastle seems to have accepted as fundamental, that, so long as the ministry possesses the confidence of the House of Commons, it enjoys full direction of its machinery – acting for good or for ill.

One thing should be added in connection with this analysis of the structure of government. Parliament in the eighteenth century, accepting the restricted franchise and venal practices, was not unresponsive to the voice of the people. That public opinion could occasionally display force in determining elections and the attitude of members, especially of the lower house on impending issues, is not to be questioned; it certainly led to the fall of Walpole, who

[84] Newcastle to the Bishop of Chester, October 25, 1753, Newcastle Papers, B. M., Add. Mss. 32737, folios 135–6. See also D. A. Winstanley: *The University of Cambridge in the Eighteenth Century* (Cambridge, 1922, pp. 35–6, 145–6) for Newcastle's activities as Chancellor.

not only enjoyed the special confidence of the King, but for years seemed to have held the House of Commons, as it were, in the palm of his hand; [85] it also later was to drive Bute from office; likewise, it unhappily compelled in 1754 the repeal of the Jewish Naturalization Act passed the previous year. Indeed, at all times public opinion had a restraining influence on the ministry and made government much more representative than the narrow limitations of the franchise would suggest.

Before bringing this chapter to conclusion further reference should be made to the complicated question of political parties in England in the middle of the eighteenth century.[86] In the words of Sir Lewis Namier, in his Romanes Lecture delivered in 1952:

> "A ruling group will always try to place its opponents under a ban, and the national consequence of the practice of Walpole and the Pelhams was that anyone who wished to play at politics and for office, adopted the name of Whig. . . . In fact everyone at Court, in office and in the centre arena was a Whig, while the name of Tories, by a process of natural selection, was left to the residuum who did not enter politics in pursuit of office, honours, or profits, that is, to the country gentlemen and to the forerunners of urban radicals." [87]

In his *Essays, Moral, Political and Literary,* which first appeared in 1742, David Hume, however, shows the confusion that existed in the minds of men respecting the terms Whig and Tory at the time he composed his essay on "The Parties of Great Britain." He declared:

> "Some, who will not venture to assert that the *real* difference between Whig and Tory was lost at the *revolution,* seem inclined to think that the real difference is now abolished and that . . . there are at present no other parties amongst us but *court* and *country;* that is, men, who by interest or principle, are attached either to monarchy or to liberty. . . . Accordingly, the enemies of the ministry, as a reproach, call the courtiers the true Tories; and, as an honour, de-

---

[85] See W. T. Laprade: *Public Opinion and Politics in Eighteenth Century England to the fall of Walpole* (New York, 1936); see also A. J. Henderson: *London and the National Government 1721–1742* (Durham, N. C., 1945), and *An Historical Essay wherein the Example, Influence and Authority of Londoners in Publick Affairs are occasionally considered and compared* (London, 1741).

[86] The topic of political parties during the reign of George III up to the outbreak of the War for American Independence will be given consideration in a later volume of this series.

[87] Sir Lewis Namier: "Monarchy and the Party System," *Personalities and Powers* (London, 1955), p. 33.

nominate the gentlemen in the *opposition* the true Whigs. The Tories have been so long obliged to talk in the republican stile, that they seem to have made converts of themselves by their hypocrisy, and to have embraced the sentiments, as well as language of their adversaries. There are, however, very considerable remains of that party in England, with all their old prejudices; and a proof that *court* and *country* are not our only parties, is, that almost all the dissenters side with the court, and the lower clergy, at least of the Church of England, with the opposition. This may convince us, that some biass still hangs upon our constitution, some intrinsic weight, which turns it from its natural course, and causes a confusion in our parties." [88]

---

[88] David Hume: *Essays, Moral, Political, and Literary* (eds. T. H. Green and T. H. Grose, 2 vols., London, 1875), I, 142–3. Connected with the problem of identifying the Whigs in the eighteenth century is that of the attitude of the men of this period and of later generations toward the interpretation of their past. This has been dealt with by Richard Pares in his *King George III and the Politicians* (Oxford, 1953), and also by Herbert Butterfield in his *The Whig Interpretation of History* (New York, 1951), and in his most recent study, *George III and the Historians* (London, 1957).

CHAPTER V

A Government of Laws

"OUR GOVERNMENT," declared the young British scholar William Smith soon after his arrival in the New World in 1752,

> "is a Mixture of Republican and Monarchial Kinds; hence we are obliged for its preservation to maintain a watchful jealousy over the Magistrates; to remove all discretionary Powers; and to secure every One's Life and Fortune by general & inflexible Laws. No action must be deemed a Crime but what the Law has plainly determined to be such; no Crime must be imputed to a man, but from a legal Proof before his Judges; And even these Judges must be his fellow Subjects, who by their own interest are obliged to have a watchful Eye over the encroachments of the Ministry." [1]

When thinking in terms of English law we are of course confronted by the vast scope of the old common law supplemented and altered by parliamentary statute – the *lex non scripta* and the *lex scripta*. Regarding the latter we find that, among the activities of the Parliament of Great Britain – outside of the great bulk of so-called "private acts" passed in each session, and designed to benefit some individual or some community – social regulatory legislation was one of the most, if not the most, important. It still extended as in the past to the fixing of prices and wages. Without going into the long history of the latter we need for our present purposes only to affirm that faith in the efficiency and desirability of such regulation

---

[1] From an open letter of July 28, 1752, to the editor of the *New York Gazette*. Soon after this Smith began his distinguished career as the first Provost of the College of Philadelphia (Smith Mss., Hist. Soc. of Penna.). See also Sir W. S. Holdsworth's *Some Lessons from Our Legal History* (New York, 1928), especially his chapter "The Rule of Law."

was still strong. For example, in 1749 Parliament reaffirmed an act passed in 1709, in the reign of Queen Anne, which in itself repealed the old *Assisa Panis et Cervisiae* (Assize of Bread and Ale), passed in 1266, in the reign of Henry III.[2] By the reaffirmed statute [3] the court of the Lord Mayor in London and the magistrates in other cities and towns were responsible for setting the assize and weight of all sorts of bread, having respect to the price of grain. In 1744 an act passed nearly a century earlier, in the reign of Charles II, fixing the retail price of coal was re-enacted with some changes which gave the justices of the quorum in any county the power to determine the price of this commodity; [4] even the rates for the carriage of goods from place to place within the county were regulated by the justices of the peace,[5] who were also given great powers in 1747 to adjudicate questions of wages and services between master and servant [6] along the line of legislation passed in the reigns of Elizabeth I and James I.[7]

However, government regulations did not prevent serious dissatisfaction with prices, especially food prices, which, incidentally, were determined by the squirearchy. In 1753 in the western part of England near Wells, hundreds of colliers visited market towns and took things into their own hands, declaring by proclamation what should be the prices of corn, meat, butter, and vegetables, and compelling the owners to sell at these rates.[8]

We now turn from mere regulatory to repressive legislation. It cannot be denied that statutory as well as the old common law penalties were very severe, and that in the application of the law there was frequently displayed a callousness in the face of human

---

[2] 51 Henry III, Stat. 6; 8 Anne, c. 18.

[3] 22 Geo. II, c. 46, Par. 21. By this, all bread was divided into five categories according to the price of the loaf, ranging from the penny loaf to the eighteenpenny loaf, and comprising white, wheaten, and household bread. For example, if the magistrates allowed the baker to charge upon the basis of the cost of wheat to him at two shillings a bushel, the household penny loaf would have three fourths of this weight and the white loaves one half; in a year of great scarcity of wheat, he would be allowed to charge upon the basis of wheat valued at the rate of 15 shillings per bushel, and the household penny loaf would contain but 6 ounces and 3 drams.

[4] 16 and 17 Chas. II, c. 2, and 17 Geo. II, c. 35.

[5] 21 Geo. II, c. 28, Par. 3.

[6] 20 Geo. II, c. 19.

[7] 5 Eliz., c. 4 and 1 Jas. 1, c. 6.

[8] R. Slade to Charles Tredway, May 12, 1753, Newcastle Papers, B. M., Add. Mss. 32731, folio 446.

suffering that leaves a most unhappy impression on the present-day investigator of the annals of the period.[9] The punishment for high treason, petty treason, misprision of treason, and other felonies was of the utmost severity. For the first, the offender was drawn and hung, if a male, or was burnt after strangulation, if a female, except in the case of important persons, for whom beheading was the penalty.[10]

Felonious offences other than treason, under the common law, were such crimes as homicide, rape, larceny, robbery, and burglary. The penalty attached to them was not only forfeiture of property, but death, except for the felonies of mayhem and petty larceny. The scope of felonious offences, moreover, had been enormously extended as the result of formal enactment by Parliament, mostly during the eighteenth century. Up to 1786, 256 offences had been from time to time expressly declared felonies by act of Parliament, and during the period under consideration there were on the statute books at least 212, of which 142 were without benefit of clergy.[11] For the less serious felonious acts, transportation was the usual punishment for the first offence with death for a repetition or for returning from transportation before the expiration of the sentence.

In making a survey of legislation during the reign of George II

---

[9] See Leon Radzinowicz: *A History of Criminal Law and its Administration from 1750* (London, 1948, I, Appendix I, pp. 611–59), for a careful analysis of statutes in force in the eighteenth century calling for the death penalty. There were writers who condemned the severity of the laws, such as William Eden (Lord Auckland), as set forth in his *Principles of Penal Law*, published in 1771; and William Godwin, in his *An Enquiry concerning Political Justice*, published in 1793. On the other hand, the Rev. Martin Madan, in his *Thoughts on Executive Justice, with Respect to our Criminal Laws . . .* , written in 1785, set forth the principle that the prevention of crime, not its punishment, was "the great end of all legal severity. . . . The terror of the example is the only thing proposed, and one man is sacrificed to the preservation of thousands." To the contrary the Italian Cesare Beccaria, who in 764 published his *Dei Delitti e delle Pene* (translated in 1880 under the title *Crimes and Punishments*), laid down the humanitarian principle that punishment should be based solely on the degree of injury that an act had inflicted on society and that mere severity of the penalty would not accomplish this object. He therefore was opposed to capital punishment, since he felt it to be a violation of fundamental law and therefore beyond the scope of state action. See Radzinowicz: *op. cit.*, I, 140–1, 277–86.

[10] See William Blackstone: *Commentaries on the Laws of England* (London, 1770), IV, 75, 98, 120.

[11] See in the *Statutes at Large* (Eyre, Strahan, and Woodfall, 10 vols., London, 1786) the Index under "Felonies." Sir Thomas F. Buxton in 1819 put the number at 223 capital offences and Sir James Mackintosh in 1823 put the number at 200. See Radzinowicz: *op. cit.*, I, 4, for comment on these writers.

one is impressed on every hand with the fact that the government was in the hands of the propertied interests of Great Britain and that the value placed on the life of the common man was not very great. It will be of value to examine some of these eighteenth-century statutes.[12]

To entice an artisan out of the Kingdom and to export utensils or machinery used in the woollen or silk manufactures of Great Britain or Ireland made one liable, by a law of 1750, to a fine of £500 and a year's imprisonment.[13] In 1742 it was provided by statute that those who stole cloth at night should forfeit treble the value by distress and sale, for the first offence; but in 1745 it was provided that theft of the same should subject the offenders to capital punishment as felons, except that the judges might order the offender transported for 14 years.[14] To increase the dimensions of woollen cloth by stretching or straining made the maker liable to a month in jail at hard labour, and as a further check on tendencies to do this the name of the maker had to be placed on the cloth, which was officially measured.[15] The malterers and coal operators, to protect their interests from dissatisfied labourers, secured a law in 1737 which provided a death penalty for those guilty either of cutting hop vines or setting fire to any coal mine, pit, or coal.[16] In 1741 stealing and destroying sheep was made a capital felony without benefit of clergy, and the following year this was extended to cattle-stealing.[17] An act passed in 1744 revived a law of the reign of Charles II[18] against theft and rapine on the northern border of England, a law

---

12 It may be pointed out that the accused in the middle of the eighteenth century enjoyed a protection denied those of an earlier period through an enactment of the year 1731 providing that all proceedings in the courts of justice in England or Wales or in the exchequer in Scotland should be in English "in words at length and in a common legible hand" under penalty (4 Geo. II, c. 26; 6 Geo. II, c. 6; 6 Geo. II, c. 14). Exceptions were made for proceedings of courts of admiralty beyond the sea, and two years later the exchequer court of Scotland was excepted.

13 23 Geo. II, c. 13.

14 15 Geo. II, c. 27, and 18 Geo. II, c. 27.

15 However, in 1736 the prohibition of the use of cotton cloth, provided for by a law passed in the seventh year of the reign of George I (7 Geo. I, stat. 1, c. 7, par. 10), which sought to encourage the woollen and silk manufactures by making illegal the use whatsoever of printed, painted, stained, or dyed calicoes produced in foreign parts, was so clarified as to free from the dangers of prosecution merchants who carried for sale printed linen and cotton cloth produced at home. See 9 Geo. II, c. 4.

16 10 Geo. II, c. 32; made perpetual by 31 Geo. II, c. 42.

17 14 Geo. II, c. 6, and 15 Geo. II, c. 34.

18 13 and 14 Chas. II, c. 22, 9 Geo. I, c. 22, and 6 Geo. II, c. 37.

of the reign of George I against evil disposed persons doing violence in disguise,[19] and a law passed earlier in the reign of George II against the breaking down of river banks.[20] Not only were these acts made capital offences, but in 1736 it was provided that anyone who should enlist in the service of a foreign power or should procure the enlistment of any British subject should suffer death without benefit of clergy.[21] Finally, in 1746, provisional bills of attainder were passed against some 47 individuals in connection with the Scottish rebellion.[22]

The above recital, brief and inadequate as it is, indicates pretty clearly the temper of the age. It must be pointed out, however, that in one important respect the law was altered in the direction of leniency. The act against witchcraft passed in the first year of James I was repealed in 1736, as was that passed in Scotland in the ninth year of the reign of his mother; both of these laws had carried the death penalty. In 1750 the only punishment for the supposed practice of witchcraft was that those who deluded others as to their powers should be imprisoned for one year, and once each quarter should stand in the pillory in the market place of some market town for one hour.[23] Again, a law passed in 1722, "An Act for the more effectual punishing wicked and evil disposed Persons going around in Disguise and doing Injuries and Violences,"[24] provided a death penalty for the wilful destruction of trees and shrubs. This was modified in 1766 to provide a penalty of transportation for seven years.[25] Even this punishment apparently seemed too severe, for in the same year the penalty for the first offence was changed to a fine of £20; for the second, one of £30, and for the third, transportation for seven years.[26] However, the time had not arrived for drastic modification of the criminal code; that was to come only in the nineteenth century.

In the matter of the enforcement of the law, we are confronted at this period by the venerable common law courts of oyer and terminer and of general gaol-delivery, with the Court of King's

---

[19] 12 Geo. I, c. 30, extending the life of 9 Geo. I, c. 22.
[20] 6 Geo. II, c. 37. The act of 1744 is 17 Geo. II, c. 40.
[21] 9 Geo. II, c. 30.
[22] 19 Geo. II, c. 26.
[23] 1 James I, c. 12 was repealed by 9 Geo. II, c. 5.
[24] 9 Geo. I, c. 22.
[25] 6 Geo. III, c. 36.
[26] 6 Geo. III, c. 48.

Bench at Westminster possessing a general appellate jurisdiction over all cases involving crimes and misdemeanours.[27] The procedure in these courts was characterized by the presence of a jury of the peers of the accused, called by Blackstone "the grand bulwark of . . . liberties." [28] There is evidence that these juries frequently acted on the side of mercy in bringing in their verdicts, but at other times they were rigid in supporting the law even when it involved capital punishment.[29] The proof of this comes readily to hand.

At the Hertfordshire assizes in the spring of 1751 John Jones was sentenced to death for returning to England before the expiration of his transportation term; according to a statement appearing in *Aris's Birmingham Gazette* the same year, more people received sentences of death at these assizes than had been known in the county within the memory of the oldest man there: one for murder, two for highway robbery, one for arson, two for horse-stealing, one for sheep-stealing, and one for stealing 40 shillings in a dwelling house. In this connection it may be pointed out that the judge reprieved the three last mentioned convicted felons.[30]

Flogging was a penalty very commonly employed, either in addition to some more severe penalty, or alone, and this was especially true in the army and navy. For example, in 1756 a court-martial sentenced Robert Jescock to suffer 1,000 lashes for desertion. In this instance the reviewing officer recommended lightening of the penalty.[31] At the Westminster sessions of the Middlesex County Court

---

27 In the case of peers accused of treason, felony, or misprision of either, there was instituted the court of the Lord High Steward to which, under terms of a statute passed in the reign of William III (7 William III, c. 3), all peers entitled to vote in Parliament were summoned. When that body was in session the trial was by King in Parliament. For the distinction between these two methods of trial see Blackstone's *Commentaries*, IV, 258–62.

28 *Ibid.*, IV, 342.

29 In the above connection Radzinowicz (*op. cit.*, I, 12) cites the case of William Yorke, but ten years of age, who in 1748 was convicted of murder in the Bury assizes. Although Chief Justice Willes respited the execution in order to secure the opinion of the other judges, it was finally unanimously decided that in order to deter other children from committing like offences the boy should be put to death. The sentence was carried out. It may be added that young Yorke's crime was premeditated. He took a five-year-old girl from bed out to a dung heap, stabbed her to death, and then buried her body.

30 *Aris's Birmingham Gazette*, March 18, 1751.

31 While approving the proceedings of the court and confirming the sentence, this officer went on to say: "but tho I am desirous of Punishing Desertion with very great severity, yet I think one Thousand lashes if properly inflicted must render a man unfit

in 1748 it was ordered by the judges that Mary Meredith be whipped at the cart's tail along Wardour until her body be bloody; at the sessions held at Hicks Hall, Katherine Downer was sentenced to be whipped from Holborn to St. Giles pond along Drury Lane, and Mary Gear from one end of Compton Street to the other. These examples from the court records have been selected at random.[32]

Transportation was one of the commonly employed penalties; quite frequently the judge substituted this for capital punishment.[33] Groups of people were frequently brought into court and ordered to be transported to the plantations.[34] A writer in 1751 stated that the Warwick assizes just closed had proved a "maiden one," for not one person was capitally convicted. He went on to state, however, that Mary Nicholls was ordered transported for seven years for stealing two silver spoons and some wearing apparel, Thomas Warringham for stealing cheese, and Thomas Drake was sentenced to be transported for 14 years for an unstated offence.[35]

What was true of England was also true of Scotland. The undesirables escaping capital penalties were herded off to the plantations. The court at Dumfries in October 1749 banished William Hamilton to the plantations for seven years for highway robbery,[36] and at Jedburgh in the same month John Young and his wife Margaret, accused of theft and felony, petitioned for banishment to America, which was granted;[37] then at Edinburgh in November one John Smith, sentenced to death for counterfeiting shillings, was allowed to accept transportation in place of this fate.[38]

---

for future service, so that if you intend to continue Jescock in the regiment, I leave it to you to mitigate his punishment as you shall judge best for the service" (General Bland to Colonel Armstrong, Aug. 3, 1756. Letter Book of General Bland, National Library, Edinburgh).

[32] See P.R.O., Middlesex County Records, Calendar of Session Books, and also Orders of the Court, January 1747–48 to December 1751, 179. Z. 1049, p. 78; 1050, p. 48; 1051, pp. 47 and 48; 1052, p. 45.

[33] Sometimes a sense of pity on the part of neighbours led to efforts to have the harsh sentences modified. The case of Ann Grant, sentenced in the Oxford assizes in 1753 to transportation for stealing a shift and an old cloak, excited the sympathy of a number of people of substance because this was her first offence. They asked the Duke of Marlborough to use his influence to secure a pardon for her; this he did. See Marlborough to Newcastle, September 3, 1753, Newcastle Papers, B. M., Add. Mss. 32732, folio 601.

[34] See P.R.O., Middlesex Court Records, Calendar of Session Books, 179 Z; see also *Aris's Birmingham Gazette*, March 4, 1751.

[35] *Ibid.*, April 1, 1751.

[36] Glasgow *Courant*, November 6, 1749.

[37] *Ibid.*

[38] *Ibid.*, November 30, 1749.

An account of the work of the circuit court at Inverness in the Highlands, as presented in the Glasgow *Courant* of October 30, 1749, will show in what summary fashion the business of dealing out justice could be carried on in Great Britain in the eighteenth century. The court met on October 14, which was a Saturday, and that morning Marjory M'Eandory was indicted for child-murder and was thereupon convicted and sentenced to be hanged on the first day of December; in the afternoon Robert Pardil was tried and found guilty of unmercifully beating a gentleman named Fraser and was ordered to be publicly whipped at the hands of the common hangmen and then to be transported for life; on Monday morning the Donald Frasers, elder and younger, were tried not only as gipsies, but the younger also for murder, of which he was convicted and ordered to be hanged December 18, while the elder Fraser for petty theft was banished; on Monday afternoon Thomas Findlater was condemned to be hanged December 29 for the rape of a child; on Tuesday one McDonald was also sentenced to be hanged on that date, for murder; the same day Elizabeth MacKenzie was indicted as accessory to the murder of her husband, but "there appearing no sufficient evidence and she petitioning for Banishment, the Lords granted it"; on Wednesday a gentleman and ten of his tenants were brought before the bar for alleged riot, were "assoiled" and dismissed, but Jean McPherson for alleged murder of her own child was on that day banished.

Such was the criminal law and such was its enforcement. Justice was not to be trifled with in Great Britain.

At the period under consideration it still held true that those brought before the court who refused to plead and who stood mute under accusation of serious crime might be put to death under the torture of great weight.[39] By accepting this fate and thus escaping trial they at least preserved their property for their dependents.

---

[39] The law declared that "notorious felons" (*les felouns escriez*) standing mute were by law to be put "to strong and hard imprisonment" (*mys en la prisone forte & dure*) (3 Ed. I, c. 12). This was changed in 1772 so as to provide that any person arraigned for felony or piracy standing mute should be convicted in the same manner as by verdict or confession (12 Geo. III, c. 20). For examples of the employment of *peine forte et dure* in the eighteenth century, see W. C. Sydney: *England and the English in the Eighteenth Century*, II, 301–2. It should be added that this was not employed in the less serious cases of felony. The accused was also given the benefit of clergy if the offence permitted it, even were he to stand mute. See Blackstone's *Commentaries*, IV, 320.

However, should the accused refuse to plead in cases of high treason, judgment of death was automatically given and the estate confiscated. Further, to strike another in the King's court so as to draw blood, entailed the loss of the right hand, and to strike another in Westminster Hall while the courts of justice were sitting involved in addition to this, imprisonment for life and forfeiture of one's goods and loss of estate for life.

Summary as was the criminal law in England, the civil law and equitable proceedings were highly involved.[40] Rousseau justly pointed out, in referring to this situation, that the fear of arbitrary judgments had led the people to submit themselves to a thousand inequitable and extravagant judgments; he also declared that the mad idea of trying to anticipate all contingencies had led them to make of their law an immense labyrinth in which both memory and reason were equally lost.[41] The indescribable complexities of English law in the year 1750 may indeed be contrasted most unfavourably with the situation within the dominions of Frederick II of Prussia, where through the autocratic power of that sovereign sweeping reforms had just been carried out in the promulgation of the "Code Frederick" and the institution of the "Systematic Plan of the Body of Laws," as well as by the summary settlement of all outstanding lawsuits.

Nevertheless, as was previously stated, Rousseau found in England the best government in Europe; his judgment was shared by both Voltaire and Montesquieu. A fair judgment of the character and spirit of the government is probably that of the well-informed but nameless Frenchman who in 1742 set forth his *"Observations sur le Royaume d'Angleterre."* [42] Naturally, he views it in the light of the system in operation in France. What are the things that to him stand out as worthy of notice? "By the English Constitution," he wrote,

---

[40] For English law in the eighteenth century see Volumes X–XII of Sir William S. Holdsworth's *A History of English Law* (12 vols., London, 1903–1938); see also Edward Jenks: *A Short History of English Law* (5th ed., London, 1939), and T. F. T. Plucknett: *A Concise History of the Common Law* (3rd ed., London, 1940).

[41] J. J. Rousseau: *"Gouvernement de Pologne,"* in *The Political Writings of Rousseau* (Vaughan), II, 480; see also Blackstone's *Commentaries*, I, 10.

[42] The text is among the Loudoun Papers, Huntington Library. This statement should be compared with that by the Portuguese traveller Gonzales who in the 1730's also expressed great admiration for the laws of England (John Pinkerton: *Voyages and Travels*, II, 127).

> "the English are a free people because no law can be made or abrogated without the consent of their representatives in Parliament. An Englishman cannot be imprisoned without a manifest breach of the law of the country, and judges cannot refuse him the habeas corpus. . . . A creditor cannot have at the same time both the person and goods of his Debtor; he may choose which it shall be. The punishment for those offences that are not capital are never arbitrary, but proportioned to the offence according to a rule made for all cases. . . . Civil Causes are conducted much after the same manner as in the jurisdiction in France and are determined by their judges, who are always esteemed for their knowledge of the Rights, Laws, and Customs of the Country. But in criminal cases where the crime is determined by the fact, criminals cannot be tried but by twelve jurymen who are taken by lot from among the Burghers of the place. The judge only informs them of the circumstances of the crime and after explaining the different points of the law regarding the case he leaves them to decide. . . . In England they never make use of the torture in order to extort from a prisoner a confession of his crime. A man cannot be condemned but upon a clear and unexceptionable Deposition upon oath. There is, however, one case and but one where torture is applied . . ."

and thereupon he described the process of *peine forte et dure,* referred to above in connection with the refusal of the accused to plead.

Other foreigners thought highly of the administration of justice in England in the eighteenth century. P. T. Grosley, for example, was impressed by the practice of setting people at liberty on bail as well as by other procedures favourable to the accused in criminal cases; [43] C. de Saussure praised the absence of torture in criminal trials; [44] and François de la Rochefoucauld asserted that in no other country were the rights of the accused so strongly upheld and respected.[45]

While in general there was equality before the law, certain exceptions may be noted here and there. The first has to do with benefit of clergy. All clerks in orders were, without branding or transportation, admitted to their privilege and at most confined for one

---

[43] *A Tour of London; or, New Observations on England* (London, 1772), II, 140.

[44] *A Foreign View of England in the Reigns of George I and George II* (trans. Mme. van Muyden, London, 1902), p. 119.

[45] *A Frenchman in England, 1784* (ed. J. Marchand, London, 1933), p. 117. For the views of the above travellers and others, see Leon Radzinowicz: *op. cit.*, I, 715–16.

year for offences that allowed this relaxation; lords of Parliament and peers of the realm were also entitled to this relaxation, but only for their first offence of this nature. Further, all commoners were liable only to be burnt on the left thumb and to suffer discretionary imprisonment for their first offence within benefit, except in the case of larceny, for which they might be transported.[46] The act against excessive and deceitful gaming, passed in 1739, carried an exception to games in any palace where the King resided; [47] the law of 1744 against rogues and vagabonds expressly excepted from all the penalties therein detailed the heirs and assigns of John Dutton of Dutton, late of the County of Chester, Esquire, deceased; [48] while the statute of 1746 punishing cursing and swearing divided people into groups with an appropriate fine for each.[49]

Considering applied government in Great Britain, up to this point attention has been mainly directed to the composition and activities of the ministry and Parliament. Granted these central organs of policy-framing, administration, and lawmaking, which were the actual sources of political power and which, taken together with the vestiges of the royal prerogative, constituted the immediate source of legal authority — with ultimate legal sovereignty since 1689 vested in the King's High Court of Parliament — [50] by what process were the mandates of the national will brought home to the people? In other words, what was the local machinery of enforcement for this will?

There were, of course, the customs, excise, and stamp officials, and the judges of assize; there were the sheriffs and lord lieutenants, each of whom had a direct contact with the central government, besides the officials of the boroughs and cities and those of the parishes, all of whom were pledged to uphold the laws of the realm and were expected to qualify for office by conforming publicly to

---

[46] 5 Anne, c. 6, Par. 5; see also Blackstone's *Commentaries*, IV, 358–67.

[47] 12 Geo. II, c. 28, Par. 10.

[48] 17 Geo. II, c. 5, Par. 29.

[49] For the everyday labourer, the common soldier, and the sailor, the penalty for swearing was one shilling; for every other person under the degree of gentleman, two shillings; and for everyone of that degree or above, five shillings. Those who defaulted payment were to spend ten days in a house of correction, with the exception of the soldier or sailor, who were instead to be committed to the stocks for a maximum period of two hours. See 19 Geo. II, c. 21, Par. 1.

[50] That is, "in the composite body of King, lords, and commons." See W. S. Holdsworth: *Some Lessons from our Legal History*, pp. 127–39, for a criticism of Blackstone's views of sovereignty.

the rites of the Church established by law through the taking of the holy sacrament after the prescribed manner.[51] The most important of these instrumentalities in the broad field of national administration operating locally were undoubtedly the justices of the quorum, whose powers, as was indicated earlier in this chapter, were steadily enlarged and whose importance, great as it previously had been, was considerably enhanced under George II.[52]

The justices of the quorum, for instance, were in 1739 given the power to make general assessments on the shire, which took the place of the several rates formerly provided for by distinct acts of Parliament.[53] In 1741 their powers were enlarged for carrying out the statutes relating to the repair and rebuilding of bridges and houses of correction and the proper disposition of rogues and vagabonds.[54] As has already been mentioned, three of these justices in any county were authorized in 1744 to fix the price of coal;[55] in 1747 they were empowered to adjudicate questions of wages and services between master and servant;[56] and in 1748 they were permitted to fix rates for the carriage of goods from place to place.[57] These powers were over and beyond those with which they had previously been clothed. So important, indeed, was the position they occupied at this period in public life, not only at the quarter sessions but at other times, that in 1745 an act was passed which provided that no person could be a justice of the peace unless possessed of £100 annual income, or entitled to a reversion valued at £300 a year.[58] Justly has England of the seventeenth and eighteenth centuries been called a squirearchy!

---

[51] 25 Chas. II, c. 2; 16 Geo. II, c. 30.

[52] For the justice of the peace see Sir Thomas Deveil: *Observations on the Practice of a Justice of the Peace . . .* (London, 1747); Richard Burn: *The Justice of the Peace and Parish Officer . . .* (2 vols., London, 1755); E. G. Dowdell: *A Hundred Years of Quarter Sessions . . . from 1660 to 1760* (London 1932).

[53] 12 Geo. II, c. 29 and 13 Geo. II, c. 18, which alter a long line of acts from 22 Henry VIII, c. 5, to 12 Anne, stat. 2, c. 23.

[54] 14 Geo. II, c. 33.

[55] 17 Geo. II, c. 35.

[56] 20 Geo. II, c. 19.

[57] 21 Geo. II, c. 28.

[58] 18 Geo. II, c. 20. W. C. Sydney, in his *England and the English in the Eighteenth Century* (II, 274), calls the county justices of this period "a boorish set of brutes, both ignorant and tyrannical." While many would merit this stricture, it is to be doubted that the majority of the justices of the peace should properly be placed in this category, admitting the limitations of their knowledge and the fact that they were in a sense born to power in their localities.

In conclusion, it may be suggested that the spirit behind the expression of the national will in the middle of the eighteenth century is probably fairly caught by the Rev. Samuel Squire. In his unsigned *An Historical Essay upon the Balance of Civil Power in England,* which appeared in 1748, he asked himself, with the contemporary situation on the Continent clearly in mind:

> "Am I, then, in any Danger of losing my Life or my Limbs, or my Liberty, by the mere Caprice of a wanton or Malicious Courtier, or the imperious Commands of a head-strong Tyrant? Is my Property safe from all-devouring Ordonnances of an absolute Monarque? Are there any other Taxes layed upon me, than such as the united Wisdom of the Nation in a free Parliament has thought expedient to propose? . . . Are not the true interests of Trade duly studied, encouraged and protected? Are not the laws of my country impartially executed, or [are they] dispenced with, by the mere Will or Prerogative of the Prince? or are they not made the invariable Rule of the King's Conduct as well as of Mine? Am I not permitted, without the least Restraint laid upon my Conscience, to serve Heaven in my own Way? . . . You may, therefore, boldly defy the best-read Historian to assign a single Reign in all our Annals when these Great Ends of Government were more religiously intended or more generally obtained than under his present Majesty's auspicious, mild, and steady Administration: nay, You may boldly challenge the most discontented and querulous of all his Subjects to point out that Nation under Heaven where he will venture to assert, that he could live so happily, in all respects, as he does in England."

To Blackstone, Montesquieu's observation was correct when the latter affirmed that England was "a land, perhaps the only one in the universe, in which political or civil liberty is the very end and scope of the constitution."[59] Granting this to be true, one at the same time is made painfully aware that the England of the eighteenth century was not the humane England or the socially minded England of today.

---

[59] *Commentaries,* I, 6; *Spirit of the Laws,* II, c. 5.

CHAPTER VI

The Mountainous Principality

TO THE WEST of England proper, bounded on the south, west, and north by the Bristol and St. George's channels and the Irish Sea, protrudes the land massif of Wales, a country of bold mountains, rushing streams, and inviting vales. Filled as it is with an unusual number of monuments and other remains – many of them most impressive – of prehistoric, Roman, Norman, and other civilizations, there broods over much of it an air of mystery. The traveller moving from the well-settled coastal plains up into the lonely mountain fastnesses is struck by the bleakness as well as the wild beauty of the surroundings. Even today only here and there in the interior do people congregate in villages. In fact, in the more inaccessible parts it is only the nimble-footed mountain sheep that seem to be able to sustain themselves and increase in numbers while grazing upon the precipitous slopes.

Who were the first inhabitants of Wales and whence came they? The answer is still a mystery. It seems to be generally agreed that they were of the same race as the ancient Iberians, whose descendants are still to be found living in isolation in the Pyrenees.[1] At least it is certain that a people of small stature and dark complexion, "the little people of the mountains," whose furtive, elusive movements are embodied in Welsh legend, were entrenched in the all but inaccessible areas of the country long after the coastal plains and the vales had welcomed waves of newcomers, large, blond people whose Celtic language is still spoken today and whose literature

---

[1] See Sir J. E. Lloyd: A *History of Wales . . . to the Edwardian Conquest* (London, 1912), I, 15.

A portion of an eighteenth-century map of England and Wales.

(New York Public Library, Division of Ma

embodies its lyric quality.[2] Following upon the heels of these Brythonic Celts came the Romans, who built military roads and encampments.[3] With their departure early in the fifth century there appeared on the scene Saxon, Danish, and Irish sea-raiders, whose efforts at conquest were sporadic and limited in effect to the more accessible parts. This was also true of the attempts of the expanding Kingdom of Mercia in the eighth century under King Offa, who finally contented himself with the building of the famous dike between the mouth of the Wye and the mouth of the Dee, to the west of which the Welsh were left undisturbed by any serious outside threats until the days of the Normans.

After overrunning England in the eleventh century, the Normans turned their attention to Wales. Seizing certain strategic elevations near the coasts and also along the eastern border that commanded the approaches to the interior, they built their great castles.[4] These strongholds had the effect of isolating the Welsh of the mountainous regions from those of the plains and vales, where the natives freely intermingled with Normans and Flemings as well as with Anglo-Saxons. Despite this differentiation, for a period of years in the thirteenth century the country was given a considerable degree of unity under the famous leader and overlord known as Llewelyn the Great.[5] But with his death and as the result of successful wars waged by Edward I, King of England, against the overlords of the country, together with his confiscation of lands and his tactful bestowal of the title of Prince of Wales on his eldest son, a basis was laid in that century for the ultimate political integration of Wales and England in the fifteenth century.[6]

In that century we come to an event of great importance in the history not only of England, but of Wales as well. In 1485 Henry Tudor – grandson of the Welshman Owen Tudor and descendant of John of Gaunt – leading Welsh forces under the Welsh red dragon

---

[2] *Ibid.*, I, 17–19.

[3] *Ibid.*, I, 47–81; see also V. E. Nash-Williams: *The Roman Frontier in Wales* (Cardiff, 1954), and F. Haverfield: *Military Aspects of Roman Wales* (London, 1910).

[4] J. E. Lloyd: *op. cit.*, II, 357–461.

[5] *Ibid.*, II 462–764.

[6] Sir Frederick Rees in his *Studies in Welsh History* (Cardiff, 1947, p. 29) makes the point that the Principality over which the son of Edward I became Prince was limited to the five shires then in existence, but that in the rest of what was then known as Wales, including the Marches, the King's writ did not run; see also W. H. Waters: *The Edwardian Settlement of North Wales . . .* (Cardiff, 1935).

banner, overwhelmed those under Richard III, King of England, at Bosworth. Richard was killed in the battle, and Henry was thereupon proclaimed king as Henry VII, to the great pride and satisfaction of the people of Wales. Although he established the powerful Council of the Marches of Wales for the purpose of suppressing the lawlessness and turbulence of the Lords of the Marches, the Principality remained under him a distinct political entity.[7] However, under his son, Henry VIII, the great alteration in its political status took place.

In 1536, by the Act of Union (27 Henry VIII, c. 26), Wales became an integral part of the Kingdom of England and Wales, and Welshmen acquired all the rights of Englishmen. The shire system was soon afterwards rounded out by act of Parliament in 1542 (34 and 35 Henry VIII, c. 26), so as to include the lands of the Lords of the Marches. In each of the shires, thereafter twelve in number,[8] a sheriff was appointed to represent the power of the Crown. Each shire was also divided into hundreds, within which a justice of the peace was established as well as two constables; for each shire courts of quarter sessions, presided over by the justices of the quorum, were also created; further, the shires were combined in judicial districts, four in number, within which were held the powerful King's Great Sessions Courts which were called upon to enforce English law and to follow English administrative practices. The use of the English language by all officeholders and in all official proceedings was likewise prescribed. As a further evidence of the union of the two nations the Welsh were accorded seats in the House of Commons.[9] They were already represented in the House of Lords by British peers with landed possessions in Wales.

Hand in hand with these constitutional and political changes there also came important alterations in the system of Welsh land tenure. The custom of gavelkind, in terms of which intestate estates had for centuries been divided equally among the heirs of the deceased, was abolished in favour of primogeniture. Moreover, while

---

[7] Henry VII held in his own hands some fifty Marches lordships and therefore ruled them directly, as he did the seven shires created by Edward I. See Sir Frederick Rees: *op. cit.*, pp. 31–2.

[8] In reality there were thirteen shires after 1542, but Monmouth was embodied in the English judicial system.

[9] See Sir Frederick Rees: *op. cit.*, pp. 34–42.

the Lords of the Marches lost their governmental authority within their demesnes, now embodied in the new shires, they, nevertheless, retained their land holdings. And with the suppression of the lesser monasteries in 1536 and the greater monasteries in 1539 throughout Wales as well as England, accompanied by the confiscation of these properties, there took place an increase in the number of great private landowners, "the new gentry," in both areas. Therefore by the middle of the eighteenth century most of the land of Wales that was not Crown land seems to have been embodied in fairly large, if not very large estates, the possessors of which were either Englishmen – frequently if not generally absentees – or Welsh who were fairly thoroughly Anglicized. These proprietors in turn leased their lands on a year to year basis.

Despite the efforts over the centuries to Anglicize the Welsh nation as a whole, they were still holding tenaciously to their language and social customs in the middle of the eighteenth century, especially those dwelling in the more mountainous regions.[10] This, to a degree, is still true today. They not only continued to speak Welsh, but adhered to the dress of their ancestors.

The following is a description of the costumes generally worn by the Welsh in the eighteenth century: "The national costume, which remained the same for centuries, consisted of coat, breeches and waistcoat of skyblue homespun with worsted stockings to match. The women made an even livelier picture in the linsey-wolsey skirts they wove themselves in pretty blue and red checks or stripes on a white ground. Under a high black hat a snowy kerchief covered the

---

10 In eastern Radnorshire English was the language of Presteign and Knighton, both east of Offa's Dyke, but to the west of them Welsh was the common language. The traveller and archaeologist Henry P. Wyndham noted in his *A Tour through Monmouthshire and Wales in . . . 1774 and in . . . 1777* (2nd edn. Salisbury, 1781, p. 18) that upon arriving at Caerphilly in Glamorganshire he had moved into a strange land: "It is observable that tho' Caerphyli is at the distance only of two miles from Monmouthshire, and separated from it by a simple brook, yet the buildings, manners, and dress of the inhabitants are as strictly Welsh as those of Merionethshire. The English language is as little understood here, as among the mountains of Carnarvon. . . ." At the same time he ventured to make the prediction, by no means fulfilled, that "possibly, within a century a traveller may meet with as much difficulty, in his researches after the remains of the Welsh language along the coasts and Marches of Wales, as Mr. Barrington did in his tour through Cornwall in pursuit of the Cornish [language], where he found but one old woman, near 90 years of age, who could speak it, and but two other old women who could understand her" (*ibid.*, pp. 18–19).

hair, and a plaided shawl or a long scarf of red flannel braided with black ribbon was worn over the shoulders."[11]

On his small leased acreage the farmer's life, except in such favoured places as the Vale of Glamorgan in South Wales and the Valley of the Dee in North Wales, was likely to be "one of ceaseless and often unrewarding toil; for, as a rule, the land was poor and hilly, and it was a heart-breaking job trying to wring a livelihood out of the stony soil and its matting of coarse grass, bracken and gorse. Up and down the steep ascents the farmer and his family, climbed and stumbled, bent double by sacks of roots, firewood, fodder for the beasts – a list of necessary burdens almost as endless as the day's chores. Scorched by the sun, withered by the wind, it was lucky if anything came to fulfillment, for the crops grew grey and stunted beside the gold and purple-headed ragwort and thistles that alone seemed to flourish."[12] George Lipscomb, who travelled through South Wales in the latter part of the eighteenth century, noted that "the women, who are in general very robust and well calculated to endure fatigue, share with the stronger sex the most arduous exertions and business of husbandry, and they are commonly seen either driving the horses affixed to the plough, or leading those which draw the harrow."[13] To another traveller in Wales "the state of the common people in the lowlands in this country, and particularly of the women, to whose lot the most laborious drudgery belongs, seems miserable, beyond the idea of an Englishman to conceive. . . ."[14]

---

[11] Elizabeth Inglis-Jones: *The Story of Wales* (London, 1955), p. 153. In Cardiganshire, according to an eighteenth-century traveller, the appearance of the costumes shifted as one passed from the northern to the southern part of the country. "The women throughout the northern part of Cardiganshire were dressed in blue jackets, with petticoats of the same colour; and sometimes [with] the addition of a blue rug over the shoulders. About the middle of the county their appearance began to vary. The blue mantle gave place to white; and in a few instances to red ones; and as we approached Cardigan, the number of the former diminished and the latter increased" (George Lipscomb: *Journey into South Wales . . . in the year 1799* (London, 1802), p. 168). In Pembrokeshire Henry P. Wyndham found the women wearing — even in the summer — "a heavy cloth gown with a hood hanging from it behind; instead of a cap, a large handkerchief, wrapped over their heads is tied under their chins. They have sometimes, tho' rarely, a small beaver hat with a very low crown." Elsewhere in Wales he found both men and women wearing "large beaver hats with deep crowns, and with broad quakering brims flapping over their shoulders" (*op. cit.*, pp. 67–8). For the Welsh dress see *Welsh Costumes and Customs* (Aberystwyth, 1951).

[12] Elizabeth Inglis-Jones: *op. cit.*, p. 155.

[13] G. Lipscomb: *op. cit.*, pp. 111–12.

[14] H. P. Wyndham: *op. cit.*, p. 151.

After visiting most parts of the Principality in the 1770's, Henry Wyndham noted that the habitations of the common people, such as farm labourers, were, as a rule, "low, mud-built hovels, raised over the natural earth, which is as deficient in point of level within, as without, [and] notwithstanding the severity of the climate, the windows are frequently destitute of a single piece of glazing. If the inhabitants wish to enjoy the light, they must at the same time suffer the cold." [15] With floors of hardened mud or gravel and roofs of turf, straw, or thatch, these painfully simple cottages often had but one room at the end of which straw or rushes were piled as beds.[16] Some of the cottages, however, more substantially built of blocks of stone, could boast of three rooms, one of which was for general living, another for sleeping, and a third for utility purposes.[17]

In the towns such humble dwellings might be interspersed with more pretentious ones. Indeed, some of the towns presented an attractive appearance in the eighteenth century, particularly in North Wales. Wrexham, Ruthin, and Denbigh were among these.[18] Visiting the latter town in 1774, Dr. Samuel Johnson noted that some of the houses were built of stone, some of brick, and a few of timber.[19] He also found that Denbighshire, bordering on England, was "built of very splendid homes." [20]

South Wales also had towns that impressed the visitor happily. Cardiff, in the Vale of Glamorgan and located at the mouth of the Taff River, was described as "a large, handsome and populous town," while Swansea, at the mouth of the Tawe, made a "handsome appearance" with its wide streets, as was true of Carmarthan on the west coast.[21] Even small villages could charm the stranger.

---

[15] *Ibid.*

[16] See G. Lipscomb: *op. cit.*, p. 168; see also Sir Leonard Davies and A. Edwards: *Welsh Life in the Eighteenth Century* (London, 1939), pp. 197–8.

[17] *Ibid.*

[18] H. P. Wyndham: *op. cit.*, pp. 163, 172.

[19] *A Diary of a Journey into North Wales in the Year 1774* (London, 1816), p. 58. For an account of home and furnishings of the High Sheriff of Anglesey, Henry Morgan (1727–1780), see G. N. Evans: *Social Life in Mid-Eighteenth Century Anglesey* (Cardiff, 1936), pp. 26–30. I. C. Peate in *The Welsh House: A Study in Folk Culture* (London, 1944) has produced the standard work on the Welsh house.

[20] *Diary*, p. 74. Wyndham was particularly impressed with numbers of fine homes in the area about Wrexham (*op. cit.*, p. 172), the most important town in Denbighshire, although Denbigh was the county seat and elected a member to Parliament.

[21] *Ibid.*, pp. 27, 36–7, and 53. Although Wyndham praised the appearance of Carmarthan, he was dismayed to find in the unimproved part of the town "a long

Little Aberarth in Cardiganshire delighted George Lipscomb, who called it "the neatest, most rural and interesting" village in Wales. "The cottages," he wrote of it, "are placed in the simplest style of irregularity, which can be imagined. They are all . . . clean, built with stone, and not like the Welsh cottages in general, covered with turf, but with the smoothest thatch, remarkably well laid on. . . ."[22] This desire for neatness in their surroundings was also manifested in South Wales by the common practice of white-washing the walls of the houses and outbuildings. After passing through Glamorganshire one traveller noted that "there is scarcely a cottage to be seen, which is not regularly brushed over every month."[23]

The air of penury hovering over most of the labouring people of Wales was exhibited not only in their very humble places of abode, but in other ways as well. It was observed that neither men nor women customarily wore shoes or stockings. But however poor they were, they were also a proud people possessed of the habit of industry, as we have noted, and were unwilling to beg. Wyndham, who knew the Continent well, wrote that Wales was the only country in Europe in which the traveller could escape the solicitations of such "abject wretches" as he found among the more impoverished groups of Welshmen.[24]

Until now we have been concerned with the Welsh of the lowlands. Many of those of the mountains lived a life even more primitive in the eighteenth century. This was particularly true of the shepherds. George Lipscomb recorded in his journal how, after descending from the heights of Mount Plinlimmon, he came to a shepherd's habitation. To him the hut presented a melancholy spectacle; there was not a chair in it, nor one single comfort to cheer "the wretched existence of its miserable inhabitants" — outside of a turf

street of mud-built hovels, the chimneys of which are erected in the street, and project some feet beyond the line of houses" (*ibid.*, p. 53).

[22] *Op. cit.*, p. 167.

[23] Wyndham: *op. cit.*, p. 37.

[24] *Ibid.*, p. 153. After traversing most of Wales, Wyndham, on reaching Conway, which was "on the great Irish road"—that is, the road running from Chester to Holyhead, whence the boats sail to Ireland — found to his surprise that the inn there was "crowded with beggars." "I don't recollect," he reflected, "to have seen one beggar, before in the whole principality" (*ibid.*, p. 150). We may surmise, in view of the numbers of Irish on their way at the time to the Chester fair, that these beggars were not Welshmen. That there was begging on Anglesey in the seventeenth century and at times in the early part of the eighteenth is indicated by G. N. Evans (*op. cit.*, pp. 193–7); but no evidence of this is found on the island in the middle of the eighteenth century.

fire which almost suffocated him, unaccustomed as he was to the smoke that arose from it. Yet, this shepherd could not be accounted poor in view of the fact that he possessed, he affirmed, more than a hundred sheep, which grazed on the mountain slopes – nor had he any rent to pay.[25] The shepherd was living, it would appear, in much the same manner as his predecessors, who for hundreds of years had occupied these same isolated mountain areas.[26] As he paid no rent, he well may have obtained a claim to the land on which his hut stood by means of an old and curious custom, that of the "one-night house." This squatter-claim device appears to have existed throughout Wales from an early period. According to it, a freehold right, in the minds of the people at least, was held to be established if a man in the course of a night could erect some sort of habitation with a roof and a chimney and by morning have a fire on the hearth.[27]

Whereas England by the middle of the eighteenth century was beginning to experience the effects of the agricultural revolution, this was not true of Wales, outside of those portions of Montgomeryshire, Denbighshire, and Flintshire which lie adjacent to English counties. In the other areas, according to contemporary testimony, most of the farmers and labourers, "miserably poor . . . hold the lands generally from year to year at rack rents." As a partial explanation of this lack of progress, it was stated that "if one, more industrious than the rest, should make any improvement, the landlord advances his rent, or turns him out. It is therefore to the interest of the farmer to let them [the lands] lie waste, as he has no certainty of a return, when he is liable to be turned out at the landlord's pleasure." The farmers therefore were accustomed "only to take care to get just sufficient by their industry to supply present want, and

---

25 Lipscomb: *op. cit.*, p. 155.

26 Giraldus Cambrensis gives a description of Welsh life in the twelfth century. The people, he said, did not live in towns, but wandered about in separate families. He noted that the sedge-covered huts they raised were but for temporary use and involved little labour; that no tables were to be found within them, or even dishes; and that on retiring for the night the family rested together upon a mat made of rushes and for protection from the cold was covered in common by a coarse rug. For a translation from the Latin of this passage in Giraldus see Wyndham: *op. cit.*, pp. 143–4.

27 In their report of 1895 the Land Commissioners had the following to say about the above practice: "It is a notable circumstance that there survives in Wales a traditional notion, erroneous in point of law, but universal, that by buidling a 'Ty-un-nos' (a 'one-night house') freehold rights could be acquired" (quoted by Eiluned and Peter Lewis: *The Land of Wales* [London, 1949], p. 27).

let the morrow provide for itself."[28] Hand in hand with this hindrance to advancement in rural life went the innate conservatism of the people, who were opposed to any change and who, as a result, disdained the use of more efficient methods of agriculture.[29]

As a rule, the chief field crops in the eighteenth century were barley and oats, with most of the lands of the farms given over to pasturage.[30] That there was much neglect of good land is indicated by the fact that, despite the increase in population, more than 1,250,000 acres of land were not being properly utilized in 1812. One half of this area, it was estimated, was fit for cultivation.[31] Another factor that contributed to the depressed condition in the eighteenth century – especially among the mountain people – was the enclosure movement by private acts of Parliament. This had the effect from 1733 onward of closing off much of the land shepherds had from time immemorial used for the pasture of their flocks.[32] No longer able to live in their accustomed haunts, at least in the old, free ways, because these Crown lands were rapidly passing into private ownership and thereupon enclosed, they were obliged to seek their livelihood either in the Welsh lowlands or in England, or, as many did, emigrate to America.[33]

---

[28] Daniel Defoe, Samuel Richardson, and others: *A Tour through the Island of Great Britain* (Dublin, 1779), II, 300.

[29] For the refusal on the part of farm labourers to exchange their primitive ploughs for the new Rotherham swing-plough introduced in North Wales about 1760 see Sir Leonard Davies and A. Edwards: *op. cit.*, pp. 14–15.

[30] Most of the farms in South Wales consisted of about fifty or sixty acres. See Walter Davies: *A General View of Agriculture and Domestic Economy of South Wales* (2 vols., London, 1814), I, 162. For Agriculture in Wales in the eighteenth century the student should consult not only the work just cited, but also the same author's *A General View of Agriculture and Domestic Economy of North Wales* (London, 1810), as well as a recent study, *The Economic History of South Wales prior to 1800* (Cardiff, 1933), by D. J. Davies.

[31] See Sir Leonard Davies and A. Edwards: *op. cit.*, p. 1.

[32] See Ivor Bowen: *The Great Enclosure of Common Lands in Wales* (London, 1914), and A. H. Dodd: "The Enclosure Movement in North Wales," Board of Celtic Studies *Bulletin*, III, Part 2 (December 1926).

[33] Lipscomb (*op. cit.*, pp. 101–3) presents a picture of migrating Cardiganshire people who were obliged to leave their ancestral abodes where they could no longer support themselves: "In the course of our morning's ride," he writes, describing his journey into the region of Mount Plinlimmon, "we met with a little horde of Welsh-men, who with their wives and children, and all that they had, were quitting their native retirement, the peaceful retreat of innocence and penury, and journeying toward Deptford, to procure employment in the dock-yard. These poor people . . . exhibited a picture of industry and patience, which could not fail to excite our admiration and pity."

If agriculture was neglected in Wales before the middle of the century, certain influences were at work to improve its condition after 1750. Various county improvement associations came into existence,[34] and turnpike roads were built, beginning in North Wales. With easier access to markets many men of wealth were led to expend large sums of money on their estates, not all of which, unhappily, brought profitable returns.

As grazing country Wales stood high throughout the century. The black cattle, which seems to have been the predominant type, and other breeds flourished in the vales and lower mountain pastures, although without preliminary pen-feeding they were not generally fit for the market. As a result, thousands of cattle were driven in great herds each year to the cattle markets of England, many of them going as far as Kent. Those from Anglesey were, in addition, forced to swim the Menai Straits. In order to make the long journey the cattle were shod and encouraged on their way by drovers and their dogs, who whenever possible avoided the main highways.[35]

We have noted that the Welsh were industrious, frugal people who had learned to be reasonably content with but little in the way of comforts. Wool, which was washed before being clipped from the backs of their sheep, was carded, spun, woven, and otherwise processed in their homes. They also produced a surplus of such articles as stockings and woollen gloves, for which Bala in North Wales was the chief market. About Wrexham very considerable quantities of flannel of the best quality were produced[36] and carried to markets such as that at Shrewsbury. Denbigh was a centre for the tanning of leather. Common utilities for the home and farm were also skillfully fashioned in most parts of Wales.

In 1750 there was little evidence in Wales of industry in the modern sense. Pottery works were operating in the area of the coal fields in Flintshire near Hawarden, and in Glamorganshire; at Neath

---

[34] H. P. Wyndham (*op. cit.*, p. 28), arriving at Cowbridge in Glamorgan, found at the inn there printed announcements of the Society for the Encouragement of Agriculture, which offered suitable premiums to encourage farmers to adopt new modes of agriculture; he noted that the scheme was supported by "ample subscriptions."

[35] See Caroline Skeel: "The Cattle Trade between Wales and England from the Fifteenth to the Nineteenth Centuries," Royal Hist. Soc. *Trans.*, 4th series, IX, 135–58; S. W. Rider and A. E. Trueman: *The Cattle Trade between England and Wales*; and G. N. Evans: *op. cit.*, 119–25.

[36] There seems to be some evidence that the Celtic people were the first to produce flannel. The wool from the mountain sheep was especially well adapted for this purpose.

some copper smelting had been going on for a century and a half. This latter enterprise was in the heart of the vast coal deposits of South Wales which stretch from Pontypool on the eastern border of Glamorganshire to St. Bride's Bay in western Pembrokeshire.[37] This coal had been drawn upon for domestic purposes as early as the thirteenth century, if not earlier.[38] Early in the seventeenth century a company received a grant to utilize the coal for the smelting of iron and other metals in South Wales, and toward the end of the century Sir Humphrey Mackworth started to exploit the coal resources about Neath for smelting the lead and copper ore from mines that he had acquired. To further his project he became identified with a mining company and as its chief driving force raised money for the building of docks and other facilities for the movement of coal on a large scale. Among the innovations that Mackworth introduced were so-called "sailing wagons on land" – wagons that operated on wooden rails that led from the mines to the sea and that were drawn by a single horse aided by sails. But the company experienced great resistance from the outside and dissension within the membership, which finally wrecked it. The Mackworth family, nevertheless, retained its properties at Neath and by the middle of the century the collieries of this town were exporting some seven thousand tons of coal, utilizing for that purpose the port of Swansea only a little more than seven miles away.[39]

Thus, beyond the fact that coal was being mined about Neath for copper and lead smelting and for export, there was little industrialization in South Wales in the middle of the eighteenth century.[40] Although Swansea, located on the bay of the same name, was a busy shipping centre for the Neath coal exports to southwestern England and to Ireland and was reputed to have the largest trade of any town in Glamorganshire, it was still noted for its cleanness, its broad and pleasant streets, its domestic manufacture of straw hats, and the possession of mineral waters that seemed to display great efficacy in the curing of human ailments. Its people still hoped, as they had

---

[37] Sir Leonard Davies and A. Edwards: *op. cit.*, pp. 86–114.

[38] E. Phillips: *A History of the Pioneers of the Welsh Coalfield* (Cardiff, 1925), p. 3; see also Charles Wilkins: *The South Wales Coal Trade and its allied Industries from the earliest Days . . .* (Cardiff, 1888), and G. G. Francis: *The Smelting of Copper in the Swansea District from the time of Elizabeth* (London, 1881).

[39] E. Phillips: *op. cit.*, p. 18.

[40] Sir Frederick Rees: *op. cit.*, p. 131.

earlier in the century, to make it a fashionable watering-place.[41] But this was not to be realized. By 1765 its industrialization was well under way. In Swansea Bay at that date a hundred ships might be seen either loading coal or about to sail fully burdened. Pottery works were constructed there as was also a large copper smelting plant, which Wyndham on a visit in 1774 found to be "perpetually smoaking"; he also mentioned a still larger smelting plant operating in that year a little way up the Tawe, at the mouth of which Swansea is built.[42] Neath he found humming with activity; he was deeply impressed by "immense copper works and iron forges, its tin works and coal mines." As he surveyed the busy scene the town presented he was impelled to reflect that "the Welsh seem . . . to be little anxious about the comforts of good houses. . . . For the large part of this trading town actually consists of more miserable hovels, than are to be found in the most indigent villages in England." [43] One may venture the view that many if not most of the people who had been gathered to labour at Neath in 1774 – especially if they had come from mountain country to the north, where the enclosure movement had forced large numbers to leave – had never lived in homes of much superior quality.

Meanwhile, in a bleak, hilly region of northeastern Glamorganshire, at Merthyr Tydfil on the River Taff, some twenty-five miles northwest of Cardiff, the coal outcropping attracted the attention of men of capital, for the most part Englishmen. In 1759 Isaac Wilkinson, an ironmaster who had already acquired ironworks near Wrexham, formed a company to smelt and forge iron near Merthyr Tydfil; in 1765 a second ironworks was established not far away by Anthony Bacon, and soon afterwards, a third in the same general area. Out of these efforts, all before the year 1775, came the Dowlais, the Cyfarthfa, and the Plymouth ironworks respectively, each of large proportions and each highly successful as the result of the happy combination of an abundance of iron, coal, limestone, water power, and industrious labourers.[44]

Although these ironworks were dependent on Cardiff for the ex-

---

[41] W. L. Jarvis: "Glimpses of Old Swansea," *Wales*, II (August 1895), pp. 368–73.

[42] H. P. Wyndham: *op. cit.*, pp. 36–7.

[43] *Ibid.*, p. 38.

[44] See Charles Wilkins: *The History of the Iron, Steel, Tin-plate, and other Trades of Wales* (Merthyr Tydfil, 1903), also his *The History of Merthyr Tydfil* (Merthyr Tydfil, 1867).

port by sea of the iron and coal they produced, that place remained throughout the eighteenth century one of slight commercial consequence. In fact, until the opening in 1794 of the Glamorgan canal leading from Merthyr to its waterfront – and the establishment of the first real dock in 1798 – coal was brought to Cardiff in panniers on the backs of horses or mules, and iron in two-ton wagons, whereupon these products were loaded on vessels at a primitive quay. Not until early in the nineteenth century were there more than two thousand inhabitants in the town. But with the growing demand of the world for coal the borough and its dock facilities expanded rapidly, with the result that when in the middle of the nineteenth century railroads were built to the mines, it became the world's greatest port for the shipment of coal.

The population of Wales in the middle of the eighteenth century was somewhere between three and four hundred thousand.[45] The Principality was divided into 12 shires,[46] 86 hundreds, and 915 parishes.[47] With the extension of the statutes of England to Wales and the granting of seats in Parliament, the forty-shilling freeholders of the shires were entitled to vote. How many were thus qualified is not clear. However, in two shires where contests for a seat in Parliament took place in the course of the eighteenth century the number of electors was respectable. In Cardiganshire in 1734 one candidate received 344 votes and his rival 340; in Carmarthenshire in 1754, the vote was 785 to 390. Each of the twelve shires was entitled to elect a member. In addition, twelve towns enjoyed the same privilege.[48]

---

[45] According to figures supplied by D. Fenning and J. Collyer in their *A New System of Geography*, which was published in 1765, Glamorganshire was supposed to have 58,000 inhabitants; Denbighshire, 38,400; Cardiganshire, 35,300; Brecknockshire, 35,300; Montgomeryshire, 33,960; Flintshire, 32,400; Pembrokeshire, 25,900; Radnorshire, 18,960; Merionethshire, 17,100; Carmarthenshire, 17,000; Carnarvonshire, 16,000; and Anglesey, once fairly densely populated, but 12,000 (*ibid.*, II, 570–6).

[46] Monmouthshire, which ethnically and culturally is to be identified with Wales, was, as has been noted, attached judicially to England in the days of Henry VIII and is therefore not considered in this connection.

[47] D. Fenning and J. Collyer: *op. cit.*, II, 570–6.

[48] These towns were Beaumaris, Brecon (Brecknock), Cardiff, Cardigan, Carmarthan, Carnarvon, Denbigh, Flint, Haverfordwest, Montgomery, Pembroke, and Radnor. In 1750 some of these towns, such, for example, as Flint, which was called "a mean place, without any market," did not compare with such a town as Wrexham, "esteemed the largest town in North Wales" with its great church and well-constructed homes that were occupied by many of the lesser gentry in Denbighshire. It will be

Those who sat in Parliament for the Welsh counties or towns in the middle of the eighteenth century constituted a group made up of members of well-established and usually wealthy landed families with influential connections. Examples of this point will illustrate Welsh parliamentary history.

Charles Edwin, who represented Glamorganshire from 1747 until his death in 1756, had sat for Westminster between 1741 and 1747; his father, Sir Humphrey, who had been Lord Mayor of London, had purchased in 1670 one of the three towns in Carmarthenshire named Llanfihangil. The member for Cardiff in 1750 was Herbert Mackworth of Knoll – son of the late Sir Humphrey a member of Parliament for Cardiganshire – who was in possession of the great Mackworth properties at Neath and elsewhere. William Owen, who represented Pembrokeshire in that year, held a seat in the House for fifty-one years, either for the county or for the town of Pembroke; his father, Sir Arthur Owen, also had represented either the county or Pembroke in Parliament. William Edwards of Haverfordwest, who sat for that town for forty-eight years, was the son of Francis Edwards, a member of Parliament between 1722 and 1726; William not only inherited in 1721 the great estates of the Rich family in Kensington, London, and elsewhere, but in 1726 came into his father's property; he was still holding his seat, as Lord Kensington of the peerage of Ireland, when he died in 1801 at the age of ninety-one. Thomas Lewis sat for Radnor from 1715 to 1761; Sir Lynch Salusbury Cotton represented Denbighshire from 1749 to 1774; and Richard Myddleton of Cherk Castle, although only twenty-one years of age, followed his father in 1747 as member for the town of Denbigh, and sat until 1788, when he voluntarily retired by accepting the Chiltern Hundreds.[49] In like manner William Vaughan in 1736 took over the seat for Merionethshire held by his father, Richard Vaughan, and continued to occupy it for the follow-

noted that no town in Merionethshire was given representation in Parliament and that in Pembrokeshire two towns enjoyed this right: Pembroke and Haverfordwest.

[49] It may be noted in passing that the above device was a means of avoiding the parliamentary law that, once having been elected to a seat in the House of Commons, one may not resign it. It was therefore customary for one desiring to give up his seat and retire to private life to accept the titular office of steward of the Chiltern Hundreds, theoretically an office of profit and thus disqualifying him to sit in the House under the terms of the officeholders statute passed in 1707. For a recent study of this see Betty Kemp: "The Stewardship of the Chiltern Hundreds," *Essays presented to Sir Lewis Namier* (ed. R. Pares and A. J. P. Taylor, London, 1956), pp. 204–26.

ing thirty-three years.[50] It may be added that even in Wales an election contest might be a very costly thing. For example, Sir Humphry Howarth, who in 1722 was obliged to contest the seat for Radnorshire and was successful, holding it thereupon until his death in 1755, was forced to mortgage his estate, "Maesllwch." It was eventually foreclosed and passed out of the hands of the Howarth family.[51]

Most of the men who were sent to Parliament in the eighteenth century from the Welsh counties and towns, moreover, were those already prominently identified with activities in the Principality. John Talbot of Lincoln's Inn, who sat for Brecknock for twenty years and who was the son of Charles, Lord Talbot, at one time Lord High Chancellor, was Recorder for Brecknock for eleven years and a justice of the Great Sessions, as well as the Auditor of the Society for the Encouragement of Learning. Then there was Sir Lynch Salusbury Cotton, who, as already indicated, represented Denbighshire for twenty-six years; for forty-seven years he was also a member of the Common Council of Denbigh. William Owen, who from 1723 to 1774 was returned either by Pembrokeshire or the town of Pembroke, was Lord Lieutenant of Pembrokeshire as well as *custos rotulorum* for three other counties; while Thomas Morgan, the member for Brecknockshire, who spent his entire adult life in Parliament, was not only Lord Lieutenant and *custos rotulorum* for that county from 1731 to the date of his death in 1769, but was also Brigadier General of its militia as well as that of Monmouthshire, in which county he likewise came into possession in 1763, as next in line, of the great Tredegar estates.[52]

In fact, of the twenty-four seats in the House of Commons allocated to Wales, not one of these in the middle of the eighteenth century was held by a real outsider, nor was one held, it also seems to be true, by a native of the Principality who was not as thoroughly at home in fashionable English society as he was in the use of the English tongue. This strong suspicion of strangers modified by a certain tolerance of the foreign culture of those long settled in the area of the seacoast — whether they were English or Flemings — was as characteristic of the great majority of the Welsh people as

[50] See W. R. Williams: *The Parliamentary History of the Principality of Wales* (Brecknock, 1895), pp. 6–175.

[51] *Ibid.*, p. 175.

[52] *Ibid.*

was their attachment to the language and mores of their ancestors – a dichotomy with many complexities.[53]

The form of local government was mediaeval. At Cardiff the constable of the ruined castle was the chief magistrate and was supported by twelve aldermen and twelve of the common council, together with two serjeants at mace and five constables. In Carnarvon, the chief officer was likewise the constable of the castle; Brecknock was governed by two bailiffs, fifteen aldermen, two chamberlains and two constables; Camarthan had a mayor and two sheriffs who were chosen from among the sixteen aldermen; Radnor was under a bailiff and twenty-five burgesses.[54]

In another respect many of the Welsh still lived in the Middle Ages. Like that of the native Irish and the Highlanders of Scotland, their world was peopled with fairies, sorceresses, ogres, and changeling elf-children.[55] An eighteenth-century writer declared: "The people of this country [Wales] are not inferior in superstition to the Laplanders; the most improbable and absurd tales of haunted houses, demons, and apparitions, are related and believed. Nor can many be found so hardy as to doubt the existence of witches, fairies, elves, and all the bugbears of a writer's tale." [56] Even the weddings in South Wales retained certain echoes of the Rape of the Sabine Women by the Romans. Mounted behind her father on a merlin, one of the native breed of horses, the bride would be chased by the bridegroom and his friends on a wild ride until overtaken, whereupon the happy couple would enter the church and be married amidst great rejoicings.[57]

In one very important respect, however, the Welsh had turned their backs on their forbears of the Middle Ages. Nowhere else in the British Isles in 1750 were there fewer Roman Catholics than in Wales; yet nowhere in these Isles were there more impressive ruins of cathedrals, churches, abbeys, and other ecclesiastical structures

---

[53] Eiluned and Peter Lewis: *op. cit.*, p. 29.

[54] D. Fenning and J. Collyer: *op. cit.*, II, 572–6.

[55] See Peter Roberts: *The Cambrian Popular Antiquities; or, An Account of Some Traditions, Customs, and Superstitions of Wales, with Observations* (London, 1815).

[56] *A Tour of Great Britain . . . Originally begun by . . . Daniel DeFoe, continued by the late Mr. Richardson . . . and brought down to the present Time* (4 vols., Dublin, 1779), II, 292.

[57] Mita Williams: "Ancient Marriage Customs," *Wales*, No. 12 (April 1895), pp. 156–63; B. H. Malkin: *South Wales* (London, 1804), p. 67; and Sir Leonard Davies and A. Edwards: *op. cit.*, p. 230.

bearing testimony to the early devotion of the Welsh to the Catholic Church. How completely they had gradually drawn away from the Roman Catholic communion is indicated by the circulation in 1776 of questionnaires in all the parishes within the diocese of Bangor, which comprehended much of North Wales. In sixty-eight replies signed by the parish priest, only one parish noted the presence of any one who was presumably a Roman Catholic; in this instance the priest referred to the presence of "two Irishmen" settled in his parish, but indicated that they had no priest to minister to them.[58]

The question may be raised why the Celts of Wales repudiated the Roman Catholic Church while those of Ireland and of much of Highland Scotland still showed intense loyalty to it in 1750. Certainly one among other factors was that the Tudors, who carried a Welsh name and were largely of Welsh extraction, were personally popular among the Welsh. It was not the case therefore of a dynasty of foreign conquerors seeking to impose their own religious settlement, as was true in Ireland. The closing of the monasteries and confiscation of their lands in the face of the denunciation of the Pope therefore led to a very different response in Wales than in Ireland. In fact, the Welsh were led in the course of the sixteenth and seventeenth centuries to accept as fully the change from the Roman Catholic to the Anglican Establishment as the Irish were led slowly but surely in the twelfth and thirteenth centuries to give up their independent, national Irish Church — for centuries the great rival of the Roman Church not only in the British Isles, but in some other parts — and to become most obedient to the authority of the papacy. The papal action in opposing Tudor ecclesiastical policy in the sixteenth century was regarded by most Welshmen, it would appear, as improper interference from outside, whereas in Ireland it was hailed. Again, the "planting" of Northern Ireland by Anglican Englishmen and Presbyterian Lowland Scots, with the confiscation of the lands of revolting Irish leaders and their followers, only intensi-

58 "The Diocese of Bangor in the Eighteenth Century," *Wales*, II (1895), 121–3, 204–7, and 567–70. This revealing document was apparently edited by the late Sir Owen Edwards, editor of *Wales*, who was at the time history tutor and fellow of Lincoln College, Oxford. It should be noted that Holywell, in the diocese of St. Asaph, where stood the shrine of St. Winifred, was a place of pilgrimage in the eighteenth century for Catholics from England, although the shrine itself had passed out of their keeping. The only part of Wales where Catholics settled in any appreciable numbers in the course of the eighteenth century was in Glamorganshire, as the result of the bringing in of skilled artisans from the Continent.

fied the loyalty of the Irish to Rome, the avowed enemy of the English monarchy. In contrast, the Welsh showed their attachment not only to the Tudors but also to the early Stuarts. Under Elizabeth their spiritual needs were recognized by the translation of the entire Bible into their language, followed in the days of James I by translation into Welsh of the authorized English version – a great concession to national pride.[59] It is perhaps not surprising therefore that while the Irish rebelled against Charles I and sought to exterminate the English and Scots settled among them, the Welsh were so attached to their King that in the course of the Great Rebellion he had nowhere on the island more loyal followers.

Nevertheless, the Established Anglican Church in Wales had, during the period under consideration, fallen on evil days. Almost everywhere once splendid ecclesiastical structures, a priceless heritage that had been the object of solicitude and adornment by the devout before the Reformation, now stood in complete or near ruin. This neglect reflected the Puritan reformers' hostility against everything these structures symbolized, especially during the period of the Commonwealth. The Anglican clergy, who were expected to perform their religious offices in them, were likewise obliged to eke out a miserable livelihood as the result of the impropriation of the revenues attached to them. The tithes designed for the maintenance of the churches were in the hands of private individuals who, as a rule, had no interest at all in their welfare. In 1721 a worthy divine, Dr. Erasmus Saunders, who was educated at Jesus College, Oxford, and was prebendary of St. David's, published in London *A View of the State of Religion in the Diocese of St. David's about the beginning of the Eighteenth Century . . . with Considerations on the Reasonableness of Augmenting the Revenues of Impropriate Churches.* In this work he dealt with the deplorable condition of the churches in South Wales, where so many were "in actual ruins; so many more are ready to fall, and almost all are robb'd and pillag'd by a sweeping Alienation of all the Tythes, as well as the Lands and Glebes once belonging to them and become the Properties of such Persons as generally seem to think themselves neither by Law nor Conscience bound to maintain the worship of God in them." He thereupon pleaded that one should see "the pitiful Condition of our once

---

[59] See Sir John Ballinger: *The Bible in Wales, a Study in the History of the Welsh People* (London, 1906).

so celebrated and noble Cathedral; or . . . the Stately Ruins of the Bishop's Palace, of the College, the Schools, the Archdeacon's and the Canon's houses at St. David's, and the like Desolation of the Collegiate Church and Houses belonging thereunto and of the Bishop's Palace at Brecon." He also referred to the desolate remains of the old collegiate church of Llandhewyfrefi in Cardiganshire, "a church once endow'd with a handsome Provision for a Dean and twelve Prebendaries; but the Endowment is now alienated to that Degree that the poor Incumbent there, though the Tythes of his Parish are said to be worth Four hundred Pounds per Ann. is obliged to content himself with about Eight Pounds Salary." [60]

Nor did the deplorable situation of the churches in Wales improve during the century. In 1774 Dr. Samuel Johnson went with his friends the Thrales to Mrs. Thrale's birthplace in North Wales, "Bodville," near which were the churches Tydweilliog and Llangwinodyle, the impropriations of which she held, apparently by inheritance. "We surveyed the churches, which are mean and neglected to a degree scarcely imaginable," wrote Johnson. "They have no pavement and the earth is full of holes. The seats are rude benches, the altars have no rails. One of them has a breach in the roof. On the desk, I think, of each lay a folio Welsh Bible of the black letter, which the curate cannot easily read." [61] The two parish churches were what were called "perpetual curacies," and were supported by the "small tithes," which provided each curate with a stipend of £6.16.6 a year. Although the Thrales were apparently deeply moved by the sad spectacle presented in each church and Mr. Thrale vowed that he would beautify them, and "if he prospers will probably restore the [great] tithes," it does not appear that he ever carried out his good intentions.[62]

Such was the characteristic situation of the Established Church among a people highly endowed with religious sensibilities, who either because of their poverty or their indifference, permitted this sorry state of affairs. It must be noted that such organizations as the Society for the Promotion of Christian Knowledge, which was espe-

[60] See Sir Leonard Davies and A. Edwards: *op. cit.*, pp. 198–9.

[61] Samuel Johnson: *A Diary of a Journey into North Wales* . . . (London, 1816), pp. 107–11.

[62] Yet the situation of the two churches was somewhat improved in the course of time. By 1809 the income of Tydweilliog was £43.19.10 and that of Llangwinodyle £46.2.2 (*ibid.*, pp. 112, n.).

cially active in Wales from the beginning of the eighteenth century down to 1740, did much to promote the pious efforts of the clergy and other religious leaders by distributing among the people Bibles and other good books in the Welsh language.[63]

Despite what has been said about the appearance of decay of the Established Church, it seems to be quite clear that most of the Welsh people were members of it in the middle of the eighteenth century; it is equally clear that many did not take their religious professions too seriously. If there was a large attendance of men at the morning service, it might well mean that they had assembled at the church not at all in a devout frame of mind but rather in anticipation of a football game or a great cock-fight, which were regularly held in the churchyard in many parishes.

For a time in the seventeenth century, especially with the triumph of Parliament in the Great Rebellion and after the death of Charles I, it did seem that a majority of the people of Wales might be prevailed upon to repudiate Anglicanism, as they had Roman Catholicism, in favour of the principles and practices of the Independents and the Baptists. Under Cromwell preachers of these faiths replaced most of the clergy of the Establishment within the Principality. With the Restoration of Charles II, however, Anglican clergymen who were still alive were restored to their livings after those who had been enjoying them were ejected as "Presbyterians" — a term of opprobrium which covered all Protestant dissenters at that time.[64]

It should be stressed that, as a group, the Welsh dissenting preachers were deeply devoted men. After being deprived of their posts, they and their successors continued to labour among those who had come under their influence. It appears that the number of conventicles they set up was rather large (on the basis of returns made after 1669 to the Archbishop of Canterbury) and that the influence of these dissenters gathered in their chapels laid the foundations, at least in some respects in the following century, for the Calvinistic Methodist Church, despite the latter's close connection with the Anglican Establishment.[65]

---

[63] See *The Correspondence and Minutes of the S. P. C. K. relating to Wales* (ed. Mary Clement, Cardiff, 1952).

[64] Thomas Rees: *History of Protestant Nonconformity in Wales* (London, 1861), p. 175.

[65] *Ibid.*, pp. 197–345.

The activities of the Quakers were as important as those of the Independents and the Baptists in the religious history af Wales toward the close of the seventeenth century. As the result of English statutes, especially the code enacted after the Restoration in 1660, they were obliged to submit to an intense type of persecution. Curiously enough, the number of Quakers was greatest during this period of imprisonment, attachment of property, and harassment in other ways for refusal to pay tithes, take the required oaths, and abide by the statute against unlawful assemblies. The leading member of the Society of Friends at this period, Richard Davies of Welshpool, Montgomeryshire, describes in his autobiography, *Account of the convincement, exercises, services and travels of Richard Davies, with some relation of ancient Friends and the spreading of Truth in North Wales,* published in London in 1744, the trials that he and his fellow Friends faced in Wales in the latter seventeenth and early eighteenth centuries. The story is told in so unaffected a manner and with so little bitterness as to be profoundly moving.

The Welsh Quakers were, by and large, people of substance, and some of them were highly educated, such as Charles Lloyd, an Oxford man who spent ten years in confinement despite the fact that he was a local magistrate. The gaol in which he was imprisoned at one period was, in fact, so filled with Quakers, Independents, Presbyterians, and Baptists that the common criminals had to be quartered in the garrets.[66] But this persecution seemed to have provided added zeal to the Society of Friends. Meetings held at Presteign, Carmarthen, Dolgelley, Rhayader, Denbigh, Bala, and Monmouth in the early part of the eighteenth century were crowded; at Monmouth fifteen hundred people assembled.[67]

But by 1731 a disturbing element had entered the picture. Magistrates no longer broke up the meetings and on occasion even granted permission to the Quakers to assemble in the town hall. The Quaker John Kelsale actually noted this change in attitude with regret. Although, he declared, people continued to come in large numbers to the gatherings, "yet I find little or no convincement follows. . . .

---

[66] See R. Williams: "Quakerism in Montgomeryshire," *Wales*, No. 21 (January 1896), pp. 7–12.

[67] "Friends in Wales," *Wales*, No. 11 (March 1895), pp. 97–9. This contribution consists of extracts taken from the diary in the manuscript volumes of John Kelsale, a schoolmaster and an ardent Friend, and were contributed by E. Griffith. The diary is continued in other numbers of *Wales*.

The government and people of the better sort are very kind and civil to friends. . . . Yea, the very priests [of the Established Church] in diverse places are seemingly, at least, loving to friends, and they being unwilling to give them offence – as they call it – are too easy toward them [that is, to the Friends] in respect to religious matters." [68]

It appears that tolerance of their views and practices was something that the Society of Friends could not combat as a destructive force to the movement. For example, Kelsale records with sorrow that at the yearly meeting in 1733 at Hay, Brecknockshire, there were "many people, but not many friends." [69] In fact, the decline of the Society in Wales was very rapid after that date. In 1776 only three Quaker families were recorded as living at Dolgelley, one family at Llangelynin, and one woman at Talyllyn. That was all in the diocese of Bangor.[70] Many Quakers, as is well known, emigrated to the British colonies in North America, among them such as Thomas Lloyd. Others, among them Charles Lloyd and John Kelsale, left Wales to settle in England, and still others died without successors to give "testimony to the truth." Even the granddaughter of Richard Davies, the chief founder of Quakerism in Wales, was married in an Anglican "steeple-house" by a priest and was thereupon disowned. In Montgomeryshire, the heart of the movement in Wales, the Quaker meeting house at Dolobran closed in 1780.[71]

The Welsh are an emotional people; their love of music, shown especially in the power of their choral singing, is indicative of this, as is their unbounded zest in field sports. Beneath the quietism of the Society of Friends was a great emotional urge. This urge, for example, led the first prominent Welsh Quaker, Richard Davies, to enter a church – which in his autobiography he called a "steeple-

---

[68] *Ibid.*, No. 14 (January 1895), pp. 264–5.

[69] *Ibid.*

[70] "The Diocese of Bangor in the Eighteenth Century," *ibid.*, No. 11 (March 1895), pp. 121–3; No. 13 (May 1895), pp. 204–7; No. 20 (December 1895), pp. 567–70.

[71] *Ibid.*, No. 21 (January 1896), pp. 7–12. In Merimethshire, near Llwyngwril, where the author of this volume was stopping in 1951 and also in 1952, is the Quaker burial ground at Llwn Du, called the "Quakers' garden." Here the body of John Goodman, who preached for 55 years and died at the age of 82, was laid to rest in 1763. He seems to have been the last of the Quaker preachers in this part of Wales to achieve real prominence. Upon inquiry it was impossible to gain information as to the presence of a single Quaker in this region where once they played so significant a role in religious life. For the dispersion of the Welsh Quakers see T. M. Rees: *A History of the Quakers in Wales and their Emigration to North America* (Carmarthen, 1925).

house" – and openly to contradict the minister, as did George Fox, the founder of the Society of Friends, on more than one occasion. For "brawling" in church Davies was thereupon placed in gaol. But there was no outlet for emotion when this practice was frowned upon by the yearly meeting of Friends and when those who had been actively hostile to the Quakers became tolerant. Many were inclined to go to sleep during the periods of quiet at the meetings, much to the distress of the more ardent Friends.

The Welsh people were therefore not backward in embracing a new call with high emotional overtones. In Wales this came with the great religious revival of 1735 which had its real beginning in the fervent preaching of the Welsh Anglican, Griffith Jones, rector of Llanddowror in Carmarthenshire. Men and women crowded to hear him preach. His fame spread throughout Wales. Another Welshman of Carmarthenshire, Daniel Rowlands, fell under the spell of his exhortations in 1735, and in that same year Howell Harris of Trevecca (Trevecka) in Brecknockshire was also deeply stirred. These two men of tremendous spiritual earnestness ignored the churches and the protests of clergymen and sought out the people wherever they could be found, calling them to repent. The effect of Harris's preaching was unprecedented. "His words fell like balls of fire on the careless and sinful multitude," it was affirmed. Thomas Rees called him "the most successful preacher that ever ascended a pulpit or platform in Wales." [72] And hymns written by William Williams, the great Welsh hymn-writer and revivalist, it is recorded, "inflamed the people" at the gatherings.

Here we have the beginnings of Calvinistic Methodism in Wales, to the spread of which George Whitefield, the great English revivalist, made an important contribution – as did the dedicated nonconforming clergy. Hand in hand with this went the organization of the so-called "Circulating Schools" for the religious education of the masses, promoted and sustained throughout his lifetime by Griffith Jones.[73] These are said by 1761 to have numbered 218, and

[72] *Op. cit.*, p. 364. For the career of Harris see H. J. Hughes: *Life of Howell Harris, the Welsh Reformer* (London, 1892); for Harris's correspondence see M. H. Jones: *The Trevecka Letters, or, The Unpublished Manuscript Correspondence of Howell Harris and his Contemporaries* (Carnarvon, 1932).

[73] See F. A. Cavenagh: *The Life and Work of Griffith Jones of Llanddowror* (Cardiff, 1930); see also Jones's *Welsh Piety; or, A farther Account of the Circulating Welsh Charity Schools. . . .* (London, 1758).

during a period of twenty-five years, up to the time of Jones's death, to have taught some 150,000 people of all ages to read. The movement also carried with it the spirit of Welsh nationalism and a revival of interest in the Welsh language and literature.

With the parting of the ways between John Wesley and George Whitefield in England, there appeared in like manner two distinct groups of revivalists in Wales – one upholding Wesleyan Methodism and [74] the other the Calvinistic Methodism of Whitefield and his patroness, the Countess of Huntingdon.[75] Although both groups of Methodists remained technically identified with the Anglican communion during the period under consideration in this series, the great spiritual movement that they promoted did not fail to arouse strong opposition on the part of clergy and laymen of the Established Church. Henry P. Wyndham, writing in his journal of a visit to Haverfordwest in Pembrokeshire in 1774, reflected fully this hostile attitude: "Methodism has extended its baneful influence even in this remote angle of our island: two chapels, of the different persuasion of Wesley and Lady H[untingto]n flourish at Haverfordwest; they seem to be dedicated to their tutelary saints, for they are only characterized by the names of their respective patrons. Both are regularly crowded; but whether superstition, novelty, or curiosity is the cause, I am unwilling to attribute it to the neglect of the pastors of the Established Church, nor did I give credit to that vulgar opinion." [76]

Out of the establishment of Methodist societies in all parts of Wales there emerged the distinctly Welsh religious denomination of Calvinistic Methodists. While adhering to the Established Church of England during the remainder of the eighteenth century, its members refused to accept its discipline. As late as 1801 they referred to their organization as "the Private Societies among the People called Methodists." However, in 1811 a clear break occurred when twenty-three ministers were ordained without permission of the Established Church and in violation of the principle of apostolical succession. In

[74] See David Young: *The Origin and History of [Wesleyan] Methodism in Wales* (London, 1893).

[75] See D. E. Jenkins: *Calvinistic Methodist Holy Orders* (Carnarvon, 1911), and W. Williams: *Welsh Calvinistic Methodism . . .* (London, 1884).

[76] Wyndham went on to say: "I have since seen, in the most retired spots in this country, a wretched cottage, nearly bursting with the fulness of its congregation; while multitudes, in a heavy rain, were swarming about the outside, imbibing with gaping mouths, the poisonous tenets of the preacher. . . ." (*op. cit.*, p. 66).

1823 a distinct confession of faith was adopted. Then in 1826, with the approval of the "constitutional deed," the Calvinistic Methodist Church became a separate denomination, having severed all connections with the Established Church. It may be said in conclusion that the release of powerful spiritual energies, combined with the social implications of the broad humanitarianism and equalitarianism that characterized the revivals (such as those of 1735 and of 1762), had profound and beneficial cultural effects upon the people of Wales, effects that were by no means limited to those most directly concerned.

But we must now turn our attention to the people of Scotland, who like those of Wales were near neighbours of the English. In the middle of the eighteenth century the Scottish civilization, too, was being influenced by the close ties, political and otherwise, that bound the three nations into one, making them collectively the people of Great Britain.

CHAPTER VII

Caledonia Gathers the Fruits of the Union

SCOTLAND in 1750 was in the midst of a great economic and social transition; this was especially true of the region about the Clyde and in the Highlands. Yet evidence is not wanting that during the period from 1707, when "An Act for an Union of the Two Kingdoms of England and Scotland" (5 Anne, c. 8) was passed, to 1745 the country at large experienced a state of "extraordinary languor and debility." Trade was inconsiderable, agriculture in the most wretched state of neglect, and manufactures of little value. Further, the people were oppressed, abject, and dispirited; the nobles, poor, proud, and haughty.[1] It seems that, profoundly and beneficially as Scotland was affected by the Union, happy results were not immediately in evidence. The contrary was true, especially in certain sections of the country, such as Lanarkshire, where the beginnings of an industrial life were placed disastrously into direct competition with the more efficiently organized system that had been evolved in England.[2]

[1] William Alexander: *Notes and Sketches Illustrative of Northern Rural Life in Scotland in the Eighteenth Century* (Edinburgh, 1877), p. 101; see also William Cunningham: *The Growth of English Industry* (3rd edn., London, 1896–1903), II, 412–13; John Struthers: *A History of Scotland, from Union to . . . 1748* (2 vols., Glasgow, 1827–8); W. L. Mathieson: *Scotland and the Union . . . to 1747* (Glasgow, 1905) and *The Awakening of Scotland . . . 1747 to 1797* (Glasgow, 1910); and Vol. III of P. H. Brown's *History of Scotland* (Cambridge, 1909).

[2] "Most of the Scottish industries, except linen, were killed by English competition," affirmed Henry Hamilton with reference to the situation in Scotland after 1707; see his *The Industrial Revolution in Scotland* (Oxford, 1932), p. 3. For the effect of the Union upon the Newmills woollen industry near Haddington see Sir John Clapham: *A Concise*

Scotland was, nevertheless, producing some commodities for exportation in the first half of the century. Grain and flour were sent abroad in moderate quantities; [3] Scottish cloth, especially plaids, which were renowned throughout Europe for their colour and fineness, likewise found a ready sale, as did Aberdeen knit stockings, which were unsurpassed in quality and constituted a valuable export by 1750; further, linen, made in many parts of the Lowlands, was undoubtedly the most important textile produced and was especially esteemed in Virginia.[4] The salt of Scotland was considered better for the curing of fish than even that made in the great salt works at Shields in Yorkshire, and as a result there was a ready demand for it, especially in Norway, Germany, and the Baltic areas.[5]

Although the Scottish fisheries did not have great importance, they did enjoy one decided advantage over others, for the herring season began earlier in the waters off Scotland than in those to the south. Glasgow traders therefore could get their fish to Spain and Portugal before the English and the Dutch; likewise, those shipping from Dundee and Aberdeen could bring their catches to the markets of the Baltic earlier than could competitors operating farther south, thus commanding the top prices. In addition, very substantial quantities of salted salmon were exported. The shipment of coal into England, especially to London, was also a source of wealth by 1750.

It is true that the sheep and cattle of the Scottish Highlands were inferior in size and usually leaner than those of England; it was therefore necessary to drive them into the Lowlands to be fattened.[6] After fattening, most of them were sold in England, especially at

---

Economic History of Britain . . . to 1750 (Cambridge, 1949), p. 238, and especially G. P. Insh: *The Scottish Jacobite Movement* (Edinburgh, 1952), pp. 51–5.

[3] In 1749, 49,664.3¾ quarters of grain and flour were exported. See "An Account of the Quantity of Grain and Flour exported from Scotland from Xmas 1707 to January 5, 1766, Custom House, Edinburgh, January 16, 1767," P. R. O., Treas. 64. 274.

[4] *The Scots Magazine* (1750), XII, 550. In 1728 more than two million yards of linen were stamped for sale; in 1750, five and a half million yards; and in 1771, almost thirteen and a half million yards. See H. Hamilton: *op. cit.*, p. 6.

[5] The iron industry of Scotland existed on a modest scale before the middle of the eighteenth century, largely as a result of English capital and enterprise. But it was not until 1759 that the great Carron iron works were established. See *ibid.*, pp. 150–3. Coal also was mined and used in the production of salt. But it was not until after the middle of the eighteenth century that the Lanarkshire coal-field was opened up with the digging of canals.

[6] As was true of Wales, the Highland regions offered very fine summer pasturage but no fodder for winter. Cattle therefore had to be driven to market in the fall or face near starvation. See H. Hamilton: *op. cit.*, pp. 19–23.

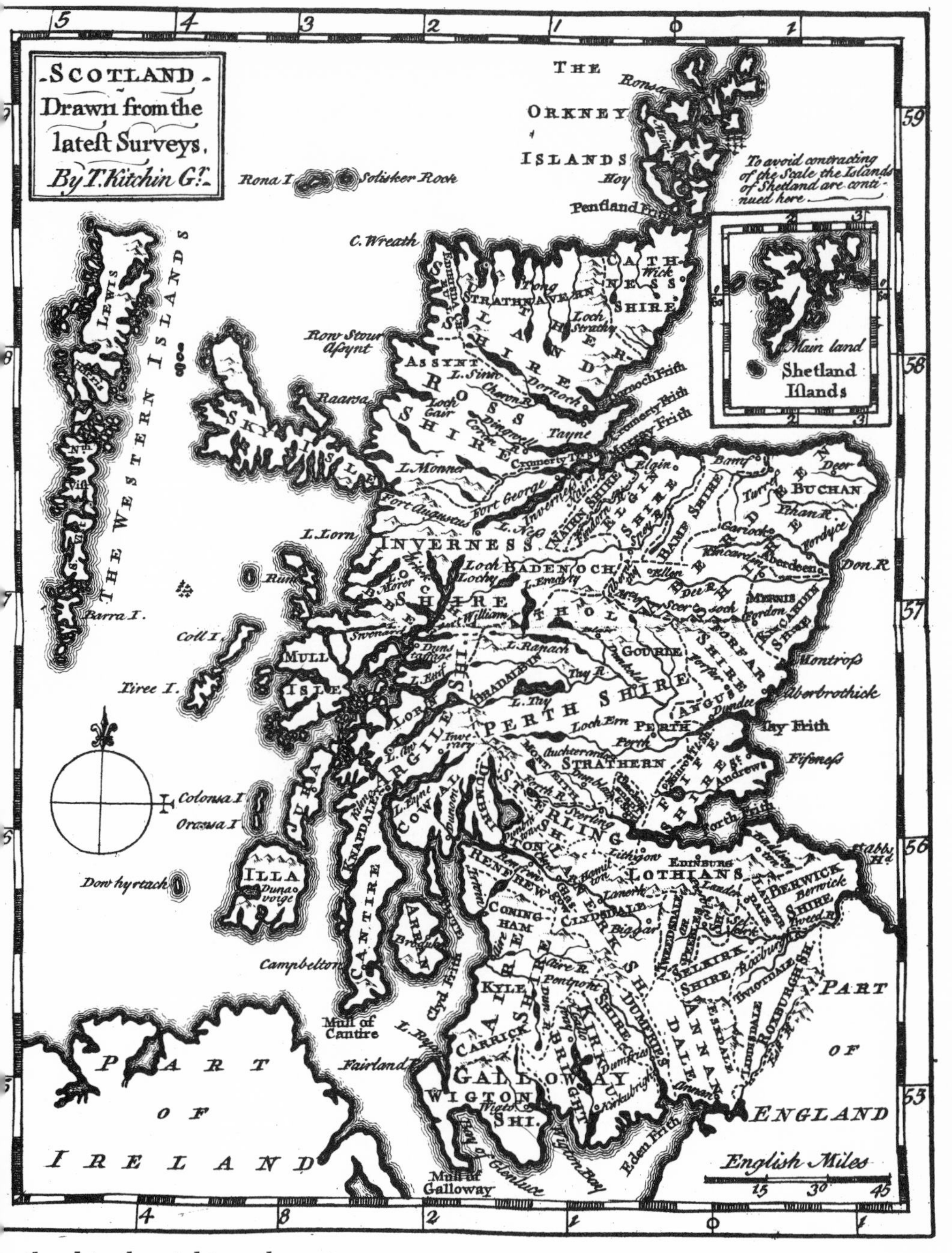

cotland in the eighteenth century.

(From T. Kitchin's *Geographia Scotiae: Being New and Correct Maps of all . . . Scotland,* 1756)

the great cattle fair at St. Faith's, where they brought substantial returns.

Thus, the frugal people of Scotland even before 1750 were helping substantially to supply the needs of other countries and, significantly, were not making great demands upon the world, with the exception of those products of North America, the West Indies, and Europe which were needed in the course of trade. In fact, in the early 1760's Scotland was the only country in Europe which without exception enjoyed favourable balances in its commercial relations with all other countries.[7]

It was stated at the beginning of this chapter that the region of the Clyde was in the midst of a great change in 1750, a change that was to make it one of the greatest industrial and commercial centres of the world. According to a report made in the year 1656, the total shipping of Glasgow consisted of twelve vessels of from 12 to 150 tons burden.[8] The town's chief export before the Union with England – an event that led to mob violence in Glasgow – apparently was herring and salmon. Even this was inconsiderable because the places with which Scotland traded principally lay to the east, which meant that the people of the towns of the east coast carried on practically all the commerce. But the Union, according to John Gibson, a Scottish merchant writing in the eighteenth century, brought about a decline of the commerce of eastern Scotland, while unexpectedly increasing that of the Clyde to an amazing degree.[9]

As soon as the treaty between England and Scotland was signed, Glasgow merchants, lacking vessels suitable for the American trade, proceeded to charter ships from Whitehaven. It has been asserted that it was not until about 1718 that the first vessel actually the property of Glasgow people sailed for the Chesapeake.[10] An account has survived of one of the earliest *legal* adventures of Glas-

---

[7] See D. Fenning and J. Collyer: *A New System of Geography* (London, 1765), II, 579.

[8] See the Report to the Right Hon. Commissioners for Appeals, November 20, 1656, in the *Literary Rambler*, IV, October 1872.

[9] John Gibson: *The History of Glasgow* (Glasgow, 1777), p. 205. According to a statement issued in 1752 at Edinburgh, the foreign trade before the Union was chiefly with France, Holland and the Baltic. The high English duties to which Scotland now became liable stopped the course of that trade and it required time before it would fall into another channel. See *Proposals for Carrying on Certain Public Works in the City of Edinburgh* (Edinburgh, 1752), p. 16.

[10] John Gibson: *op. cit.*, p. 207; see also H. G. Graham: *The Social Life of Scotland in the Eighteenth Century* (London, 1909), pp. 129–30.

gow merchants in the tobacco trade: a ship was loaded with goods and entrusted to a captain who knew nothing of keeping accounts, but was a man of great shrewdness. Upon his return he was asked how the adventure had succeeded; he could not tell, but threw upon the table a large stocking, called a "hogger," filled to the top with money.[11]

By 1735 the city is said to have had sixty-seven ships, some of which sailed to America; others to the West Indies, Gibraltar, the Straits, Holland, Stockholm, and Ireland; and the rest sailed in the coasting trade.[12] By 1750 the number could hardly have been much fewer than one hundred.[13]

To supply the cargoes for these ships local industries were stimulated, new manufactures introduced, the rhythm of the life of the town quickened. Master craftsmen – it appears from ordinances passed in the year 1746 at the request of the craft guilds of the shipwrights and the masons – were pushing their journeymen to a maximum of effort.[14]

---

[11] This delightful story is contained in the scrap-book of Dugald Bannatyne, an eighteenth-century merchant. See *Statistical Account of Scotland* (Edinburgh, 1845), VI, 228–31. In fact, Scotsmen had been greatly interested in the tobacco trade in the seventeenth century either as interlopers, or by taking up residence in England, or by buying tobacco at Whitehaven or Liverpool to sell to Holland or Sweden. See Theodora Keith: "Scottish Trade with the Plantations before 1707," *Scottish Historical Review*, VI, 32–48, and especially J. M. Price: "The Rise of Glasgow in the Chesapeake Tobacco Trade, 1707–1775," *William and Mary Quarterly*, 3rd ser., XI, 179–99, and T. C. Barker: "Smuggling in the Eighteenth Century: The Evidence of the Scottish Tobacco Trade," *Virginia Magazine of History and Biography*, LXI, 387–99, which indicates how expert Scottish merchants had become before the Union in the circumvention of the trade and navigation system with respect to tobacco imports.

[12] John Gibson, *op. cit.*, p. 209.

[13] The following shipping news for the last week in March 1750 as printed in the *Caledonia Mercury* of April 9, will indicate the importance of the commerce of the Clyde:

"Grennock, March 31. Sailed *The Mary*, Dundas, *The Boy*, Campbell, and *The Diligence*, Dunlop, all for Virginia with Bale goods; *The Meriam*, Tomlinson, for Jamaica with Herrings and Bale goods, *The Mary and Jean*, Gardner, for Bristol with Pitch and Tar, *The Friendship*, Peterson, for Virginia in Balast, *The Kingston*, Chrisholm, for St. Christopher with Bale goods and Herrings; *The John and Robert*, Craig, and the *Adventure*, Man, both for Rotterdam with tobacco, *The Nancy*, *Gray*, for Hamburg, and *The Blossom*, Craig, for Dunkirk, both with tobacco; *The Duke of Cumberland*, Brown, *The Molly*, Gray, and *The Bugle*, Fleming, all for Virginia with Bale goods; *The Loving Anna*, Kelly, for Norway with Tobacco; *The Sprightly*, Campbell, for Isley with Flaxseed, iron, etc."

[14] On March 19, 1746, the Burgh approved an act regulating the hours of employment of journeymen which provided that none should be hired except upon the basis of

Indeed, a splendid new burgh had come into existence by 1760. Richard Pocock, who toured the British Isles, noted in that year that two of Glasgow's streets measured nearly a mile in length, with other streets crossing at right angles. He described the houses – most of them four stories high and some five – as finely built of hewn stone, and he added that several merchants had "grand houses"; [15] John Gibson a few years later declared: "Every stranger is charmed with the appearance of Glasgow." [16]

With this newly acquired wealth came a change in the habits of the people. In the early part of the century the style of living was moderate and frugal. Among the wealthiest of citizens a home with more than one so-called "public room" was hardly to be found, and even this – the dining room – was seldom used except in the entertainment of guests, since the family usually ate in the bedroom of the master. "Their unpretending manner," declared Dugald Bannatyne, "is shown by the customary form of invitation, which was 'to eat an egg' with the host, and when they wished to indicate that one was not of their society they said 'that he had never cracked a hen's egg in their home.'" [17] This lack of display is further indicated by their manner of carrying on business. For example, a merchant engaged in the Virginia trade during the early days of this growing commerce, desiring to settle his accounts with those who had furnished goods for the voyage, would customarily invite his associates to a public house for a glass of wine – for which they themselves paid.[18]

About the year 1735 the first of the great mansions of the tobacco merchant princes was built; this was followed by others. "It was with a certain degree of reverence, and even of awe," wrote a contemporary in later years, "that in my boyish days, I contemplated the gorgeous mansions of these lordly merchants fenced in from the

---

the accustomed hours, which were from six in the morning till eight at night for shop-work and from eight in the morning to seven at night for house-work. See *Extracts from the Records of the Burgh of Glasgow* (eds. Sir James D. Marwick and Robert Renwick, 6 vols., Glasgow, 1908–14), IV, 224–6.

[15] Richard Pocock: *Tours in Scotland, 1747, 1750, 1760* (ed. D. W. Kemp, Edinburgh, 1887), pp. 49–52. For an account of housing in Glasgow see Marjorie Plant: *Domestic Life of Scotland in the Eighteenth Century* (Edinburgh, 1952), pp. 21–3.

[16] John Gibson: *op. cit.*, p. 132.

[17] From the scrap-book of Dugald Bannatyne in the *Statistical Account of Scotland* (ed. Sir John Sinclair, Edinburgh, 1791–9), VI, 228.

[18] *Ibid.*, see also H. G. Graham: *op. cit.*, pp. 133–5.

humble dwellings of the lower classes by their iron palisades and boundary walls and built upon a scale almost equal in strength to the castles of our ancient feudal barons."[19]

Extravagance of living and ostentation now made their appearance in Glasgow with frequent entertainments and heavy drinking. Finally, a group of the wealthier merchants – among them the Cuninghames, the Glassfords, the Houstouns, the Ritchies, and the Spierses – came to occupy a highly privileged position in the life of the town.[20] There was, in fact, a walk near the Merchants' House at the Cross of the Tolbooth where they alone might promenade in their long scarlet cloaks and bushy wigs, much to the envy of lesser folk.

It is said that four young men of talent and spirit were largely responsible for the rise of Glasgow to a position of first importance in the commercial world. They were William Cuninghame of Lainshaw, John Glassford of Douglastown, James Ritchie of Bushby, and Alexander Spiers of Elderslie. Spiers was the greatest of the tobacco importers. It was estimated that his house alone brought to Europe one twelfth of the entire amount secured from the Chesapeake region. John Glassford was also one of the world's greatest merchants. He is said to have owned in his own name twenty-five ships and their cargoes. Through the efforts of these and other merchants, the town, including Greenock and Port Glasgow, by 1771 was importing from America more than 46 million pounds of tobacco, from Ireland more than one million yards of linen cloth, from the West Indies more than 175,000 gallons of rum, and from Portugal more than 30,000 gallons of wine, together with less impressive totals of sugar, wool, salt, linen yarn, and Honduras logwood.[21] As for Glasgow's exports, most of the tobacco secured from the Chesapeake was sent

---

[19] "Reminiscences" in *Glasgow Past and Present* (Glasgow, 1856), III, 338.

[20] Glasgow overseas enterprise, it may be pointed out, took the form, as a rule, of companies or partnerships in the eighteenth century. The following were among the most important: John Glassford & Co., Glassford & Munro, Glassford, Gordon, Montcath & Co., Alexander Houstoun & Co., James Brown & Co., Finley, Hopkins & Co., William Cuninghame & Co., Cuninghame, Findlay & Co., and Cuninghame, Brown & Co. Although these companies competed with one another for business they were, in the words of J. M. Price (*William and Mary Quarterly*, 3rd ser., XI, 191), "closely associated by ties of joint interest and kinship."

[21] See J. M. Price: *William and Mary Quarterly*, 3rd ser., XI, 180, and John Gibson: *op. cit.*, pp. 213–39. Further details respecting the Glasgow tobacco trade are dealt with in the next volume of this series, in the chapter entitled "The Chesapeake Bay Staple."

to France, Holland, Germany, Scandinavia, and Ireland; the French government, which had established a monopoly, took almost one half of the total supply and much of the remainder went to Rotterdam. Boston took the Scottish glass and linen, as did Philadelphia and Virginia, the latter colony purchasing a million yards of linen in 1771; while to Dublin the town sold more than 100,000 gallons of West India rum.[22]

The River Clyde by the middle of the eighteenth century was therefore the scene of feverish activity. Its waters teemed with great and small craft; along its banks were extensive wharves; its shipyards were busy, and its warehouses crammed with the commodities of foreign lands. Such were the fruits of the enterprise of Glasgow's men and of the opportunities afforded by the Act of Union!

In the light of what has been said one need not wonder that the town had been hostile to Charles Edward and his claims in the recent Jacobite rebellion. It had everything to lose and nothing to gain from his program of disrupting the Union in case he were unable to secure the English throne for his father and himself. The cry "break up the Union and free Scotland," meaning the restoration of the Stuarts to the Scottish throne, might echo well enough in the Highland glens, but for Glasgow it would have been a disaster of the first magnitude, even in 1745.

In September of that year Charles appeared before the defenceless but unfriendly town and demanded £15,000 to protect it from his Highlanders, finally compromising, however, at £5,500. Upon his departure the inhabitants armed themselves with weapons secured from Edinburgh and sent off a force to the army opposing him. As a result of this hostile act he compelled the merchants to reclothe his army when he returned the following December. Glasgow's loyalty to the Crown and the Union was given special recognition by the British Parliament in 1749, when it granted the town £10,000 as reimbursement for what was extorted by the rebels.[23]

Although it occupied a place of great importance in the commercial life of the United Kingdom, Glasgow had to yield along other lines to the superior claims of Edinburgh. The latter, situated in the

---

[22] In 1771 Glasgow exported 558,237 pounds of glass, 1,503,872 pounds of wrought iron, 3,270,325 yards of linen cloth, 128,887 gallons of rum, and 43,890,709 pounds of tobacco, 21,280,000 pounds of the latter going to France. See Gibson: *op. cit.*

[23] *Extracts for the Records of the Burgh of Glasgow*, VI, 214–19, 236–9, 300–2.

heart of one of the most fertile sections of the Lowlands, was not only the capital city and the metropolis of Scotland, but was the chief center of that vigorous intellectual life to which reference will be made later in this chapter.[24]

Already the city was famed as a medical center. Its progressiveness, moreover, was indicated by the existence of numerous benevolent institutions, such as one for elderly couples and another for the relief of female orphans. A splendid royal infirmary had been built through the liberality of great numbers of people – even journeymen, masons and others engaged in its erection, contributed a portion of the labour. High Street continued by Canongate, from Holyrood Palace to the Castle, was known as the Royal Mile. It was considered in 1750 to be perhaps the world's finest thoroughfare, lined as it was with many splendid and impressive buildings, which were occupied by trade guilds and private individuals of distinction.

It was in Edinburgh, too, that each May the General Assembly of the Established Church of Scotland met in the Cathedral of St. Giles under the presidency of some man of distinguished station in life, who, as Lord Commissioner, represented the King. The city was planted upon the ridge of a hill which admitted of but one good street, and the narrow lanes leading from this were, because of their steepness, narrowness, and dirtiness, considered only as unavoidable nuisances. "Confined by the small compass of the walls," it was stated in 1752, "the houses stand more crowded than in any other town in Europe, and are built to a height that is almost incredible."[25]

Although Edinburgh possessed nothing like the commercial importance of Glasgow in 1750, there was a very great advance – especially after the crushing of the rebellion of 1745 – in the amount of shipping employed at Leith, which served the city as a port. This increase was doubtless brought about by the opening up of the West

---

[24] The standard work on Edinburgh in the eighteenth century is that by Hugo Arnot: *The History of Edinburgh . . .* (Edinburgh, 1788); see also W. Maitland: *History of Edinburgh* (Edinburgh, 1753); B. Chambers: *Tradition of Edinburgh* (Edinburgh, 1847); Michael Joyce: *Edinburgh: The Golden Age, 1769–1832* (London, 1951); and H. G. Graham: *The Social Life of Scotland in the Eighteenth Century* (pp. 110–21), a work already cited.

[25] *Proposals for Carrying on Certain Public Works in the City of Edinburgh* (Edinburgh, 1752). For an account of housing in Edinburgh see Marjorie Plant: *The Domestic Life of Scotland in the Eighteenth Century*, pp. 19–21. Many of the houses had as many as fourteen stories, housing the same number of families, one to a story.

India trade. In 1744 only 2,285 tons of shipping belonged to that place, whereas by 1752 the amount had increased to 5,703 tons.[26]

Indeed, the gradual commercial progress of the Lowlands not only about the Clyde, but to the east was evident by the middle of the eighteenth century. Two concrete examples of industrial advancement may also be noticed. The production of aqua-vitae jumped from 185,997 gallons during a seven-year period before 1745 to 723,150 gallons during a corresponding period before 1752; the amount of linen manufactured during a five-year period before 1732 was valued at only £662,938 sterling, whereas for a five-year period ending in 1751 it was valued at £1,607,608.[27] Since 1746, when the rebellion was suppressed, a most surprising revolution had, in fact, taken place in the trade, husbandry, and manufactures of the Lowlands. It was asserted that these activities "which had hitherto proceeded only by slow degrees, now began to advance with such a rapid and general progression, as almost exceeds the bounds of probability. They are no longer the detached efforts of Aberdeen, of Glasgow, of Dumfries, or any other single town but . . . the combined force of the whole nation which seems at length to be exerting itself." [28]

The spiritual life of Lowland Scotland, it need hardly be said, was dominated by Calvinistic doctrines. After the struggles of the sixteenth and seventeenth centuries, the Lowlanders had succeeded in establishing the Presbyterian Church as the national church. It was governed not by an episcopal hierarchy – as was the Anglican Church – but by a General Assembly. This body alone was competent to settle all questions fundamental to the Establishment. In maintaining uniformity and church discipline throughout the country it was assisted by thirteen provincial synods; below these were something over sixty presbyteries, which were responsible for the welfare of the individual kirks.[29]

---

[26] *Proposals for carrying on certain public works in . . . Edinburgh.*

[27] *Ibid.*

[28] *Ibid.*

[29] The Presbyterian clergymen were supported by tithes that had been fixed 120 years previous to 1750. At that earlier period it was provided that no clergyman's stipend should be below 800 marks or eight chalders of victuals — roughly 96 bushels. As calculated in the eighteenth century the minimum stipend was well below £40. See *The Scots Magazine* (1750), XII, 154–5. The chief work on the Church of Scotland for the period under consideration is John Cunningham's *The Church History of Scotland* . . . (2

The Scottish clergymen of the eighteenth century were educated and intellectual, even if narrow in their views, and, it may be said in passing, nowhere else did the great American theologian of the middle of the eighteenth century, Jonathan Edwards, find so sympathetic a hearing for his learned treatises as among the ministers of Scotland, who were of course in harmony with his Calvinistic teachings. Outside the Establishment were the Seceders, who had broken away largely over the issue of lay presentation to church livings — in opposition to the Moderate party — and who had something approaching a hundred meeting houses.[30] The Anglicans still were divided into those who would take the oaths and those who would not, that is, the nonjurors. As a group the nonjurors had shown much sympathy for the Young Pretender and were, as in England, under a cloud.[31] Finally, there were the Roman Catholics, who had their greatest strength in the Highlands, where some regions were almost solidly loyal to Rome.[32]

---

vols., Edinburgh, 1859, republished in 1882); see also *Annals of the General Assembly of the Church of Scotland from . . . 1739 to . . . 1766* (ed. Nathaniel Morren, 2 vols., Edinburgh, 1838–40).

[30] For the seceders see John McKerrow: *History of the Secession Church* (Edinburgh, 1848); see also [John Brown]: *An Historical Account of the Seceders . . .* (Edinburgh, 1766).

[31] According to an act passed in 1746 (19 Geo. II, c. 38, *Statutes at Large* [Eyre and Strahan], VI, 328–31), nonjuring pastors were prohibited from officiating in Episcopal meeting-houses in Scotland without duly qualifying themselves by securing the proper licenses from the Crown; those resorting to such a meeting-house were liable to six months' imprisonment for the first offence and for the second, transportation for life.

[32] It was asserted in 1753 that "in Moydart, Knoydart, Arisaig, Morar, Glengary, Braes of Lochaber, Glenroy, Strathglass, Strathdon," and in some other extensive regions of the Highlands, including many of the western islands, Catholic priests were still exercising great influence over the minds of the people, preaching "up to them indefeasible hereditary Right. . . . And the Youth in the within mentioned countries are very early byassed and corrupted in their Principles with Popish books, rebellious Songs, Pamphlets, Declarations and Manifestos put into their hands by these Priests." This, the writer declared, was the case despite the earnest endeavours of the Society for the Propagation of Christian Knowledge. "Popery is daily prevailing in the foresaid Places; The Number of Priests there is considerable . . . there is likewise a number of Papists' schools . . . tho' the Masters and Teachers of these schools have taken the oaths to the present government politically to disguise their Principles which they believe they may safely take because they can get absolution whenever they please to apply for it" (Gilbert MacPherson to the Duke of Newcastle, B. M., Add. Mss. 32731).

With reference to the Macdonalds, the Earl of Stair, writing at the end of the seventeenth century, declared: "That's the only popish clan in the Kingdom and it will be popular to take severe course with them" (*Papers Illustrative of the Political Condition of the Highlands of Scotland, from 1689 to 1696* [ed. J. MacConechy, Glasgow, 1845], p. 53).

The Scottish Roman Catholic priests, however, had been accused of deep complicity in the rebellion, and the attitude of the authorities toward them was consequently by no means tolerant.[33] These priests had previously been responsible not only for the spiritual welfare of their Highland Catholic communicants, but also for what education existed among them. An act passed in 1746 required an oath of allegiance to George II from those serving as chaplains and as teachers in the Highlands,[34] and many priests, because of their devotion to the Stuart cause, could not qualify and were consequently liable to arrest and imprisonment.[35] Numbers of them were either driven out or apprehended, leaving their charges without spiritual leaders and teachers. This presented an opportunity for Protestantism, and by the middle of the century the Scottish branch of the Society for Propagation of Christian Knowledge had taken up the work of weaning the Catholic Highlanders away from their old religious attachments. Teachers were placed in their midst, and in the late 1750's the Society was busy with the making of a translation of the New Testament into Gaelic, which the scholar Macfarlane was commissioned to carry through to completion.[36]

The people of the Highlands were, as a rule, poor, many of them indigent — for the glens were badly overpopulated — [37] yet they were

---

[33] "Had a letter from Lieut. Nicholson, from Stomney, acquainting me he had sent Torkell McLeod, a Popish priest, over on board the brig for being guilty of high treason. The prisoner, it seems, was drinking with a sargeant and three other men of Lieut. Nicholson's party when he made use of his treasonable expressions in saying the King was a rebel, and he could prove him so" (Capt. John Barlow, Island of Uist, to Headquarters, June 30, 1753, *Glasgow, Past and Present,* II, Appendix).

[34] 19 Geo. II, c. 39, and 20 Geo. II, c. 51, *Statutes at Large* (Eyre and Strahan) VI, 336–7, 391–2.

[35] For example, on August 13, 1754, General Bland's secretary transmitted a warrant to the commanding officer at Bernera "to convey the Popish Priest from Bernera to the Talbooth of Edinburgh" (Bland Letter Book, National Library). For the Catholic Church in Scotland in the eighteenth century see Volume IV of Alphons Bellesheim's *History of the Catholic Church in Scotland* (trans. D. O. H. Blair, Edinburgh, 1887–90).

[36] See the minutes of the Society for the Propagation of Christian Knowledge for March 23, 1758, Lang Manuscripts, University of Edinburgh. For the efforts to improve conditions in the Highlands during the period under consideration see the excellent article by John Mason: "Conditions in the Highlands after the 'Forty-five," *Scottish Historical Review,* XXVI, 134–46.

[37] In 1727 the Glasgow Highland Society was founded. Its members were either born in the Highlands or descended from those who were. The purpose was charitable and especially directed to the education of poor but worthy Highland boys so that they might be useful in church and state. See *Extracts from the Records of the Burgh of Glasgow,* VI, 332–6. Two years previous the Buchanan Society was founded in the same city

brave and hardy and famed for their loyalty to the clan and chieftain. They were accustomed to live on the simplest of fare, such as milk, curds, whey, a little oatmeal with occasional oat and barley cakes, or porridge, sometimes with a piece of salt meat in it. Pocock declared that they went on foot with wonderful expedition, using the Highland trot, and that in Sutherlandshire the post travelled from Dornoch to Edinburgh and back, a total distance of two hundred miles, in four days and seemed to make nothing of it.[38] Their manner of life, of course, produced these qualities of ruggedness and simplicity. For example, during the summer those with cattle went into the high mountains where they lived in crude huts called "shealings."

At the same time it appears that many of the Highlanders lacked industry. An officer on duty in Northern Scotland, a Captain Johnston, declared that they were so lazy that rather than repair their houses – though they had wood for the cutting and bracken to thatch the roofs for the pulling – they allowed them to remain open to wind and water even during the winter; nor would they take the trouble to plant a few greens or roots to give themselves a supply of food.[39] On the other hand, Pocock stressed the fact that they were, in general, extremely hospitable, charitable, civil, polite, and sensible.[40]

Under the extraordinarily complicated feudal-patriarchal system

---

for the care of the poor of that name and especially for furnishing boys the necessary apprentice fee of one hundred marks. See *ibid.*, VI, 375–7.

In 1745 it was estimated that there were 57,000 wandering beggars in the Highlands living either by charity or robbery. See Edward Burt: *Letters from a Gentleman in the North of Scotland* (London, 1818), II, 355–6. This does not take into account as many more who were indigent and required help, living "in a state of semi-starvation and habitual idleness" (Audrey Cunningham, *The Loyal Clans* [Cambridge, 1932] p. 467).

[38] Richard Pocock: *Tours in Scotland, 1747, 1750, 1760*, pp. 127–8. For the Highlands in the middle of the eighteenth century see *The Highlands of Scotland in 1750 from Manuscript 104 in the King's Library, British Museum* (ed. Andrew Lang, Edinburgh, 1898). For a description of the types of dwellings in the Highlands see Marjorie Plant: *The Domestic Life of Scotland in the Eighteenth Century*, pp. 29–31.

[39] See Johnston's report of November 12, 1752, *Glasgow, Past and Present*, II, Appendix; see also H. G. Graham's *The Social Life in Scotland in the Eighteenth Century* (2 vols., London, 1899), I, 184 and 225. A contrary view respecting the indolence of the Highlanders was expressed by Edward Burt, writing in the days of William III. See his *Letters from a Gentleman in the North of Scotland* (2 vols., London, 1754, II, pp. 20–1), in which he shows the eagerness of men to be profitably employed. Some clans were more enterprising than others, especially the Campbells.

[40] *Op. cit.*, p. 128.

that prevailed into the middle of the century, the lands of the Highlands were largely in control of a few lords, heads of great clans as a rule, having superiorities and heritable jurisdictions and in receipt of bonds of "manrent" from lesser chieftains.[41] The latter in many cases were rewarded with lucrative "wadset-rights" to Highland lands,[42] and in turn leased these to gentlemen of the clan, frequently cadets of their families, who were commonly known as "good men" or "tacksmen."[43] The tacksmen in turn released the same lands to the actual tenants, who ordinarily held only small plots of ground, an average it appears, of about twenty-six acres each.[44] On every large estate there were the so-called "kindly tenants," who for one reason or another enjoyed a privileged position both in law and practice, frequently holding their lands at a nominal rental and transmitting this favour to heirs and assignees.[45] They might have important holdings or be among the class of cottars who occupied but an acre or two and who acted as day labourers;[46] the latter would annually pay for their rental, on the average, some five shillings and tenpence in English money, three pounds of butter, a little oatmeal, and three sixteenths of a sheep, with the landlord possessing a lien on the grain crop, which he might seize for arrears of rent. A few specific examples will serve to illustrate the question of land tenure in the Highlands in the year 1750.

On the lands formerly belonging to James Drummond of Perth in the Parish of Mulhill there were 144 tenants, who in 1748 paid an average rental of £50 Scots money, or £4.3.4 sterling. Many of these people owed, in addition, services and rent in kind, such as butter, wedder (that is, the meat of a wether, or mutton), meal, bear (a coarse barley), swine, cheese, capons, geese, and other types

---

[41] For example, the Duke of Argyll, head of the Campbell clan, enjoyed bonds of manrent obtained by his ancestors from the heads of the Camerons and the Macleans, which made the latter, in theory, legally dependent upon the former.

[42] Gilbert MacPherson to the Duke of Newcastle, May 1, 1753, B. M., Add. Mss. 32731.

[43] See A. McKerral: "The Tacksman and His Holding in the South-West Highlands," *Scottish Historical Review*, XXVI, 10–25; see also Audrey Cunningham: *op. cit.*, p. 446, and H. G. Graham: *op. cit.*, p. 224.

[44] William Alexander: *Notes and Sketches Illustrative of Northern Rural Life in the Eighteenth Century* (Edinburgh, 1877), p. 13.

[45] George Douglas Campbell, eighth Duke of Argyll: *Scotland as it was and is* (New York, 1887), p. 13.

[46] William Alexander: *op. cit.*, pp. 14–16; see also the article by John Mason: "Conditions in the Highlands after the 'Forty-five," *Scottish Historical Review*, XXV, 134–46.

of poultry; some were also liable to winter cattle, some to cart peat, coals, and bark, and some to aid in shearing. In addition, these Drummond tenants paid the whole of the King's cess, or land tax, and the King's mail, and carried other public burdens.[47] The 106 tenants on his lands of Cargill and the Barony of Stobhall paid rentals that average £39 Scots money, or some £3.6.4 sterling, and were also liable for kain (that is, small produce), such as oats, horse corn, lambs, meat, bear, capons, wedder, eggs, linen cloth, and straw.[48] Rents on one estate in Fife varied from £62.13.4 to 13*s.* 4*d.* Scots money.[49] The following terms of rental may be considered typical: "For one-eighth part of the Five Merkland of Balleichtriel £28 money rent; one "F" [Firkin] of Bear, one "F" [Firkin] of Horse Corn, 2 sheep, 2 lambs and 12 days service of one man." [50] From this it is evident that the rentals, considering the quality of the soil and the limited uses to which it could be put, were not light.[51]

The ancient methods of agricultural economy survived in most of Scotland well into the eighteenth century.[52] The land, as a rule, was not enclosed. Each husbandman would furnish two of the eight oxen required to draw the great plough. The four who contributed oxen

---

[47] See "Forfeited Estates Papers," Public Record Office, Treas. 64. 245.

[48] *Ibid.* These tenancies were designated as either "pendicles" or "ploughs" or "rooms." The "pendicle" was apt to be smaller than the "plough" or "room"; for example, one tenant held "half a plough and a pendicle thereof." There was also "penny land" "half-penny land," and "farthing land" in the rent rolls of Perth, Aberdeen, and Inverness (*ibid.*, Treas. 64. 249). Some of the "rooms" rented for more than £100 Scots money on the estate of one Oliphant in Perthshire, while none of the "pendicles" equalled £50 (*ibid.*, Treas. 64. 248 (20) b). The "plough," cultivated by four tenants as a rule, was equal to 104 acres. See Arthur Birnie: "Some Aberdeenshire Leases of the Eighteenth Century," *Economic History Review*, IV, 465.

[49] "Forfeited Estates Papers," P.R.O., Treas. 64. 248 (14) b.

[50] *Ibid.*, Treas. 64. 248 (40) a. "In some instances a merk may be less than an acre; in others perhaps equal to two acres. Every merk again consists of so much arable ground, and of another part which is only fit for pasturage" (Stair's *Institutes* [Edinburgh, 1830], p. 299).

[51] Frequently the so-called "bondage work" required of the tenants in addition to payments was an important item. Take, for example, the requirement of "6 hands for the peat moss, 4 hooks a day in harvest, 4 horses a day in mucking, 4 horses a day in harrows, 2 long arrages yearly, 2 servants for pulling up the fauld dykes yearly" (Arthur Birnie: *op. cit.*, IV, 466).

[52] H. Hamilton: *op. cit.*, pp. 13–36. William Alexander affirms that up to the close of the eighteenth century, with a few exceptions, the old modes of tillage were in universal use, in spite of the efforts of agricultural reformers who, for example, as early as 1723 organized the Society of Improvers in the Knowledge of Agriculture in Scotland. See his *Notes and Sketches of Northern Rural Life*, p. 24; see also the article by Arthur Birnie "Ridge-Cultivation in Scotland," *Scottish Historical Review*, XXIII, 194–211.

for the same plough had lands – at least in the earlier part of the century – lying adjacent. Under this "runrig," or alternate strip system, the total holdings of these tenants, called a "plough," might be somewhat more than one hundred acres, but frequently was much less as a result of population pressure on the estates. The lands were planted with oats and barley.

Wheat was rarely cultivated in Scotland outside the Lowlands, where it was grown successfully and profitably, especially in the region of Midlothian. It appears that potatoes were first experimented with at Kilsyth in 1739, but the general cultivation of them in Scotland did not come for about twenty years. It is said that in the early part of the century nine tenths of the corn produced in the country was raised within five miles of the coast.[53] Indeed, communication by land up to the period of the Rebellion of 1745 – despite the previous efforts of the government at road construction – was generally so difficult that carts were little used in most places; only one or two could be found in the average Highland parish. All accounts left by travellers seem to agree that the civilization of the more remote sections of Scotland was of a most primitive type.

All that has been said serves not only to indicate the isolation of the groups living within the fastnesses of their mountain glens, but helps to explain the continued vitality, in spite of the superimposition of feudal institutions often in conflict with it, of the patriarchal form of government – a form that by the middle of the eighteenth century had disappeared from almost every other part of Europe. The authority and will of the chief was still, as of old, ordinarily sufficient to determine for the clan the gravest issues of peace and war.

Thus, in 1715 the Camerons, the Macdonalds, the Macleans, the Glenmoriston Grants, the Farquharsons, the Atholl Highlanders, the Robertsons of Strowan, the Gordons, the Breadalbane Campbells, the Mackintoshes, the Drummonds, the Mackenzies, the Macleods, the Macphersons, the Macdougalls joined the revolt of the Earl of Mar in favour of the Old Pretender as a result of the decisions of their leaders. In 1745, when the Young Pretender, Charles Edward, appeared, Cameron of Lochiel, Macdonald of Keppoch, Macdonald of Clanranald, Macdonald of Glengarry, Macdonald of Glencoe, and Stewart of Ardsheal agreed to bring out their men; these were later

---

[53] William Alexander: *op. cit.*, pp. 19, 101.

joined by the men of Atholl, by the Mackenzies of Shian, the Macphersons of Cluny, the Mackinnons, the Ogilvies, the Gordons, the Farquharsons, the Frasers, the Macleods, and the Grants of Glenmoriston. However, the Campbells, the Monroes, the Macdougalls, the Macleans, the Macdonalds of Sleat – the most powerful of the Macdonald clans – in the main either hung back and remained quiet or, as did the Campbells under Archibald, third Duke of Argyll, rallied strongly to the aid of the government.[54]

The Highlands in 1750 were under military police. Although the rising in favour of the Young Pretender had been crushed on the bloody field of Culloden in 1746, much bitterness and restlessness survived the disaster. This was caused not only by the merciless methods taken by the Duke of Cumberland in stamping out the rebellion, but also the provisional attainting of its leaders by Parliament, the consequent setting up of special courts of oyer and terminer for the estates,[55] as well as by legislation against both the wearing by civilians of the Highland dress and the carrying or concealing of arms.[56] In fact, the British government had determined to do away once and for all time with the old order of things in the Highlands by breaking up the feudal and clan systems and by reforming the manners of the people.

It appears that the inhabitants of the mountains in northern Scot-

---

[54] That the Highlanders, however, on rare occasions refused blind obedience and took sides opposed to that of their chief is well attested. For an excellent example involving the Atholl Highlanders at the time of the Revolution see James Browne: *History of the Highlands and of the Highland Clans* . . . (Glasgow, 1843), IV, 406.

[55] By the provisional act of attainder of 1746, 43 Scottish noblemen and gentlemen were mentioned by name as liable to attaint unless they submitted before July 13 of that year (19 Geo. II, c. 26). This was followed by the erection of certain special courts of oyer and terminer which gave sentences of attaint against the supporters of Charles Edward; that in and for the County of Surrey of July 22 attainted 51, that of September 26 in and for the County of Cumberland and held at Carlisle attainted 76, that of October 7 and in and for the County of York attainted 70 (P.R.O., Treas. 64. 243). Finally, to bring the Highlands into thorough subjection an act was passed in 1748 relating to high treason and misprision of treason and for the trial of these crimes. This not only abrogated the necessity of taking down in writing the evidence used to incriminate those suspected, but made it lawful to imprison people in the King's forts. See 21 Geo. II, c. 19, *Statutes at Large* (Eyre and Strahan), VI, 405–7.

[56] 19 Geo. II, c. 39, and 21 Geo. II, c. 34, *ibid.*, VI, 332–8, 415–21. The problem of the Highland dress after legislation forbidding the use of the tartan is discussed by Marjorie Plant in "Clothes and the Eighteenth Century Scot," *Scottish Historical Review*, XXVII, 1–24.

land, secure in their inaccessible glens, had never as a group submitted to the laws that were supposed to govern all Scots. For more than a century before the Union attempts had been made, but with indifferent success, to bring the dwellers of these wild regions into submission. It is therefore easy to understand how many, if not most, Highlanders well into the eighteenth century apparently considered themselves all but independent of the rest of Scotland. As a result those most advantageously situated for the purpose – such as the broken clan of Macgregors and the Macdonalds of Glencoe – forced the Lowlanders along the Highland border to pay a tribute called "black meal" for the protection of their cattle.[57]

It must be pointed out that, quite beyond the characteristic lawlessness referred to above, the majority of the Highland chiefs did not consider the Hanoverians their real and lawful rulers. This was even true of some who remained quiet during the risings. To them the new royal line was at best made up of successful usurpers who had not the slightest interest in the welfare of the Highlands, where the great feudal jurisdictions were supported in the face of growing resentment, it appears, on the part of dependent chieftains and their followers.[58] For this reason, among others, the Highlanders were deeply involved in intrigues to place the Stuarts on the throne; they joined the futile risings by the Earl of Mar in 1715 and in 1719, when the Spaniards flung into the Highlands a handful of troops. This was followed by the program of pacification instituted by General George Wade, which included not only attempts to disarm the in-

---

[57] "Memorial touching the Bill now pending for disarming the Highlands" among the Newcastle Papers of this period (B. M., Add. Mss. 33049, folios 253–61) declared: "The colour made use of in demanding and receiving this contribution was this. The Chief or some leading man of the nearest clan, touched as he said by the sufferings of his neighbours in the Low Countries, would gladly furnish a standing Guard, called a Watch, of 50 or 100 armed men as the case might require, continually to Guard the Passes by which goods robbed must be carried off by the Robbers, provided the district whose Cattle he undertook to defend would enable him to maintain such a force by paying him a certain annual contribution, and the Tribute being paid, he restrained his own Robbers, and actually defended against the inroads of his neighbors. Thus, the Highlanders found their account in being armed, and shared in the fruit of their neighbors' industry without labour, for this Tribute called Black Meal became universal, and was paid without exception by all the Lowlands, bordering on the armed Highlands."

[58] Audrey Cunningham: *The Loyal Clans*, pp. 507–8. In this connection see *Superiorities Display'd, or Scotland's Grievance by reason of the Slavish Dependence of the People upon their Great Men; upon account of Holdings or Tenures of their Lands, and of the Many and the Hereditary Jurisdictions over Them* (Edinburgh, 1746).

habitants, but a comprehensive program of road-building and fort- and barracks-construction.[59]

Substantial as the achievements of Wade in some respects were, much still remained to be accomplished among many of the clans whose ways of living were described as little less than barbarous by most of the writers of the period, and whose outlook on life was still in most respects certainly antinational, if not antisocial. Therefore, the Lowlanders and the English Whigs united in demanding a policy of "thorough" to bring about a fundamental change.[60]

Among the Highlanders there were, it should be understood, those elements in Northern Scotland which were not included in the above censure. Some of the clans, such as the Mackays, had remained loyal not only in 1715 and in 1719, but also in 1745, and were even used effectively by the government in the work of subjugating their neighbours after Culloden, especially by enlisting them in the regular service, as were those embodied in Loudoun's Highland companies. However, the disaffected elements controlled the heart of the Highlands. In the words of Bishop Sherlock:

> "The Country of the Rebellious Clans is a vast tract . . . now forfeited to the Crown & lying contiguous in the heart of the Highlands, it divides the well affected Clans, some of them lying to the North and some to the South: The forfeited country being put under a proper Governm^{t} supported by a sufficient military force, w^{d} not only be kept quiet itself, and in time civilized; but it w^{d} be a barrier agst the *now* well affected Clans should they ever alter their mind; to wch there wants nothing but an alteration in the affection of the Chief. . . ." [61]

In the light of this situation it is not surprising that after the suppression of the rebellion a sweeping program of reconstruction of the government of the Highlands should have been drawn up by the ministry.

Under the title "Heads of Regulations in Scotland," the program

---

[59] For a careful analysis of the problem as it existed in the 1740's see the "Memorial touching the Bill now depending for disarming the Highlands," B. M., Add. Mss. 33049, folios 253–61.

[60] Thomas Wentworth's policy in Ireland before 1639 is most commonly designated as the rule of "thorough." The Scottish Highland policy after 1746 may be compared to it.

[61] Bishop Sherlock to Edward Weston, June 10, 1746, C. F. Weston Underwood Papers, Hist. Mss. Com. *10th Report*, p. 291.

outlined the following: 1. The abolition of all private jurisdictions, such as regalities. 2. The holding of circuit courts twice a year in the chief towns of the counties. 3. The granting to all vassals having from their lands an income of £40 sterling per annum the privilege of purchasing the same from their superior so as to hold them directly from the Crown. 4. The making of the criminal processes in Scotland less expensive and more simple, as in England. 5. The placing of military forces in every rebellious district of the Highlands. 6. The sending of riding judges into each district every two months. 7. The strict enforcement of the acts referred to previously forbidding the wearing of the Highland dress. 8. The transporting to the plantations for life of common people engaged in the late rebellion. 9. The regranting of the lands of the proprietors of Lochaber and "other thievish districts" to suitable persons. 10. The compelling of all government officials to qualify for the service.[62]

In Scotland there had survived, as has been suggested, the system of heritable jurisdictions which made some of the chiefs and chieftains of the clans doubly powerful. These jurisdictions were in the form of so-called regalities, justiciaries, shrievalties, stewardies, bailieries, constabularies, clerkships, and offices of forester and coroner. The most important was that of Hereditary High Justiciary, possessed by only one family — that of Argyll — the jurisdiction of which comprehended the whole of Argyllshire, a number of the Western Islands, and several other districts on the mainland belonging to or depending upon that family. This office carried with it high and low justice in all criminal matters and stood in equality with the High Court of Justiciary at Edinburgh. It was limited only by the ability of the Crown to pardon those meeting with its condemnation.

Of hardly less importance in Scotland were other hereditary jurisdictions. The lords of regality could, by means of their bailies, judge capital and other criminal causes as well as practically all civil questions, subject only to an appeal to the Court of Sessions and Court of Justiciary. This was also true of the jurisdiction exercised by hereditary stewards and hereditary bailieries; the hereditary sheriffs had a sheriff's court within the county and possessed great influence in the election of members of Parliament. The power enjoyed by many of those with heritable jurisdictions may be appreciated when one considers that a barony, of which there were many in Scotland,

---

[62] "Heads of Regulations in Scotland," B. M., Add. Mss. 33049, folio 230.

might have an extent of from thirty to sixty miles, including not only the lands belonging directly to the lord, but also those of which he was the feudal superior.[63]

In fact, one is hardly guilty of exaggeration in saying that the hereditary offices distributed among the great families, great landowners, and certain heads of clans endowed them with almost the last increment of power over their dependents. In effect these offices gave them legally the power of life and death – through the grant of "pit and gallows" – over the great majority of Highlanders.

While it is true that Scots convicted by those possessing hereditary jurisdictions were theoretically entitled to an appeal to the King's courts at Edinburgh, in practice a poor man could take no such step because at this period the cost of an appeal in Scotland was all but prohibitive – far beyond that, for example, in the English courts. The following statement prepared in connection with the jurisdiction bill illustrates the point:

> "Whoever considers the powers that the Proprietors of Hereditary jurisdictions have over poor people, who live within their respective Territories, must perceive the bad use that may be made which these powers naturally give and the very great difference there is between the security which the body of the Commons of England have, from that which is enjoyed by the body of the Commons of Scotland." [64]

A bill was therefore framed to do away with most of these jurisdictions – with the exception of that of High Constable of Scotland – vesting the powers in the King's courts; further, the courts of barony were reduced by it to the consideration of minor cases. This bill was presented to Parliament by Lord Chancellor Hardwicke early in the year 1747. Its progress through the houses was aided by the fact that it comprehended the making of due compensation to those who would lose these powers – if they had been loyal to the House of Hanover.

There was, nevertheless, a certain amount of determined opposition on the part of some individuals who insisted that Parliament had solemnly pledged itself to refrain from any such action by accepting

---

[63] For a careful analysis of these jurisdictions see a "Paper of Amendments & Additions proposed to be made to the Scots' Jurisdiction Bill, with some Reasons for the Amendments," B. M., Add. Mss. 33049; see also G. P. Insh: *The Scottish Jacobite Movement* . . . (Edinburgh, 1952), pp. 153–64.

[64] "Paper of Amendments & Additions proposed . . . to the Scots' Jurisdiction Bill," B. M., Add. Mss. 33049.

the Articles of Union, the twentieth of which read: "That all heritable Offices, Superiorities, heritable Jurisdictions, Offices for Life, and Jurisdictions for Life, be reserved to the Owners thereof as Rights of Property, in the same manner as they are now enjoyed by the Laws of *Scotland*, notwithstanding this Treaty." Opponents further urged that the bill would give the Crown a dangerous increase of power by placing under the absolute direction of the Crown the election of the forty-five commoners of Scotland to Parliament. Under the bill, it was argued, the Crown would control Scottish elections through the sheriffs, who with or without hereditary jurisdiction were vastly more powerful within the counties of Scotland than in England. The Duke of Argyll, however, was one of the most powerful supporters of this measure. This must have made a deep impression, since no one stood to lose as much as he himself.[65] The bill therefore passed over all protests, with a provision allowing the courts to determine in each case the value of the claims for the jurisdictions thus assumed by the Crown.[66]

The year following, the old system of ward-holding, whereby the Scottish nobility had been able to enrich itself at the expense of the rightful owner of property, was also changed to that of "blanch" or "feu" holding, which allowed those in temporary possession of such property only nominal benefits.[67]

By means such as have been described the once great powers of the old Scottish lords and chiefs were finally swept away. One last measure in the year 1752 crowned the efforts of Parliament in this direction. Out of the vast confiscations that took place in the late 1740's the estates of Simon, Lord Lovat; George, Earl of Cromarty; John Drummond; Archibald Macdonald; and Alexander Robertson of Strowan were now, as the result of a bill introduced by the Lord Advocate of Scotland, annexed to the Crown inalienably for the pur-

---

[65] In addition to his dukedom, Argyll enjoyed other great honours and offices, among them Marquess of Kintyre; Heritable Justice-General of the Sheriffdom of Argyll, the Western Isles, and elsewhere; Heritable Sheriff, Lord Lieutenant, and Commitiar of the said isles; Admiral within the same bounds, and Heritable Master of the Household in Scotland.

[66] See *Parliamentary History* (Hansard), XIV, 2–57, 149. The act in question is 20 Geo. II, c. 43. Parliament ultimately paid £152,237.15.4 for the rights, although almost £600,000 had been the total of the demands. This involved some 161 claimants and some 250 heritable or life jurisdictions. See C. S. Terry: "Jacobitism and the Union," *Cambridge Modern History*, VI, 118–19.

[67] P.R.O. (England), Treas. 17. 15, pp. 498–505; 20 Geo. II, c. 50.

pose of applying the rents and profits thereof for the better civilizing and improving of the Highlands.[68]

As may be imagined, it was no easy thing to administer effectively for the Crown the forfeited estates in many regions where local influences still supported those who had been previously identified with the overlordship of these lands. Before the act referred to above, for example, Major-General Churchill, in command in the Highlands, was impelled to address repeated communications to the Duke of Newcastle regarding the forfeited estates of the Camerons, the Macdonalds, and the Stewarts, which he claimed were still possessed by Jacobites, most of whom had been in the late rebellion. He asserted that those who were well affected to His Majesty were turned out and vengeance threatened against any who should bid for the Crownlands against the friends of the former proprietors.[69]

The unsettled state of affairs in the country was, moreover, manifested in other ways. Even as late as 1753 it was reported from Inveraray that the Highlanders, despite the efforts to disarm them, had in reserve a sufficient number of guns, blunderbusses, side-pistols, swords, dirks, and targets concealed in dry mosses and below the thatch or the outcoverings of their houses to arm eight thousand men, and that many followers of the Pretender – who had escaped with him to France and had entered the service of the French King – were back in Scotland rounding up recruits. The names of some twenty-three of these officers were given by an informer together with their present rank; he further declared that with the aid of the Catholic priests they were busy stirring up the people into a rebellious attitude, telling them that they were slaves and assuring them that the kings of France, Spain, and Prussia would now come to the support of their real King.[70]

---

[68] 25 Geo. II, c. 41; see also *Parliamentary History* (Hansard), XIV, 1235–71. For the repeal of this law, whereby the King was impowered to grant forfeited estates to loyal heirs of the former proprietors, see 24 Geo. III, Sess. 2, c. 57. The student is again referred to the article by John Mason: "Conditions in the Highlands at the 'Forty-five," *Scottish Historical Review*, XXVI, 134–46, for a study of attempts to improve conditions on the forfeited estates.

[69] See letter of John West of the Treasury Board to the Barons of the Exchequer in Scotland, July 10, 1751, P.R.O., Treas. 17.15.

[70] Gilbert MacPherson of Inveraray to the Duke of Newcastle, May 1, 1753, B. M., Add. Mss. 32731. The French military service made a great appeal to Highlanders, many of whom received commissions. However, to enlist in foreign service without a license was a capital offence. So long as England and France were at peace, little interest seems to have been taken in this aspect of Scottish affairs, but with the beginning of hostilities

In order to bring the Highlands to a state of order, suppress the notorious and ancient evil of thieving – especially the driving of cattle – [71] prevent and punish enlistments in the French service, and discourage the activities of the Catholic priests, garrisons were scattered soon after Culloden in all the glens where disorder or disloyalty had prevailed. Royal Commissioners, appointed to manage the forfeited estates, also carried on the program General Wade instituted earlier in the century, and performed, among other duties, the really useful service of making new roads and straightening old ones. This not only served immediate police purposes, but, taken together with the earlier efforts in this direction, ultimately had a profound influence on the whole Highland region by bringing it out of its isolation.

The correspondence among the officers in charge of the various military districts and that between their commanding officers, Major-Generals Bland and Churchill, throws much light on conditions in northern Scotland in the middle of the century. It sets forth in the blunt language of soldiers the observations of men who were in daily contact with the people. A few items taken from the garrison reports will indicate the rather barbarous conditions found in certain regions.

Captain John Beckwith, writing from Loch Arisaig on June 11, 1752, declared that an extensive district on the northeast side of the Loch was entirely inhabited by thieves. "I may say entirely," he affirmed, "for there is but one man whose villainy is in dispute." Captain Walter Johnston, announcing from Invercomrie on June 21 of the same year the capture of a Cameron, "a notorious plunderer," stated further that he had received word that "two other Camerons with Sergeant Moore and one McIntire" were driving cattle by the pass called Glengolairdy and that the sheriff substitute of Perth-

military detachments became very active in rounding up these local recruiting officers or those in the enemy service who returned into these regions. See the Letter Book of General Bland for the Year 1756, National Library, Edinburgh.

[71] On July 4, 1750, Lieutenant James Hartley, writing from Ruthven to military headquarters, declared that the gentlemen of Badenoch had made up a list of the thieves living in that region. They agreed to find sufficient evidence against the most notorious either to transport them to the New World or to hang them. As to those guilty of second degree villainies, they covenanted not to harbour or to permit them to settle upon their domains. Finally, with respect to a third group, they agreed to receive them upon proper security of good character and conduct for three years to come (*ibid.*).

For an excellent account of the Highland cattle thieves of the eighteenth century see the Introduction to Sir Walter Scott's *Rob Roy*.

shire had desired his assistance in apprehending twelve thieves. In the same letter Johnston declared that he was seeking evidence against Commissary Besset, "who by the confession of Alexander Breck . . . appears to have been art and part concerned with and a resetter and harbourer of most of the Lochrannoch thieves these many years past." On November 14 he further wrote: "It is a truth well known that the inhabitants of Rannoch in general but especially upon the estate of the late Strowan are notorious thieves. . . . It is no great wonder. . . . Since from the earliest settlement of the Camerons, McDonalds, Kennedys, McGrigors, Robertsons, which are the prevailing names here, thieves have always been protected by men of estates who kept them to join in every rebellion." [72]

It also appears that thieves swarmed even on some of the great estates of those who, outwardly at least, were seeking to suppress them. The Isle of Mull, for example, two thirds of which was said to be the property of the Duke of Argyll, was a nest of thieves, and the officers who sought to bring them to justice at Inveraray found to their dismay that they were liberated upon the verbal assurances of some of their patrons.[73]

The military detachments, however, were a powerful weapon, and their presence was gradually becoming decisive, especially as they were furnished with information by men in governmental pay who

---

[72] "Selections from Reports addressed by Military Officers stationed in the Highlands," for the years 1752 and 1753, *Glasgow Past and Present*, II, Appendix, pp. 599–631.

[73] See letter from General Humphrey Bland to the Duke of Argyll, September 29, 1754, Bland Letter Book, National Library, Edinburgh. In this body of correspondence there is a letter written by William Alston to George Douglas on October 3, 1754, which indicates the grimness that characterized the officials who had determined to stamp out thieving. It relates the case of an alleged thief known as the Piper, who refused to accept the sentence of banishment of the previous circuit court and instead was "running his letters against the Procurator Fiscal in order to force on his trial." Two others were doing the same. "If their scheme succeeds to operate their Liberation without a trial it will be attended with the worst consequences . . . the only Remedy is that these Rogues be tried at Inverness . . . before the Session set down . . . but it is incumbent upon you and indeed you cannot do a more important service to the government than instantly to find evidence to hang that Dog of a Piper; when you take the Precognition put such of the witnesses under Bail whom you suspect may withdraw themselves and whenever your proof is compleat either to hang or Banish him send it to Mr. —— and a copy to the L[d]. Advocate. You must attend to this that the hanging one who forces on his own trial in this manner will effectively prevent all evil practices for the future, so that your hanging the Piper now by his own folly, is become the most important service you can do for the state" (*ibid.*).

associated with their cattle-driving neighbours.[74] It was especially fatal to the morale of the clans when members were busy bringing to justice their fellow clansmen. No association, indeed, can survive the breakdown of loyalty to it.[75]

Out of the prevailing confusion, a new order gradually appeared.[76] By 1756 General Humphrey Bland was able to write that the laws were observed in every corner of the Highlands and that every man was secure in his property. The most notorious offenders, he declared, had been hanged; others had been transported; still others put on board the fleet; many had fled the Kingdom; and the enlistment of several in the army had been winked at.[77] One was now able, he affirmed, to travel in safety from one end of the Highlands to the other; only here and there did the tartan appear among the common people, nor were arms in the hands of civilians.

Thus by the middle of the eighteenth century the old Highlands of romance, of adventure, of cattle-driving, of chiefs and clans and fiery crosses, were, through the processes just described, rapidly disappearing never to return. Soon Lowlanders were moving in to set up new communities and to introduce handicrafts.

Nevertheless, the aftermath of the subjugation of the Highlands and its transformation is not a pleasing picture. Despite the eventual restoration of the forfeited estates [78] and the return from abroad of exiled leaders, the population suffered indescribable miseries in the course of the changing economic order. This brought with it, among other things, a new attitude toward land and the profits therefrom even on the part of old proprietors formerly bound by the ancient Scottish institution of "kindness," and resulted in the virtual de-

---

[74] See General Bland to George Ross, July 31, 1756, for a statement regarding the effectiveness of the use of special funds for this purpose (*ibid.*).

[75] In the bringing to justice of one Rory Macdonald, a Captain Macdonald (McDonald) was active, for which he found himself loaded with indignities; it appears he was, however, strongly supported by the government. See James Stuart to Captain McDonald of Knock, September 11, 1754, *ibid.*

[76] By September 1754, the Regiment of Buffs quartered at Glasgow was ready to return to England. It was given out that the military patrols could now be withdrawn from Inveraray, Tarbet, Saltcoats, Irwin, Ballantrae, Stranraer, and Dumfries, although General Skelton's regiment was dispersed in those parts of the Highlands which still demanded attention. See General Bland to the Commissioners of the Customs, September 23, 1754, *ibid.* On the islands, especially, there was still difficulty not only with thieving, but also with violations of the laws regarding the wearing of the national dress and the carrying and secreting of arms. See General Bland to Captain Salt, August 26, 1754, *ibid.*

[77] *Ibid.*

[78] See 24 Geo. III, c. 57.

population of great regions — known in Scottish history as "the Clearances" — for ultimate utilization in sheep-raising.[79] In connection with this it was sought, but rather unsuccessfully, to convert herdsmen and agricultural labourers into fishermen and artisans by directing the landless Highlanders to coastal towns and villages, a process that resulted in the emigration and expatriation of thousands from their beloved glens.[80]

Because of the splendid record in Europe of the Highland "Black Watch"[81] the British government increasingly sought the services of this martial race of men in the armed forces. Under Pitt, in the course of the Great War for the Empire, numerous Highland regiments were raised and played their part with great distinction under their natural leaders. What is more, these regiments, recruited from the various clans and officered by men who had in many instances been traditionally hostile to one another in the old and bitter clan feuds, not only served to obliterate the old hatreds in face of the common enemy, but also in the course of times created in the Highlands a truly remarkable spirit of loyalty to the Hanoverian line.[82]

An important aspect of Scottish eighteenth-century history must now be emphasized before concluding this chapter. This has been fittingly called the Scottish renaissance of learning — a renaissance that had as centres the four universities of Edinburgh, Glasgow, St. Andrews, and Aberdeen. By 1750 it was exerting a powerful

---

[79] Factors other than the spread of sheep-raising, such as the increase in population and the increase in large cattle farms, were responsible for depopulation of areas in Scotland, see H. Hamilton: *op. cit.*, pp. 69–73.

[80] See I. C. C. Graham: *Colonists from Scotland: Emigration to North America, 1707–1783* (Ithaca, N. Y., 1956), pp. 1–104; see also Margaret I. Adams: "The Highland Emigration of 1770," and her "Eighteenth Century Highland Landlords and the Poverty Problem," *Scottish Historical Review*, XVI, 280–93, XIX, 1–20, 161–79; Audrey Cunningham: *op. cit.*, Chap. XII; and Alexander Mackenzie: *History of the Highland Clearances: or, a strange return by the Highland Chiefs for the fidelity of the Clans* (Inverness, 1881), pp. xi, xii, 22–3, 26, 47, 61, 88, 112–13, 146.

With respect to the encouragement of the fisheries along the Highland coasts, Josiah Tucker in his *A Brief Essay on the Advantages and Disadvantages which respectively attend France and Great Britain with regard to Trade* (London, 1750, pp. 115–16) put forth the proposal that a fishery on the northern coast of Scotland be subsidized by the granting to the undertakers a double premium on herring caught and cured there and exported to foreign markets. He saw great advantages attending such an enterprise.

[81] The Black Watch, made up of loyal Highlanders, came into existence in 1729; in 1751 its name was changed to 42nd Regiment or Highland Regiment; later the earlier name was restored.

[82] For a history of the Highland regiments down to 1812, see James Browne: *A History of the Highlands* (Glasgow, 1843), IV, 133–384.

influence on the intellectual life of Scotland and far beyond its borders.

The causes for this mid-eighteenth-century cultural flowering in Lowland Scotland are still obscure, but emphasis has recently been placed by scholars on the influence of the Scottish bar, members of which, because of the close relationship of Scottish law with Roman law, studied abroad, especially at Utrecht and Leyden, and brought home many challenging ideas in the fields of philosophical and historical thought.[83] It is equally clear that ideas of the possibility of human betterment and enlargement of human understanding, ideas that found expression in the British Isles in the seventeenth century and the early part of the eighteenth – in such organizations as the Royal Society of London for Improving Natural Knowledge and in groups for social amelioration, including the movement to spread education among the masses – must have had an influence on Scottish thought and aspiration.[84] This must have been true also of the closer contacts with London that came about with the establishment of the British Parliament as a result of the Union of England and Scotland in 1707.[85] Manifestly, there developed an urge among Scots during the early part of the eighteenth century to widen their horizons and with this widening to cast off evidence of provincialism.[86]

This brings us to the activities of Francis Hutcheson (1694–1746), author of *A System of Moral Philosophy,* who, it appears, played a leading role in bringing about the Scottish renaissance. Of Presbyterian Ayrshire stock, he was born in Ireland and educated at the University of Glasgow, where in 1729 he was to be called to occupy the chair of moral philosophy.[87] His lectures created great interest and stimulated such students as Adam Smith (1722–1790),[88] who in 1751 was appointed to the chair of logic at Glasgow before he was transferred to that of moral philosophy. From his labours emerged

---

[83] See John Clive and Bernard Bailyn: "England's Cultural Provinces: Scotland and America," *William and Mary Quarterly,* 3rd ser., XI, 200–13.

[84] See John Mason: "Scottish Charity Schools of the Eighteenth Century," *Scottish Historical Review,* XXXIII, 1–13.

[85] See Clive and Bailyn: *op. cit.,* XI, 208.

[86] This applied not only to thought, but to manner of speech as well.

[87] For his life see W. R. Scott: *Francis Hutcheson* (Cambridge, 1900); Hutcheson's *A System of Moral Philosophy* (2 vols., Glasgow, 1755) appeared posthumously.

[88] Dugald Stewart (1753–1828), whose "Account of the Life and writings of Adam Smith" is embodied in *The Collected Works of Dugald Stewart* (Edinburgh, 1854–1860), X, 82, *passim,* stresses the influence on Smith of Hutcheson's lectures.

in 1776 the classic *Wealth of Nations,* challenging the preconceptions of the seventeenth-century state system of mercantilism. David Hume (1711–1776) as a young scholar also looked up to Hutcheson and corresponded with him.[89] But Hume, who greatly surpassed him in profundity of thought, was later to challenge many of his basic conceptions.[90] Not without reason has Hume been called "the acutest thinker in Great Britain in the eighteenth century, and the most qualified interpreter of its intellectual tendencies."[91] In fact, his writings, embodying a thorough-going skepticism, help to bridge the gap between such seventeenth-century writings as Robert Boyle's *Origin of Forms and Qualities* (1666), and John Ray's *The Wisdom of God Manifested in the Works of the Creation* (1691) and such nineteenth-century writings as Charles Darwin's *Origin of Species* (1859) and Herbert Spencer's *First Principles* (1862).

Another Scot whose achievements during this period won him a reputation that was far from local was Principal William Robertson (1721–1793) of Edinburgh University. He, in fact, has been ranked as one "of the four great historians of the eighteenth century," in company with Voltaire, Hume, and Gibbon.[92] In 1759 appeared his *History of Scotland,* which went into many editions; in 1769, his *Reign of the Emperor Charles the Fifth* in three volumes; and in 1777, his *History of America* in two volumes. Rising above mere narration and description in his histories, he stressed, whenever the opportunity afforded, the importance of general ideas with respect to political and social developments. The name of Henry Home, Lord Kames (1696–1782), philosopher, jurist, and friend of Benjamin Franklin, must also be included among the names of those who contributed to this Scottish renaissance. His *Essays on the Principles of Morality and Natural Religion* appeared in 1751, followed in 1761

[89] For excerpts from this correspondence see W. R. Scott: *op. cit.,* pp. 115–27. For Hutcheson's influence upon other men and for an exposition of his views on human rights and colonial liberty see the excellent paper by Professor Caroline Robbins: " 'When Is It That Colonies May Turn Independent': An Analysis of the Environment and Politics of Francis Hutcheson (1694–1746)," *William and Mary Quarterly,* 3rd ser., XI, 214–51.

[90] The most complete edition of Hume's writings is *Essays and Treatises on Several Subjects* (4 vols., London, 1777).

[91] See the article on Hume by Leslie Stephen in the *Dictionary of National Biography.*

[92] See J. B. Black: *The Art of History, A Study of Four Great Historians of the Eighteenth Century* (London, 1926). For a life of Robertson by a contemporary see that by Dugald Stewart, published in London in 1801.

by his *Introduction to the Art of Thinking;* in 1762 he gave the public his *Elements of Criticism* in three volumes and in 1774, his *Sketches of the History Man* in two volumes. In addition to these works he produced many writings relating to the history of Scottish law.[93]

Nor is the list of illustrious Scots of the eighteenth century limited to writers. There was the noted chemist Joseph Black (1728–1799), who although born in Bordeaux and reared in Belfast, was of Scottish ancestry. Black lectured at both Glasgow and Edinburgh; his paper on "Experiments upon Magnesia alba, Quicklime and other Alkaline Substances," presented before the Philosophical Society of Edinburgh in 1755, helped to lay the foundations of quantitative analysis and was placed second only to Newton's paper on "Optics" as a model of philosophical investigation; likewise, his *Lectures,* published soon after his death,[94] were used throughout the scholarly world. Indeed, a contemporary, the French chemist the Comte de Fourcroy (1755–1809), praised him as the "Nestor of the chemistry of the eighteenth century."[95]

Closely associated with Black at Glasgow University for some time from 1757 was young James Watt (1736–1819), who served in the capacity of mathematical instrument maker. Under the encouragement given by Black and others Watt began his career as an inventor. Out of his scientific experiments in the properties of steam and in closely related fields came a series of important inventions which resulted in his improved steam engine. But he did not stop there, for he made other valuable contributions in the fields of chemistry and mechanics and showed himself to be a man of great scientific learning.

There must also be mentioned James Ferguson (1710–1776), the astronomer and mechanical genius whose *Astronomy Explained on Sir Isaac Newton's Principles* appeared in London in 1756 and be-

---

[93] See A. F. Tytler, Lord Woodhouselee: *Memoirs of the life and Writings of the Honourable Henry Home of Kames* (2 vols., Edinburgh, 1807), which contains letters written by Franklin, Hume, and others to Lord Kames.

[94] *Lectures on the Elements of Chemistry* . . . (ed. J. Robison, 2 vols., Edinburgh, 1803), in which is included a life of Black.

[95] See article on Joseph Black, which quotes from Hoefer's *Histoire de la Chemie* (vol. II, p. 353), *Dictionary of National Biography*; see also a recent very important study of Black's early career by Henry Guerlac in *Isis* (vol. 48, pp. 124–51) under the title "Joseph Black and Fixed Air: A Bicentenary Retrospective, with Some New or Little Known Material" that corrects some statements in the *Dictionary*.

came the standard treatise in this field; James Gibbs (1682–1754), the architect of many English churches and that architectural masterpiece, the Radcliffe Library at Oxford; and Robert Adam (1728–1792), also an architect, who with his brothers constructed the famous Adelphi Terrace in London and who also was a master of the interior decoration of homes.

As some of these Scots were closely associated with England in their work, their achievements have also been mentioned in the chapter of this volume on "Social and Antisocial Forces." Over and beyond their effect on eighteenth-century English culture was their influence on the British colonies, especially with respect to higher education. James Blair (1653–1743), who was educated at the University of Edinburgh, was the chief founder of William and Mary College as well as its president up to the time of his death; William Smith (1727–1803), who held a degree from the University of Aberdeen, was the first Provost of the College, Academy, and Charitable School of Philadelphia, later to become the University of Pennsylvania; and John Witherspoon (1723–1794), a graduate of the University of Edinburgh and a noted Scottish Presbyterian divine, became president of the College of New Jersey at Princeton in 1768. Further, as a result of the efforts of two Pennsylvania medical students trained at Edinburgh, John Morgan and William Shippen, the first American school of medicine was established by the College of Philadelphia in 1765. The two became the first professors in this school and were shortly afterwards joined by two other Pennsylvanians, Adam Kuhn and Benjamin Rush, both likewise trained at Edinburgh, to round out the medical faculty.[96] But enough has been said to indicate how proper it is to stress the existence in Lowland Scotland by 1750 of an extraordinarily vigorous and fruitful burst of intellectual energy, the like of which the country had never before experienced.

If both the Lowlands and the Highlands of Scotland were in the process of great transformations, the same cannot be said of Ireland. We must now turn to a consideration of some of the problems created by conditions peculiar to this country which set it apart from the rest of the British Isles.

---

[96] See G. S. Pryde: *The Scottish Universities and the Colleges of America* (Glasgow, 1957), pp. 10–39.

CHAPTER VIII

Native Hibernians and Transplanted Britons

THE IRISH by the middle of the eighteenth century were beginning to emerge from some of the gloom of the conquest period of the two preceding centuries, a gloom almost as intense as that which had overshadowed the English in the eleventh and twelfth centuries in the course of the Norman Conquest. Conditions, however, were still far from satisfactory from the point of view of the great masses, who were principally agriculturists, or who, if they were not, at least lived on the land. Ireland presented in 1750 great contrasts of wealth and poverty. "Should a foreigner," declared a writer in 1740, in the midst of the great famine, "see the great Flocks of Sheep and Herds of Cattle which cover our Land and the Rich among us parading in foreign Silks and living sumptuously, he must needs imagine that all the rest of our People are well fed and clothed, but he will soon be convinced of the contrary when he finds such Numbers so naked and starving, and that Wool, Beef and Butter, which should be the Portion of the Poor are sent abroad to purchase Luxuries for the Rich."[1] "I live there, my lord, in the County of Tipperary, in a county abounding in Pasture," wrote a gentleman in 1741, "where vast tracts of land are held by *single* Persons, where not only Farmers, but Gentlemen Keep from three to six, or seven, nay eight thousand acres in their own Hands, stocked for the most part with Sheep without any Inhabitants but Herdsmen and Shepherds, a few, a very few cottiers to do the necessary

1 *Essays and Observations on Trade*, published by a Society of Gentlemen in Dublin (Dublin, 1740), p. 15.

Drudgery or rather Slavery about their Houses." [2] "I have already noticed," declared another in 1746, "that this County [Waterford] abounds with Cattle, which are increased more of late than ever, numbers having converted large Tracts of Arable Land into Pasture by which means several Villages have been deserted by their inhabitants." [3] Such was the picture of rural Munster in the middle of the eighteenth century!

Many of the cultivators who had formerly occupied lands that at this period were given over to grazing had been impelled when the lands were enclosed to betake themselves to inferior soils in the mountains. There they secured small farms and turned to raising potatoes and a little oats with which to maintain themselves and their families. All went well for a time, but in the early 1740's two successive winters brought severe freezes that destroyed the chief dependence, the potato crop, and left most of these poor people in desperate circumstances. Deserting their miserable habitations to descend into lower regions, these hill dwellers wandered about helpless and exposed, begging and thieving. Unfortunately, corn was scarce and dear in the parts to which they came, and after a time the charity of most of the farmers was exhausted.[4] The result was stark tragedy.

It was estimated that one third of the cottiers of Munster died of plague and starvation during this famine. "Multitudes," declared an eyewitness,

> "have perished and are daily perishing under Hedges and Ditches, some by Fever, some by Fluxes, and some through downright cruel want, in the utmost agony of Despair. I have seen the Labourer en-

---

[2] *A letter from a Country Gentleman in the Province of Munster to His Grace the Lord Primate of All Ireland. Written at Cashel, May 25, 1741* (Dublin, 1741).

[3] *The Ancient and Present State of the County and City of Waterford* (Dublin, 1746), p. 282.

[4] "Is it really just to expect that the Provinces of Leinster and Ulster should support the Poor of the Province of Munster, while the Gentlemen and Farmers of Munster, . . . who hold such vast tracts of Land in their own Hands under Stock, contribute little or nothing to their Relief though they engross so great a share of the Land and Riches of the whole Kingdom? Do they not at the time of Scarcity, *generally* suffer their own few tenants and Cottars to perish for Want: In so much that 'tis much to be feared, if People die for three months to come in such Numbers as they have done for three months past, there will not be Labourers enough found to bring in and save the next Harvest? I say, generally, for his Grace, the Archbishop of Cashel, not only employs but feeds hundreds daily at his Door, together with Mr. Damer, and some few Others" (*A Letter . . . to His Grace the Lord Primate of All Ireland* [Dublin, 1741]).

"A New and Accurate Map of the Kingdom of Ireland from late Surveys" [1750].

(New York Public Library, Division of Maps)

> deavouring to work at his Spade, but fainting for want of food and forced to quit it, I have seen the aged Father eating Grass like a Beast, and in the Anguish of his soul wishing for his Dissolution. I have seen the helpless Orphan exposed on the Dunghill and none to take him in for fear of Infection, And I have seen the hungry Infant sucking at the Breast of the already expired Parent." [5]

An unforgettable picture of human woe!

The disaster of the early 1740's was caused not only by unusual climatic conditions, but also by certain tendencies in rural economy which are clearly brought out in the preceding statements: the tendency on the part of owners or lessees of lands in southern Ireland to turn their rich arable acres into sheep walks and cattle pastures, thus freeing themselves of all responsibility for the welfare of those who previously had occupied them; the habit of the cultivators of this region most improvidently to place their chief dependence for a livelihood on the potato, at the same time showing a sense of attachment to Ireland so strong, in fact, that when the lands they had formerly possessed were enclosed, they preferred a most precarious existence on the mountainsides of their native country to expatriation and a new life.[6]

Why did Irish landowners prefer cattle and pastures to cultivators and cornfields?

"I have often wondered," queried Robert Molesworth earlier in the eighteenth century,

> "how it comes to pass that we should be so long a time, and so unusually Ignorant of the *English* manner of managing our Tillage and lands as we now are; or if we formerly knew them how we came to fall off from that Knowledge and the Practice of it to such a degree, that the English tenants who pay double the Rent to their Landlords for their acres (which are much shorter than *Irish* Acres) are able

[5] *Ibid.* Scotland in the early part of the eighteenth century was overwhelmed by a tragedy of almost equal proportions because of the failure of crops to mature.

[6] It is true that many thousands of native Irish had left the island earlier in the eighteenth century, especially for France; enlistment in the military service of that country was still going on in 1750; but it does not appear that at the latter date this service was being accepted by large numbers. Those who were going to the Continent were in most instances unattached young men — the native Irish families were still bound to the soil. See *The Scots Magazine* (1750), XII, 151. There was, however, a steady movement of unattached native Irishmen to Newfoundland, but the number that went in any one year was small; more were sent to the colonies after being convicted of crimes and after the judges had commuted their capital penalties to transportation.

notwithstanding to supply us with Corn at a moderate Price, over and above the incidental charges of Freight, Porterage, etc. and the hazard of the Seas, whilst we are often starving, though our soil if rightly managed does not come behind the best in *Britain,* take one with another?"

The answer to this query he finds to be in the difference in industry and skill between the English and the Irish,

> "for we see that an *English* Farmer on a small Holding (sometimes not exceeding twenty Acres) shall live clean and comfortably, cloath himself, Wife, Children, and Family decently, eat warm victuals once every day, if not oftener, pay his Rent punctually, whilst the condition of the Irish Farmer on *a large Farm* is the very reverse of all this. Whoever makes a step into *Cheshire* shall be convinced of the truth as soon as he puts his foot on shore."

He then continues to analyze the problem presented to the Irish landlord:

> "I know nothing is more commonly said, than *Give your Tenant a good Bargain, Set him a long Lease, or a Lease of Lives, and you prevent these Mischiefs; He will Build, Plant, Improve, Live Neatly, and surrender your Farm at the expiration of his time in good Condition.* This may sometimes prove true, but I know by sad experience that none of these encouragements are sufficient unless your tenant be both an understanding man in the way of Husbandry and a diligent honest Man; so that it seems necessary to enforce by Laws such a Course of Husbandry, as shall constrain others of a contrary Disposition, to thrive and live Comfortably whether they will or no, and at the same time provide that the Landlord receives no Damage by the ill treatment of his Land. I have known some Tenants starve on half the Rent which others have grown rich upon!" [7]

It is undoubtedly true that the average Irish tenant of this period was neither very sober nor very industrious. Every holy day he sought to make a day of idleness and intemperance, and in order to carry on farming and other operations it appeared necessary to fix the holy days which were to be observed by labourers and servants.[8]

---

[7] Robert, Viscount Molesworth: *Some Considerations for the Promoting of Agriculture and Employing the Poor* (Dublin, 1723), pp. 4–6.

[8] 7 Wm. III, c. 14, *The Statutes at Large, Passed in the Parliament held in Ireland: from the Third Year of Edward II, A. D.* 1310, *to the Twenty Sixth Year of George III, A. D.* 1786 inclusive, published by Authority (13 vols., Dublin, 1786), III, 286–8; cited hereafter as *Irish Statutes.*

"And this restraint is most necessary," declared Sir Richard Cox in a charge that he delivered to the grand jury at Bandon-Bridge in 1740 – a charge that was not particularly complimentary to the native Irish. "For," he continued, "there is not in the whole World a more superstitious or a more lazy people than *Irish* papists.[9] The number of Days they are allowed by this Law to rest, are Eighty-six in the year; and yet it is a Grievance they loudly complain of, that they are not permitted to add as many more." He then concluded: "I need not tell you, that Industry is the Support of Society, and that this Nation more often feels the want of it, than any other Country, except Spain, that we know. Idleness is not the Vice of Protestants." [10]

In other words, landlords, whether they were native Irish or transplanted Britons, were confronted continuously by the problem of tenants who lacked the zeal, whether justifiably so or not, to cultivate the land that they had rented. Unless conditions were quite satisfactory to them, these tenants were inclined, especially if unattached, to wander away from their holdings as did their Scottish Highland kinsmen, to become sturdy beggars. These able-bodied tramps, not to be confused with the legitimate objects of mercy, swarmed the roads of Ireland in the 1740's, and many not content to ask alms "swaggered and bullied the poor Inhabitants to a compliance with their Demands for Diet and Lodging." [11] According to Judge Cox, "the miserable cottages of the greater Part of the Housekeepers are always liable to the Resentment of these." [12]

The tenant problem was undoubtedly complicated by the fact that lands had become more valuable in Ireland with the development of the foreign trade of the island in the course of the eighteenth century. It appears that new price levels for commodities had been established, and as a result, there was an inevitable tendency for leases to rise in value following a universal economic trend. Molesworth reasoned in this fashion regarding the advance of rentals:

---

[9] Dr. George O'Brien in his *The Economic History of Ireland in the Eighteenth Century* (Dublin, 1918), gives great attention to combatting this common charge that the native Irish were lazy.

[10] Sir Richard Cox: *A Charge Delivered to the Grand Jury at Bandon-Bridge, January 17, 1740* (Dublin, 1741).

[11] *Ibid.*

[12] *Ibid.*

"For the Tenant must not imagine the Landlord wrongs him by demanding an increase of Rent proportionable to the current rate of the product of his Farm. If every Barrel of Bread-Corn, Drink-Corn, or Horse-Corn, if Wine, Flesh, Fish, and all other necessaries for House-Keeping, stand the Landlord in double now, to what it did thirty or forty years ago, then the Landlord puts no hardship on his Tenant if he asks double the old Rent and if he gets it, 'Tis plain the Landlord is not a farthing the Richer. I have known many good old Tenants complain and cry out at their Landlords unjustly and in a humour throw up their Farms, rather than comply with such a demand, when another able Tenant has taken it, perhaps at treble the old Rent, then have I seen the old Tenant repent his own oversight and non-complyance, when it has been too late to remedy it." [13]

There is, however, a point beyond which a rental cannot be pushed and remain an economic rent. This is brought out in a communication of 1762 relative to the agrarian outbreaks that occurred in Munster in that year:

"Some landlords in Munster," affirmed the writer,

"have set their lands to cottiers far above their value, and to lighten their burden, allowed commonage [14] to their tenants by way of recompense; afterwards in spite of all equity, contrary to all compacts, the landlords enclosed these commons, and precluded their unhappy tenants from the only means of making their bargains tolerable. . . .

"It is not uncommon in Munster to charge from 4 to 5 guineas per acre for potato-ground; but we shall suppose the price but four guineas, that is, ninety-one shillings; the daily wage of labourers is four pence per day; there are three hundred and sixty-five Days in the year of which fifty-two are Sunday, and suppose but thirteen holidays, the remainder is but three hundred working days, the wages for which is an hundred shillings, that is, nine shillings above the price of their land; [of] which five shillings are paid for the tythe; and two for hearth money; and the remaining two go toward the rent of their cabins. What is left? Nothing—And, out of this nothing they are to buy seed for their garden, salt for their potatoes and rags for themselves, their wives and children. It must be observed that in calculating I have mentioned three hundred working days, though it is known, from the greater number of holidays ob-

[13] *Some Considerations for the Promoting of Agriculture and Employing the Poor*, pp. 7–8.

[14] This is the right of pasturage for their live-stock on the general grazing lands of the estate.

served in that part of the Kingdom than in any other, from the number of wet and broken days, joined with the natural laziness of the people, there are not above two hundred days, for which they are paid– What an aggravation does this make in the account? And will the best crop of potatoes enable them to maintain a family, often six or eight persons, under the difficulties we have mentioned?" [15]

There has survived a statement which follows of the actual charges that the agricultural labourer was obliged to meet in the 1780's which is so illuminating that it is well to present it at this point, although it must be kept in mind that rentals undoubtedly had advanced over those of the period under consideration:

"The rates paid by the Cottagers in Ireland, particularly in the southern and western counties, for rents, dues, etc. will surprise the reader; they appear almost improbable. The following statement was made on an average amongst several thousands of these people:

Rent per annum for cottage		£2. 5.6
Expense of rent for potatoes		–.18.–
For grass		£2. –.–
Turf		–.11.4½
Hay		–.15.–
Corn grinding		–.10.–
Tax on one hearth		– 2.–
Tythes for potatoes		– 3.3
Tythes for Corn		– 1.–
Tythes for Turf		– 1.7½
Tythes for Hay		– 3.3
Tythes for poultry		– –.8
Small dues		– 5.5
		7.17.1
His wages in summer	£3. 4.9	
His wages in winter	2.11.18	
		5.16.7
Deficiency in earning behind expenditures		£2. 0.6

"This deficiency he is left to his own industry to make good at the time the iron-handed Squire does not want his service." [16]

[15] "An Inquiry into the Cause of the Outrages Committed by the Levellers or White-boys in the Province of Munster," *Dublin Magazine*, April 1762, reprinted in *A Candid Inquiry into the Causes and Motives of the Late Riots in the Province of Munster* (London, 1766).

[16] *A Congratulatory Address to His Majesty from the Peasants of Ireland* (Dublin, 1786), p. 16.

To study these figures intelligently it would of course be necessary to ascertain the value of the commodities that with effective labour could be raised upon the land thus rented, taking into account the time required of the cottager to secure by day wages or otherwise the amount necessary for payment of the rent to his landlord. The problem, moreover, of comparing land rents in Ireland with those in Great Britain is especially complicated by the fact that native Irish families, unlike those of Lowland Scotland, Wales, and England, were not inclined to turn to handicrafts to supplement the family income. It seems to be true that Irish rentals and public dues were lower than similar rentals and exactions in Great Britain. But the earning capacity of the Irish was much less. In Great Britain, outside of the Highlands, the entire family of a small land-tenant customarily worked from dawn until dusk, caring for the fields, spinning and weaving, or otherwise occupied gainfully. Such industry, as a rule, was not to be found among the native Irish. Women and children seldom worked, and the men only by fits and starts.

In 1744 the rentals in southern Ireland seem characteristically to have run from between £1 and £2 an acre. This is indicated by the numerous advertisements for leases of larger units of land containing the rental value of the smaller allotments, although some of these undoubtedly had a higher value. Take, for example, the lands of William Wall of Coolna Mucky in County Waterford, which lay principally in and about Carrick-on-Suir in County Tipperary: Timothy Neal was renting 6 acres "with a good house" with a lease for 31 years from March 1739 at a yearly rental of £6.12.3; Gregory Fitzpatrick, 13.01 acres at a yearly rental of £10.18.7; James Escontt, 30 acres with a lease for three lives from March 1732 at a yearly rental of £18.09; and Patrick Ryan, 22 acres, out of lease, set at will at a yearly rental of £16.18.[17]

Some of the rentals are larger than these and presuppose either the subleasing or the grazing of the lands. John Jephson was the tenant of "the lands of Ballynagranach," 145 acres, with lease of 3 lives renewable forever, paying 5 guineas on the renewal of each life and at a yearly rental of £72.11. The tenant of this land had a profit rent of £40 yearly by it. Sir John Osborne had "part of the lands of Newtown Annex, 130 acres. Lease for 3 Lives yet in Being. Yearly

---

[17] See *Pue's Occurrences* for January 1 and 15, 1745.

rents £101."[18] The rentals in County Limerick corresponded to those above.[19]

In northern Ireland, in the region of the Protestant settlements, the rentals were apparently somewhat lower because the lands were of less value. For example, on the estate of Viscount Dungannon in County Down, his agent, one A. Hill, Esq., rented to John McCullough 52 acres, 3 roods, and 4 perches for his own life and that of his two sons, and a grandson; the lease was dated November 1754, and called for a yearly rental of £17, fees of 8/6, and duties of £1.1.6.[20]

A study of the Dungannon rent roll for the year 1766 discloses the fact that the average rental brought in somewhat under £9 per annum. In a list of 114 of these rentals, 82 were for parcels of land less than twenty-four acres in extent. Of the latter, 17 were for units of between ten and fifteen acres and 27 for those of less than ten acres. Of the parcels over twenty-four acres in extent, 21 were for units containing between twenty-five and fifty acres; 10 for units between fifty and seventy-five acres, and one a parcel of more than seventy-five acres. The total rent rolls amounted to £1,881.12.5.[21]

As in Scotland, throughout Ireland the practice was firmly established among great landowners of turning over to individuals large bodies of land with the intention that they would in turn sublease them to advantage. For example, a William Stewart of Killymoon held of the Primate of Armagh sixty-four bodies of land, the largest of which was 527 acres, the smallest, one rood and 10 perches.[22]

There is abundant evidence that in the middle of the eighteenth century the value of agricultural lands was rising in Ireland, as it had for some decades. This is illustrated by the tenancy of one Robert Young, who held 43 acres in County Waterford which paid £28.18 yearly rent and were leased for 21 years; in 1736 a statement was made in a newspaper advertisement that the lease when

---

[18] *Ibid.*

[19] For example, the lands of Lewis Ormsby, lying in County Limerick, advertised in *Pue's Occurrences* on November 19, 1745, carried a rental comparable to the above.

[20] "A Rent Roll of Part of the Estate of the Rt. Hon. Lord Visct. Dungannon in the County of Down for one year's Rent Fees and Duties ending at All Saints, 1766," Public Record Office of Northern Ireland, Belfast.

[21] *Ibid.*

[22] A map joined to the return on the Stewart rentals bears the date 1726. See Public Record Office of Northern Ireland.

out would advance £10 yearly, making of course an increase of more than one third on the rental.[23] It is very natural that the tenants should have been opposed to these advances, even if the prices of the commodities they sold were also enhanced in value. To prevent any increase upon the termination of their leases, it was asserted, they only too frequently set to work to ruin their landlords and were themselves also ruined.

Molesworth declared, for instance, that

> "the Tenant when he finds he cannot renew upon his own Terms, toward the latter end of his Lease does all he can to destroy his Farm, by turning up all the green Sward of it, and Plowing it all (sometimes even the Meadows), by taking false crops, Pitt-Fallowing and neglecting to Manure it, selling off all the Hay, Straw, and other Fulture of it, not giving it due Seasons, suffering the Houses, Fences and other Conveniences or Ornaments of it to run to decay without any sufficient Remedy to the Landlords for all this Waste. . . . These Practices have enforced most Landlords of late either to endeavour to tye up their Tenants from plowing at all (they being desirous to see the green side of their Land remain uppermost) or else to take their Estates into their own Hands and Management, and turn Husbandmen themselves till they can bring their land into good Heart again by letting it run waste for four or five Years." [24]

One of the greatest difficulties, according to this writer, was the attitude of the tenant regarding the amount of land required for his needs. "He will not be satisfied," Molesworth affirmed,

> "unless he has a long Lease of Lives of forty, fifty, or sixty Years, that he may sell it; and 'tis rare to find a Tenant in *Ireland*, contented with a Farm of moderate size. He pretends he cannot maintain his Family with less than a hundred Acres, nay (if at any distance from Town) two or three hundred Acres. Now I say, that this (for a Plowing Farm) is more than any Man of moderate Fortune and Stock can manage. His contrivance, therefore, is to bring in one or more Partners, or Cottagers, who shall pay him one third more per Acre than he pays by his Lease to his Landlord; he himself not having money or stock to sett his Affairs a going for so large a quantity of Land. These partners or Cottagers being not only Beggars and Thieves, but generally Harbourers of such, are the Destroyers of all Farms. [In England] you seldom hear of such a thing as a Sub-

[23] See *Pue's Occurrences*, January 15, 1744–1745.

[24] Robert Viscount Molesworth: *Some Considerations for the Promoting of Agriculture and Employing the Poor*, pp. 7–8.

Tenant or Tenant's Tenant; every man resides on his own Farm, and manages it in Person, whereas here you will often see three or four Setts of Tenants, one under another, who all live by that Difference. . . . And the last poor miserable Tenant must make what he can of the Farm by all the evil Usage of it imaginable . . . and 'Tis ten to one, that this man breaks and runs away, but not till he has destroy'd the Farm, at least his part of it." [25]

Further, according to Sir Richard Cox, in Munster a practice had survived which had been banished from other parts of the Kingdom: that of burning the grain crop in the straw to save the trouble of separating the grain from the straw and chaff in the customary manner. Against this a statute had been framed in the preceding century under Charles I.[26] The law, he declared, refers to "a natural, lazy disposition possessing the people who will not build proper protections for their stock or barns to thresh and store their corn in, but the better to enable them to be flitting from their Lands, and to deceive his Majesty of such Debts as they may be owing at any time, and the Landlords of their Rents, do for the great part instead of threshing, burn their corn in the straw. . . ." He then stated that "the Reasons for this Law are as strong in some parts of the County as they were at the time of enacting it. The same ill Husbandry, Improvidence, and lazy Disposition possess the Inhabitants." [27]

These unfortunate practices of the tenants seem to have acted as a great discouragement to landlords to continue their lands in cultivation. This was especially so because it was expensive and difficult to secure ejectments of undesirable tenants who either neglected to pay their rent or insisted on holding on after their leases had expired. One writer of this period affirmed that to secure the removal of a tenant from land he was holding against the will of the owner came "to as much expense as the value of the Inheritance." He therefore demanded that a more speedy and less expensive method be contrived for putting landlords in possession of lands under these circumstances.[28]

Many were the suggestions thrown out from time to time for bet-

---

[25] *Ibid.*, pp. 11–13.

[26] 10 & 11 Chas. I, c. 17, *Irish Statutes*, II, 171–2.

[27] *A Charge delivered to the Grand Jury in County Cork, Bandon-Bridge*, 1740 (Dublin, 1740), pp. 21–2.

[28] G. E. Howard: *Queries Relative to Several Defects and Grievances in Some of the Present Laws of Ireland* (2nd edn., Dublin, 1761), p. 6.

tering conditions in Munster. After the calamitous famine of the early 1740's a proposal was made for improving agriculture by drawing down from northern Ireland some of the industrious Protestants, who were to set an example for the native Irish tenants. "I know a Papist Lord," declared a gentleman of Tipperary in 1741, "who intends at a considerable expence, to bring a colony from the North and give them good encouragement to settle on his estate. And I hope Protestant Noblemen and Gentlemen will not be more blind to their own Interests, as well as to the general good of their Country." [29] The solution, however, of this difficult problem of securing a proper utilization of the lands of southern Ireland was sought, as we have noted, in another direction. The more enterprising landlords, whether Protestant or Roman Catholic, turned from tillage to grazing.

The majority of the native Irish – despite their well-known natural talents and personal charm, of which no misfortune has ever robbed them – were living on a deplorably and undoubtedly an unnecessarily low level in 1750. It was asserted that the average dwelling cost less than ten shillings to build and that three fourths of the people consumed little more than milk, potatoes, and salt [30] – a standard probably to be compared only with that of the Scottish Highlanders, the Welsh mountaineers, the people of the fen country in eastern England, the peasants of Picardy, the Polish and Russian serfs, and some of the peasants of the Rhine region, all of whom were existing in a state of wretchedness in the first half of the eighteenth century. Many in Ireland were too poor to pay the hearth tax and were therefore permitted to compound by paying a lump sum for the cabins of a particular district; others, still more unfortunate, were furnished with certificates of exemption from taxes by the government.[31]

In his exhortation to the Roman Catholic clergy of Ireland, George Berkeley, then Bishop of Cloyne, declared in 1749, in great solicitude and pity: "The House of an Irish Peasant is the cave of Poverty: within, you see a Pot and a little straw; without, a Heap of Children tumbling on the Dunghill." Then he went on to affirm:

---

[29] *A Letter from a Country Gentleman in the Province of Munster To His Grace the Lord Primate of All Ireland* (Dublin, 1741).

[30] *State of the Trade in Ireland* (Dublin, 1758), pp. 12–13.

[31] Charles Smith: *The Ancient and Present State of County of Kerry* (Dublin, 1765), p. 77.

"In this fertile and plentiful Island, none can perish for Want but the Idle and Improvident, none who have Industry, Frugality, and Foresight, but may get into tolerable, if not wealthy Circumstances. Are not all Trades and Manufactures open to those of your Communion? have you not the same free Use, and may you not make the same Advantage of Fairs and Markets as other men? do you pay higher Duties, or are you liable to greater Impositions than your fellow Subjects? and are not the public Praemiums and Encouragements given independently to Artists of all Communions? have not, in fact, those of your Communion a very great Share of the Commerce of this Kingdom in their Hands? and is not more to be got by this than by purchasing Estates or possessing civil Employments,[32] whose possession are often attended with larger expences? It will be said, the Hardness of the Landlord cramps the Industry of the Tenant. But if Rent be high and Landlord rigorous there is more need of Industry in the Tenant. It is well known that in *Holland* taxes are much higher and Rents both of Land and Houses than in Ireland. But there is no Objection or Impediment to the Industry of the People, who are rather animated and spurred on to earn a Livelihood by Labour that is not to be got without it. . . .

"Was there but Will to work, there are not wanting in this Island either Opportunities or Encouragements. Spinning alone might employ all idle Hands (Children as well as Parents) being soon learned, requiring neither Wit nor Strength, but suited to all Ages and Capacities. The Public provides Utensils, and Persons for teaching the use of them, but the Public cannot provide a Heart and Will to be Industrious!" [33]

---

[32] Catholics, under terms of laws to be described later, could neither purchase real estate nor serve in public office.

[33] *A Word to the Wise:* or, *An Exhortation to the Roman Catholic Clergy of Ireland.* This first appeared in 1749 and was printed in 1752 in *A Miscellaneous Containing Several Tracts on Various Subjects left by Berkeley.* A reply to this address appeared in the Dublin *Journal* of November 18, 1749. It is in form of a "Letter from The Roman Catholic Clergy of the Diocese of Dublin." Berkeley had appealed to the clergy to use their influence with their own people to turn from idleness to industry and thereby lift the cloud of wretchedness. In their reply the clergy expressed their highest sense of gratitude for this manifest solicitude on the part of this great man for the welfare of the people of Ireland. "And they take the Liberty in this public manner to return their sincere and hearty Thanks to the Worthy Author, assuring him that they are determined to comply with every Particular recommended in it to the utmost of their Power. In every Page," they declared, "it contains a Proof of the Author's extensive charity. His Views are only toward the public Good: The means he presents are easily complied with, and his manner of treating Persons in this Circumstance so very singular, that they plainly shew the Good Man, the polite Gentleman, and true Patriot."

In view of what has been said about conditions in Ireland in 1750, the present-day student who approaches in a spirit of detachment the problem of the misery of the native Irish in the eighteenth century is beset with many questions. Irish historians stress the great artistry, industry, and unusual civilization in general of the Irish during the early Christian centuries.[34] Certainly by the eighteenth century little enough of this had survived. What is the explanation?

Undoubtedly the wars of conquest had had a most depressing effect upon the people as they would have had upon any group. But conquest probably peculiarly affected the Irish, a nation endowed with intense loyalties. The destruction of the clan system of the septs, the denial to the occupiers of land customary rights existing under the old Brehon law, the substitution for their outlawed chiefs English and also Scottish landlords toward whom there could be no loyalty — all these things were as wormwood to them. Never did they reconcile themselves to these changes, even with the passing of generations. Added to these was the effort to deprive them of the last of their consolations, their religion, by many restrictive statutes and the taking away of their beloved churches for use by the Anglican state establishment.

To a people less emotional, less subject to despair, more inclined toward sober rationalization than the Irish — as, for example, the Jews, a race harried about the earth, as they have been for two thousand years and more, yet rising above every calamity — such things might have been borne with a certain equanimity, and out of the ashes of national disaster and humiliation new energies might have appeared phoenixlike with a new determination to lose nothing essential of the great racial heritage. But not so the Irish. For only too many of them bitterness clouded the horizon of life, and discouragement sapped away whatever ambition they might have possessed.

During the period under consideration the conditions confronting the Irish tenant, even the ambitious tenant who sought to live by tillage alone, were peculiarly distressing. All that has been stated previously indicates that Ireland, as the result of the opening up of the great West Indian markets and the great demand for raw wool, was faced by a situation having many factors in common with the England of the fifteenth and sixteenth centuries, when the lords of

---

[34] See especially P. W. Joyce: *Social History of Ancient Ireland* and Alice S. Green: *History of the Irish State to 1040.*

manors in many parts of the country – after the Black Death and the consequent price disturbances and failure of the Statute of Labourers to accomplish its purpose – growing weary of the struggle with their tenantry, found that corn lands could be more profitably employed as sheep walks. Then, as Sir Thomas More, an eyewitness, remarked in his *Utopia:*

> "The Increase of Pasture . . . by which your sheep, which were naturally mild, and easily kept in order, may be said now to devour men, and unpeople, not only villages but towns: for wherever it is found that the sheep of any soil yield a softer and richer wool than ordinary, there the nobility and gentry, and even those holy men the abbots, not contented with the old rents which their farms yielded nor thinking it enough that they, living at their ease, do no good to the public resolve to do it hurt instead of good." [35]

Many peasants of southern Ireland in the eighteenth century, like many peasants in sixteenth-century England, found themselves in competition with a mode of agricultural economy which could dispense with their services. This dilemma could be met successfully only by unusual resourcefulness and industry, by the forsaking of old standards and inefficient and slothful methods of mediaeval tillage, and by combining with the new methods some handicraft. In each instance the peasants were unprepared to accept the challenge of a competing system and to adapt themselves to changing conditions, and they were, as a consequence, brushed aside and into the ditches.[36]

Such a crisis in agriculture is comparable to that which faced the handicraftsmen in England at the end of the eighteenth century in the erection of the great factories run by machinery. There is, however, this distinction: the craftsmen with all their enterprise or initiative, could not hope to compete with the whirling machinery; for the agricultural labourers the possibility existed – whether in England of the sixteenth century or Ireland of the eighteenth – of bringing the produce of their labour much more successfully into competition with the sheep and the cattle.

In northern and eastern Ireland and in the towns of southern Ire-

[35] *Ideal Commonwealths* (ed. Henry Morley, London, 1886), p. 12.

[36] See in the above connection A. H. Johnson: *The Disappearance of the Small Landowner* (Oxford, 1909), pp. 40, 51, 53, 55, 56, 58; also E. H. Gay: "The Enclosure Movement in England," *Papers and Proceedings of the American Economic Association* (1904), pp. 158–9.

land conditions were different from those just described. Unlike the native Irish, the English and Scottish peoples in these localities were not deeply rooted to the soil; their forefathers had come into these parts in the spirit of adventure and with the hope of bettering their condition; most of them also appear to have come with notions of thrift and industry well established. They not only turned to farming but, as a rule, combined this activity successfully with weaving wool or linen.[37]

However, in 1699 the English Parliament passed the famous Woollen Act,[38] which prohibited the export from the English plantations of any wool, woollen yarn, or woollen manufactures of any kind, and limited the exportation of Irish woollens to England. Duties ranging from 10 to 20 per cent were levied upon these Irish exportations for the purpose of adequately protecting English producers faced by higher manufacturing costs.[39]

That this did not seem unjust to the Irish House of Commons — which was particularly solicitous respecting all things that adversely affected the Protestants in Ireland — is indicated by its declared will-

---

[37] It would appear that the industries referred to above had been long established among the native Irish, at least in some parts of the island, but, except for the cruder products, little was produced by them in 1700. For an account of this see George A. O'Brien's *The Economic History of Ireland in the Seventeenth Century*, pp. 68–75, 176–92, 225–35.

[38] 10 and 11. Wm. III, c. 10. The preamble of the act declared: "Forasmuch as Wooll and the Woollen Manufactures . . . are the greatest and most profitable commodities of this Kingdom [England] on which the Value of Lands and the Trade of the Nation do chiefly depend: And, whereas great Quantities of the like Manufactures have of late been made, and are daily increasing in the Kingdom of Ireland and in the English Plantations in America, and are exported from thence to foreign Markets, heretofore supplied from England which will inevitably sink the Value of Lands and tend to the Ruine of the Trade, and the Woollen Manufactures of this Kingdom, for the Prevention whereof . . ." (*Statutes at Large* [Eyre and Strahan], IV, 7–11).

This fear of the disastrous effects of competition in the wool industry of Ireland was still present in 1753. It found expression in the debate in the British House of Commons on the bill to relax the restrictions on the importation of wool from that island, in the course of which Robert Viner said: "It is certain that all the lands in England are higher rented than lands in Ireland, and that the expence of agriculture in England by reason of our numerous taxes far exceed that in Ireland." He was supported by Thomas Whichcot, who declared: "I think it next to a demonstration that, until the rents and the taxes in England be reduced as low as they now are in Ireland, or those in Ireland raised as high as they are at present, or may hereafter be, in England . . . it is impossible for our farmers to afford selling their wool, or our spinners their woollen yarn, near so cheap as the same commodities may be sold in Ireland" (*Parliamentary History*, XIV, 1298–9, 1308).

[39] William Cunningham: *Growth of English Industry and Commerce*, II, 296–300.

ingness to protect England's woollen trade from injury from Ireland by the encouragement of Irish linen and hempen manufactures and by its imposition of additional export duties upon Irish woollens.[40]

This legislation limiting the exportation of woollen goods undoubtedly struck a severe blow at the Irish industry and it appears that a great many of the looms ceased producing. The act apparently most seriously affected the weavers who had come into Ireland in recent years from the western part of England, especially from Devonshire. Happily, however, the Irish market was not ruined for Irish weavers, and there are indications that the woollen industry was much more important in Ireland in 1750 than has been allowed by previous writers.[41]

According to a statement prepared by the Dublin Society and published in its *Essays* in 1750, there were four kinds of woollen cloth imported into Ireland: the "old drapery," the "new drapery," "prunella," and "shagy," and the average value of these imports was a trivial £14,000 for the three years preceding the report,[42] which would indicate that the home market, especially for the cheaper grades of woollens, was practically in the hands of the Irish manufacturers. This is borne out by the author of the very able *Representation of the State of the Trade of Ireland,* published in 1750, who asserted that tobacco was the only imported commodity that all classes of the Irish people consumed; that only 500,000 out of 2 million enjoyed a standard of living which enabled them to purchase other types of imports; and that the remaining three fourths of the people secured locally their wool, their linen, and other necessities of life.[43] Manifestly, most of the woollens for the first group were also locally produced. Someone writing from Waterford in 1751 had the following comment to make on the production of woollens:

---

[40] The duties were as follows: on broadcloth of twenty shillings' value, 4s.; on serges, bays, or new drapery of twenty shillings' value, 2s. See 10 Wm. III, c. 5, *Irish Statutes,* III, 472–3.

Malacky Postlethwaite, in his *Britain's Commerical Interest Explained* . . . (London, 1759, Vol. I, 147), argued that since the woollen manufacturing supports England and her ability in turn to support the other parts of the Empire, she must not be deprived of this source of her strength. At the same time he took the position that "the flourishing linen industry" should be left to Ireland and Scotland.

[41] See 5 Geo. II, c. 21, *Irish Statutes,* III, 472–3, for significant evidence.

[42] The chief item was "old drapery," an expensive fabric at 15 shillings a yard which amounted to £10,827 of the total; the "new drapery," at 2s. 6d. a yard, was valued at £2,293. See *Dublin Society Essays* (Dublin, 1750), pp. 8–10.

[43] *Representations of the State of the Trade of Ireland* (Dublin, 1750), p. 13.

> "The Linen Trade, which was introduced in this place in 1746 has increased to such a degree as surpasses our most sanguine Hopes; and amongst the many good Consequences attending so valuable a manufacture to the Poor, (which are very apparent to us, who live upon the spot) it is giving [taking the] Place of the Woollen Manufacture, now carried on to a great extent in this Country, under so many Restraints; and if Liberty was granted to export striped and check'd Linnens from the Kingdom, the Woollen Manufactures in England, I am persuaded, would soon find the benefit of it. The people must eat, and it is the same thing to them whether they get their Bread from Linnen or the Woollen Manufacture; one of them, I think they ought to have without Restraint, otherwise they must keep what share they can of both." [44]

The importance of the industry in the 1740's is indicated, moreover, by a study of bonds given by Irish merchants who desired to export wool and woollen goods to England and also by the bonds given by British merchants who had contracted to import such commodities from Ireland into England.[45] One thing that doubtless stimulated the working up of wools was an act passed in the year 1737 in the British Parliament, taking the duties off woollen and bay yarn imported from Ireland.[46] Be that as it may, it is clear by the port records referred to that between 1739 and 1743 quantities of raw wool and yarn – and cloth totalling hundreds of thousands of yards and made up of friezes, flannels, shags, draperies, and stuffs – came into England from Ireland, in addition to woollen rugs, blankets, hats, and stockings. It appears that the greatest sale of these commodities was in Wales, where the shaggy, heavy, and coarse types of Irish cloth were apparently especially appreciated by the mountain folk.[47]

It must not be supposed that all the woollens produced at this period in Ireland were rough, cheap materials. In southern Ireland

[44] "Extract of a letter from Waterford," March 8, 1751, in the Birmingham *Gazette*, April 8, 1751.

[45] See "An Account of all Bonds taken in the Ports of Dublin, etc. for the Lading of Wool, etc. 1739–1743," and "An Account of the Bonds taken in the Ports of Bideford, etc. for the Lading of Wool, etc. in Ireland and Importing the same, 1739–1743," P.R.O., Treas. 64. 282, No. 2 and 3. These bonds were required by 10 Wm. III, c. 5, reaffirming the regulations provided for by 14 and 15 Charles II, c. 9, Sec's 42–44, *Irish Statutes*, II, 488; III, 472–3.

[46] 12 Geo. II, c. 21.

[47] Milford Haven in Pembrokeshire was the leading port interested in the importation of these Irish woollens, although they were also brought into Bideford and Liverpool.

at Carrick-on-Suir, in County Tipperary, there was a flourishing manufacture of ratteens, which a writer in 1746 declared "our nobility and gentry often find to be a most light, warm, and commodious wear in winter." He went on to say that the inhabitants had brought this weaving to a state of great perfection so as to make it the equal of the finest of cloth and worth from three to thirty shillings a yard. "It is incredible what numbers are employed in that little Town in this manufacturing, men, women, and children finding sufficient work." [48]

That the importation of Irish worsteds into England in 1750 was considered a matter of no little significance is indicated by the disturbances that took place at Tiverton in Devonshire in January of that year. "We have had," declared a correspondent, "great disorder and some skirmishes between the wool-combers and weavers of this town, on account of the merchants introducing Irish worsteds; the magistrates read the riot act, which not being effectual, the military power was called in which prevented further mischief, but the wool-combers refusing to work, a stop was put to all trade." [49]

Indeed, the export of raw wool from Ireland to England reached its maximum in 1710, when 258,208 stones or more than three and a quarter million pounds of wool were sent; there then took place a rapid decline in this export until in 1727 only 49,784 stones or less than 700,000 pounds were entered.[50] This might suggest one of several things: that less wool was being produced in Ireland, that more was being smuggled to France,[51] or that more was being worked up

[48] Charles Smith: *The Ancient and Present State of the County and City of Waterford* (Dublin, 1746), p. 281.

[49] *Gentleman's Magazine* (1750), XX, 41.

[50] "An account of the Quantity of Wool Imported from Ireland into England in Twenty Years from Christmas, 1708 to Christmas, 1728," Custom House, February 25, 1729, P.R.O., Treas. 64. 273. In 1773, 11,073 hundreds or 1,240,176 pounds were imported (*ibid.*, Treas. 64. 274). It appears that only one fourth the amount of wool was exported to England in 1749 as was exported from Ireland during the last seven years of the reign of Charles II. The license fees at the earlier period averaged £4,000 and in 1749 they amounted to only £509.6.9 (*ibid.*, Treas. 14. 13, p. 57).

[51] The volume of wool smuggled each year after the passing of the Woollen Act was doubtless very great, but the amount was probably not much greater in the middle of the eighteenth century than earlier. A gentleman who visited Cork in 1748 declared: "Running of Wool, though there is a strict Act of Parliament against it, will be continued. Not long ago a large quantity was shipped on board several vessels, in sight of the soldiers that were sent to prevent it, who were outnumbered, and obliged to retire" (*A Tour through Ireland by Two English Gentlemen* [Dublin, 1748], p. 93). The chief smuggling operations at this place were carried on at Spike Island, in whose harbour small vessels at high tide could steal unobserved by the officers at Cork.

into woollens in Ireland. The available evidence points in the last-named direction. There was, indeed, the most serious opposition among the Irish weaving interests to the exportation of wool and especially woollen yarns to meet the English demand. Moreover, the skill of Irish weavers was respected by foreigners. This is indicated in the beginning of the century by the enticement of these handicraftsmen to France and other countries after the passing of the Woollen Act in 1699; [52] this was true also in the middle of the eighteenth century.

According to a report made by Lord George Sackville to the Lords Justices in Ireland in 1753, there was in progress a "systematic seduction of Irish woolworkers to Spain." [53] In 1750 it was also asserted that the best of the Irish weavers went to Great Britain for employment and that none but the worst and most indolent were employed at home, "which is one Reason why, it is found by experience, that an Irish Manufacturer will not do as much work in two Days as an English Manufacturer in one." [54] All this at least indicates that the Irish woollen industry was far from dead. Indeed, *The Gentleman's Magazine* for February 1750 printed the following significant item:

> "Dublin, Feb. 5 was a great rising of journeymen weavers to prevent the exportation of wool, or bays yarn and a company of foot was obliged to assist in suppressing them." [55]

If the English were afraid that the unrestrained exportation of Irish woollens would destroy their own chief industry, they apparently up to 1750 felt they had nothing to fear from Irish linen. In line with the well-established policy of the home government of seeking to develop staples for various parts of the Empire which would not compete with staples produced elsewhere within it, encouragement

---

[52] "But this English persecution in Trade had the same effect with the French persecution in Religion, for soon after the Irish weavers settled in France and laid the Foundation of the Woollen Manufactures almost in all Parts of Europe, . . . much more rivalled England than Ireland could ever have done, not only drawing after them Irish Wool and Yarn, but by enabling them to work up their own foreign Wool at the same Time. . . . And now they can undersell not only England but the Irish too" (*ibid.*, p. 19).

[53] "Calendar of Miscellaneous Letters and Papers Prior to 1760," State Paper Office, Dublin.

[54] *The State of Trade in Ireland* (Dublin, 1750), p. 8.

[55] *The Gentleman's Magazine*, XX, 91. For a much fuller account see Dublin correspondence of February 6 in *Aris's Birmingham Gazette* for February 19, 1750.

had been given to the people of Ireland by both the British and Irish parliaments to produce and export this manufacture. In 1704 the colonial trade was thrown open to Irish linens.[56] Moreover, the Irish Parliament at the same time provided that no export duty should be laid upon such products,[57] and two years later granted a bounty of five shillings per hogshead on imported hemp seed and as much as twopence a yard for the export of canvas sailcloth – this was advanced to as much as fourpence a yard in 1745.[58] Further to encourage the industry, additional duties were placed upon imported linens,[59] and in 1715 further bounties were granted on the export of flax and hemp manufactures.[60]

It is true that in 1717 the British Parliament was led, it would seem as a result of protests on the part of British linen weavers, to make clear that the privilege of exporting Irish linens freely to the plantations could be continued only on condition that the Irish Parliament repeal the heavy duties upon British white and brown linens imported into Ireland,[61] duties that bore especially heavily upon the Scottish weavers.[62] This the Irish Parliament proceeded to do.[63]

By 1750 great quantities of Irish linen were passing into Great Britain for local consumption. Again the British weavers became articulate under this heavily subsidized competition, with the result that Parliament was led to provide that countervailing import duties equal to the Irish bounty on canvas exports to Great Britain should be levied.[64] Indeed, by the middle of the century the production of linens was by far the most important manufacture in Ireland. Between the years 1727 and 1736, 54,578,702 yards of linen were exported into England,[65] and it is significant that the amount exported in the last year was twice that for the first. Irish linen, as the result

[56] 3 and 4 Anne, c. 8, continued by 3 Geo. I, c. 21.

[57] 4 Anne, c. 4, sec. 5, *Irish Statutes*, III, 74.

[58] 6 Anne, c. 9, secs. 1 and 3; 19 Geo. II, c. 6, secs. 54–6, *Irish Statutes*, III, 132, VI, 742–3. In this connection see G. F. Zook: "Economic Relations of England and Ireland, 1660–1750," *The Historical Outlook*, XIII, 242.

[59] 8 Anne, c. 2, *Irish Statutes*, IV, 188–90.

[60] 2 Geo. I, c. 13, sec. 3, *ibid.*, IV, 378.

[61] Levied under 14 and 15 Chas. II, c. 8 and c. 9, *ibid.*, II, 457–9.

[62] 3 Geo. I, c. 21, par. 1, *Statutes at Large* (Eyre and Strahan), V, 107.

[63] 4 Geo. I, c. 6, *Irish Statutes*, IV, 448–52; see also G. F. Zook: *loc. cit.*, XIII, 242–3.

[64] 23 Geo. II, c. 32, *Statutes at Large* (Eyre and Strahan), VI, 503–4.

[65] "An account of the quantities of Irish Linen Imported into England from Christmas, 1727 to Christmas, 1736," Custom House, London, March 14, 1737, P.R.O., Treas. 164. 273.

of being placed on the free list while the linens of other countries were dutiable, easily controlled the English market, although lesser amounts were brought into England from Germany, Flanders, Holland, and Russia.[66] In addition to this encouragement, the Irish Parliament added a policy of subsidization. In 1710 the so-called Linen Board was instituted to consist of 72 Trustees, 18 from each province, who had the disposal of funds set aside by Parliament for the encouragement of the industry. From 1710 to 1725 the sum of £49,134.10.21.2 was appropriated to this end from the duties, and from 1725 to 1758, £66,000.[67] In 1725 a committee, appointed to investigate the state of the hempen and linen manufacture reported:

> "The effect of these Laws hath been, that Ulster has universally run into the manufacture of Linens and Yarns, by which their rent is in great measure paid, their land improved in value and their Poor maintained. The provinces of Leinster, Munster, and Connaught, have every one of them laid a foundation to begin and carry on the same manufactures, and some good cloth is now yearly made in every one of these Provinces. Connaught is remarkable for making great quantities of a very good and useful Yarn." [68]

To give additional encouragement to the three last-named provinces £50,000 was appropriated between 1733 and 1758 from the duties on calicoes, teas, and other articles. In fact, it was asserted that a total sum of £165.134.10.2 was set aside down to 1757 by the Irish Parliament to subsidize linen production and exportation.[69] By the late 1740's the working up of flax had surpassed its production, for it was then necessary to import this article; in 1748, 17,293 hundredweight were brought into the island and by 1751 the annual amount was 24,779 hundredweight, of which 16,564 came from Great Britain and the rest from the Baltic and Holland.[70] Linen as an industry in some places supplanted woollens; this was true of

---

66 "An account of the Quantity of Linen Cloth both Plain and Figured Imported into England from Christmas 1759 to Christmas 1765," Custom House, London, Nov. 24, 1766, P.R.O., Treas. 64. 274.

67 See both Thomas Prior: *An Essay to Encourage and Extend the Linen Manufacture in Ireland. By Praemiums and other Means* (Dublin, 1749), and Robert Stephenson: *An Inquiry into the State and Progress of the Linen Manufacture of Ireland . . .* (Dublin, 1757), pp. 96–100.

68 *Ibid.*, p. 93. For the growth of linen manufacturing see C. Gill: *The Rise of the Irish Linen Industry* (Oxford, 1925).

69 Robert Stephenson: *op. cit.*, p. 101.

70 *Ibid.*, p. 92.

Waterford in Munster, which up to the 1740's had been famous for its friezes,[71] but turned from this woollen fabric to linens.[72] By 1750 the annual exportation of linens to England from Ireland had reached a total of 9,077,712 yards and in 1751 the high total of 11,703,545 yards. The combined total of all the linen imported into the Kingdom from Holland, Flanders, Russia, and Germany was only one fourth that amount.[73]

Not only did the British desire Irish linen to supplement what they produced to meet their own needs, but the colonies were also offering a splendid market to which this manufacture could be directly shipped in Irish vessels.[74] "You can send nothing which will sell better here than Irish linens of all sorts as high as 2/ per yd. and a few ps. at 2/6 to 3/," wrote William Faris from North Carolina to William Dobbs in 1750.[75] In 1748 British merchants were exporting to the colonies more than a million yards of this linen as against less than seventy thousand ells of their own produce.[76] This export, moreover, was subsidized by statute, Irish and British linens benefiting equally. The bounty law ran from 1743 to 1750 and was supplemented by subsequent legislation.[77] By this act a bounty amounting to one penny was paid on every yard of linen exported valued between sixpence and twelvepence per yard and a halfpenny on linen worth less than sixpence. It appears that in certain branches of the industry English manufacturers had established a superiority. According to one writer, they had by the late 1750's surpassed the Irish "in Huckaback Table Linen in Yorkshire, in good sheeting in Lancashire, and in three quarters and half wide Linens, called Dowless, in Somersetshire and in Devonshire." [78]

---

[71] Charles Smith: *The Ancient and Present State of the County and City of Waterford* (Dublin, 1746), p. 281.

[72] *Aris's Birmingham Gazette*, April 8, 1751.

[73] "An Account of Foreign Linen Imported in England from Christmas, 1748 to Christmas 1753," Custom House, January 9, 1755, P.R.O., Treas. 64. 274.

[74] G. F. Zook: "Economic Relations of England and Ireland, 1660–1750," *Historical Outlook*, XIII, 243.

[75] The date of this letter is February 19, 1759–60. See Dobbs Papers, Public Record Office of Northern Ireland.

[76] "Linens exported to the British Colonies, 1741–1753," Custom House, London, January 9, 1755, P.R.O., Treas. 64. 284. The English ell was 45 inches.

[77] See 15 Geo. II, c. 29; 18 Geo. II, c. 24 and c. 25; 22 Geo. II, c. 42, *Statutes at Large* (Eyre and Strahan), VI, 186–9, 272–4, 443.

[78] See *An Inquiry into the State and Progress of the Linen Manufacture of Ireland* (Dublin, 1757), p. 119.

In addition to the amount of linen exported, in the late 1730's the island was making 12,500,000 yards for home consumption, according to *A Letter from a Merchant who had left off Trade in relation to the British and Irish Linen Manufactures.*[79] The writer pointed out that England made 21,000,000 yards for its eight million people, Scotland made 16,500,000 yards for its two million, and Ireland the above total for a population equal to that of Scotland. Indeed, one authority on Ireland writing in 1750 included linen among those few commodities that all classes of the Irish population enjoyed.[80]

What about the rewards of those engaged in this handicraft? It was estimated that a weaver, after paying all deductions, was able to lay aside eightpence a day and that a flax dresser would earn on an average of a shilling a day, which indicates that these skilled workmen were receiving a compensation from three to six times the reward of an agricultural labourer.[81] But weaving demanded constant industry whereas potato-raising appealed to the easygoing, rather shiftless ways of life of most of the native Irish of this period.

It is a curious fact that neither the Gaelic peoples in Ireland nor those in Scotland ever took readily to the sea, and it is true that both native Irish and Scottish Highlanders frequently starved in sight of waters teeming with fish to be had for the catching, which were left for the Lowlanders, the English, and especially the Dutch to exploit. Even in the days of James I the Dutch resorted to Irish waters to fill their boats, and this was true in 1750. There were, of course, a few men of enterprise in Ireland who profited by this opportunity.

Londonderry in the north, it may be noted, had an interest in the herring fishery, as did Youghal and Bantry in the south. In 1749 one Richard Mead of Bantry, County Cork, caught and cured 380,000 fish and in 1748 John Young, also of Bantry, caught and cured 482,590 herrings and 231 barrels of sprats.[82] But this untold wealth was ignored by most Irishmen, who preferred apparently to pay rack-rents than pull an oar and handle the seine in rough waters.

A proposal, it is true, was made in 1750 that a fund of £25,000 be raised for employing 250 ships and 39,000 people in the fisheries,

---

[79] The above work is quoted in *An Inquiry into the State and Progress of the Linen Manufacture of Ireland* (Dublin, 1757), p. 122.

[80] *Representation of the State of the Trade of Ireland* (Dublin, 1750), p. 13.

[81] *An Inquiry into the State and Progress of the Linen Manufacture of Ireland*, p. 123.

[82] *Some Consideration on the British Fisheries with a Proposal for Establishing a General Fishery on the Coasts of Ireland* (Dublin, 1750), pp. 8–10.

and in this connection it was pointed out that the waters of Ireland abound in "cod, whiting, haddock, hake, bass, mackerel, ling, and mullet, besides various flat fish such as turbot, sole, plaice, flounder and ray." The writer urged that these would not only furnish the tables of the better circumstanced at a lower rate than then existed, but would yield a prodigious supply of wholesome food for the industrious poor, "who at present feed in such a Manner, that it is shameful even to mention." [83]

Reference has been made to the growth of grazing at the expense of tillage in southern Ireland. What was loss to the agricultural population was gain to the trading element that drew upon this enlarged supply of beef and dairy products for export. Although the British Parliament had not modified the policy — adopted in 1663 — of refusing to allow the importation of Irish cattle [84] it nevertheless threw open to the people of Ireland the plantation trade in meat and butter. This relaxation led to very great activity in Irish commerce, especially at Cork, which in 1750 was the most important center on the island for the export trade. Indeed, it was asserted in 1748 that since 1718 a new city, "which the industrious inhabitants have gained from the sea or marshy Ground," [85] had been added to the old Cork. A writer in the year 1750 declared that Cork was thrice as large as it was forty years previous, and that its commerce had increased in the same proportion.[86] Its trade in beef, besides butter and tallow, was enormous. Between the middle of August and Christmas of each year almost one hundred thousand black cattle were purchased from the grazers and slaughtered there.[87] Into Cork harbour came ships of various nations. "We counted sixteen then at anchor, among which were seven Portuguese, that were taking in Beef, Tallow, and Hides," declared a gentleman who visited the town in 1748.[88] He was especially impressed in approaching the city. "Here the eye is entertained with innumerable pleasant Seats . . . which bespeaks the Opulence of the City we are now drawing near to." [89] In the city itself he found an enlightened state of affairs, not-

[83] *Ibid.*, p. 11.

[84] 18 Charles II, c. 2, *Statutes at Large* (Eyre and Strahan), III, 278.

[85] *A Tour Through Ireland by Two English Gentlemen* (Dublin, 1748), p. 89.

[86] Charles Smith, *The Ancient and Present State of the County and City of Cork* (Dublin, 1750), p. 315.

[87] *Ibid.*, pp. 410–14.

[88] *A Tour Through Ireland*, p. 55.

[89] *Ibid.*, p. 56.

ing the existence among other establishments of several printing offices and also book shops "as well stocked with ancient and modern Learning as many in London." [90] Cork at this period was probably the greatest centre in the world for the export of meat products. The estimated value of the 70,000 cattle shipped to England before the import prohibition of 1663 referred to was £140,000; but the value of the meat and butter trade under the new trade dispensation was estimated at £400,000 in 1750, which did not take into account the value of the hides sold principally to France, Spain, and Portugal and the value of the tallow, which was placed at £70,000.[91] This, of course, helps to explain the vast increase in the value of Irish exports during the first fifty years of the eighteenth century.

But Cork was not alone in her prosperity; Kinsale was described at this period as "a handsome, populous, and rich town" with a large provision trade, especially with Flanders, Holland, France, and the West Indies; Waterford and Youghal, also, in Munster, were flourishing through weaving and commerce, and Youghal carried on some fishing, as has been indicated. In Ulster there was Belfast, the chief commercial centre of the region, which enjoyed an active trade with Scotland, while Londonderry, called, as was Kinsale, "a handsome town," was beginning to acquire wealth through the West India trade carried on in British bottoms. In Leinster there were Drogheda, Carlingford, and Dundalk, and the capital of the Kingdom, Dublin – all places of wealth and commerce. Finally there was Galway in Connaught, "a neat and rich city," the metropolis of the western part of Ireland.[92]

Considering the commercial relations between England and Ireland at this period, it may be said that these testify to the fairly rapid growth of wealth, although not to the elevation of the standard of living of the great body of agricultural workers in the latter country. In the year 1700, according to the official figures, the total value of the exports of Ireland to England was £233,853.6.3, while that of the imports from England to Ireland was £261,115.15.10 1/2; by 1740 the amounts were respectively £390,565.7 and £628,-288.9.4, and by 1750 respectively £612,808 and £1,316,600.2.2.[93]

[90] *A Tour Through Ireland*, p. 99.

[91] *A Representation of the State of Trade of Ireland* (Dublin, 1750), p. 18.

[92] For descriptions of the various towns of Ireland of this period see D. Fenning and J. Collyer: *A New System of Geography* (London, 1765), II, 607–17.

[93] B. M., Add. Mss. 29903. Malachy Postlethwaite, in his *Britain's Commercial Interest Explained* . . . (London, 1757), gives the following as Ireland's chief exports:

Despite what has been said about Ireland's industrial and commercial activities as evidences of progress, it is undeniable that the island suffered extremely from absenteeism. Men of wealth preferred to go abroad, especially to England, to spend their income, rather than to lay it out in Ireland. It was a matter of observation at this period "that no people in Europe are so meanly provided with houses and furniture in proportion to their incomes, as the men of estates in Ireland." [94] Thomas Prior in 1745 estimated that £627,799 was drained out of the country each year by absentees. Of this total he figured that £204,200 was taken out by those who had possessions in Ireland they never saw.[95] It was generally felt that a very considerable group of people were receiving great benefits from Ireland, but were making no adequate return and by no means sharing equally in the carrying of the public burdens. A writer calling himself "Philo-Patriae," in "A Letter to a member of the Parliament of Ireland," demanded in 1745 that these people should be compelled to contribute a special tax of a shilling on the pound out of the clear profits of their estates.[96]

Ireland was not alone in experiencing the disadvantages that flowed from the indisposition of men of wealth to remain at home and give themselves over to improving their estates and the condition of those dependent upon them. St. Christopher, Jamaica, Barbados, Antigua, and South Carolina were seriously affected, especially the first four named, by the residence in England of a large proportion of the planters of wealth and ability. On the continent of Europe provincial France was almost certainly the victim of the royal policy of encouraging the nobility to resort to Versailles, where they lavishly spent the money wrung from their peasants, to the

---

"cattle (meat), hides, tallow, butter, cheese, honey, wax, hemp, timber, pipe-staves, woven rugs, shag-mantles, friezes, ratteens [ratins], comlets, with wool and woollen cloth, salmon, herring and other fish, together with lead, tin, and iron" (*ibid.*, Vol. I, 61). He failed, incidentally, to mention linen goods.

[94] Charles Smith: *The Ancient and Present State of the County and City of Cork* (Dublin, 1750), p. 252.

[95] Thomas Prior: *A List of Absentees of Ireland* (Dublin, 1745). Lists were published also in 1729, 1757, and 1783. In 1767 the estimate of the grand total drained from Ireland by absentees was £869,302.14.9 and in 1783 it had mounted to £2,085,394 (*ibid.*, ed. of 1783). See also Alexander Thom & Sons: *A Collection of Tracts and Treatises* (2 vols., Dublin, 1860–1) for additional information on absenteeism.

[96] The letter referred to above is printed in Prior's *List of Absentees of Ireland.* For a discussion of the proposed absentee tax see "Memoirs of Charlemont's Political Life," 1755–1783, in Hist. Mss. Com. *12th Report,* Appendix, Part X, Vol. I, 36–8.

utter neglect of all local interests. Nevertheless, assuming the existence of the evils of absenteeism as well as other evils that afflicted the country, to one Irishman at least, the Earl of Orrery, the condition of the island was in 1751 so vastly improved over its former state, especially in comparison with the dark days of the famine, that he was constrained to declare:

> "The present state of Ireland is as flourishing as possible. Agriculture is cultivated; arts and sciences are encouraged; and in the space of eighteen years, no kingdom can be more improved. Ireland, in relation to England, may be compared to a younger sister, lately come of age, after having suffered all the miseries of an injured minor, such as, law suits, encroachments upon her property, violation of her rights, destruction of her tenants, and every evil that can be named. At length, time, and her own noble spirit of industry, have entirely relieved her; and, some little heartburnings excepted, she enjoys the quiet possession of a very ample fortune, subject, by way of acknowledgment, to certain quit-rents payable to the elder branch of her house: and let me add, by experience, that, take her all in all, she cannot have a greater fortune than she deserves." [97]

We must now turn from the economic aspects of Irish civilization in the eighteenth century to consideration of its social and political atmosphere.

---

[97] Remarks on the *Life and Writings of Jonathan Swift* (1751), p. 127.

CHAPTER IX

The Dependent Kingdom

ONE WOULD NOT be far wrong in saying that Ireland in the middle of the eighteenth century could be controlled only by the civil authorities acting in conjunction with military forces. To illustrate this state of affairs it may be noted that in 1743 the Irish Commissioners of the Revenue appealed to the Lords Justices for military aid in collecting quit-rent arrears in the Longhrea district in County Galway, and that in 1746 military assistance was asked "to distrain for composition rent" in that same region. Again, at Sligo the revenue officers wrote in 1748 that since troops were removed it had been impossible to enforce the revenue laws; in 1749 military assistance was demanded to restrain smuggling near Ross Castle; and in 1752 the collector of Newport in County Mayo protested against the withdrawal of troops from that town. During the latter year the grand jury of County Tyrone represented to the government the necessity of replacing troops (which had been withdrawn) for the purpose of clearing "torie" robbers from the mountains. Finally, appeals came from both counties Limerick and Donegal in 1753 for military aid to assist the civil authorities in carrying out orders of the courts.[1]

The poverty of the native Irish as a group has already been stressed. This was productive of crime. Many also were goaded with a sense of injustice and deep-lying resentment against the government, which will explain a great deal of the active discontent.[2]

---

[1] For the above and other items see "Calendar of Miscellaneous Letters and Papers, Prior to 1760," State Paper Office, Dublin.

[2] With respect to local government, without reference to the central administration of Ireland, all power was likely to be in the hands of the great landowners, or, if not, at

Others had fallen victim to intemperate habits that bred commotions. "It is frightful," declared one, William Henry, in 1753, "for a sober person to travel into some market-towns in the evening of a market; but especially on a Fair Day." He then went on to say: "What Outrages are committed at County Feasts? at Races, at Cock fights – What Havoc at Funerals? In other Counties where the spirit of whiskey prevails, the spirit of the law is laid aside. No Sheriff can execute a Process if a notorious Whiskey drinker is enquired after for Debt, for Breach of the Peace or for Murder, but Fellow-Drunkards raise the county to defend him." [3] A Dublin gentleman wrote at this period: "That there are more Robberies, Rapes, Murders, and Outrages of every kind in this Kingdom, than in any other five Nations in Europe, our daily Papers must evince. It is well known that there are several Places in and about this city, where not any Number of Bailiffs dare go to execute any Process of Justice." [4] The island was indeed a prey to lawlessness.

In most of the countries of Europe the religious and ecclesiastical systems were made to serve the purposes of the state, especially in the maintenance of law and order. This was not true of Ireland. The explanation for this divergence lies in the fact that the religion established by law was not the preference of an overwhelming majority of the people, who in reality clung tenaciously to the ministrations of a church that was barely tolerated by the government. Although, according to the best available information, the population of Ireland in 1750 was probably double or triple that of a century previous, the membership of the Anglican Established Church of Ireland, created during the reign of Elizabeth I, had not grown with this increase. County Cork possessed 75 parishes and within 41 of these the churches were in ruins; [5] in County Waterford, where there were 29 parishes in 1746, 16 churches were in ruins and services were

least in those of royal appointees. The counties were controlled by a high sheriff, justices of the peace, and constables, high and petty. Writing of the Province of Connaught, one enlightened English traveller called the landlords "haughty and tyrannic . . . The will and pleasure of these chiefs is absolute law to the poor inhabitants that are connected with them . . ." ([John Bush]: *Hibernia Curiosa. A Letter from a Gentleman in Dublin to his Friend at Dover* [London, 1768], pp. 27–30).

[3] *An Earnest Address to the People of Ireland Against the Drinking of Spirituous Liquors.* (Dublin, 1753), pp. 22–3.

[4] *Queries Relative to several Defects and Grievances in some of the present Laws of Ireland* [By George Edmund Howard.] (2nd ed., Dublin, 1761), pp. 20–1.

[5] "A State of the Parishes in the Diocese of Cork" in Charles Smith's *The Ancient and Present State of the County and City of Cork* (Dublin, 1750), I, 70–9.

being held only in 7 parishes.[6] This was probably typical of the parishes within both the provinces of Munster and Connaught, for Lecky points out that in County Clare in 1763 no Protestant church existed in 62 out of 76 parishes; the rectors of most of the remaining 14 parishes were non-resident.[7] Undoubtedly one reason for this non-residence of ministers within certain parishes was the existence of a sentiment so hostile to their presence that they could not abide there in personal safety. Further, there was a noticeable tendency to strengthen a few churches within a diocese at the expense of the weaker parishes, as in that of County Cork, in which the livings of 29 of the parishes were attached to some ecclesiastical office removed from the parish and generally united with the cathedral.

However, considerable energy was manifested within some of the dioceses in promoting the larger interests of the Church of Ireland. Nicholas Forster, Bishop of Raphoe in County Donegal, a declared enemy of pluralities and non-residence who died in 1743, restored many churches, erected chapels of ease within his larger parishes, and founded several charity schools, all at his own expense.[8] When William King was promoted from the bishopric of Derry in 1702 to the archbishopric of Dublin, he found that the greatly increased Protestant population was in need of additional churches within his province, and erected 19 new churches, rebuilt 7, and restored 14. The explanation for this activity is that in the course of the seventeenth century many weak parishes had united. King now proceeded to separate them and to settle a resident clergy, which, incidentally, he helped to maintain from his own private fortune.[9] Peter Brown, a man of great austerity and piety who became Bishop of Cork and Ross in 1709, was also active in church restoration and many of the structures within his diocese were rebuilt. His greatest problem, however, was the finding of conveniently located glebes and habitations for his clergy, as his diocese was more in need of these than

[6] "A State of the Parishes in the Diocese of Waterford," in Charles Smith's *The Ancient and Present State of the Town and County of Waterford* (Dublin, 1746), pp. 40–1.

[7] W. E. H. Lecky: *History of Ireland in the Eighteenth Century* (5 vols., London, 1892), II, 19.

[8] *The Whole Works of Sir James Ware Concerning Ireland* (revised and improved by Walter Harris, Dublin, 1764), I, 283. The set of these Works used by the author is one annotated in the handwriting of the Rt. Rev. W. Reeves, Lord Bishop of Down, Connor and Dromore, and possessed by Trinity College, Dublin.

[9] *Ibid.*, II, 363–9; see also *A Great Archbishop of Dublin, William King, D.D., 1650–1729* (ed. Sir C. S. King, London, 1908).

most other parts of the Kingdom.[10] Despite difficulties encountered, it appears that by 1750 the problem of non-residence of the clergy had been largely overcome in both his bishopric and that of Cloyne.[11]

It was the hope of the government, of course, that the clergy would succeed in winning over the population to conformity with the legally established faith. This was due perhaps not so much to any fervent missionary zeal for Anglicanism on the part of the Crown officials but to the conviction that Ireland would never become loyal to King and government so long as it was loyal to a foreign ecclesiastical power that for almost two centuries had shown a rather consistent hostility to England. Many of those who received appointments and benefices to promote this political objective had not the first qualifications for so great and difficult a task. There were, of course, some able and devoted churchmen in Ireland: such as Thomas Rundle, who Pope – in writing to Swift – declared "will be a friend to the human race wherever he goes";[12] Hugh Bolter, Archbishop of Armagh, who died in 1742; and Bolter's contemporaries the Archbishop of Cashel and Sir Thomas Vesey, Bishop of Killaloe, whose death, according to Sir James Ware, was deeply mourned as the passing of "a Father, Brother, Friend and Companion," a man of great generosity about whom it was said that the "tythes of a parish belonging to his see he never would receive." These men and others were widely known for their charities and philanthropic spirit and their deep solicitude for their charges.[13] But such men lacked support. In truth, under the best of conditions the difficulties of the task of changing the religion of the people were insuperable – the great mass of the native Irish clung with unswerving loyalty to their ancestral faith.[14] This same devotion to Roman

10 *The Whole Works of Sir James Ware*, III, 571–2.

11 "I can aver from an experience of 30 years, that there have been very few non-residents among the clergy of the dioceses of Cork and Cloyne, where the late unhappy disturbances broke out at first and raged with the greatest violence" (*A Vindication of the Conduct of the Clergy by a Southern Clergyman* [Dublin, 1788], p. 52).

12 *Works of Dean Swift* (Scott Edn.), VIII, 366.

13 *The Whole Works of Sir James Ware*, I, 133; III, 598–9; *A Letter from a County Gentleman in the Province of Munster To His Grace the Lord Primate of All Ireland* (Dublin, 1741).

14 The case of the Irish Roman Catholics is strongly stated by Charles O'Conor in *The Case of the Roman Catholics of Ireland . . . fully Explained and Vindicated* (Dublin, 1755). For the ecclesiastical history of Ireland see also P. F. Moran: *Spicilegium Ossoriense: being a Collection of Letters and Papers Illustrative of the History of the Irish Church from the Reformation to the Year 1800* (3 vols., Dublin, 1874–84); W. D.

Catholicism was, nevertheless, not manifested by the native Irish aristocracy or upper middle class.

According to the Irish "Convert Rolls," [15] between the years 1703 and 1727 some 450 people took the oaths and secured certificates to testify to their change of faith from the Roman Catholic to the religion of the Established Church of Ireland; between the latter year and 1751 almost 1,600 took out certificates. Of this number, 786 supplied no information to indicate their station in life; but 1,163 enjoyed some title or other distinction, such as "Earl," "Lord," "Viscount," "Baronet," "Sir," "Hon.," "Gent.," "Esq.," "Mr." In contrast, only 10 were described as yeomen, 24 as farmers, 25 as merchants, and 8 as doctors. The geographical distribution of these converts was wide, but especially large numbers were identified with counties Dublin, Galway, Clare, Mayo, Tipperary, Kerry, and Cork – all but the first among the most predominantly native Irish counties at this period.

The turning to Protestantism of the greater part of those Irish Catholics possessed of large estates is also stressed by a contemporary, the patriotic Earl of Charlemont, who associated intimately with many of them in public life. Writing in the 1770's, he affirmed that the "greater part of the old Catholic gentry, had, either from conviction or convenience, conformed to the established and ruling religion. . . ." [16] Even in the diocese of Elphin in County Roscommon, where the Catholics, it was asserted, outnumbered the Protestants fifty to one, the gentry as a group were Protestant by 1720 and were said to be very loyal to their religion.[17]

The motivations that led the great body of the native Irish aristocracy to Protestantism are not stated in the Convert Rolls. Was it to protect some larger group interest, some family interest, or merely to further some selfish personal interest? Doubtless many may have repeated cynically the sentiment attributed to Henry IV of France, who accepted Roman Catholicism with the remark that Paris was worth a mass. Many may, on the other hand, have remained secretly

Killen: *The Ecclesiastical History of Ireland* (2 vols., London, 1875); *History of the Church of Ireland from the earliest Times* (ed. W. A. Phillips, 3 vols., London, 1933–4); and J. S. Reid: *History of the Presbyterian Church in Ireland* (3 vols., Belfast, 1834).

[15] See "Convert Rolls and Certificates," Public Record Office, Dublin. These rolls cover the period from the beginning of 1703 to September 4, 1775.

[16] See "The Manuscripts and Correspondence of James, First Earl of Charlemont," Vol. I, 1745–1783, in the Hist. Mss. Com., *12th Report*, Appendix, Part X, Vol. I, 43.

[17] *The Whole Works of Sir James Ware Concerning Ireland*, III, 536.

devoted to Catholicism, seeking primarily to promote its interests from the new vantage point of political power. That this was done, and most effectively, James, Earl of Charlemont bears testimony. In referring to former Catholics now possessing political power, he declared that, connected by both blood and friendship with their fellow native Irish, they were induced "to love, assist, and protect, as far as in them lay, their former brethren. . . ."[18] The tremendous significance of this movement of the native Irish upper classes into the ranks of the Anglicans has hardly been adequately stressed by students up to the present. For, freed from the disabilities that affected their fellow Irishmen, they were able indubitably to exert a high degree of influence upon government as electors, as members of the Irish Parliament, as royal councillors, as local magistrates, as large landholders, as a proud and ancient aristocracy, and as bankers and great merchants. On the shoulders of these converts, therefore, fell the heavy responsibility of protecting the interests of their politically submerged compatriots.

At this point it is well to consider the political disabilities of Roman Catholics in Ireland in the middle of the eighteenth century. In spite of their great numerical preponderance, which in some localities ran as high as fifty to each Protestant,[19] they had not only been deprived of their earlier privilege of sitting in the Irish Parliament, but also of the right to vote at elections, to be members of borough corporations, to act as justices of the peace, to hold any local office, to practice before the bar, to possess arms, to join the army or navy, to acquire any interest in land for more than thirty-one years, and to possess a horse valued at more than £5.[20] These

---

18 "Lord Charlemont's Memoirs . . . 1755–1783," Hist. Mss. Com., *12th Report*, Appendix, Part X, Vol. I, 45.

19 "My diocese" wrote Henry Downs, Bishop of Elphin, in 1720, "is about 70 Irish miles in length yet has not above 20 clergymen in it, & but one Parsonage house & that is the Dean's . . . about which I think the Papists are more numerous than at Killala, being 50 to 1 Protestants" (*Works of Sir James Ware*, III, 536).

20 The following statutes placed the above restrictions on Catholics: 3 Wm. and Mary, c. 2 (English), *Statutes at Large* (Eyre and Strahan), III, 443–7; 7 Wm. III, c. 5; 10 Wm. III, c. 8 and 13; 2 Anne, c. 6; 6 Anne, c. 6; 8 Anne, c. 3; 2 Geo. I, c. 10; 6 Geo. I, c. 10; 1 Geo. II, c. 9, sec. 7; 9 Geo. II, c. 3, sec. 13, *Irish Statutes*, III, 260–7, 487–96, 512–4; IV, 12–31, 121–6, 190–216, 342–8, 533; V, 224–5; VI, 185. An English statute passed under Anne likewise disqualified Catholics from purchasing forfeited estates and narrowly limited their right to lease lands (1 Anne Stat. 1 c. 32). The statute regarding the possession of horses above a certain value reflected the dread excited by the superb Irish cavalry that all but turned the battle of the Boyne into an Irish victory. It also echoed the disability of English Roman Catholics. For the penal laws in Ireland see

laws, with the exception of the first-named, had issued from the Irish Parliament, which was, as will be made clear, quite under the power of the English Crown.

In addition to these legal incapacities, there was the act to prevent Catholic priests from entering Ireland; the exclusion of Catholics from Trinity College in Dublin — as well as from the English universities — through religious tests; the denial to Catholics of the right to teach or the right to send their children abroad to be instructed; the limitation of the right of free testament, so that the eldest son, if a Protestant, would receive an estate that otherwise would be equally divided among all the sons; and, finally, the disabilities facing the Protestant who married a Catholic and whose children were educated as Catholics.[21] All this combined to produce a code quite comparable to the intolerant legislation that disgraced the statute books of many Continental countries of this period as the result of religious bigotry developed in the course of the Reformation and the wars of religion that followed.

Although the Irish religious code was remarkable among all other codes because of the numerical preponderance of those adversely affected, it was certainly not notable because of rigorous application.

Certain of the acts creating disabilities very naturally were enforced much more rigidly than others, among them those that related to the political activities of Roman Catholics; this was especially true with respect to the exercise of the franchise, to office-holding, and to membership in Parliament. Nevertheless, that there was relaxation regarding the enforcement of even these laws seems to be true. For example, a report of the Trustees appointed by Parliament for the sale of forfeited estates in Ireland, issued in 1700, pointed out that in the last assize for County Galway, where forty persons were brought for trial for the late Rebellion, a majority of the jury which had them in charge were officers in King James's

---

H. B. Parnell: *A History of the Penal Laws against the Irish Catholics, from the year 1689 to the Union* (4th edn., London, 1825), P. F. Moran: *The Catholics of Ireland under the Penal Laws in the Eighteenth Century* (London, 1899), and William Burke: *The Irish Priests in the Penal Times* (1660–1760) . . . (Waterford, 1914).

[21] In the above connection see 9 Wm. III, c. 3; 2 Anne, c. 3; 7 Geo. II, c. 5 and 6; 13 Geo. II, c. 6; 19 Geo. II, c. 13, and 23 Geo. II, c. 10, *Irish Statutes*, III, 349–53; IV, 5–6; VI, 13–21, 495–504, 765–6; VII, 42–4. W. E. H. Lecky (*A History of Ireland in the Eighteenth Century*, I, Chap. 2) provides a full discussion of Irish disabilities.

army "and adjudged within the Articles."[22] This also shows the difficulties of a practical nature that stood in the face of enforcement of the restrictive code. The Convert Rolls which cover the eighteenth century, also show that some Catholics were actually officeholders and officers in the army at the time they were renouncing their religion in favour of that of the state. One held a vice-treasurership of Ireland, another was the Treasurer of County Longford; there were counsellors at law, barristers at law, attorneys of the exchequer, attorneys of common pleas, and students of Trinity College among the names on these Convert Rolls.[23] This relaxation of the laws extended to other areas as well.

For example, despite the formal prohibition against sending Catholic children abroad to be educated, a stream of young men went to Louvain and to Lisbon to be trained in institutions under the control of the Dominican Provincial of Ireland.[24] Many hundreds or even thousands were being quietly instructed by Catholic teachers in various parts of Ireland.[25] In his charge to the grand jury at the general quarter sessions in County Cork in 1740, Sir Richard Cox declared that the law passed in the reign of Anne to restrain Catholics from teaching was being violated in the county.[26] "These are the men," he complained, "who lay the Foundations of that lamentable Ignorance in which the *Irish* Papists are bred. They indeed teach a little bad *Latin*, but much superstition and more Treason." Sir Richard made clear the attitude of the dominant minority regarding the enforcement of legislation against Catholics:

> They [the Catholics] should recollect that they are at all times in the Power of the Law and are barely connived at in the Practice of their Religion. This should instruct them not to utter the least contemptuous expressions of the established Religion; which in its Nature is

---

[22] See *The Second Report of the Trustees Appointed by Parliament for the Sale of Forfeited Estates in Ireland* (London, 1700), No. 1, p. 5.

[23] See "Convert Rolls and Certificates," Public Record Office, Dublin. These rolls are arranged alphabetically.

[24] See the transcription of the "Fottrell Papers" in the Lennox-Conyngham Collection, Public Record Office, Belfast.

[25] P. J. Dowling: "Illegal Education: A Study in Irish History," *Dublin Review* (1929), pp. 206–7.

[26] Sir Richard Cox: *A Charge Delivered to the Grand Jury at a General Quarter Sessions of the Peace held for the County of Cork at Bandon-Bridge, Jan. 13, 1740* (Dublin, 1741), pp. 12–13.

very indulgent in matters of Conscience: For the Possessors of it may be provoked by the too insolent Behaviour of Papists, to make them feel the weight of that Law which hangs over them." [27]

The Irish penal code comprehended at least the idea that Roman Catholics should be allowed to enjoy the services of a parish priest, provided he fulfilled the requirements of the law regarding registration.[28] In the middle of the century more than a thousand of these priests were labouring among the people and gathering them together in chapels where they worshipped undisturbed.[29] In addition to these secular priests there were the Dominicans, who in the face of the laws against the regular clergy,[30] returned to Ireland in the early part of the eighteenth century and before 1739 had established or re-established some thirty-six communities, some of these in populous centres such as Dublin, Cork, Waterford, and Limerick, and others in rural places. These Dominicans were highly educated men who displayed real devotion to their labours and were noted as teachers. They must have exerted a very great influence in certain sections of Ireland.[31]

In other words, there was a vast difference in eighteenth-century Ireland between what was legally permitted and what was tolerated and connived at. This lax enforcement by the British of the penal laws against the Catholics in Ireland in 1750 was in striking contrast to the rigid enforcement of such laws against non-Catholics in France, Spain, and Portugal. Moreover, it is not without significance that one of the most able opponents of some of the persecuting statutes previously described was none other than George Berkeley, Bishop of Cloyne of the Church of Ireland, who declared in his *Queries:* "A relaxation of some of the Laws in this Kingdom against the further Growth of Popery, hath been a question which hath a good deal exercised the Understanding and Reasonings of Men for

[27] *Ibid.*, p. 7.

[28] See 2 Anne, c. 7, and 4 Anne, c. 2, *Irish Statutes*, IV, 31–3, 71–2.

[29] These places of worship were not hidden away. For example, in the "View of Cork" prepared to go with Charles Smith's *The Ancient and Present State of the County and City of Cork* (1750, opposite page 394) the "Mass House" is designated, as well as other prominent buildings.

[30] It may be pointed out that for the purpose of the law friars were treated as regulars.

[31] For an account of Dominican activities in Ireland in the eighteenth century see the "Fottrell Papers," Public Record Office, Belfast.

these some Years past."[32] His opposition to the laws that, for example, prevented a Catholic from purchasing lands, taking long leases, or securing his money by mortgages was most emphatic. In other words, Irish Roman Catholics did not lack champions even among the Anglican clergy.

That the way to prosperity was not closed to Irish Catholics of energy and ambition, in spite of the cruel injustice of the code, is indicated by the fact that in the course of the eighteenth century the leading business men, the wealthy merchant class, the principal bankers, and money lenders were identified with this group. It is even asserted by the Earl of Charlemont that many members of Parliament were deeply indebted to them "and consequently to a great degree dependent on them."[33]

Ireland was, of course, a dependency of the Crown of England, and its religion was established upon a basis that was not out of harmony with the principle of *cujus regio ejus religio* – a solution of the religious problem laid down in the Peace of Augsburg in 1555 for the states within the Holy Roman Empire. Under laws passed by the Irish Parliament all people living within the Kingdom were expected to support the church establishment irrespective of religious preferences, which was quite in accordance with the conceptions that prevailed in both Protestant and Catholic countries of that period. In this connection the point has been generally stressed by writers that the forced contribution of tithes can be justified only if the majority of the people favour the religion maintained by these contributions. There is much that may be said in favour of this point of view.

Many would, however, urge that the rights of a minority in a matter of conscience are as precious when it comes to this principle as are the rights of the majority. Speaking with historical retrospect, it has been actually less of a financial hardship as a rule, all things being equal, for a majority to pay to support a church it does not

---

[32] *Queries Relative to Several Defects and Grievances in Some of the Present Laws of Ireland* (2nd edn., Dublin, 1761), pp. 29–48; Nicholas Taaffe, five years later, in his *Observation on Affairs in Ireland . . .* (London, 1766) also pleaded for measures of toleration for Irish Roman Catholics.

[33] Hist. Mss. Com., *12th Report*, Appendix. Part X, Vol. I, 45–6. That the leading merchants were largely Irish Catholics is also indicated by the author of the *State of Trade in Ireland* (Dublin, 1750); see, further; *Queries Relative to Defects in the Laws* (Dublin, 1761), p. 35.

favour and in addition to contribute to the maintenance of its own religion than for a small minority to attempt to do the same.

That the native Irish nevertheless considered this compulsory support of the Church of Ireland a grievance is not surprising. The forced payment of tithes has not always been acceptable even to conformists and more than once has become a great issue in the history of Europe. Witness not only the German Peasant Revolt early in the sixteenth century, when intense hatred was expressed against such exactions, but also the equally intense hatred of them by the French peasantry preceding the outbreak of the French Revolution, as indicated by the *cahiers*.

Accepting the fact that, from the point of view of present-day thought, the forced contribution to any religious establishment is indefensible, and particularly the dragooning of those out of sympathy with the purposes of the Establishment, something may be justly said in favour of the Church of Ireland of the eighteenth century. It exhibited an attitude of such restraint in the imposition of dues as would seem to indicate that it was not unmindful of the reluctance with which the great mass of impoverished Irishmen contributed to the support of an ecclesiastical system not only alien to them, but one that many of them intensely disliked.

Moreover, although the dissenters in England were expected to pay tithes on some forty-five different commodities, which they did, but most reluctantly, Irishmen were obliged to pay on only nine, or, where potatoes were tithed as they were in Munster, on ten.[34] It may be urged that the number of articles subject to tithe is not so significant as the amount of produce that would be left to the individual after meeting the various exactions of landlord, state, and church. In the case of the native Irish it was surely little enough, at least for the agricultural labourers who refused to turn to handicraft to supplement their earnings. They naturally looked for relief from the load of their rack rent, their hearth tax, and their tithes, and they logically enough fastened on the Church for attack in the middle of the century. They were doubtless encouraged by some landlords who sought to divert their attention from rack rents to what at the worst was a minor grievance. The rental per plantation-acre in Munster, for instance, was between 5 and 7 guineas, whereas the

---

[34] *An Impartial Discussion of the Subject of Tithes Addressed to Members of Both Houses of Parliament* (Dublin, 1786).

tithe on the same amount of land would range between 5 and 10 shillings, depending on the value of the crop. They were also doubtless encouraged to resist the tithe-gatherers because there appeared a greater likelihood of success in a contest with the clergy than against the government or the landlords. For the former were, by their very position in rural Ireland, weak.

As we have seen, it was only in the Province of Munster that the potato was tithable. This was raised to the exclusion of almost every other field crop because of its enormous yield per acre in comparison to grains and other farm produce. Without the potato tithe the Munster clergy, who were in the main dependent upon these local dues, would have starved; but to collect it meant friction, for the peasantry was well aware that elsewhere in Ireland potatoes were exempt. It is therefore no wonder that corn stacks were burned in County Cork in the summer of 1750 as the result of a dispute about the tithing of potatoes.[35]

That moderation was shown in most cases in levying the tithes seems to be clearly indicated. In the eighteenth century a good crop of potatoes would yield from £15 to £20 per plantation-acre; the real value of the tithe for this was from £1.10 to £2. It appears, however, that the clergy generally "sold" the tithe for the best acre for not more than £10 shillings and frequently it would go for as low as 5 shillings, with the cultivator always enjoying the privilege of buying the tithe at this price before it was offered to another.[36] There were, it appears, some exceptional cases in which a greater tithe was charged than was customary.[37] This gave an excellent weapon to the enemies of the Establishment and led to such disturbances as the White-Boys and finally brought Henry Grattan into the field in opposition to tithes. It is, however, of interest to note that the agrarianism of the White-Boys in the 1760's was largely fomented by a clergyman of the Church of Ireland, Nicholas Sheeby,

[35] See "Calendar of Manuscripts, Letters, and Papers Prior to 1760," under dates July 25, August 10, 15, and 16, 1750, Public Record Office, Dublin.

[36] See *Considerations on the Present Disturbances in the Province of Munster*, by Dominick Trent, Esq. (Dublin, 1787), pp. 37–8.

[37] See "The Case of the Rev. Mr. Hare against the Estate of Mrs. Strange in the parish of Bally Sheepene," which involved the legality of charging 32 shillings per acre, for something over 20 acres of potatoes, based upon the assessed value of the crop. Although the court awarded Mr. Hare £33.1.4, the latter refused to take more than £10, which had been the basis that he had offered for settlement to the agent of this estate (*ibid.*); see also *A Vindication of the Conduct of the Clergy by a Southern Clergyman* (Dublin, 1788).

parish priest of Clogheen in County Tipperary, who, characterized by his contemporaries as "the person most of all obnoxious on this occasion," was finally apprehended, hanged, and quartered.[38]

Thus far little has been said specifically of that numerous body of people living especially in northern Ireland who, Presbyterian in religion, were racially a mixture of Scottish and English stocks with perhaps here and there some very slight mixture of native Irish blood and who may be accurately described as Ulster Scots.

The first important influx of Scottish Lowlanders into the north of Ireland had come under James I.[39] Numbers continued to arrive in the course of the seventeenth century, but it appears that this movement reached its greatest acceleration under William III, when, it is estimated, at least 50,000 immigrants came from Scotland between 1690 and 1697. Almost all of them were Presbyterians.[40] This great increase of Presbyterian Scots was viewed with mixed feelings by the Church of Ireland. The Establishment was happy to see such powerful accessions to Protestant strength, especially because the Scots were known for their militant qualities; it was also gratified to see a region that had been wasted by recent dynastic struggles filled with people known for their industry and frugality, most of whom brought with them skill as linen workers.

Nevertheless, the Anglicans of northern Ireland did not want to be driven from the positions of power which they had so long enjoyed in the local and central government, nor did they want to see any alteration in the religious establishment. With many of the municipalities and counties captured in elections by the Presbyterian Scots, it must have seemed to the Anglicans that submergence by this new element would be at hand unless steps were taken to ward off the danger. This was averted by an act of the year 1703, an act ostensibly passed with the object of preventing the further growth of Roman Catholicism, but containing clauses designed to apply to the dissenters.[41] It provided that all public officers in Ireland should take the sacrament of the Lord's Supper according to the rites of

[38] *A Candid Enquiry into the Causes and Motives of the Late Revolt in Munster* (London, 1766).

[39] Highlanders came to Ulster in the days of Elizabeth I.

[40] See *Ulster Journal of Archaeology* (1858), Vol. VI. For the history of the Ulster Scots see J. S. Reid: *History of the Presbyterian Church in Ireland, comprising the Civil History of Ulster . . .* (ed. W. D. Killen, 3 vols., Belfast, 1867), and W. T. Latimer: *A History of Irish Presbyterians* (Belfast, 1902).

[41] 2 Anne, c. 6, sec. 16–18, *Irish Statutes*, IV, 22–5.

the Established Church. This act was comparable to the Test Act in England, passed in the reign of Charles II, and could be avoided only by those willing to engage in occasional conformity, a practice against the convictions of most Presbyterian officeholders, who thereupon resigned their posts.

The political disability created by an act of 1703 was naturally resented by those affected by it. Further, when the favourable leases offered to the new immigrants had expired, the landlords proceeded to raise the rents in many places above what, it was insisted, was the real value of lands, or at least beyond what could be paid out of their produce if any tolerable subsistence be allowed to the farmers even exerting their utmost industry.[42]

Deprived not only of opportunities for political advancement and influence, but also of favourable conditions for earning a livelihood, thousands of Ulster Scots now directed their thoughts to a new migration — this time to America.

At first little attention was paid to the movement. By 1718, however, it had reached such proportions that the Lords Justices felt impelled to bring it to the attention of the Lord Lieutenant. "We have had accounts," they declared, "from most parts of the Kingdom, especially the North, of very great numbers of Protestants, with their families, shipping themselves off for New England and other parts of the West Indies. A List has been laid before us of upwards of 1200 who have gone from two Ports in the North this summer and we understand that many others, since that list was given us, have transported themselves from these ports as well as from this Port [Dublin]." [43] The stream of emigration assumed the proportions of a flood when at least 13,000 persons annually were carried from Ulster to the New World.[44] Expedients of various kinds were employed to check this, but without avail; among these was a plan for diverting the Ulster emigrants from going to America in favour of the Province of Connaught.[45]

---

[42] See the letter without date to the Lords Justices, enclosed in their communication to the Lord Lieutenant of March 8, 1728–29, and printed in connection with the article "Ulster Emigration to America," by the Rev. W. T. Latimer in the *Journal of Proceedings of the Royal Society of Antiquaries of Ireland* (1902), XXXII, Part 4, pp. 388–92.

[43] *Ibid.*, p. 387.

[44] See W. E. H. Lecky: *History of Ireland in the Eighteenth Century*, I, 274.

[45] In 1758 the Rev. William Henry, D.D., of Urney wrote to the Lord Lieutenant praying for disused arms. In this letter he stated that he had promised the men who

It need not be assumed that all those who went from Ireland to America laboured under pressing economic difficulties. "There are some who are settled at easy rates," wrote in 1729 Francis Iredel and Robert Craghead, two Presbyterian clergymen who had been appointed by the government to investigate the causes of this alarming exodus. These ministers pointed out the influence of letters from friends in America encouraging Ulstermen to follow them, "promising them liberty and ease as the reward of their honest industry." [46] But their investigation confirmed the earlier reports that the increased land rentals, together with other payments such as the tithes, had greatly impoverished many tenants and that religious disabilities deprived the ambitious among them of political careers. So anxious were many to get to America that they sold their services for a term of years as indentured servants in payment of the ocean passage. It is interesting to note that nothing is said – in the above list of causes for emigration, data for which were gathered from various parts of Ireland for the report of 1729 – about the discouragements faced by those who worked in wool, which, immediately after the passing of the Woollen Act of 1699, did most certainly send large numbers of weavers out of the Kingdom.[47]

It is, of course, extremely easy to fall into the error of exaggeration when dealing with such an episode as the emigration to America of the people of Ulster. To assume that as a group the people of this province were impoverished, oppressed, and consequently bore hatred toward government, would be a distortion of the facts. The letters of the Lords Lieutenants and the Lords Justices, and the report of a committee of Presbyterian ministers are uniform in stating that the greater part of those leaving were well affected to the King's government. The loyalty of the Presbyterian ministry – "who had a share of the Royal Bounty" – to His Majesty's government was especially stressed by the Lord Lieutenant in his communication of February 11, 1729.[48] This is in harmony with the sentiments expressed in "The Humble Address of the Presbyterian Ministers

---

would go into Connaught from Ulster "A Bible and Backsword to defend it, and to every woman a Prayer Book and Spinning Wheel" ("Calendar of Miscellaneous Letters and Papers Prior to 1760," Public Record Office, Dublin).

[46] This report is inserted as a part of the article on "Ulster Emigration to America," referred to above and printed in the *Journal of the Proceedings of the Royal Society of Antiquaries of Ireland,* Vol. XXXII, Part 4.

[47] *Ibid.*

[48] *Proc. Royal Soc. Antiq.,* XXXII, Part 4, p. 388.

and Gentlemen in the North of Ireland in behalf of themselves and the rest of their Persuasion," passed at a meeting of the General Synod on June 19, 1722. One must assume the sincerity of so solemn a pronouncement, voluntary as it was in nature. The opening words are as follows:

> "We, your Majesty's most Dutiful and Loyall Subjects, beg Leave with all humility to repeat our most thankful acknowledgments of the Many blessings we have enjoyed under your Majesty's Auspicious Government since your happy accession to the Imperial Throne of these Kingdoms." [49]

Almost forty years later, in the summer of 1761, the General Synod went on record again in words of such extravagant loyalty to George III that it would do well to quote these also:

> "With hearts full of veneration for the memory of Y^r Royal grandfather under whose auspicious reign these nations enjoyed invaluable blessings, we your Majesty's most dutiful & loyal subjects, the Presbyterian ministers of the Northern association in Ireland, take the first opportunity of our annual meeting to congratulate your majesty . . . and to express our unfeigned affection and inviolable attachment to Y^r Majesty's person and government.
>
> "Your Majesty's Protestant dissenting subjects in the North of Ireland, are a numerous body, the main strength of the Protestant interest in this part of the Kingdom, of well Known Zest for the success of your illustrious house and our ancestors in times of Danger have always been ready to sacrifice their lives & fortunes for its defence & support. We beg leave to assure Your Majesty that nothing shall be wanting on our part to cherish & cultivate the same loyal & hereditary spirit." [50]

Although America offered great inducements to those in northern Ireland who were not happily situated, and there were many such, one must not think in terms of a population devoid of resources. Many towns of Ulster were handsome in appearance and the people of her countryside were renowned for their success as weavers of fine linens. That the well-informed, even in America, were under the impression that Ulster was an impoverished region is surely dis-

---

[49] "Records of the General Synod," III, 1722–1737, under date of June 19, 1722. These records are in the Presbyterian Historical Society Library at Belfast.

[50] This address is in the Minutes of July 3, 1761, of the Synod that met at Londonderry; see *ibid.*, Vol. IV, 1738–1762.

proved by the appeals made by American Presbyterians to the people of this province to come to their assistance financially. In 1754 the Rev. Gilbert Tennent, a leading American missionary, appeared at the synod of northern Ireland with a petition from the Presbyterian synod of New York and the trustees of "the infant college of New Jersey," as well as from many of the inhabitants of the neighbouring provinces, which supplicated for such assistance for the college as this synod should think proper, "particularly for Saturdays Collection in the several Congregations." [51] This was granted. Further, in 1761 we find the synod engaged in the task of "the collection of funds for the American Ministers." [52]

The emigration to America is, indeed, but one phase of the Lowland Scottish odyssey.[53] Of these fearless border men – either from the Highland border or that facing England – the more restless and dissatisfied were lured to northern Ireland in the seventeenth century. There they settled along a new frontier, facing new dangers; most of them, their children, and grandchildren acquired more or less important interests, some intermarrying with their English and, much less frequently, with their Irish neighbours and becoming, finally, deeply rooted there, though they always remained a border people. But among these the more restless and dissatisfied looked for a new frontier, which they found in the first half of the eight-

---

[51] *Ibid.*, Vol. IV, 1738–1762, under date of 1754.

[52] See the "Minutes" of the Synod for 1761, which was held in Londonderry, *ibid.*

[53] As early as the end of the seventeenth century the term Scotch-Irish was at least occasionally applied by some residents of America to people of Scottish ancestry who came from Ulster. These people resented the appellation because, in the words of the Scot Lord Adam Gordon, it indicated "a spurious race of mortals"; nor did they want to be called "Irish," which they likewise felt was a misnomer. These Ulster Scots, nevertheless, are to be distinguished in American history from the people who came directly to America from Scotland. While it is true that the Lowlanders who emigrated to the New World were, as was true of the Ulster Scots, Presbyterian in religion, they did not become frontiersmen, as a rule, nor did they, as a group, espouse the cause of American independence, as was the case with the former, but — settled in communities of their own, apart from their Ulster kinsmen — were among the most loyal supporters of King George III. For a discussion of these interesting points see I. C. C. Graham: *Colonists from Scotland: Emigration to North America, 1707–1783* (Ithaca, N. Y., 1956), pp. 18–19; see also G. S. Pryde: "The Scots in East New Jersey," New Jersey Historical Society *Proceedings*, n.s., XV, 3, n. 2.

In this series, for the sake of accuracy in nomenclature, the term "Scotch-Irish" has been avoided. In place of it the term "Ulster Scot" or "Ulster Presbyterian" has been employed. As the *Oxford Dictionary* points out, the people of Scotland do not refer to themselves as "Scotch," but as "Scots" or "Scottish," and limit the use of the word "Scotch" to indicate such things as a breed of dog or a favourite drink.

eenth century east of the Allegheny Mountains in America, facing the Indian country. Most of those who went there, after some shifting, especially to the south, established permanent abodes in this region. However, again the more restless and dissatisfied among their offspring sought in the latter part of the eighteenth century a new frontier beyond the mountains. This mighty journeying of border Scots thus continued ever westward, generation after generation, a new region always luring the residue of restless, dissatisfied men until the vanguard of these hardy pioneers had established its home in the wilderness of the final American frontier.[54]

Granted the fact of the increase in land rentals, which brought dissatisfaction, and rightly so, to the tenant class of both northern and southern Ireland, it must be admitted that under the circumstances this was an evidence of increasing value of the things the land was capable of producing. In fact, in the eyes of many contemporaries, Ireland in the middle of the eighteenth century was enjoying a very considerable degree of prosperity.[55] The bankers John Willcocks and John Dawson of Dublin were circulating – before their failure in 1755 – some £300,000; [56] and by that year there was a surplus in the national treasury, it appears, of £600,000.[57] Arthur Dobbs, whose home was in Northern Ireland (and who in 1754 became Governor of North Carolina), considered that Ireland was so advantageously situated financially that he proposed in a letter to the Earl of Holderness – in connection with a plan for exploiting the resources of the Hudson Bay region – that the Hudson's Bay Company be bought out "upon condition of Ireland paying the purchase and being at the sole expense of settling and Improving

---

[54] For a fairly recent study of the Ulster Scots in both Ireland and the New World, see Maude Glasgow: *The Scotch-Irish in northern Ireland and in the American Colonies* (New York, 1936). The activities of the Ulster Scots in America will be considered in subsequent volumes of this series.

[55] "Ireland," affirmed the Primate in 1752, is in "the midst of peace and prosperity" (B. M., Add. Mss. 32727, folio 267).

[56] Morris Adderley to the Earl of Charlemont, March 4, 1755, Hist. Mss., Com., *12th Report*, Appendix, Part X, Vol. I, 208.

[57] *Ibid.* The surplus arose from the following sources: the old hereditary revenues by common law, which comprehended crown rents, composition rents, and casual revenue — which at this period produced only £17,000 annually — and the vastly more important hereditary revenue by statute law, composed of quit-rents, excise, tonnage and poundage, wine and strong drink licenses, and hearth money. See "The Present state of the public Revenue of Ireland with a short account of the Funds from which it arises," B. M., Add. Mss. 32735, folios 250–1.

and defending those countries, which can no ways hurt but greatly increase the Trade as well as the sale of the Manufactures of Britain and Ireland." He went on to declare that "the Revenue of Ireland is now in so happy a situation as to pay our debt [that is, the debt of Ireland], be able to make the purchase and be at the whole expense without any new tax or encroaching upon the Revenue granted for the support of the Establishment and all exigencies and emergencies of government." [58] This was true despite the disgraceful manner of loading the country with pensions for people, many of whom never saw – and never cared to see – Ireland.[59]

It is hardly necessary to repeat that the government of Ireland was completely under the authority of that of Great Britain. The latter was represented on the island by the Lord Lieutenant, William Stanhope, Earl of Harrington, from 1747 to 1751, and Lionel Cranfield Sackville, Duke of Dorset, from 1751 to 1755. Dorset had also spent some five years in that office in the 1730's. In authority, actual exercise of day-by-day power, and the splendour of his office

[58] Arthur Dobbs to the Earl of Holderness (undated), Dobbs Papers, Public Record Office of Northern Ireland.

[59] For example, Lady Yarmouth, the mistress of George II, received £4,000; this was granted to the Earl of Cholmondeley and to Sir William Yonge for the Countess. Augustus Schultz received £1,000; Henry William Lawman, £1,000; Francis Fane, £800; Henry, Earl of Grantham, £1,500; William, Earl Cowper, £1,000; William, Earl of Jersey, £1,500 — to name only a few of the recipients. In 1751 William, Earl of Harrington, received £2,600; in 1755 Richard Arundell, £2,200; Thomas Pitt, Esq., £1,000; and Sir Thomas Robinson, £2,000. See Treas., Out-Letters (Ireland), P.R.O., T. 14. 13, pp. 32–4, 40, 85, 94, 128, 130, 132–3, 143, 149, 156, 164, 168, 170, 174, 182, 184, 188–9.

There were undoubtedly many people enjoying Irish pensions who had a legitimate claim on the government. This is especially true of the recipients of the smaller sums, some as low as two shillings a day or £36.10 a year. It also appears that the adding of pensions by the ministers had come to the point of making the King sensitive. Newcastle, in a letter to his brother Henry, has left behind an interesting description of an interview with George II, whom he sought to persuade to make such a grant while in Hanover. "He went on exclaiming against loading Ireland," declared the Duke, "I said everything I c^d^ as to poor Mrs. Selwin, Her long services, Her compassionate case, etc. He often said she was a very good woman & at last upon my urging all I c^d^ said it is time enough when I come to England. So y^t^ tho' with a very ill Grace He will certainly do the Thing" (Thomas Newcastle to Henry Pelham, October 12, 1752. Newcastle Papers, B. M., Add. Mss. 32733, folio 75). The evil here described was characteristic of eighteenth-century Europe, and the abuse seems to have gone to very great lengths in some of the continental countries, especially in France and Spain.

It should be made clear that no gift or pension under a penalty of double the value against any person who accepted either could be made out of the hearth money tax, which was appropriated entirely to public service. This was the one tax that practically all Irishmen were obliged to pay. These pensions were therefore paid out of the other hereditary revenues. See B. M., Add. Mss. 32735, folios 250–1.

there was no one in the British Empire – except the King – to be compared to the Lord Lieutenant of Ireland. In public he was attended by a great body of horse guards, and at his Council that met in Dublin Castle there appeared the most important civil and ecclesiastical officials of the Kingdom. During his protracted absences in England, the Primate of Ireland, at this period George Stone, really acted as a deputy; in doing so he also served in his regular capacity as one of the Lords Justices.[60]

One of the greatest responsibilities of the Lord Lieutenant, outside of the preservation of law and order, was the proper control of the Irish Parliament.[61] This bicameral body consisted of a House of Lords composed of 4 archbishops, 35 earls, 45 viscounts, 12 bishops and 35 barons,[62] and a House of Commons of some three hundred members elected for life or until the King dissolved it or died.[63] That a seat in the Parliament was highly esteemed by Irishmen is indicated by the fact that £4,000 was paid in 1753 to secure one, in spite of the advanced age of the King.[64] This body, however, enjoyed limited power under the binding force of the famous statute of Drogheda of 1495, generally known as Poynings's Law. According to it, the initiation of legislation was, at least in theory, limited to the English Privy Council, as was the final approval of all acts, which were automatically sent to England and only after passing the Great Seal were returned to Ireland.

It is easy to underestimate the responsibility – in view of the restraints of Poynings's Law – that rested on the members of the Irish Parliament for guaranteeing to Ireland tranquillity, prosperity, and

---

[60] For a study of the office of Lord Lieutenant in the eighteenth century see J. L. McCracken: "The Irish Viceroyalty, 1760–73," in *Essays in British and Irish History in Honour of James Eadie Todd* (London, 1949), pp. 152–68. For lists of Irish officials and other useful information respecting the government of Ireland see R. Lascelles: *Liber Munerum Publicorum Hiberniae* (1152–1827); or *The Establishments of Ireland* (2 vols., London, 1824–30 [1852]).

[61] "The two houses of Parliament are infinitely superior, in point of grandeur and magnificence, to those of Westminster," wrote an English traveller who visited Ireland in 1764. See [John Bush]: *Hibernia Curiosa. A Letter from a Gentleman in Dublin to his Friend at Dover, Kent* . . . (London, [1768]), p. 9.

[62] See *Journals of the House of Lords of the Kingdom of Ireland*, covering the years between 1634 and 1800 (8 vols., Dublin, 1779–1800).

[63] See *The Journals of the House of Commons of the Kingdom of Ireland, from 1613 to 1800* (20 vols., Dublin, 1796–1800).

[64] Lord Bruce to the Earl of Charlemont, August 8, 1753, Hist. Mss. Com., *12th Report*, Appendix, Part X, 186.

good government. The wide range of its activities can, in fact, be appreciated only after an examination of the Irish statutes at large.[65]

For example, Parliament passed acts to encourage tillage, to subsidize the export of corn, to promote the linen industry, to provide for the construction of good roads, and for the draining of bogs. It determined the relation between master and servant and took steps to uphold the public order and to foster the charity schools, which, in England at least, were accomplishing a great and good work. The Irish Parliament, however, was the instrument of a privileged group, privileged politically, ecclesiastically, and socially; its laws were directed not only toward the support of the Established Church of Ireland while discouraging both the Catholics and the Protestant dissenters, but also toward the maintenance of the power of the landed aristocrats as against the poor and discontented peasantry. In spirit at least, if not in form, it was a typical eighteenth-century European instrument of government, neither very much worse nor very much better than could be found contemporaneously in almost any one of a dozen continental countries.[66]

At the period under consideration a great struggle was taking place within the Parliament of Ireland between two groups: one supporting the measures of the Lord Lieutenant and the Lord Primate and recruited largely from the landholding aristocracy;[67] the other made up of a combination of pro-Catholics, bankers, and others who rallied around a few opposition officeholders such as Henry Boyle, who was both Speaker of the House and Chancellor of the Exchequer; Anthony Malone, Prime Serjeant; Thomas Carter, Master of the Rolls; John Gore, Counsel to the Commissioners of the Revenue; and the Earl of Kildare.

---

65 See *The Statutes at Large* (20 vols., Dublin, 1786–1801) covering the years from 1310 to 1800.

66 For a critical analysis by the Irish patriot Charles Lucas of the constitution of Ireland in the middle of the eighteenth century see his *The Political Constitution of Great Britain and Ireland asserted and vindicated . . . ; and the Grievances, which each . . . has suffered . . . set forth . . . to the free citizens of Dublin* (2 vols., London, 1751). Yet Lucas pays but slight attention to the situation of the great mass of native Irish, despite his charge that the English instead of uniting the Anglo-Irish and native Irish drove both to rebellion (pp. 132–41).

67 "I have the support of the best and most creditable men in public office, and of the Country Gentlemen of the greatest properties and most decent characters. By which means the Privy Council and the House of Lords are almost entirely with us, and the House of Commons already at an Equal Ballance," affirmed the Primate, George Armagh in a letter written May 26, 1752; see B. M., Add. Mss. 32727, folios 264–9.

The two opposing groups were rather evenly matched, except that no one in Parliament supporting the government could equal Prime Serjeant Malone either in sheer ability or in the tenacity with which he held to his opposition. Of him it was said by his chief opponent, the Primate (George Stone, Archbishop of Armagh, as we have already mentioned), that "if all the favours of the Crown had been poured into his lap, he would not the less have persisted in his resolution." [68] Malone, of Catholic extraction, with Catholic connections, and the leader of the pro-Catholic group, had already aroused the "Whigs," that is, the Protestant Irish gentry, to action when they saw him gradually gathering to himself the chief influence of the House of Commons. He now began an attack against the government on the issue of the disposal of the public funds, constantly and boldly denying the right of the King to dispose of a shilling in the Treasury of Ireland without authorization of the Irish Parliament. As a result, he finally prevailed upon other officeholders to join with him in opposition to the policies of the Lord Lieutenant.[69]

Behind all this open warfare was the attempt on the part of the Primate to do away with the system of so-called "undertakers," who had been able, as a rule, to give the government a House of Commons that was complaisant. Malone, Boyle, and Carter, the chief of these undertakers, had become too powerful, it appears, to suit the Archbishop; he therefore proceeded to assume control of the chief sources of patronage.[70] This led to reprisals.

The occasion that was seized upon by the opposition to harass the Lords Justices was the introduction into Parliament of the money bill, by means of which the government was seeking to wipe out the national debt. This debt in the year 1748 stood at £365,500 – as against the debt of Great Britain of £78,000,000, plus interest charges amounting to £3,000,000 annually. By 1751 it had been lowered to £237,501, and by 1753 only £77,500 remained.[71]

[68] George Armagh to [the Earl of Holderness], Dec. 24, 1753, *ibid.*, 32433, folios 541–6.

[69] George Armagh to [Newcastle?], Nov. 17, 1753, *ibid.*, 32733, folios 266–8.

[70] "Lord Charlemont's Memoirs of his Political Life, 1755–1783." Hist. Mss. Com., *12th Report*, Appendix, Part X. Vol. I, 5.

[71] P.R.O. (London), Treas., 14. 13 pp. 139–41. See, for example, 25 Geo. II, c. 2, *Irish Statutes*, VII, 104–11, passed in the year 1751 for the payment of £120,000, together with the interest on the balance of the debt. For a full account of the struggle between the court party and the opposition over the above issue see J. L. McCracken: "The Conflict between the Irish Administration and Parliament, 1753–6," *Irish Historical Studies*, III, 159–79.

Indeed, as the result of rather careful management of the public funds and the continued rise of taxes on such luxuries as wines, silk, hops, china, and lacquered ware, and another on all salaries, profits of employment, fees, and pensions, the surplus in the Irish Treasury in 1753 was £400,000 in excess of the amount required to liquidate the debt. The teller of the Exchequer, Nathaniel Clements, was lending this surplus to various Irish bankers, most of whom were Roman Catholics – and therefore disqualified for government office or for the purchasing of landed estates – who were nevertheless free to engage in business and were dominant not only in finance, but in trade, as has already been emphasized.

It is not clear whether the government money bill was opposed because at this period the Irish funds carried a 4 per cent interest rate against a 3 per cent interest rate on the British consolidated debt – and therefore were a most desirable investment that interested parties sought to retain – or whether the bankers did not want the loans to them disturbed – as would be the case when certain sums were called into the Exchequer for the liquidation of the debt – or whether other motives worthy or unworthy were at work. Be that as it may, the opposition to the government money bill was sufficient to prevent its passing in the form intended. Thereupon the royal authority in England altered the bill, adding certain words to the preamble which signified the King's "previous consent" to the proposed appropriation, and sent it back to Ireland to be repassed.[72]

The excitement in and out of Parliament at this implied encroachment of the royal prerogative on the Irish Parliament now grew to white heat. Members who had never previously taken their seats hastened to Dublin. The opposition contended that the amendment vested a power in His Majesty to draw money at all times from the Treasury without control, without making himself accountable for it, and without appropriating it to the specific uses for which it was raised. It was asserted that, should the alteration to the bill be allowed to stand, the money might even be carried to Hanover to be spent. To men like the Earl of Charlemont, it was the old issue between King and Parliament involving the royal prerogative. In the final division the government was defeated by a vote of 122 to 118.

---

[72] This preamble as altered read as follows: "Whereas your Majesty was graciously pleased to signify that you would consent and recommend it to us that so much of the money . . ."

Although Parliament was hardly representative of the nation and was packed with placemen, the episode is not without very real significance in Irish constitutional history.

According to Duke of Dorset's analysis of the political situation in Ireland, the Speaker, Henry Boyle, through his having succeeded to "the Direction of the Influence which the late Lord Burlington's estate gives over the Boroughs in that Part of the Country," had some 40 members at his back, while the family of the Gores, with Malone attached to it, accounted for 30 more, and Kildare for 10. These 80 members made up "the standing body of opposition." This nucleus was augmented by some 40 more, men "who delight in opposition, & of others who always seek the shelter of a majority; which before the session began was given out to be very ample on the side of that Party." [73] As for the government support, it came not only from the powerful Ponsonby family, which could answer for 50 members, but also from a majority of officeholders, from gentlemen of independent fortune, and from friends of the Lord Lieutenant, the Primate, and the Chancellor. It is, however, of interest that 17 officeholders and men of great power in the government voted with the opposition, among them Nathaniel Clements, Teller of the Exchequer, who, it was declared, "has the command of the money in the Treasury which he lends in large and small sums, and by this means has more people in his power than any other officer," and Sir Richard Cox, Collector of Customs at Cork.[74]

The defeat of the government on the question of accepting the alterations made by the King in Council was, at its worst, so far as the immediate issue was concerned, only a deeply humiliating thing. Early in the following year Dorset called together a group of the most influential of his supporters to consider what should be the next move. Among these were the Primate, the Lord Chancellor, the three chief judges, and the Attorney General and Solicitor General. They arrived at the conclusion to recommend to His Majesty, that — under the authority of his sign manual — he should order the disposition of the money to the same uses for which it was designed by the rejected bill. This they felt would not only be a clear vindication of the right of the Crown to dispose of the surplus, but would com-

[73] Dorset to Newcastle, January 14, 1754, B. M., Add. Mss. 32734, folios 39–42.

[74] George Armagh to [the Earl of Holderness?], Dec. 24, 1753, *ibid.*, 32433, folios 541–6.

bine with it "an act of graciousness from His Majesty to the public." [75] This was done, and acting upon this recommendation the King took the necessary steps to wipe out the remainder of the national debt of Ireland, much to the satisfaction of those supporters of the royal prerogative in Irish affairs who took it as an indication that the King was determined not to allow Ireland to drift away from its imperial moorings as the result of this manifestation of nationalistic sentiment.[76]

The Lord Lieutenant and his supporters did not stop here. Those leaders of the opposition who held government posts were disciplined. Speaker Boyle was stripped of his Chancellorship of the Exchequer and the post of Lord Justice; the Master of the Rolls, Carter, was dismissed, as were the Prime Serjeant, Malone, the Quartermaster General, Colonel Dilkes, and the Collector of the Customs at Cork, Sir Richard Cox.[77] The power of the prerogative group was further displayed when, two years later, Boyle made his submission so complete that he was placed on the pension list with £2,000 a year for thirty-one years.[78]

Defeated as the opposition to the government was in its immediate objective, it did accomplish some things of importance: it rejected a bill altered according to His Majesty's desires; it expelled from the House the Surveyor General, Neville, for waste of the public money in barrack construction; it brought to bear the force of public opinion along constitutional lines upon public matters.[79] Moreover, it taught the people of Ireland a secret of which they had been ignorant hitherto: that government might be seriously embarrassed and checked, even if but temporarily, by an opposition in Parliament, and that this opposition might look forward to even more successful attempts to vindicate the authority of the national

---

[75] Duke of Dorset to the Duke of Newcastle, February 5, 1754, *ibid.*, 32734, folios 122–6.

[76] For the general consideration of Irish public finance see T. J. Kiernan: *History of the Financial Administration of Ireland to 1817* (London, 1930).

[77] Thomas Adderley to the Earl of Charlemont, April 19, 1754, Hist. Mss. Com., *12th Report*, Appendix, Part X, Vol. I, 192; see also Duke of Dorset to [Newcastle?], April 27, 1754, B. M., Add. Mss. 32735, folios 188–90.

[78] P.R.O. (London) Treas. 14. 13, pp. 88–9.

[79] The student should consult R. B. McDowell's *Irish Public Opinion, 1750–1800* (London, 1944), for a detached study of pamphlet literature relating to Irish affairs. This literature is also listed (pp. 265–91).

legislature as against the Crown.[80] As for Anthony Malone, the leader of this movement and the most influential among those supporting in Parliament the native Irish interest, he must, despite his earlier record as an "undertaker," be considered in many respects the forerunner of the great Henry Grattan.[81]

80 "Lord Charlemont's Memoirs of his Political Life, 1735–1783," Hist. Mss. Com., *12th Report*, Appendix, Part X, Vol. I, 7.

81 Malone later became Chancellor of the Exchequer. He deeply impressed contemporaries with his great powers and enlightened views. See W. E. H. Lecky: *History of Ireland*, I, 463, II, 62, 205.

CHAPTER X

Summarization

SPECIFIC ECONOMIC, social, and political developments that characterized the civilization of England, Wales, Scotland, and Ireland in the middle of the eighteenth century have been described at some length in this volume. It now remains to attempt to summarize them.

Of the four countries, England was by far the most dynamic and progressive in 1750. Before the Union with Scotland it had created a series of flourishing North American and West Indian colonies and had fastened upon Hudson Bay and Newfoundland. It had also brought into existence the highly successful United East India Company, which enjoyed, so far as the peoples of the British Isles were concerned, a monopoly of trade with the vast area to the east of the Cape of Good Hope; and it had established a series of factories on the western coast of Africa through the activity of men of the sea.

The population of England surpassed the combined population of the three other countries, as did its wealth by any standard of measurement which might be used. It had more arable land than was true of the other three taken together and more of it was under cultivation. (England proper has 32,547,009 acres; Ireland, 20,860,601; Scotland, 19,069,500; and Wales, 4,780,470.) England was also filled with flourishing cities, towns, and villages as well as pleasant country seats, all of which provided evidence of prosperous and progressive conditions. For in both the centres of population and in many rural areas there was intensive productive activity as the result of the processing of the resources of mines, farms, and grazing areas as well as products secured in the course of foreign trade, such as cotton, silk, and tobacco.

Further, England possessed in 1750 the world's greatest navy and the world's greatest merchant marine. Facing the continent of Europe near at hand, it was favoured by the fact that the estuary of the Thames, its chief river, was most advantageously located for the development of commerce on a vast scale with the mainland and also with other parts of the outside world. Moreover, it possessed in its capital, London, not only the leading city of the British Isles, but one that embraced within its metropolitan boundaries a greater population than the entire Principality of Wales. London, in fact, was a magnet that drew to itself men of talent and means from all parts of the British Isles and beyond – it also drew others who were no asset. The explanation for this is not difficult to find in view of the fact that it was the seat of the government of the British Empire as well as of Great Britain. The City was also the headquarters for most of the larger overseas trading companies, the Bank of England, and many other important business enterprises, not to mention leading cultural and philanthropic organizations.

Nevertheless, other parts of the British Isles had something of importance to contribute to the general economic well-being of the whole. Ireland, for example, led the other three countries as a producer of linen; it also surpassed them as an exporter of barrelled beef, the processing and shipping of which was concentrated at Cork, a place of opulence. Scotland stood first in certain woollen manufactures such as plaids and stockings and was also a great producer of linen. Glasgow, which led even London in the import and re-export of New World tobacco, was a thriving commercial port whose men of enterprise were destined to make the Clyde the chief ship-building centre of the world. Poor as Wales was in the middle of the eighteenth century, it excelled in the manufacture of flannel, the high quality of which reflected the skill and industry of its artisans. This flannel was also superior because the wool from the backs of the Welsh mountain sheep was peculiarly well suited for this type of cloth. The pastures of Wales and its mountain grazing lands also provided thousands of cattle yearly for the English market. In addition, the Principality had great economic potentialities in the form of ore beds and vast seams of coal – the latter ultimately to make Cardiff the most important port in the world for the shipment of coal.

Despite the existence of this degree of economic progress in each of the four countries of the British Isles, there were simultaneously groups sharing little enough in the prevailing prosperity, groups whose standard of living would be considered shockingly low today. Such were the backwash of most of the towns, many of the Welsh of the mountains, most of the Scottish Highlanders and the native Irish dwelling among their bogs. Whether their condition was better or worse in the eighteenth century than in the sixteenth century or the fourteenth or the twelfth, surviving historical records do not give a completely satisfying answer. Their manner of eking out a livelihood was primitive and faced with hazards. Intensely conservative in their outlook on life, with minds enslaved by ignorance and superstition, they usually spurned innovation in thought and action. In fact, the betterment of their condition came only as the result of the relentless operation of economic and social forces beyond their control as individuals which forced an alteration in their manner of life — be it by migration, by a change in occupation, or otherwise.

With its greater population and wealth, England also enjoyed a superiority in many other fields over other portions of the British Isles. Throughout them the English language was favoured by people of cultivation — most books, pamphlets, and newspapers, wherever printed, appeared in English. Oxford drew young men from Scotland to Scottish-founded Balliol College and young Welshmen to Jesus College, which apparently was the chief object of Welsh interest in higher education from the days of its creation in the reign of Elizabeth I. Scotland, however, in 1750 maintained four universities, and Edinburgh was certainly unsurpassed as a centre for the training of those seeking to enter the medical profession. Further, among the chief contributors to the rich intellectual and cultural life of England in the eighteenth century were to be found Scots, Irishmen, and Welshmen enriching philosophy, religion, history, law, *belles-lettres,* and architecture.

An outstanding characteristic of the civilization of the British Isles in 1750 was the part played by what may be properly called the *élite.* This group of superior social standing was made up of the nobility, the country gentry, those of the learned professions, military and naval officers, and also great merchants and financiers. An *élite* also was to be found in every country of Europe at this period, composed of the same elements, if such elements existed. The origins of this social order lead back to the dawn of civilization on the Continent, to leadership acquired by strong warlike men, to the later institution of feudalism and chivalry, to the still later rise of the towns and the possession of privileges accorded to them, to the prestige attained by men of unusual business, legal, or political capacity who moved up from the lower ranks of society by the acquisition of wealth or as the result of the display of talent in public affairs. In some countries a sharp line divided the nobility from the masses. This was not true in the British Isles. There was constant movement upward of those who were ambitious for social advancement and possessed the qualifications for highly successful accomplishment. Indeed, the British nobility in 1750 was, by and large, relatively new, in terms of aristocratic lineage; much the same was true of the lesser aristocratic order, the gentry. The fact that the children of the nobility who did not inherit a title were simply commoners in the eyes of the law ensured a connecting link between the peerage and the rest of the nation. The existence of this constant pressure from below had important political and social implications not only for that period, but for the future.

Those who had attained a place among the *élite* were the effective custodians of political power in the British Isles in the middle of the eighteenth century. Active members of the Parliament of Great Britain or of Ireland were, it need hardly be added, almost sure to be identified with the dominant Whig party. The chief interest of most politicians as legislators – except in times of crisis or when great questions of state were up for discussion and decision – seems to have been centred upon obtaining personal advantages or, at best, purely local objectives. To further these within the bounds of a one-party system of government they were perforce led to divide into groups. Each group tended to attach its fortunes to the leadership of some powerful individual, generally of the nobility. In Great Britain he might at the time be outside the ministry, but more likely was identified with it; in Ireland this powerful individual would be either in opposition to or in support of the administration of the Lord Lieutenant.

Nevertheless, whatever group or groups might be in power, it was government by the *élite* in the British Isles. In view of this, it would have been surprising had not legislation in both Great Britain and Ireland been what would be called class legislation. This was the case. Further, those who enforced the laws were recruited – at least for most positions of real responsibility – from the same social stratum of the population which enacted them. Naturally, they favoured public measures in harmony with their own particular aims and ideals. Thus, the aristocratic landowners sought to maintain the prosperity of agriculture, and the merchants and financiers that of trade and the industry that promoted its expansion. In doing so they were able – as a result of restrictions placed in the laws directed against combinations of labourers and other unlawful activities on the part of dissatisfied people – to absorb a much larger percentage of the national income at the expense of the rest of the nation than would be possible today with legislation especially motivated by aims of social amelioration.

While it is true that an *élite* was in control of national and local government in both Great Britain and Ireland in the middle of the eighteenth century, it should at the same time be observed that there were checks upon it. For example, the franchise was by no means limited to this group, nor was service on juries, nor the exercise of the multitude of lesser offices which were quite necessary for the smooth operation of the affairs of state. Further, there was an alert, free press quick to denounce injustice and consequently feared by every politician. In other words, there were limits beyond which those in position to give direction to government measures in Great Britain and even in Ireland could not go in favouring narrow, selfish interests against those of the generality of the people. What may be called class legislation had therefore to be based upon the avowed assumption that it was designed to promote the national welfare. Had those who governed flagrantly disregarded this principle in the making and enforcement of laws, Great Britain could hardly have escaped the sort of social and political revolution that was destined to engulf France in 1789, with the flaming hatred of the Third Estate directed against a privileged nobility that squandered the substance wrung from the peasantry in frivolities at Versailles to the utter neglect of local interests. In this connection it is well to bear in mind that neither the British nor the Irish nobility enjoyed any such tax exemption as was accorded that of France. From the highest to the lowest – outside of those held to be the special objects of mercy – people were expected to pay taxes, and their weight in 1750 rested chiefly on the well-to-do landowners and consumers of luxuries in Ireland as well as in Great Britain.

Of the three countries brought into some sort of union with England, Wales was most closely integrated in 1750. Politically it was a part of England after 1536, when the Welsh acquired all the rights and responsibilities of Englishmen, including representation in the

House of Commons. Under the voluntary Act of Union of 1707 the Scottish people were permitted to retain their systems of civil and criminal law and legal administration as well as their nationally established Presbyterian Church. In creating the Parliament of Great Britain, elected Scottish peers took their seats in the House of Lords, as did elected members of the commonalty of Scotland in the House of Commons. All laws passed by the Parliament thereupon were applicable to both countries, with the only restrictions on its power indicated by the reservations embodied in the Act of Union. By this same Act all trade barriers were eliminated, which established equality of trade with the English overseas colonies.

Under the terms of Poyning's Law — otherwise known as the Statute of Drogheda, enacted by the Irish Parliament in 1495 — all English statutes passed prior to the eighteenth year of the reign of Henry VII were made applicable to Ireland. Those of later date were applicable only when Ireland was specifically named in them or unless adopted by the Irish Parliament. The English Privy Council possessed under this law the initiative in Irish legislation, with the local Parliament limited to the acceptance or rejection of proposed legislation. In order to clarify the constitutional relationship between Great Britain and Ireland, the British Parliament passed a statute (6 George I, c. 5) declaring its authority to make laws that would "bind the Kingdom and the People of Ireland," although the latter were not represented in this august body. Moreover, there was no trade equality between Great Britain and Ireland: the English trade and navigation acts as well as other discriminatory legislation operated against it in most respects, as did such legislation against the English colonies in the New World, whose inhabitants in like manner were unrepresented in the British Parliament. The eventual solution of the problems involved in the subordination of Ireland to Great Britain seemed to statesmen of a later generation to lie in a legislative union between the two countries. This was ultimately carried into effect in 1801, but without realizing a happy reconciliation between the two nations, such as had been hoped for, for example, by the younger Pitt.

Before bringing this volume to conclusion certain broad generalizations may be made respecting the civilization of the British Isles in the middle of the eighteenth century. It was in a very real sense a civilization of transition. The agricultural revolution was already well under way, striking at the ancient modes of rural economy and characterized by the enclosure movement. The industrial revolution was about to begin, bringing with it the destruction of domestic handicraft in favour of power-operated factories filled with men, women, and children tending the complicated machines.

Again, it was a period of transition in things of the spirit. By 1750 the intolerance and bigotry of the sixteenth and seventeenth centuries had shaded into latitudinarianism and tolerance on the part of many leaders in church and state. The spread of this tolerant attitude in turn was to bring about the repeal of laws passed during these earlier centuries which had placed grievous disabilities upon religious nonconformists. In fact, these laws were an anachronism in 1750. Anglicanism was established in England and Wales, and Presbyterianism in Scotland, whereas the Congregational Church was publicly supported in three American colonies. Two other colonies were definitely opposed to any type of religious establishment, and the proliferation of religious sects characterized most of the Empire. There was also the stark fact that, despite all efforts during a century and a half to wean the native Irish from Roman Catholicism, they were as loyal to it as they ever had been – even in the face of desertion by a goodly number of Irishmen who by and large could be numbered among the *élite.*

In the field of intellectual history the middle of the eighteenth century also was a period of transition. The philosophical concepts and static cosmology that found favour in the sixteenth and seventeenth centuries were giving way to concepts that came to the forefront in the nineteenth and twentieth centuries, concepts based on evolutionary hypotheses and the resulting inductive reasoning flowing from advances in pure science.

It was also a period of social transition. Social forces were already operating – such as the Methodist revival – which would introduce a new quality of humanity into law-enactment and law-enforcement, and add to the sense of the dignity and worth of the individual. These forces culminated in the abolition of the British slave trade and later of slavery throughout the Empire.

Finally, it was a period of transition in constitutional arrangement and political organization which would transform the English monarchy – based to a degree, even after the Glorious Revolution, on the older monarchical principles of the sixteenth and seventeenth centuries – into the democratic monarchy of the nineteenth and twentieth – based upon full acceptance of the fact that Parliament, with its elected House of Commons, was the custodian of the great Crown powers and as such responsible for their wise employment by those exercising executive authority. This evolution of the constitution of Great Britain was to add immeasurably to the stability of the monarchy, purify politics, and introduce a new sense of honour in public affairs. Out of these constitutional and political changes was to emerge a new quality of statesmanship embodying among other things a real solicitude for the welfare of dependent peoples — especially for those of Ireland — leading in the nineteenth and twentieth centuries to a variety of measures by means of which it was hoped at length to bind them in friendship to the peoples of Great Britain.

Index

A NOTE ON THE AUTHOR

Lawrence Henry Gipson is Research Professor of History, Emeritus, at Lehigh University. He was born in Greeley, Colorado, and at an early age went to live in Idaho. After being graduated from the University of Idaho, he entered Oxford as the first Rhodes Scholar from the state of Idaho. Later he was called to three institutions for the purpose of bringing into existence departments of history and government: the College of Idaho, Wabash College, and Lehigh University. The thesis for his doctorate at Yale is the first of Professor Gipson's many published books and articles on historical topics. He has received many distinctions, among them election to the Harold Vyvyan Harmsworth Chair in American History at Oxford. Since his return to America the following year Professor Gipson has been giving his undivided attention to the completion of his series The British Empire before the American Revolution, *and to the revision of its first three volumes.*

A NOTE ON THE TYPE

This book is set in Linotype Caledonia. Caledonia belongs to the family of printing types called "modern face" by printers — a term used to mark the change in style of type-letters that occurred about 1800. Caledonia is in the general neighborhood of Scotch Modern in design, but is more freely drawn than that letter.

This series was designed by W. A. Dwiggins, and composed, printed, and bound by The Plimpton Press, Norwood, Massachusetts.